CHURCH DOG

For further resources, including the forewords to the original 14-volume edition of the *Church Dogmatics,* log on to our website and sign up for the resources webpage: http://www.continuumbooks.com/dogmatics/

KARL BARTH
CHURCH DOGMATICS

VOLUME III

THE DOCTRINE
OF CREATION

§ 45–46

THE CREATURE II

EDITED BY
G. W. BROMILEY
T. F. TORRANCE

t & t clark

Published by T&T Clark
A Continuum Imprint
The Tower Building, 11 York Road, London, SE1 7NX
80 Maiden Lane, Suite 704, New York, NY 10038

www.continuumbooks.com

Translated by G. W. Bromiley, J. W. Edwards, O. Bussey, Harold Knight, J. K. S. Reid, R. H. Fuller, R. J. Ehrlich, A. T. Mackey, T. H. L. Parker, H. A. Kennedy, J. Marks

Copyright © T&T Clark, 2010

Authorised translation of Karl Barth, *Die Kirchliche Dogmatik III*
Copyright © Theologischer Verlag Zürich, 1945–1951
All revisions to the original English translation and all translation of Greek, Latin and French © Princeton Theological Seminary, 2009

British Library Cataloguing-in-Publication Data
A catalogue record for this book is available from the British Library

ISBN13: 978-0-567-26198-4

Typeset by Interactive Sciences Ltd, Gloucester, and Newgen Imaging Systems Pvt Ltd, Chennai
Printed and bound in Great Britain by CPI Antony Rowe, Chippenham, Wiltshire

PUBLISHER'S PREFACE TO THE STUDY EDITION

Since the publication of the first English translation of *Church Dogmatics I.1* by Professor Thomson in 1936, T&T Clark has been closely linked with Karl Barth. An authorised translation of the whole of the *Kirchliche Dogmatik* was begun in the 1950s under the editorship of G. W. Bromiley and T. F. Torrance, a work which eventually replaced Professor Thomson's initial translation of *CD I.1*.

T&T Clark is now happy to present to the academic community this new *Study Edition* of the *Church Dogmatics*. Its aim is mainly to make this major work available to a generation of students and scholars with less familiarity with Latin, Greek, and French. For the first time this edition therefore presents the classic text of the translation edited by G. W. Bromiley and T. F. Torrance incorporating translations of the foreign language passages in Editorial Notes on each page.

The main body of the text remains unchanged. Only minor corrections with regard to grammar or spelling have been introduced. The text is presented in a new reader friendly format. We hope that the breakdown of the *Church Dogmatics* into 31 shorter fascicles will make this edition easier to use than its predecessors.

Completely new indexes of names, subjects and scriptural indexes have been created for the individual volumes of the *Study Edition*.

The publishers would like to thank the Center for Barth Studies at Princeton Theological Seminary for supplying a digital edition of the text of the *Church Dogmatics* and translations of the Greek and Latin quotations in the original T&T Clark edition made by Simon Gathercole and Ian McFarland.

London, April 2010

HOW TO USE THIS
STUDY EDITION

The *Study Edition* follows Barth's original volume structure. Individual paragraphs and sections should be easy to locate. A synopsis of the old and new edition can be found on the back cover of each fascicle.

All secondary literature on the *Church Dogmatics* currently refers to the classic 14-volume set (e.g. II.2 p. 520). In order to avoid confusion, we recommend that this practice should be kept for references to this *Study Edition.* The page numbers of the old edition can be found in the margins of this edition.

CONTENTS

§ 45-46

MAN IN HIS DETERMINATION AS THE COVENANT-PARTNER OF GOD

That real man is determined by God for life with God has its inviolable correspondence in the fact that his creaturely being is a being in encounter— between I and Thou, man and woman. It is human in this encounter, and in this humanity it is a likeness of the being of its Creator and a being in hope in Him.

1. JESUS, MAN FOR OTHER MEN

Real man lives with God as His covenant-partner. For God has created him to participate in the history in which God is at work with him and he with God; to be His partner in this common history of the covenant. He created him as His covenant-partner. Thus real man does not live a godless life—without God. A godless explanation of man, which overlooks the fact that he belongs to God, is from the very outset one which cannot explain real man, man himself. Indeed, it cannot even speak of him. It gropes past him into the void. It grasps only the sin in which he breaks the covenant with God and denies and obscures his true reality. Nor can it really explain or speak of his sin. For to do so it would obviously have to see him first in the light of the fact that he belongs to God, in his determination by the God who created him, and in the grace against which he sins. Real man does not act godlessly, but in the history of the covenant in which he is God's partner by God's election and calling. He thanks God for His grace by knowing Him as God, by obeying Him, by calling on Him as God, by enjoying freedom from Him and to Him. He is responsible before God, i.e., He gives to the Word of God the corresponding answer. That this is the case, that the man determined by God for life with God is real man, is decided by the existence of the man Jesus. Apart from anything else, this is the standard of what his reality is and what it is not. It reveals originally and definitively why God has created man. The man Jesus is man for God. As the Son of God He is this in a unique way. But as He is for God, the reality of each and every other man is decided. God has created man for Himself. And so real man is for God and not the reverse. He is the covenant-partner of God. He is determined by God for life with God. This is the distinctive feature of his being in the cosmos.

[204] But this real man is actually in the cosmos. He is on earth and under heaven, a cosmic being. He belongs to God, but he is still a creature and not God. The one thing does not contradict the other, but explains it. If we are to understand man as the creature of God, we must see first and supremely why God has created him. We must thus regard him from above, from God. We must try to see him as God's covenant-partner, and therein as real man. This is what we have done in the preceding section. But if we are to understand him as God's covenant-partner—which is our present task—we must return to the fact that God has created him and how He has done so, regarding him as a cosmic being, as this particular cosmic being. It is in this distinction from God, in his humanity, that he is ordained to be God's covenant-partner. In this continuation of theological anthropology we now address ourselves to all the problems which might be summed up under the title "The Humanity of Man." Our presupposition is that he is the being determined by God for life with God and existing in the history of the covenant which God has established with him. Only in this way—and we shall not allow ourselves to be jostled off the path which we have found—is he real man, in this being which consists in a specific history. But we must now see and understand this real man as a being distinct from God, as the creature of God, and to that extent as a being here below. It is as he is not divine but cosmic, and therefore from God's standpoint below (with the earth on which and the heaven under which he is), that he is determined by God for life with God. The creation of God, and therefore His positing of a reality distinct from Himself, is the external basis and possibility of the covenant. And the covenant itself is the internal basis and possibility of creation, and therefore of the existence of a reality distinct from God. We must now ask concerning man, the covenant-partner of God, from the cosmic standpoint, in his life here below, in distinction from God, and to that extent in his humanity. If we do not do this, we shall certainly have seen and understood the content of his being, but not the form inseparable from the content.

The question which will occupy us in this section is the necessary transitional question which borders and links the two essential ways of viewing him. Between the determination of man as God's covenant-partner on the one side, and his cosmic and creaturely being on the other, there is obviously an inner relationship, since we have to do with one and the same subject. His humanity can hardly be something which stands in alien remoteness from the fact that in this humanity he is the being which exists in this covenant-history. The man who, seen from above, from God, is the covenant-partner of God and real man as such, can hardly fail to be recognised in what he is below, in his distinction from God. He cannot be radically and totally hidden from himself in this distinction, as though he were a different being altogether. His divine determination and his creaturely form, his humanity, are certainly two very different things, as Creator and creature, God and man, are different. But they cannot [205] contradict each other. They cannot fall apart and confront each other in neutrality, exclusion or even hostility.

To be sure, there may be an actual antithesis. The covenant-partner of God can break the covenant. Real man can deny and obscure his reality. This ability for which there is no reason, the mad and incomprehensible possibility of sin, is a sorry fact. And since man is able to sin, and actually does so, he betrays himself into a destructive contradiction in which he is as it were torn apart. On the one hand there is his reality as God's covenant-partner which he has denied and obscured. And on the other, as something quite different and not recognisably connected with this reality, there is his creaturely form, the humanity which runs amok when it is denied and obscured in this way, and plunges like a meteor into the abyss, into empty space.

In relation to this dreadful possibility and reality even Holy Scripture speaks of two men, a first who is of the earth, earthy, and a second who is the Lord from heaven (1 Cor. 15^{47}). The very fact that the one who is really first has become the second, and the one who is really second the first, is an indication of the actual confusion to which there is reference in this passage. There is a similar indication in 2 Cor. 4^{16}, where in reference to a monstrous contra-diction we are told that the outward man perishes, but the inward man is renewed from day to day. And when Col. 3$^{9f.}$ tells us that we are to put off the old man and put on the new, we have to remember that what is here called the old is really the new which has illegitimately obtruded itself and which we ought never to have put on, whereas the new is really true and proper man, and to that extent the old and original man which could be put off only in the reckless folly of sin. The confusion indicated in all these apostolic sayings is attested indeed by the very fact that they have to speak of two distinct men in hostile confrontation. It is to be noted, however, that only with relative infrequency does the Bible speak of man in this antithesis.

The good creation of God which now concerns us knows nothing of a rad-ical or absolute dualism in this respect. We cannot blame God the Creator for what sinful man has made of himself. We do despite to Him if in relation to the human creatureliness of His covenant-partner we begin with the actual antith-esis, making the contradiction in which he exists a basic principle, and thus overlooking or contesting the fact that he exists originally and properly in an inner connexion and correspondence between his divine determination and his creaturely form, between his being as the covenant-partner of God and his being as man. The fact that of all cosmic beings he belongs so particularly to God necessarily affects him particularly as the cosmic being he is. As the cre-ative operation by which he is brought into being is a special one, so he himself as the one actualised by this work is a special creature, standing in connexion and correspondence with his divinely given determination. If God gives him this determination, whatever else he may be he is obviously one who is deter-mined by it, a being to which this determination is not strange but proper. His [206] humanity cannot, therefore, be alien and opposed to this determination, but the question of a correspondence and similarity between these two sides of his being necessarily arises. Our present question is how far his humanity as his creaturely form corresponds and is similar to his divine determination, his being as the covenant-partner of God.

Presupposing that it does in fact correspond to it, we may say that it does so indissolubly and indestructibly. To be sure, the correspondence and similarity may be covered over and made unrecognisable by the sin of man. It may well be that in consequence of the sin controlling human life we no longer see them at all in ourselves or others or human society, or do so in confused pictures which can be perceived and explained only with the greatest difficulty. It may well be that what we can actually see is so doubtful and equivocal that we despair of finding any solution for the problems involved. This is indeed the case to the extent that man is actually a sinner. We have to reckon with the fact that the similarity is indeed covered over and made unrecognisable. At this point, therefore, we undoubtedly have to do with a mystery of faith which can be disclosed only as we refer to God's revelation. On the other hand, if our creaturely form, humanity, has this similarity to our divine determination, the correspondence and similarity cannot possibly be taken away from it or destroyed. The power of sin is great, but not illimitable. It can efface or devastate many things, but not the being of man as such. It cannot reverse the divine operation, and therefore the divine work, that which is effected by God. Sin is not creative. It cannot replace the creature of God by a different reality. It cannot, therefore, annul the covenant. It cannot lead man to more than a fearful and fatal compromising of his reality, his determination. And so his humanity can be betrayed into the extreme danger of inhumanity. It can become a picture which merely mocks him. But man can as little destroy or alter himself as create himself. If there is a basic form of humanity in which it corresponds and is similar to the divine determination of man, in this correspondence and similarity we have something constant and persistent, an inviolable particularity of his creaturely form which cannot be effaced or lost or changed or made unrecognisable even in sinful man. And the task of theological anthropology is rightly to point to this inviolable and constant factor, so that it is seen as such. Theological anthropology as a doctrine of man as the creature of God has to do with constants of this kind. The being of man as the soul of his body is another unassailable and constant factor of this kind, as is also his being in time. With these anthropological mysteries of faith we shall have to deal in the further course of our exposition. But we must first consider the supreme constant to be found in the mystery of the correspondence and similarity between the determination of man and his humanity.

[207]   The practical significance of this question must not be missed. If the humanity of man genuinely corresponds and is similar to his divine determination, this means that the mystery of the being and nature of man does not hover indefinitely over human creatureliness. It touches and even embraces man below as well. In the form of this correspondence and similarity it dwells in him too. Even in his distinction from God, even in his pure humanity, or, as we might say, in his human nature, man cannot be man without being directed to and prepared for the fulfilment of his determination, his being in the grace of God, by his correspondence and similarity to this determination for the coven-

4

ant with God. Even here below he does not exist in neutrality, but with a view to the decision and history in which he is real. Consciously or unconsciously, he is the sign here below of what he really is as seen from above, from God. And so he is wholly created with a view to God. It is not, of course, that he is intrinsically recognisable as this sign. Even in respect of this natural correspondence and similarity of human nature there is no natural knowledge of God. Even in this matter we are concealed from ourselves, and need the Word of God to know ourselves. But in this respect too, in our humanity as such, there is something in ourselves to know. In virtue of this correspondence and similarity, our humanity too has a real part in the mystery of faith.

But what is the right way to this mystery? Everything depends upon our finding the right way at this critical point in our investigation, and therefore in this transitional question. And here, as in theology generally, the right way cannot be one which is selected at random, however illuminating. The arbitrarily selected way would be one of natural knowledge inevitably leading into an impasse. We must be shown the right way. And the way which we are shown can only be the one way. We must continue to base our anthropology on Christology. We must ask concerning the humanity of the man Jesus, and only on this basis extend our inquiry to the form and nature of humanity generally.

That Jesus, who is true man, is also true God, and real man only in this unity (the unity of the Son with the Father), does not destroy the difference between divinity and humanity even in Him. And if in respect of this unity we have to speak of a divinity, i.e., a divine determination of his humanity too, it is not lacking in genuine humanity. There is a divinity of the man Jesus. It consists in the fact that God exists immediately and directly in and with Him, this creature. It consists in the fact that He is the divine Saviour in person, that the glory of God triumphs in Him, that He alone and exclusively is man as the living Word of God, that He is in the activity of the grace of God. It consists, in short, in the fact that He is man for God. But there is a humanity of the man Jesus as well as a divinity. That He is one with God, Himself God, does not mean that Godhead has taken the place of His manhood, that His manhood is [208] as it were swallowed up or extinguished by Godhead, that His human form is a mere appearance, as the Roman Catholic doctrine of transubstantiation maintains of the host supposedly changed into the body of Christ. That he is true God and also in full differentiation true man is the mystery of Jesus Christ. But if He is true man, He has the true creaturely form of a man, and there is thus a humanity of the man Jesus. Therefore, as we turn to the problem of humanity, we do not need to look for any other basis of anthropology than the Christological. On the contrary, we have to realise that the existence of the man Jesus is quite instructive enough in this aspect of the question of man in general.

This time we can state the result of our investigation at the very outset. If the divinity of the man Jesus is to be described comprehensively in the statement

5

that He is man for God, His humanity can and must be described no less succinctly in the proposition that He is man for man, for other men, His fellows. We are now considering Jesus here below, within the cosmos. Here He is the Son of God. Here He is distinguished as a man by His divinity. But here He is human, Himself a cosmic being, one creature among others. And what distinguishes Him as a cosmic being, as a creature, as a true and natural man, is that in His existence He is referred to man, to other men, His fellows, and this not merely partially, incidentally or subsequently, but originally, exclusively and totally. When we think of the humanity of Jesus, humanity is to be described unequivocally as fellow-humanity. In the light of the man Jesus, man is the cosmic being which exists absolutely for its fellows.

We must first return to some earlier statements. The man Jesus is, as there is enacted a definite history in which God resolves and acts and He Himself, this man, fulfils a definite office, accomplishing the work of salvation. He does this in the place of God and for His glory. He does it as the One who is sent for this purpose. The Word and grace of God are exclusively at work in Him and by Him. He does it for God. This is again His divinity. But the humanity in which He does that for which He is sent is that He is there in the same totality for man, for other men. In no sense, therefore, is He there for Himself first and then for man, nor for a cause first—for the control and penetration of nature by culture, or the progressive triumph of spirit over matter, or the higher development of man or the cosmos. For all this, for any interest either in His own person or intrinsically possible ideals of this kind, we can find no support whatever in the humanity of Jesus. What interests Him, and does so exclusively, is man, other men as such, who need Him and are referred to Him for help and deliverance. Other men are the object of the saving work in the accomplishment of which He Himself exists. It is for their sake that He takes the

[209] place of God in the cosmos. Their deliverance is the defence of the divine glory for which He comes. It is to them that the Word and grace of God apply, and therefore His mission, which is not laid upon Him, or added to His human reality, but to which He exclusively owes His human reality as He breathes and lives—the will of God which it is His meat to do. From the very first, in the fact that He is a man, Jesus is not without His fellow-men, but to them and with them and for them. He is sent and ordained by God to be their Deliverer. Nothing else? No, really nothing else. For whatever else the humanity of Jesus may be, can be reduced to this denominator and find here its key and explanation. To His divinity there corresponds exactly this form of His humanity— His being as it is directed to His fellows.

We again recall the clear-cut saying in Lk. 2[11]: "Unto you (men) is born this day in the city of David (the reference is to the son of Mary) a Saviour (i.e., your Deliverer)." He is the Son of Man of Daniel 7, who establishes the right of God on earth and under heaven by helping to his right the man who is vainly interested in himself and all kinds of causes—sinful and therefore lost man. He protects the creation of God from threatened destruction. He gives it (secretly and finally openly) its new form free from every threat. And He does this by liberat-

6

ing man from the threat of the devil and his own sin and the death which is its ineluctable consequence. This is His divine office. And in this office alone, as the New Testament sees it, He is also human and therefore a cosmic being. This being the case, we can readily understand why the New Testament can find no room for a portrayal or even an indication of the private life of the man Jesus. Naturally, it does not deny that He has this. It speaks clearly enough of His birth, of His hunger and thirst, of His family relationships, His temptation, prayer and suffering and death. But it discloses His private life only by showing how it is caught up in His ministry to His fellows which is the concrete form of His service of God. Hence the private life of Jesus can never be an autonomous theme in the New Testament. This is true even of His private life with God. The Johannine discourses contain extensive expositions of the relationship of the Father to the Son and the Son to the Father, but they do not attribute any independent aim to this relationship. In the strict sense, they do not stand alone, but tirelessly aim to show that the man Jesus is for others, near and distant, disciples, Israel and the world, and to show what He is for them, for man. What He is in His relationship as the Son to the Father is not something which He is and has for Himself. He does not experience or enjoy it as a private religious person. He is it as a public person. He manifests it in His relationship to His disciples and through their mediation to the whole world of men. It thus acquires at once the form of a specific action in relation to men and on their behalf. Hence Phil. 2$^{6f.}$: "Who, being in the form of God, thought it not a prey to be equal with God: but made himself of no reputation, and took upon him the form of a servant." Or again, 2 Cor. 8^9: "Though he was rich, yet for your sakes he became poor, that ye through his poverty might be rich." Or again, Heb. 12^2: "Who for the joy that was set before him endured the cross, despising the shame." Or again, Heb. 2^{14}: "Forasmuch then as the children (of Abraham) are partakers of flesh and blood, he also himself likewise took part of the same; that through the power of death he might destroy him that had the power of death, that is, the devil; and deliver them who through fear of death were all their lifetime subject to bondage." Or again, Heb. 2$^{17f.}$: "Wherefore in all things it behoved him to be made like unto his brethren, that he might be a merciful and faithful high priest in things pertaining to God .... For in that he himself hath suffered being tempted, he is able to succour them that are tempted." Or again, Heb. 4^{15}: "For we have not an high priest which [210] cannot be touched ($\sigma \nu \mu \pi \alpha \theta \hat{\eta} \sigma \alpha \iota$) with the feeling of our infirmities; but was in all points tempted like as we are." Or again, the whole sequence of the life of Jesus as recounted by Peter in his address at Cæsarea in Acts 10^{38}, in which we are told that Jesus of Nazareth was anointed with the Holy Ghost and with power, and went about as a Benefactor ($\epsilon \dot{\nu} \epsilon \rho \gamma \epsilon \tau \hat{\omega} \nu$), "healing all that were oppressed of the devil." According to the New Testament, this sympathy, help, deliverance and mercy, this active solidarity with the state and fate of man, is the concrete correlative of His divinity, of His anointing with the Spirit and power, of His equality with God, of His wealth. It is genuinely the correlative of His divinity, so that the latter cannot have any place in the picture of His humanity, as, for example, in the form of His "religious life," but, on the presupposition of His divinity, His humanity consists wholly and exhaustively in the fact that He is for man, in the fulfilment of His saving work. Similarly, His prophetic message and miracles, His life and death, stand under the sign of this relationship. He is wholly the Good Samaritan of Lk. 10$^{29f.}$ who had compassion on the man who fell among thieves and thus showed Himself a neighbour to him. And if the parable concludes with the words: "Go, and do thou likewise," this is equivalent to: "Follow thou me," and in this way a crushing answer is given to the question of the scribe: "And who is my neighbour?" He will find his neighbour if he follows the man Jesus. Our first and general thesis can be summed up in the formula of the second article of the creed of Nicea-Constantinople: *qui propter nos homines et salutem nostram descendit de coelis et incarnatus est*[EN1]. The fact that the Son of God became identical with the man Jesus took place *propter nos*[EN2], for the sake of His fellow-men, and *propter salutem nostram*[EN3], that He might be their Good Samaritan.

In clarification, however, we must dig more deeply and say that in the being of the man Jesus for His fellows we have to do with something ontological. To be sure, the fact that He is a merciful Neighbour and Saviour is indicated and expressed in His words and acts and attitudes, indeed in the whole history of which He is the free Subject. But it is not the case that as this free Subject—for His is the divine freedom—He might have been something very different from the Neighbour and Saviour of His fellows, with a total or partial interest in Himself or a cause. That His divinity has its correlative in this form of His humanity, that it is "human" in this specific sense, i.e., in address to other men, is not arbitrary or accidental. Jesus would not be Jesus at all if we could say anything else concerning Him. He is originally and properly the Word of God to men, and therefore His orientation to others and reciprocal relationship with them are not accidental, external or subsequent, but primary, internal and necessary. It is on the basis of this eternal order that He shows Himself to be the Neighbour and Saviour of men in time.

He was the Head of His community before the existence or creation of all things in Him (Col. 1[17f.]). For God "hath chosen us in him before the foundation of the world" (Eph. 1[4]). "Whom he (God) did foreknow, he also did predestinate to be conformed to the image of his Son, that he might be the firstborn among many brethren" (Rom. 8[29]). He was this first-begotten even when He came into the world (Heb. 1[6]). And so an indefinite number of men are "given" Him, to use an expression which frequently recurs in the Fourth Gospel. They belong to the Father, and He has given them to Jesus (Jn. 17[6]). He will not let them perish (Jn. 6[39], 18[9]), nor can any pluck them out of His hand (10[29]), but they hear His Word (17[8]) and He will be glorified in them (17[10]). What has taken place and takes place between Him and them is only as it were the execution of an order which is valid and in force without either His or their co-operation, but both for Him and them. And the same is true of what will take place between Him and them. "I ascend unto my Father, and your Father; and to my God, and your God" (Jn. 20[17]), namely, "to prepare a place for you," and then to return "and receive you unto myself; that where I am, there ye may be also" (Jn. 14[2f.]). And yet that which is resolved concerning Himself and these men is undoubtedly willed by Jesus too: "Father, I will that they also, whom thou hast given me, be with me where I am" (Jn. 17[24], cf. 12[26]).

[211]

It is of a piece with this that the solidarity with which Jesus binds Himself to His fellows is wholly real. There is not in Him a kind of deep, inner, secret recess in which He is alone in Himself or with God, existing in stoical calm or mystic rapture apart from His fellows, untouched by their state or fate. He has no such place of rest. He is immediately and directly affected by the existence of His fellows. His relationship to His neighbours and sympathy with them are original and proper to Him and therefore belong to His innermost being.

[EN1] who for the sake of us human beings and our salvation came down from heaven and became incarnate

[EN2] for our sake

[EN3] for the sake of our salvation

They are not a new duty and virtue which can begin and end, but He Himself is human, and it is for this reason that He acts as He does.

We recall at this point the remarkable verb σπλαγχνίζεσθαι[EN4], which in the New Testament is used only of Jesus Himself and three closely related figures in the parables. The word denotes a movement in the "bowels" (in the sense of the innermost or basic parts). "To have mercy," or "to have pity," or "to have compassion," are only approximate translations as this movement is ascribed to the magnanimous king in relation to the hopeless debtor in Mt. 18^{27}, or the Samaritan on the way from Jericho to Jerusalem in Lk. 10^{33}, or the father of the prodigal son in Lk. 15^{20}, but especially as ascribed to Jesus Himself in face of the leper (Mk. 1^{41}), the two blind men at Jericho (Mt. 20^{34}), the dead man at Nain and his mother (Lk. 7^{13}), the hungry crowd in the wilderness (Mk. 8^2 and *par.*) and especially the spiritual need of the Galilean masses: "because they fainted, and were scattered abroad, as sheep having no shepherd" (Mt. 9^{36}). The term obviously defies adequate translation. What it means is that the suffering and sin and abandonment and peril of these men not merely went to the heart of Jesus but right into His heart, into Himself, so that their whole plight was now His own, and as such He saw and suffered it far more keenly than they did. ἐσπλαγχνίσθη means that He took their misery upon Himself, taking it away from them and making it His own. There is certainly no suggestion of a passive mood or attitude or the mere feeling of a spectator, as the word "sympathy" might imply. This is made perfectly plain by Mk. 9^{22} where the father of the epileptic boy says: "If thou canst do anything, βοήθησον ἡμῖν σπλαγχνισθείς ἐφ' ἡμᾶς[EN5]". It is not in vain, but with the immediate consequence of practical assistance, that Jesus undergoes this inner movement and makes the cause of this man His own. He knows at once what to do. And the other stories in which the expression occurs speak similarly of effective help, and the parables of resolute decisions. The verb obviously refers to the action of Jesus, but it tells us that this has an inward source and is the movement of the whole man Jesus.

And this leads us to the further point that if the humanity of Jesus is origin- [212] ally and totally and genuinely fellow-humanity this means that He is man for other men in the most comprehensive and radical sense. He does not merely help His fellows from without, standing alongside, making a contribution and then withdrawing again and leaving them to themselves until further help is perhaps required. This would not be the saving work in the fulfilment of which He has His life. Nor would it serve the glory and right of God, nor help to their right the fellows for whom He is there. For it would not alter their state and fate as sinners fallen victim to death. It would not deal with the root of their misery. The menacing of the cosmos by chaos and the assault on man by the devil are far too serious and basic to be met by external aid, however powerful. And so the being of Jesus for His fellows really means much more. It means that He interposes Himself for them, that He gives Himself to them, that He puts Himself in their place, that He makes their state and fate His own cause, so that it is no longer theirs but His, conducted by Him in His own name and on His own responsibility. And in this respect we have to remember that so long as the cause of men was in their own hands it was a lost cause. Their

---

[EN4] he had pity
[EN5] have compassion on us, and help us

judgment was just and destruction inevitable, so that anyone taking their place had necessarily to fall under this judgment and suffer this destruction. In His interposition for them the man Jesus had thus to sacrifice Himself in this cause of others. It was not merely a matter of His turning to them with some great gift, but of His giving Himself, His life, for them. It was a matter of dying for them. And if the cause of His fellows was really to be saved and carried through to success, if they were really to be helped, an unparalleled new beginning was demanded, a genuine creation out of nothing, so that the One taking their place had to have the will and the power not merely to improve and alleviate their old life but to help them to a basically new one. Interposing Himself for them, the man Jesus had thus to conquer in this alien cause. He could not merely, relieve His fellows of their sin and bear for them its punishment, as though it were enough to set them in this neutral state and wipe the slate clean. He had also to give them the freedom not to sin any more but to be obedient where they had previously been disobedient. To be their Deliverer He had thus to rise again for them to a new life. This is the saving work by which the devilish onslaught on man is repulsed, the menacing of cosmos by chaos overcome and the divine creation inaugurated in a new form in which the glory and right of God are no longer bounded and can no longer be called in question by any adversary. The humanity of Jesus implies that in the execution of His mission as the incarnate Son of God He is for men in this comprehensive and radical sense. It implies that all other men can confidently keep to the fact that this sacrifice was offered once and for all for them, that this vic-

[213] tory was won once and for all for them, that the man Jesus died and rose again once and for all for them.

A sum of the whole message of the New Testament may very well be found in the question of Romans 8³¹: "If God be for us, who can be against us?" This is quite in harmony with the introductory preaching of Jesus according to the Synoptists (Mk. 1¹⁵ and *par.*): "The kingdom of God is at hand," i.e., God has acted to establish His right among men and therefore to help men to theirs. But it is to be noted that the reality indicated has the concrete form of the man Jesus. He, as the Son of God, the Messiah, the Son of Man, is the indicated Deliverer. "God for us" in the New Testament is not the general proclamation of the love of God and His readiness to help. For it means that Jesus is for us. The immediate continuation in Rom. 8³² is that He "spared not his own Son, but delivered him up for us all," and so "how shall he not with him also freely give us all things?" The preposition ὑπέρ *c. Gen.* (less frequently περί and διά, and only once, in Mk. 10⁴⁵ and *par.*, ἀντί) denotes this concrete form of the central declaration of the New Testament. Its meaning "for" signifies for the advantage or in the favour or interests of someone. It can also signify for the sake of a definite cause or goal. It can finally signify in the place or as the representative of someone. In the innumerable passages in the New Testament in which it is said of Jesus Christ that He acted ὑπέρ, the genitive points directly or indirectly to persons. In the majority of cases it is "for us" or "for you," i.e., the men of the community which recognises and confesses Jesus Christ, for His own in this immediate sense. In Eph. 5²⁵ it says expressly for the ἐκκλησία ᴱᴺ⁶, in Jn. 10¹¹ for the sheep (of the Good Shepherd), in Jn. 15¹³ for His friends, and in Jn. 17¹⁹ for His

---

ᴱᴺ⁶ church

disciples: "For their sakes I sanctify myself." Only once in the New Testament, as demanded by the context, is it "for me" (Gal. 2²⁰). In these cases the first and third meanings intercross. Jesus acts on behalf of these men, and in their place. The second meaning (of action for a cause or goal) arises where it is explicitly said "for our sins" (Gal. 1⁴, 1 Cor. 15³, 1 Pet. 3¹⁸, 1 Jn. 2²). In these cases what is signified is that He acts because the men referred to are sinners who must be helped, and therefore to expiate and remove their sins as the ground of the impending judgment. Gal. 1⁴ makes the express addition: "That he might deliver us from the present evil aeon, according to the will of God and our Father." And there are some passages where the circle of those to whom this applies still seems to be open outwards. Even in Mk. 10⁴⁵ and *par.* the reference is to the many for whom Jesus will give His life as a ransom, and Calvin himself did not dare to give to this πολλοί^{EN7} the meaning of a restricted number of men. In Jn. 11⁵¹ᶠ· we have the remarkable saying that Jesus was to die for the people "and not for that nation only, but also that he should gather together in one the children of God that were scattered abroad." The same extension is to be found even more plainly in 1 Jn. 2²: "He is the propitiation for our sins: and not for ours only, but also περὶ ὅλου τοῦ κόσμου^{EN8}." And so in 2 Cor. 5¹⁴⁻¹⁵ there is the twofold ὑπὲρ πάντων ἀπέθανεν^{EN9}; in 1 Tim. 2⁶ we are told that "he gave himself a ransom ὑπὲρ πάντων^{EN10}" in Heb. 2⁹ we read "that he by the grace of God should taste death ὑπὲρ παντός^{EN11}"; and most powerfully of all Jn. 6⁵¹ tells us that "the bread that I will give is my flesh, which I will give ὑπὲρ τῆς τοῦ κόσμου ζωῆς^{EN12}"—a saying which finds an exact parallel in the well-known verse Jn. 3¹⁶, where we read that "God so loved the world, that he gave his only begotten Son." What Jesus is "for us" or "for you" in the narrower circle of the disciples and the community He is obviously, through the ministry of this narrower circle, "for all" or "for the world" in the wider or widest circle. And in the majority of the relevant passages this action of Jesus for others (His disciples, His community, the many, all, the world) is His death and passion. This is the primary reference of the more general expressions which speak of His self-offering for men. But we must see the work in its totality. If it is the one side that He "was delivered for our offences," there is also the other that He "was raised again for our justification" (Rom. 4²⁵). It must not be forgotten that as the New Testament sees it the man Jesus who was given up to death is identical with the Lord now living and reigning in the community, and that this Lord again is the One whose universally visible return is for the community the sum of their future and of that of the world. He has overcome death in suffering it. He has risen again from the dead. And it is in this totality that He is "for men." He removes the sting of sin by taking it to Himself, by being made sin (according to the harsh expression of 2 Cor. 5²¹), by dying for men as though their cause were His. But this delivering-up in our place, in which the traitor Judas is the strange instrument of the will of God, is something which He endures in the omnipotence of the Son of God, executing the divine commission and offering an acceptable sacrifice to God. It is not merely that He suffers Himself to be offered, but He Himself makes the offering, and triumphs in so doing. What is accomplished by Him is the destruction of human sin and the death which is its consequence. And it is done effectively and positively. In His resurrection He reveals Himself as the One He is—the genuine, true and righteous man, the real man, who kept the covenant which all others broke. He kept it in His self-offering, in His death for their sin. The divine and the human fulfilment of the covenant are one and the same in the act of obedience on the part of Jesus, in this final

[214]

EN 7 many
EN 8 for the whole world
EN 9 he died for all
EN10 for all
EN11 for every man
EN12 for the life of the world

crisis of His saving work. He did this too, and He did it for men, in their favour, for the sake of their cause, and in their place. It was "an offering and a sacrifice to God for a sweet-smelling savour" (εἰς ὀσμὴν εὐωδίας EN13, Eph. 5²) which He offered "for" us. That is to say, He made us possible and acceptable and pleasing to God, representing us in such a way that we are right with Him. Continuing in the passage in Rom. 8 with which we began, we can thus read that there can be no complaint against the elect of God because God justified them, and no condemnation because Jesus Christ died and is risen again, being now at the right hand of the Father and making intercession for us (ὅς καὶ ἐντυγχάνει ὑπὲρ ἡμῶν, Rom. 8³³ᶠ·). But it is the Epistle to the Hebrews which reveals most frequently the positive significance of ὑπέρ EN14. Jesus as πρόδρομος ὑπὲρ ἡμῶν EN15 has passed through the veil into the sanctuary (6²⁰). He has appeared ὑπὲρ ἡμῶν EN16, in the presence of God (9²⁴). He ever lives εἰς τὸ ἐντυγχάνειν ὑπὲρ αὐτῶν EN17 (7²⁵). It is also to be noted that according to Paul's account the "for" has a place in the blessing of the bread at the institution of the Lord's Supper: τοῦτό μού ἐστιν τὸ σῶμα τὸ ὑπὲρ ὑμῶν EN18 (1 Cor. 11²⁴), and it is similarly used in the blessing of the cup according to the Synoptists: τοῦτό μού ἐστιν τὸ αἷμά μου τῆς διαθήκης τὸ ἐκχυννόμενον ὑπὲρ πολλῶν EN19 (Mk. 14²⁴ and par.). But if the body and blood ὑπὲρ ὑμῶν EN20 or ὑπὲρ πολλῶν EN21 undoubtedly refer back to the life of Jesus offered in His death, the decisive event in the Supper is not this recollection as such, but present participation in the fruit of this sacrifice. The offering of My body and blood has for you the effect that as you eat this bread My life is given to you as yours, and that as you drink of this cup you may live with joy and not with sorrow, as innocent and not condemned. As I have given my life for you, it belongs to you. You may live and not die. You may rejoice and not mourn. Do this ("in remembrance of me") as you eat this bread and drink this cup. Proclaim in this way the Lord's death till He come (1 Cor. 11²⁶), i.e., until His presence, already experienced here and now with this eating and drinking, is revealed to all eyes.

This is the humanity of the man Jesus—the concrete form of His humanity. And the following implications are to be noted.

There is implied first that Jesus has to let His being, Himself, be prescribed and dictated and determined by an alien human being (that of His more near and distant fellows), and by the need and infinite peril of this being. He is not of Himself. He does not live in an original humanity in which He can be far more glorious perhaps in virtue of His divine determination. No, the glory of His humanity is simply to be so fully claimed and clamped by His fellows, by their state and fate, by their lowliness and misery; to have no other cause but that of the fatal Adam whom He now allows to be really the first, giving him the precedence, ranging Himself wholly with him for his salvation as the second Adam. If there is indeed a powerful I of Jesus, it is only from this Thou, from fallen Adam, from the race which springs from him, from Israel and the sequence of its generations, from a succession of rebels, from a history which

[215]

EN13 for a sweetsmelling savour
EN14 who also maketh intercession for us
EN15 the forerunner for us
EN16 for us
EN17 to make intercession for them
EN18 this is my body, which is for you
EN19 this is my blood of the new testament, which is shed for many
EN20 for you
EN21 for many

is the history of its unfaithfulness. He is pleased to have His life only from His apostles, His community, those whom He called His own and who constantly forsook and forsake Him. He is pleased to be called by them to His own life, to be given the meaning of His life by them. He is pleased to be nothing but the One who is supremely compromised by all these, the Representative and Bearer of all the alien guilt and punishment transferred from them to Him.

There is also implied that His being is wholly with a view to this alien being; that He is active only in the fact that He makes its deliverance His exclusive task. He moves towards the Thou from which He comes. Disposed by it, He disposes Himself wholly and utterly towards it, in utter disregard of the possibility that another task and activity might better correspond to His divine determination and be more worthy of it. After all, what are these fellow-men? What are to Him all these representatives of the human race, the more pious and noble and the less? Why should He not choose and adopt an original work, completely ignoring these pitiable figures in its execution? Well, He does not do so. He finds it worth His while to live and work for His fellows and their salvation. He does not hold aloof from them. He does not refuse to be like them and with them and in that comprehensive sense for them. He gives Himself freely to them. He has only one goal: to maintain the cause of these men in death and the conquest of death; to offer up His life for them that they may live and be happy. He therefore serves them, without prospect of reward or repayment, without expecting to receive anything from them which He cannot have far better and more richly without them. He therefore interposes Himself for Adam, for the race, for Israel, for His disciples and community.

"Whosoever of you will be the chiefest, shall be servant of all" (Mk. 10⁴⁴). The man Jesus is the chiefest. He "came not to be ministered unto, but to minister" (v. 45). This is attested by what He said at the institution of the Lord's Supper in the Synoptists and what He did in the foot-washing in John. And He makes no demand upon His own in this respect which He has not first inimitably demonstrated with the act of His own life, thus giving it the character of a demand which can be understood only as the proclamation and offer of the grace of God manifested in Him. [216]

We could hardly see the man Jesus as attested in the New Testament if we closed our eyes to the twofold fact that His being is both from and to His fellows, so that He is with them, and in this way man in His distinctive sovereignty. If we see Him alone, we do not see Him at all. If we see Him, we see with and around Him in ever-widening circles His disciples, the people, His enemies and the countless millions who have not yet heard His name. We see Him as theirs, determined by them and for them, belonging to each and every one of them. It is thus that He is Master, Messiah, King and Lord. "Selfless" is hardly the word to describe this humanity. Jesus is not "selfless." For in this way He is supremely Himself. The theme of the New Testament witness is a kind of incomparable picture of human life and character. What emerges in it is a supreme I wholly determined by and to the Thou. With this twofold definition Jesus is human.

And there is obviously no distance, alienation or neutrality, let alone opposition, between this human definition and the divine. His humanity is not, of course, His divinity. In His divinity He is from and to God. In His humanity He is from and to the cosmos. And God is not the cosmos, nor the cosmos God. But His humanity is in the closest correspondence with His divinity. It mirrors and reflects it. Conversely, His divinity has its correspondence and image in the humanity in which it is mirrored. At this point, therefore, there is similarity. Each is to be recognised in the other. Thus even the life of the man Jesus stands under a twofold determination. But there is harmony between the two. As he is for God, so He is for man; and as He is for man, so He is for God. There is here a *tertium comparationis*[EN22] which includes His being for God as well as His being for man, since the will of God is the basis and man the object of the work in which this man is engaged.

For a true understanding, we can and must think of what is popularly called the twofold law of love—for God and the neighbour (Mk. 12^{29-31} and *par.*). It is no accident that it was Jesus who summed up the Law and the prophets in this particular way. He was speaking primarily and decisively of the law of His own twofold yet not opposed but harmonious orientation. He declared Himself, and therefore the grace of God manifested in Him, to be the sum of the Law. The two commandments do not stand in absolute confrontation. It is clear that Jesus did not regard love for God and love for the neighbour as separate but conjoined. Yet they are not identical. In Mt. 22^{38} the command to love God is expressly called the first and great commandment, and the command to love the neighbour is placed alongside it as the second. God is not the neighbour, nor the neighbour God. Hence love for God cannot be simply and directly love for the neighbour. Yet the command to love the neighbour is not merely an appended, subordinate and derivative command. If it is the second, it is also described as like unto the first in Mt. 22^{39}. A true exposition can only speak of a genuinely twofold, i.e., a distinct but connected sphere and sense of the one love required of man. It has reference to God, but also to the neighbour. It has the one dimension, but also the other. It finds in the Creator the One who points it to this creature, fellowman. And it finds in this creature, fellow-man, the one who points it to the Creator. Receiving and taking seriously both these references in their different ways, it is both love for God and love for the neighbour. Thus the structure of the humanity of Jesus Himself is revealed in this twofold command. It repeats the unity of His divinity and humanity as this is achieved without admixture or change, and yet also without separation or limitation.

[217]

We must now take a further step, for it is not only by way of His utter obedience to God, but because and in the course of it, that He so fully serves His fellows. The saving work in which He serves His fellows is not a matter of His own choice or caprice but the task which He is given by God. Its execution has nothing to do, therefore, either with the fulfilment of a duty or the exercise of a virtue. For He exists and lives in His saving work. He would not be the One He is if He lived in the execution of another work or in any sense for Himself or a cause alien to this work. He cannot be at all, and therefore for God, without being for men. Hence it is the glory of the One who has commissioned and sent Him, of God, which is revealed and proclaimed in the fact that He is for

---

[EN22] basis of comparison

men. In this there is disclosed the choice and will of God Himself. God first and not the man Jesus is for men. It is He, God, who from all eternity has established the covenant of grace between Himself and man, and has pitied and received Him, pitying and receiving this particularly threatened and needy creature within the threatened cosmos of His creatures and for its deliverance and preservation. The whole witness and revelation of the man Jesus in time, the whole point of His life and existence, is that within the cosmos there should be declared as good news and operative as saving power the fact that God Himself is for man and is his covenant-partner. God interposes Himself for him, sharing his plight and making Himself responsible for his life and joy and glory. God Himself is his Deliverer. He wills a free man in a free cosmos—freed from the threat to which man has culpably exposed himself and which he is powerless to avert. The God who willed and resolved this, and acted in this way in His incarnate Son, is the basis of the saving work of the man Jesus which has man—His fellow-men exactly as they are—as its object. It is not by accident, then, that Jesus is for man as He is for God. Between His divinity and His humanity there is an inner material connexion as well as a formal parallelism. He could not be for God if He were not on that account for man. The correspondence and similarity between His divinity and humanity is not merely a fact, therefore, but has a material basis. The man Jesus is necessarily for His fellows as He is for God. For God first, as the One who gives Him His commission, as the Father of this Son, is for man. This excludes any possibility of the man Jesus not being for man as He is for God.

Titus 3^4 gives us the clear-cut description of the incarnation: ὅτε δὲ ἡ χρηστότης καὶ ἡ [218]
φιλανθρωπία ἐπεφάνη τοῦ σωτῆρος ἡμῶν θεοῦ [EN23]. It is to be noted that in company with "kindness" (and in explanation of it) "love" seems here to be almost a quality of God Himself. It is almost integral to His very nature and essence to be our Saviour, ὁ σωτὴρ ἡμῶν θεός [EN24]. We must be careful to understand this properly. God is not a creature, nor is He necessarily bound to any creature. It is His free decision and act to be "God our Saviour" and the Friend of man. But in this decision and act, in this self-determination to be our Saviour and Friend, we have an eternal presupposition of His creative work and therefore of all creatures. The One who came with the incarnation of His Word could not be other than He was. In His majesty and freedom God willed from all eternity to be for men "God our Saviour." The covenant fulfilled in time is a covenant resolved and established in God Himself before all time. There was no time when God was not the covenant-partner of man. What appeared, therefore, in the epiphany of the man Jesus was not an accidental manner or disposition of this man, a moral disposition of this creature, but the χρηστότης [EN25] of the Creator, which is identical with His φιλανθρωπία [EN26]. This is the inner necessity with which Jesus is at one and the same time both for God and for man.

And now we must take a last and supreme step. There is freedom in God, but no caprice. And the fact that from all eternity God pitied and received man,

---

[EN23] But after that the kindness and love of God our Savior appeared
[EN24] God our Savior
[EN25] love of humanity
[EN26] love

the grounding of the fellow-humanity of Jesus in the eternal covenant executed in time in His being for man, rests on the freedom of God in which there is nothing arbitrary or accidental but in which God is true to Himself. God for man, participating in and making Himself responsible for him, securing for him fellowship with Himself and therefore His saving help—this whole mystery of the man Jesus is rooted in the mystery of God Himself, which is no mere fact or riddle, but full of meaning and wisdom. And as the mystery of the man Jesus is disclosed to us, we cannot say of the even higher mystery of God Himself that it is simply hidden from us and its meaning and wisdom are unattainable. If "God for man" is the eternal covenant revealed and effective in time in the humanity of Jesus, in this decision of the Creator for the creature there arises a relationship which is not alien to the Creator, to God as God, but we might almost say appropriate and natural to Him. God repeats in this relationship *ad extra* a relationship proper to Himself in His inner divine essence. Entering into this relationship, He makes a copy of Himself. Even in His inner divine being there is relationship. To be sure, God is One in Himself. But He is not alone. There is in Him a co-existence, co-inherence and reciprocity. God in Himself is not just simple, but in the simplicity of His essence He is three-fold—the Father, the Son and the Holy Ghost. He posits Himself, is posited by Himself, and confirms Himself in both respects, as His own origin and also as His own goal. He is in Himself the One who loves eternally, the One who is eternally loved, and eternal love; and in this triunity He is the original and source of every I and Thou, of the I which is eternally from and to the Thou and therefore supremely I. And it is this relationship in the inner divine being [219] which is repeated and reflected in God's eternal covenant with man as revealed and operative in time in the humanity of Jesus.

We now stand before the true and original correspondence and similarity of which we have to take note in this respect. We have seen that there is a factual, a materially necessary, and supremely, as the origin of the factual and materially necessary, an inner divine correspondence and similarity between the being of the man Jesus for God and His being for His fellows. This correspondence and similarity consists in the fact that the man Jesus in His being for man repeats and reflects the inner being or essence of God and this confirms His being for God. We obviously have to do here with the final and decisive basis indicated when we spoke of the ontological character, the reality and the radical nature of the being of Jesus for His fellow-men. It is from this context that these derive their truth and power. The humanity of Jesus is not merely the repetition and reflection of His divinity, or of God's controlling will; it is the repetition and reflection of God Himself, no more and no less. It is the image of God, the *imago Dei*[EN27].

The "image"—we must not forget the limitation implicit in this term. If the humanity of Jesus is the image of God, this means that it is only indirectly and

---

[EN27] image of God

16

not directly identical with God. It belongs intrinsically to the creaturely world, to the cosmos. Hence it does not belong to the inner sphere of the essence, but to the outer sphere of the work of God. It does not present God in Himself and in His relation to Himself, but in His relation to the reality distinct from Himself. In it we have to do with God and man rather than God and God. There is a real difference in this respect. We cannot, therefore, expect more than correspondence and similarity. We cannot maintain identity. Between God and God, the Father and the Son and the Son and the Father, there is unity of essence, the perfect satisfaction of self-grounded reality, and a blessedness eternally self-originated and self-renewed. But there can be no question of this between God and man, and it cannot therefore find expression in the humanity of Jesus, in His fellow-humanity as the image of God. In this case we have a complete disparity between the two aspects. There is total sovereignty and grace on the part of God, but total dependence and need on that of man. Life and blessedness may be had by man wholly in God and only in fellowship with Him, in whom they are to be sought and found. On God's side, therefore, we have a Saviour and Deliverer. And He does not enter into alliance with a second God in His eternal covenant with man as revealed in Jesus Christ. Nor does man become a second God when He takes part in this covenant and is delivered by this Deliverer. The one who enters into this covenant is always the creature, man, who would be absolutely threatened without this help and lost if thrown back upon his own resources. It is in the humanity, the saving work of Jesus Christ that the connexion between God and man is brought before us. It is in this alone that it takes place and is realised. Hence there is disparity between the relationship of God and man and the prior relationship of the Father to the Son and the Son to the Father, of God to Himself. [220]

But for all the disparity—and this is the positive sense of the term "image"—there is a correspondence and similarity between the two relationships. This is not a correspondence and similarity of being, an *analogia entis*[EN28]. The being of God cannot be compared with that of man. But it is not a question of this twofold being. It is a question of the relationship within the being of God on the one side and between the being of God and that of man on the other. Between these two relationships as such—and it is in this sense that the second is the image of the first—there is correspondence and similarity. There is an *analogia relationis*[EN29]. The correspondence and similarity of the two relationships consists in the fact that the freedom in whicih God posits Himself as the Father, is posited by Himself as the Son and confirms Himself as the Holy Ghost, is the same freedom as that in which He is the Creator of man, in which man may be His creature, and in which the Creator-creature relationship is established by the Creator. We can also put it in this way. The correspondence and similarity of the two relationships consists in the fact that the eternal love

---

[EN28] analogy of being
[EN29] analogy of relation

17

in which God as the Father loves the Son, and as the Son loves the Father, and in which God as the Father is loved by the Son and as the Son by the Father, is also the love which is addressed by God to man. The humanity of Jesus, His fellow-humanity, His being for man as the direct correlative of His being for God, indicates, attests and reveals this correspondence and similarity. It is not orientated and constituted as it is in a purely factual and perhaps accidental parallelism, or on the basis of a capricious divine resolve, but it follows the essence, the inner being of God. It is this inner being which takes this form *ad extra*^{EN30} in the humanity of Jesus, and in this form, for all the disparity of sphere and object, remains true to itself and therefore reflects itself. Hence the factuality, the material necessity of the being of the man Jesus for His fellows, does not really rest on the mystery of an accident or caprice, but on the mystery of the purpose and meaning of God, who can maintain and demonstrate His essence even in His work, and in His relation to this work.

For this final step in our exposition we may refer to a narrow but sharply defined and therefore distinct line in St. John's Gospel. In this Gospel, and most strikingly in chapter 17, it emerges in a number of distinctive expressions which form a special group in the Gospel to the extent that they all indicate that the relationship of Jesus to the disciples is not original, but an exact copy of the relationship in which He stands to the Father and the Father to Him.

This first and original relationship is unmistakeably characterised in these passages, and distinguished from the second, by the fact that it is not within the creaturely world but outside it, before and above the whole history which is played out in the cosmos, and therefore in God Himself. According to Jn. 17^5 there is a glory from which Jesus already comes as man, "which I had with thee before the world was." "I have glorified him," is said by the voice from heaven in 12^{28}, and in 1^1 He is the Word which was in the beginning with God. He is not, then, "of the world" ($17^{14\ 16}$). The Father loved him (15^9, $17^{23\ 26}$). But this aorist does not carry a historical reference to what was, but to what is as it was, to what continues as it began in that pre-temporal beginning. Hence Jesus is in the Father (10^{38}, $14^{10\ 20}$, 17^{21}), the Father is in Him (10^{38}, 14^{10}, $17^{21\ 23}$), and He and the Father ("we") are one (10^{30}, $17^{11\ 22}$). And so He is sent by the Father into the world ($17^{3\ 8\ 18}$ etc.). This is the original, the relationship within the divine being, the inner divine co-existence, co-inherence and reciprocity.

And in full correspondence and similarity there is the relationship between God and man represented within the creaturely world, as a history played out in the cosmos, in the man Jesus, in His fellow-humanity, in His relationship to His disciples. We remember that the men concerned, in the first instance His disciples, belong properly to the Father, and that it is He who first loved them (14^{21}, 16^{27}, 17^{23}). But they are given by Him to the Son, and therefore to Jesus. Why? The basic answer is given by the word from heaven in 12^{28}: "I have both glorified him, and will glorify him again." The point is that the glory proper to Jesus in His relationship as Son to the Father is repeated and reflected on this new level and in this new relationship. "And now, O Father, glorify me ... with the glory which I had with thee before the world was." "I pray ... for them which thou hast given me ... and I am glorified in them." In accordance with the fact that the Son is not of the world, the same can be said of the disciples ($17^{14\ 16}$). In accordance with the fact that the Father is in Him, He is in them (17^{23}). In accordance with the fact that He is in the Father, they are in Him, Jesus (14^{20}). In

[221]

---

^{EN30} outside of God

accordance with the fact that He and the Father are one, they are to be one ($17^{11\ 22}$), and "no man is able to pluck them out of his hand" (10^{29}). Finally, in accordance with the fact that the Father has sent Him into the world, He sends them (17^{18}). And if we now read: "Neither pray I for these alone, but for them also which shall believe on me through their word; that they all may be one; as thou, Father, art in me, and I in thee, that they also may be one in us: that the world may believe that thou hast sent me" (17^{20-21}), we are obviously reminded even in this context of the bursting of the inner circle of the community outwards in favour of all men, of the whole world. He who is already glorified by the Father in His relationship to Him is again glorified in them, in His relationship to men. Thus the divine original creates for itself a copy in the creaturely world. The Father and the Son are reflected in the man Jesus. There could be no plainer reference to the *analogia relationis*[EN31] and therefore the *imago Dei*[EN32] in the most central, i.e., the Christological sense of the term.

Our starting-point was the question of the inner relationship between the determination of man as the covenant-partner of God on the one side and his creaturely and cosmic nature, his humanity, on the other; of the relationship which is not affected even by the sin of man, and therefore persists even in sinful man. We asked how far man's humanity may in all circumstances be a sign of his divine determination. We asked concerning the mystery of faith of the reference to the grace of God grounded in human nature as such. We have given a first answer to this question in relation to the man Jesus. The answer is that the inner relationship in this man is a relationship of clear agreement because His humanity, in correspondence and similarity with His determination for God and therefore with God Himself, as God's image, consists in the [222] fact that, as He is for God, He is also for man, for His fellows. This gives us a valid basis on which to take up our true question—the anthropological question, directed to all men generally, of this relationship, of the sign given to man in His humanity, of the mystery of faith of the reference to the grace of God in human nature itself.

2. THE BASIC FORM OF HUMANITY

We now turn from the man Jesus to other men—to man in general. Christology is not anthropology. We cannot expect, therefore, to find directly in others the humanity of Jesus, and therefore His fellow-humanity, His being for man, and therefore that final and supreme determination, the image of God. Jesus is man for His fellows, and therefore the image of God, in a way which others cannot even approach, just as they cannot be for God in the sense that He is. He alone is the Son of God, and therefore His humanity alone can be described as the being of an I which is wholly from and to the fellow-human Thou, and therefore a genuine I. In this respect we do not even have to take

---

[EN31] analogy of relation
[EN32] image of God

into account the fact that all other men are sinners and have turned aside from God. This means, of course, that their humanity (in more or less complete antithesis to this description) actually develops from their contradiction of the Thou to fresh opposition, and cannot therefore be a genuine I. But let us assume that there is in every man at least a serious even if hopeless striving in the other direction. The difference between Jesus and ourselves is still indissoluble. It is quite fundamental. For of no other man can we say that from the very outset and in virtue of his existence he is for others. Of no other man can we say that he is the Word of God to men, and therefore that he is directly and inwardly affected by them, or sent, commissioned and empowered to be and act in their place and as their representative, interposing and giving himself for all others, making their life possible and actual in and with his own, and thus being for them, their guarantor, in this radical and universal sense. There can be no repetition of this in anthropology. We are the victims of idealistic illusions if we deck out the humanity of man generally with features exclusive to that of the man Jesus. Man generally may mean and give a great deal to His fellows, but he cannot be their Deliverer or Saviour, not even in a single instance. On the contrary, he is the being on whose behalf the man Jesus is that which is peculiar to Him.

On the other hand, when we ask concerning humanity in general, the fact of the distinctive humanity of Jesus clearly points us in a certain direction and warns us no less clearly against its opposite.

[223]   If the humanity of Jesus consists in the fact that He is for other men, this means that for all the disparity between Him and us He affirms these others as beings which are not merely unlike Him in His creaturely existence and therefore His humanity, but also like Him in some basic form. Where one being is for others, there is necessarily a common sphere or form of existence in which the "for" can be possible and effective. If other men were beings whose humanity stood under an absolutely different and even contradictory determination from that of Jesus, it would be idle and confusing to call both Jesus and these others "men." For in the two cases the term would refer to quite different beings which would be better denoted by different terms. It would also be difficult to see how the "man" Jesus could be for and from and to other "men," how He could be inwardly affected by their being, how He could be called and sent to be their Saviour and commissioned and empowered to accomplish their deliverance, how He could interpose Himself with His human life for these other beings, acting and suffering and conquering in their place and as their Representative. The whole distinction of His humanity would thus fall to the ground as quite impossible.

On the other hand, it would also be hard to see how these others could become what Christians are called in Rom. 14[15] and 1 Cor. 8[11]: the beings or brothers for whom Christ died; those who are helped by the death of Christ, for whose human existence His death can mean deliverance. The creaturely nature of these beings cannot be alien or opposed to that of Christ, for all the disparity.

2. *The Basic Form of Humanity*

Where the saving work of the man Jesus is possible and effective in others, where there is this fellowship between Him and others, we have to ask concerning a co-ordination between Himself and others which is not just established by this fellowship but presupposed in the fact that it is made possible and actual. We have thus to ask concerning a basic form of the humanity of other men, of man in general, in which there is given and revealed the presupposition of the fact that the man Jesus can be for them. Is it true that the character of the humanity of the man Jesus as fellow-humanity is not an accident but is grounded in the will of God? Is it true that in this character of His humanity Jesus is the image of God? We have seen that this question is to be answered in the affirmative, and on what grounds. But is it not also true that this God is the Creator not merely of the man Jesus but of all men, so that in the form, and especially in the basic form, of the humanity of all men we have to see the creaturely essence which they are given by God? On these basic assumptions, a theological anthropology is forced to recognise that the question of that presupposition is not merely legitimate but necessary.

We cannot, therefore, stop at the Christological assertion that the man Jesus is for others. We have also to ask in respect of others how far as men they are beings which can be represented by the man Jesus in His suffering and conquering. We have to ask what it is that makes them possible for the covenant which is revealed and operative for them, which God has concluded with them, in this being of Jesus. We have to ask what it is that makes them capable of entering into covenant with God as the creatures of God.

Self-evidently, we do not ask concerning a worth or merit on the basis of which man has a claim to be the covenant-partner of God and to have the man Jesus act on his behalf. There is no claim of this kind; no claim of the creature against the Creator. It is the inconceivable grace of God that He takes him to Himself, that in the fellow-humanity of Jesus the free choice of the divine will is revealed and exercised as love for man. But since it is revealed and exercised in this way, since this God who is inconceivably gracious to him is the Creator of man, of every man, then the creatureliness of man, his human nature, his humanity, cannot be alien to this grace of God (no matter how inconceivable its address to it) but must necessarily confront it as it were with a certain familiarity.

We must be clear what we mean even when we speak of being capable of entering into covenant. We do not ask concerning an ability on the part of man to take up the relationship to God in covenant with Him, to be His covenant-partner. His creaturely essence has no power to do this. He can do it only as God makes him His partner, as He calls him to take up this relationship, as he exists as the one who is summoned to do so. It is again the inconceivable grace of God that He concludes this covenant with man, that He calls him to it, and sets him in a position to respond. But since He does this—He who is also man's Creator—this is only to say again that man's creaturely essence cannot be alien or opposed to this grace of God, but must confront it with a certain familiarity. If for the restoration and defence of His glory in the cosmos the grace of God has claimed the man Jesus, this shows at least that human creatureliness is not regarded as unsuitable or unserviceable, but as adapted to be employed to this end. We do not ask, then, concerning a capacity to enter into covenant which man himself has to actualise, but concerning that which makes him as the work of His Creator possible, serviceable, adapted and well-pleasing as His covenant-partner before all other creatures, and to that extent capable of entering into covenant.

Here, too, we can and must ask concerning a certain correspondence and similarity. If God had given to man a nature neutral and opposed to His grace and love and therefore to the fellow-humanity of Jesus, alien and antithetical from the very outset to covenant-partnership with Himself, how would He have made him the being marked off for this partnership? A second creation would have been needed to make this partnership possible and actual. And this second creation, in contrast to the new creation attested in Scripture, would have to be regarded as a contradiction of the first, materially altering [225] and even replacing it. If we are to avoid this conclusion, there has to be a common factor, and therefore a correspondence and similarity, between the determination of man for this covenant-partnership and his creatureliness, between the humanity of Jesus and that of man generally.

Again, we cannot stop at the mere assertion that the man Jesus is the image of God. But in relation to other men we have to ask how far as men they are beings with which Jesus can be ranged as the image of God. If God has in this One, and only in this One, His own image in the cosmos; if it is the inner essence of God which has its creaturely correspondence and similarity in His fellow-humanity, in His being for men, how can this be denied to those for whom He intervenes, to whom God has turned so seriously and totally in this One? If this One is their Saviour and Deliverer—He whose humanity is to take their place and give His life for them—and if as such He is the creaturely image of God Himself, how can they be creatures which completely lack this image, which do not at least prefigure and indicate it, when they are creatures of the same God and determined as such for covenant-partnership with Him? We emphasise again that there can be no question of their being simply and directly that which Jesus alone is. They are not simply and directly the covenant-partners of God as His creatures; they are destined to become this. And this means concretely that they are destined to participate in the benefits of the fellow-humanity of that One, to be delivered by Him. In their creatureliness they have need of the fact, and they are promised, that He, the One who is the image of God, is for them. What they themselves are in their relationship to God depends on this determination. Its reality, therefore, is not in themselves, but in Him, that One. But this determination, this reality, is genuinely present and is to be taken seriously in Him. From the very first, even in their creatureliness, they stand in the light which is shed by Him. But if they are in His light, they cannot be dark in themselves, but bright with His light.

2. *The Basic Form of Humanity*

We thus ask concerning their brightness in His light. To that extent we ask concerning the image of God in which every part as such has a share; concerning the correspondence and similarity with the essence of God peculiar to humanity as such. If it were not wholly proper to it, how could it be compatible with the essence of God to give Himself to solidarity with man as He has done in making the covenant with Himself the meaning and purpose of its creation and therefore the determination of its humanity, in Himself becoming man in Jesus Christ? For all the disparity, there is here presupposed a common factor, a parity, not merely between Jesus and other men, but, because between Jesus and other men, between God and man generally.

When we ask: What is humanity, human creatureliness? we must first ask: What is its basic form? In other words, to what extent does human essence correspond to the determination of man to be the covenant-partner of God? Our criterion in answering this question is the humanity of the man Jesus. If, for all the distance, there is between His humanity and ours a common factor, a similarity for all the dissimilarity, now that we turn to ourselves, to man generally, we must first make a great distinction and differentiation in respect of the human essence presupposed in our question. We cannot start with the assumption that there is a known and accepted picture of man and humanity before which we can pause and from the contours of which we can read off that which corresponds and is similar in man to the humanity of Jesus, and therefore supremely his participation in the image of God actualised in the humanity of Jesus. In theological anthropology there can be no question of giving a theological meaning to a given text (in this case a picture of man assumed to be generally known and accepted). This procedure would merely arouse the justifiable suspicion that the text itself (the known and accepted picture of man) is the constant and certain factor, whereas the theological interpretation is variable and uncertain like any other. No, in theological anthropology what man is, is decided by the primary text, i.e., by the humanity of the man Jesus. And the application of this criterion means that a whole sphere of supposed humanity is ruled out as non-human from the very first, and cannot be considered, because that which in it is regarded and alleged to be human stands in a contradiction to the humanity of Jesus which denies the essential similarity between Him and us and therefore excludes the possibility of the human creature as a covenant-partner of God, thus destroying the unity of creation and covenant. It is against any line of anthropological investigation and exposition which results in this denial, exclusion and destruction that we are warned *a limine*[EN33] by our Christological basis, even though we may seem to have very good reasons for accepting the picture of man proposed. We do not have to regard as human, as the essence of man which God created good, that which measured by this criterion is non-human, i.e., not yet or no longer human. On the contrary, in the application of this criterion we are free to

[226]

[EN33] from the outset

23

excise from the proposed picture of man all those features which are incompatible with the similarity which we presuppose for all the dissimilarity between the man Jesus and us other men. That which is incompatible with this similarity is *ipso facto*[EN34] non-human.

The excision with which we must begin will be as follows. It is not yet or no longer seen what humanity is when there is ascribed to man an existence which is abstract, i.e., abstracted from the co-existence of his fellows. No enriching, deepening or heightening of the concept of humanity in other directions, even religious, can excuse, make good or compensate this basic defect. If we see man in and for himself, and therefore without his fellows, we do not see him at all. If we see him in opposition or even neutrality towards his

[227] fellows, we do not see him at all. If we think that his humanity is only subsequently and secondarily determined, as an incidental enrichment, by the fact that he is not alone, we do not see him at all. If we do not realise and take into account from the very outset, from the first glance and word, the fact that he has a neighbour, we do not see him at all. At this point we have no option either to be tolerant or intolerant. We can only exclude. If a picture of man does not satisfy this demand, it has nothing whatever to do with the human essence in question, and it cannot be brought under discussion. We ask concerning the brightness of man in the light of the man Jesus, in the light of the fact that the man Jesus is for him, and therefore can be for him, because between the man Jesus and this other man there is similarity as well as dissimilarity. A man without his fellows, or radically neutral or opposed to his fellows, or under the impression that the co-existence of his fellows has only secondary significance, is a being which *ipso facto*[EN35] is fundamentally alien to the man Jesus and cannot have Him as Deliverer and Saviour. To be sure, He is the Deliverer and Saviour of sinful man, and therefore of the man who denies His fellow-humanity, acting as though he had no God and no neighbour, and therefore showing himself to be supremely non-human. But this does not mean that this sinner has ceased to be a man, or that we are allowed or even obliged to interpret His inhumanity as his humanity or the work of sin as the good creation of God. Even the sinful man who denies his humanity and in a blatant or more refined way turns his back on his fellows stands in the light of the humanity of Jesus. He acts contrary to his humanity, and he cannot be excused the guilt which he incurs by projecting a picture of man according to which his inhumanity—his isolation from his fellows, or neutrality or opposition in relation to them, or the casualness of their significance for him— belongs to his humanity as a possibility of the nature which he has been given by his Creator. No, even as he denies it, his creaturely nature stands in the light of the humanity of Jesus, and it is bright in this light, accusing him of shining in his inhumanity not only against God and his neighbour but also primarily

[EN34] for that very reason
[EN35] for that very reason

and finally against himself, and yet not ceasing to bind him to his Saviour and Deliverer. To sin is to wander from a path which does not cease to be the definite and exclusive path of man even though he leaves it. The fact that man sins does not mean that God ceases to be God and therefore man man. In this context, too, we must say that man does not accomplish a new creation by sinning. He cannot achieve any essential alteration of the human nature which he has been given. He can only shame this nature and himself. He can only bring himself into supreme peril. But the fact that he has in the man Jesus his Saviour and Deliverer is the pledge that he has not ceased to be a man, a being ordered in relation to this Jesus. The fact that the Good Shepherd has acted on behalf of His lost sheep shows that He does not give it up for lost but still [228] numbers it with His flock and deals with it as His own and not an alien possession. This is what makes the idea of a man without his fellows, in any form, quite intolerable. This is what rules it out from the very first. Theological anthropology cannot enter the sphere where this man without his fellows is considered as a serious possibility. It knows man well enough as the man of sin, but not as the man who actualises his creaturely nature in his sin, whom God has created for this actualisation. It cannot blame God for what man has made of himself. And it cannot exculpate man from the permanent reproach of the transgression with which he denies the truth, the truth of his Creator and his own truth. We take sin lightly if we spare sinful man this reproach, giving him the evasion that as a sinner he has forfeited and lost his humanity, or that God has created him in a humanity in which he can choose either to be man or not, and in which inhumanity is more probable than humanity. Every supposed humanity which is not radically and from the very first fellow-humanity is inhumanity. At this point a distinction must be made *a limine*EN36, and humanity must be protected against its decisive and definitive destruction. If we take away fellow-man from the picture of man, and describe the latter as a being which is alien, opposed or casual in relation to him, we have not merely given an inadequate or partially false representation of man, but described a different being altogether. There is nothing else for it. In this respect theological anthropology must be quite pitiless in its opposition to every attempt to seek real man outside the history of his responsibility to God. The very reality of man in his responsibility before God necessarily gives us the negative rule for an understanding of the basic form of his humanity—that in no circumstances may it be sought in that abstraction, in a humanity without the fellow-man.

At this point two marginal observations may be made on the general theological situation, especially at the present time.

1. The last war, with all that led up to it and all its possible consequences, has posed afresh the problem of humanity from the particular angle of the question of the rights, dignity and sanctity of the fellow-man. Humanity stands at the crossroads. In its future development as

---

EN36 from the outset

humanity, will it be for man or against him? Behind the political, social and economic possibilities there stands always with the same urgency, if in different forms, the necessity of this decision. The lot may be cast one way or the other according to the various anthropological views more or less consciously adopted. And it may well be that an anthropology and ethics of compromise is no longer adequate because the dynamic of a resolute humanity without the fellow-man may perhaps steal a march on all mediating positions and finally dominate the field with fatal consequences. Those who cannot approve this development are seriously asked to-day whether they are capable of producing from their own anthropology and ethics an equally and even more dynamic championship of the fellow-man. And the further question then becomes insistent, as it is already, whether any anthropology or ethics is able to do this apart from the Christian. A whole-hearted adoption of this position is possible only where the hostility, neutrality and antithesis between man and man is radically overcome,

[229]   i.e., in the presupposed concept of humanity, and known and rejected as inhumanity. Where this is not the case, there can be only half-way teachings, and it is doubtful whether even a delaying action can be successful against the assault of a humanity without the fellow-man. The exclusiveness which dares—because it must—to repudiate this humanity as inhumanity *a limine*[EN37] and without discussion is not possible, as far as one can see, except on the basis of a Christian and theological anthropology and ethics.

2. But all that glitters is not gold, and we cannot accept as genuine Christian and theological anthropology everything that claims to be such. Where the claim is justified there will necessarily be ruthlessness at this point, i.e., in the rejection of all humanity without or against the fellow-man. And this raises the question of its criterion and its consistent application. If it has a Christological basis, then, as we have seen, it has a criterion which will prove to be divisive from the very first, at the very first sight of the object. A humanity without the fellow-man will necessarily be abandoned as inhuman at the very first step. Humanity for man will remain as the only possibility. But in modern theology it is not the rule to base anthropology on Christology and therefore to use this criterion from the very outset. The question arises whether the same radicalness and ruthlessness are really possible on the other paths which are more customary. Perhaps they only lead again to mediating and therefore indefensible positions. Perhaps this type of Christian and theological anthropology cannot offer any effective resistance to the onslaught of a humanity without the fellow-man. And in the light of its lack of radicalness and ruthlessness the question then arises whether it can really claim to be a Christian and theological anthropology at all.

We have to rule out the possibility of a humanity without the fellow-man. Hence we must not discuss it. But it will be worth our while to consider briefly what we are ruling out, what conception of man we are passing by without discussion. We may begin by admitting that it is not self-evident that it should be ruled out in this way, and thus passed by without discussion. In doing this, we follow the higher right of theological necessity. But on behalf of the rejected humanity which is either without or against the fellow-man, or pays him only casual attention, it may be argued that it is not only infinitely more appealing but even self-evident on a non-theological view. If we bracket the Christian judgment, does not the word "man" immediately and at bottom definitively conjure up a being which is basically and properly for itself, so that although it may be vaguely recognised in others it can and is seen immediately and directly only in the self? According to this constantly victorious concep-

---

[EN37] from the outset

tion humanity consists in the fact that I am, that I am for myself, and neither from nor to others. In certain circumstances this "I am" can have a powerful radius. And it is not to be subjected to a moralistic judgment and condemnation as limitation or self-seeking. For after all, it will somewhere embrace others as well. The only trouble is that basically and properly it is without them or against them or only secondarily and occasionally with them and for them. "I am"—this is the forceful assertion which we are all engaged in making and of which we are convinced that none can surpass it in urgency or importance; the assertion of the self in which we can neither be replaced by any nor restrained by any. "I am" means that I satisfy myself even in the sense that I have to do justice to myself, that I am pressingly claimed by myself. "I am" means that I stand under the irresistible urge to maintain myself, but also to make something of myself, to develop myself, to try out myself, to exercise and prove myself. "I am" means further, however, that in every development and activity outwards I must and will at all costs maintain and assert myself, not dissipating and losing myself, but concentrating even as I expand, and getting even as I give. It means that I must and will acquire and have personality. But the radius is even wider than this. "I am" means that I may and must live; that I may and must live out my life in the material and spiritual cosmos, enjoying, working, playing, fashioning, possessing, achieving and exercising power; that I may and must in my own place and within my own limits—and who is to say where these are to be drawn?—have my share in the goods of the earth, in the fulness of human knowledge and capacity, in the further development of human technique and art and organisation. These are powerful projections of the "I am" outwards into space and time and its truth and poetry, or rather its poetry and truth, its myth and history. And to these projections there certainly belongs the fashioning of a relationship to what is called "heaven" in the Bible and "God," "the gods," or "the divine" elsewhere; the construction of a positive or negative, believing or sceptical, original or conventional position with reference to the ultimate limits and mystery of life, the incomprehensible which will finally confront all our comprehension. And inevitably in this onward progress of the "I am" the encounter with fellow-men will have its own specific and determinative part; the burning questions whether this or that person is important or indifferent to me, whether he attracts or repels me, whether he helps and serves or obstructs and harms me, whether he is superior to me or I can master him and am thus superior to him. To these projections there also belong the dealings with him, with all the selection and rejection, the conflict, peace and renewal of conflict, the constant hide-and-seek, the domination and dependence, the morality and immorality which these dealings inevitably involve and without which life would certainly be much easier and simpler but also much poorer and duller. The only thing is that here too we have a projection of the "I am" outwards. Even the many forms of our fellows are ultimately elements in our own myth or history, not found but invented and decked out by us, and merely speaking the words which we put on their lips. There are

[230]

merely more or less serviceable or unserviceable figures in our own play, drawn into ourselves to the extent that we have in some way transformed them into something that belongs to us. In their genuine otherness and particularity they are without like the rest of the cosmos. Originally and properly within I

[231]   am still alone by myself: in my freedom in relation to the whole cosmos; with my poetry and truth; with the question of my needs and desires and loves and hates; with my known and sometimes unknown likes and dislikes; with my capacities and propensities; as my own doctor, as the sovereign architect, director, general and dictator of the whole, of my own earth and heaven, my cosmos, God and fellow-men; as the incomparable inventor and sustainer of myself; in first and final solitude. Within this total conception there is naturally an infinite range of colours and contours, of nuances and emphases, to the final and apparently self-exclusive extremes. It is a unity only in general. In detail the variations are so great as to make the common features almost unrecognisable. It never repeats itself. It constantly takes on new forms not only in the different ages and cultures, not only in the distinction of individuals, but also within their own specific development, in youth and maturity and age, in the changing stations and circumstances of life. But we should not be misled. The "I am" may often be less powerfully at work as the basis and beginning of all things. We may not always see that in everything else we really have projections of this I. Our fellows in their otherness and particularity may often be more forcefully and obstinately and pertinently at work than our depiction suggests. Yet the overwhelming unity of the whole remains—of an attempted humanity in which the fellow-man has no constitutive function. And, if for a moment we suspend our Christian judgment, we at once recognise that it is the most obvious thing in the world to answer the question of humanity with perhaps a more profound and purified and convincing modification of this view. We have to realise what it means that theological anthropology cannot grasp this most obvious of all possibilities, but must reject it *a limine*[EN38].

By way of illustration we may refer to Friedrich Nietzsche. We do this for two reasons. He developed this conception of humanity with unequalled logic and perspicacity. And in his refusal to evade its deepest root and supreme consequence, in his enthusiastic acceptance of them, he resolutely and passionately and necessarily rejected, not a caricature of the Christian conception of humanity, but in the form of a caricature the conception itself. He shows us how necessary it is that we for our part must less violently but no less resolutely reject the conception of humanity of which he is a classical exponent.

In 1888 Nietzsche wrote his *Ecce homo*, which was published in 1908. This is an autobiography, of the same genre as Augustine's and Rousseau's *Confessions*, but with no admission of mistakes, and constituting an unequivocal final testimony for the future interpretation of the author. Shortly after writing it, Nietzsche was declared to be afflicted with an incurable mental sickness. It was understandable that Franz Overbeck, one of his closest friends, should at first prevent its publication. But he was not justified on material grounds, for whether Nietzsche was already ill or not when he wrote this book there can be

---

[EN38] from the outset

no doubt that in it he rightly perceived and summed up the final intentions of his purposes and work as they had marked him from the very first.

On the first page of *Ecce homo* we read in heavy type the statement: "Hear me, for I am he; do not at any price mistake me" (Krönersche-Klassiker-Ausgabe, 307). And even more menacingly on the final page, again in heavy type: "Am I understood?—Dionysius against the Crucified ... " (p. 433). The first saying is a bizarre but genuine form of the first and final proposition of humanity without the fellow-man. Nietzsche liked to see it represented in the form of the ancient Greek god Dionysius. The second is the repudiation of Christianity self-evident on the basis of this humanity.

"Hear me, for I am he; do not at any price mistake me." We shall first try to see what this means. Goethe too, whom Nietzsche usually although not always mentioned respectfully as a precursor, wanted to be regarded and estimated as "he," with a certain solemnity and joyous reverence making himself and his way and culture and work the theme of special consideration and explanation, and having an obvious consciousness of himself. But Nietzsche was basically and properly self-consciousness and nothing more. His angrily uncertain: "Do not at any price mistake me" and later his eager: "Am I understood?" would have been quite unthinkable on the lips of Goethe. Goethe was on the same path as Nietzsche, an exponent of the same "I am," but he knew when to stop, and said certain ultimate things about this beginning and end either not at all or very seldom and with great caution. He knew how often and not unjustly he was praised for keeping to the golden mean. He could do so, and necessarily, because his self-consciousness was continually filled with the most attentive and deeply interested world-consciousness. The quiet fulfilment of almost uninterrupted work in the world outside gives to his picture, and his occasional self-portraits, the character of a cheerful sanity in which he could not be tempted by any anxiety lest he should be confused with others, because he was far too worldly wise even to make this a matter of debate. But Nietzsche was the prophet of that humanity without the fellow-man. He did not merely reveal its secret; he blabbed it out. He was in a non-classical form what Goethe was in a classical. Apollo did not content him; it had to be Dionysius. Was he no longer sure of himself, as Goethe so obviously was? He once described himself as a victim of decadence, an example of the decline of the human type which he thought to be perfect and sometimes found to be represented and actualised in certain respects in Goethe. Did he perhaps really speak the final word of this humanity? At any rate, he had to cry out something which was in Goethe, and to which he occasionally gave expression, but which he wisely preferred to keep to himself—the fact that in a last and deepest isolation he and he alone was the eye and measure and master and even the essence of all things. What Goethe quietly lived out Nietzsche had to speak out continally with the nervous violence of ill-health.

Basically, when he was not engaged in polemics but spoke positively, Nietzsche never spoke except about himself. If we study him, it constantly strikes us how little he deals with material and objective problems. What he himself was not, if it did not repel him and he it, interested him only as a paradigm and symbol, or, to use his own expression, a projection of himself. And even when he repelled, and was repelled, it was only because the object concerned either could not be used as a paradigm of himself (like Christianity), or could no longer be put to this service (like the later Wagner). Nietzsche was originally a Greek philologist, but he no longer needed Greek philology when he had discovered Dionysius as "the one root of all Greek art," as the "philosophising god," and this Dionysius was none other than himself, Friedrich Nietzsche. For a while he devoted himself with fiery energy to natural science under the banner of evolution, but when probably in this sphere he had discovered the "will to power" as the supreme and proper form of human existence—and this, of course, as an unmistakeable but impressive symbol of his own will—the subject did not present him with any further interest or problems. He wrote concerning "Schopenhauer as

Educator," but the instructive Schopenhauer was admittedly he himself. And he magnified Wagner so long as he could find and represent in him himself and his own paganism—which was no longer possible after the personal injury done him by Wagner's *Parsifal*, in which he discerned a pilgrimage to Canossa. "Delight in things, it is said, but what is really meant is delight in oneself through the medium of things" (*Menschliches, allzu Menschliches*, 366)—this is something which Goethe could never have admitted. Nietzsche did not merely admit it; he openly championed it as a maxim. In fact, he never really had any other. And so Zarathustra too—and there was little need for the pride with which Nietzsche expressly assures us of the fact—is none other than he himself, and this time the true Nietzsche. Nietzsche admits that by his ophthalmic affliction he had been redeemed from "the book" and had not read for many years—"the greatest benefit which I have ever experienced" (*Ecce homo*, 384). For to read as the scholar reads is not to think but simply to answer to an attraction, to react. "I call it criminal that at the crack of dawn, in all the youth and freshness of his powers, the scholar—a decadent—should read a book" (p. 349). There is apparently only one exception: "As I see it, it is one of the most singular distinctions that anyone can evince to take up a book of my own:—I myself will guarantee that he will take off his shoes, not to speak of boots .... When Doctor Heinrich von Stein once honestly complained that he could not understand a word of my Zarathustra, I told him that this was quite usual. To have understood, i.e., experienced six sentences of it is to be lifted on to a higher mortal plane than 'modern' men can reach" (p. 355). Nietzsche was of the opinion that with his Zarathustra he had given humanity a greater gift than any so far given (p. 309). He declared that in comparison with it the rest of human activity was poor and limited; that a Goethe or a Shakespeare could not last a single moment in this atmosphere of tremendous passion and exaltation; that face to face with Zarathustra Dante was merely a believer and not one who creates truth, a masterful spirit, a destiny; that the authors of the *Veda* were priests and unworthy to unloose the shoes of a Zarathustra. And this is only the least to be said concerning it, giving no conception of the distance, the "azure isolation" of the work. "The spirits and qualities of all great souls put together could not produce a single speech of Zarathustra" (p. 40of.). Naturally this sounds disordered. But it is the position which Nietzsche indicated, and to the representation of which he dedicated his life's work. And what is this position but the "I am" of humanity without the fellow-man, except that this time it is adopted without condition or restraint, in all its nakedness? I am—in "azure isolation." Nietzsche often thought that he lived in indescribable wealth in this isolation, and these were the moments when he could beseechingly and yet also angrily point to the fact that he had infinite things to give, that infinite things were to be received from him. But then he had to contradict himself, for how could he give wealth and life and joy in this isolation? On the contrary, "when I have given myself for a moment to my Zarathustra, I walk up and down the room for half an hour, unable to master an unbearable spasm of sobbing" (p. 432).

> "The desert grows: woe to those who fight it,
> Stone grates on stone, the desert gulps and swallows,
> And dreadful death looks gleaming brown
> And cowers—life is a cowering ...
> Forget not man, hired out to pleasure,
> Thou art the stone, the desert, thou art death" (p. 447).

And how is Zarathustra to be anything for others or give anything to them? If there were others, he would not be Zarathustra. "First give thyself, O Zarathustra" (p. 471). But he cannot do this even if he desired now that it has been and is his necessity and triumph to be "6,000 feet beyond man and time" (p. 391). "The whole fact of man lies at a dreadful distance below him" (p. 309).

2. *The Basic Form of Humanity*

"Alone!
And who would dare
To be a guest,
Thy guest? ... " (p. 449).

To whom is he, the superman, the absolute "I am," to give himself? And if there is some-one, will he thank him for this or any gift?

"Who can love thee,
The unattainable?
Thy blessing makes all dry
And poor in love
—a thirsty land ... " (p. 470).

To this very day Nietzsche has been much admired and honoured and loved. But he had no use for the fact; he could not love in return. Nothing is more striking than that he had no use at all for women. "They all love me," he could say, but without any satisfaction. He can only ignore them or heap upon them scorn and his choicest invective. And in his very rejection of them he regards himself as "the first psychologist of the eternal-feminine" (p. 363). Yet in addition he cannot repay or be faithful to even the best and most sincere of his male friends. "At an absurdly early age, when I was only seven, I knew that no human word would reach me, but has this ever caused me any obvious concern?" (p. 353). "An extreme candour towards me is for me a necessary condition of existence; I cannot live in conditions of insincerity .... This means that my intercourse with men constitutes no little problem of patience; my humanity does not consist in fellow-feeling with men, but in restraint from fellow-feeling .... My humanity is a continual self-conquest." It is also to be noted, of course, that Nietzsche described the contempt for man, misanthropy, as his greatest danger, and one from which he thought that he had finally redeemed himself. But how? By fleeing to a height "where there are no companions to sit at the well" and drink with him.

"On the tree of the future we build our nest;
Eagles will bring us solitary ones food in their beaks.
Not food which the unclean may eat,
For they would think they were eating fire,
And burn their mouths.

We have no homesteads here for the unclean,
To their bodies and spirits our fortune
Would be an icy cavity,
And we shall live over them like strong winds,
Neighbours of the eagles and the snow and the sun,
Like strong winds" (p. 329f.).

In this way Zarathustra is lord even of misanthropy. But how? "Man is for him something unshaped, material, an ugly stone which needs the sculptor." His only impulse towards man is that of the hammer to the stone.

"Oh, ye men, in the stone there sleeps a picture,
The picture of all pictures!
Oh that it must sleep in the hardest and ugliest stone!
My hammer rages furiously against its prison,
And pieces fly from the stone,
But what care I!" (p. 406f.).

[235]   Has he ever been obviously concerned that man is either unattainable or attain able only in such a way as to cause a repugnance from which he must seek that lofty refuge with the eagles and strong winds? And yet Zarathustra does frequently seem to be very greatly troubled by this inaccessibility. It is intrinsic to the superman, to Dionysius, to Zarathustra to be almost torn asunder by sorrow at having to be the superman, Dionysius, Zarathustra.

> "The world—a door
> To a thousand deserts silent and cold!
> Who has lost
> What thou lost, can find no rest.
>
> Thou standest pale
> Condemned to winter wandering
> Like smoke
> Always seeking the cold heavens.
>
> Fly, bird, rasping
> Thy song like a wilderness-bird!—
> Conceal, thou fool,
> Thy bleeding heart in ice and disdain!
>
> The crows cry
> In whirring flight to the city.
> —Soon it will snow
> And woe then to him who has no home!"
> (*Fröhl. Wiss.*, 392 f.).

The only thing is that he soon rises up again like the eagle, scorning himself for his weakness, and finding joy and exultation and self-glory in the very thing which pains him:

> "Yea, I know whence I derive!
> Insatiable as the flame,
> I burn and consume myself.
> All I touch is light,
> And what I leave a cinder.
> I am indeed a flame!"
> (*Fröhl. Wiss.*, 30).

Which prevails—the complaint or the rejoicing? "I know my fate. The memory of something dreadful will be linked with my name, of an unparalleled crisis, of the most profound clash of conscience, of a decision conjured up against everything that has so far been believed and demanded and held sacred. I am no man; I am dynamite" (*Ecce homo*, 422). Is this complaint or rejoicing, or both? In the same breath Nietzsche can call himself both the incomparable bearer of good news and the "destroyer *par excellence.*" "I am easily the most terrible man there has ever been, but this does not mean that I am not also the greatest benefactor." He promises that only because of him are there renewed hopes. And yet he prophesies: "There will be wars such as never were on earth. Only after me will there be high politics on earth" (p. 412, 423f.). According to view or inclination, we can be deaf to his true message, rejecting or believing either the one or the other, the *evangelion* or *dysangelion*[EN39], but his real

---

[EN39] gospel, good news or anti-gospel, bad news

2. *The Basic Form of Humanity*

place is beyond good and evil, not merely like that of a Hercules choosing between the two, but genuinely as the place of the superman, who conjoins good and evil and evil and good in himself, and is thus, like Voltaire, "a *grandseigneur*^{EN40} of the spirit" (p. 380), "the first true man" (p. 423). It is thus that Nietzsche is he, and declares the fact, proclaiming himself and refusing to be mistaken. "I am the first immoralist" (p. 377, 386, 424). Immoral does not mean non-moral. There is no point in making him a bogeyman in this sense. His immoralism consists in the fact that he has the question of morality behind him, that like God he is without "tables," that he "invents" his own categorical imperative (*Der Antichrist*, 216), that he is his own table. With the conclusion of the *Götzendämmerung* in the same year, 1888, there followed indeed a "seventh day; the stroll of a God along the Po" (*Ecce homo*, 413). The one who strolls in this way along the Po is the great "he" whom Nietzsche proclaims and whom he will not have mistaken for any other.

[236]

A clever man of our own day has called Nietzsche "the greatest horse-coper of any age." It cannot be questioned that we have here a genuine short circuit, a genuine deception and self-deception. But I should hesitate to accept that severe judgment because it would apply to too many things and people whose last intentions are merely represented with less restraint and we might almost say with greater honesty by Nietzsche. Goethe, Hegel, Kant and Leibniz would come under the same condemnation, and not just a specifically German spirit, but the spirit of all European humanity as fashioned and developed since the 16th century. Outside Germany it has become customary to-day to represent and castigate Nietzsche as one of those who must bear responsibility, and even primary responsibility, for preparing and making possible National Socialism. There is something in this. But it must not be forgotten that Nietzsche directed his most scathing terms against the German nationalism of his age, the age of Bismarck, so that any contribution he made to its development was highly indirect. More positively, dismissing Germany as the "plain" of European culture, he liked to remember that he was half-Polish by descent, and valued no literature or culture more highly than the French. And was he not the man who at the very height of the age of Bismarck expressed the view that it would be worth looking for a time to Switzerland to escape the opportunist outlook prevailing in Germany? And, like so many others, he praised Italy, and historically the Italian Renaissance, as his true home, perversely maintaining that he found his superman most adequately portrayed in its most notorious representative, Caesar Borgia. But the Italian Renaissance was the mother and model not merely of Italian but of all European humanity in the modern age. And so Nietzsche-Zarathustra emphatically wished to be understood as a European, as the best and only and final European. If his representation of humanity is "horse-coping," the same is true at root—a hidden and suppressed, but very real root—of a number of others as well. And if Nietzsche prepared the ground for National Socialism, the same may be said with equal justification of other manifestations and expressions of the European spirit during the last centuries. It is thus a very serious and responsible undertaking genuinely to oppose the humanity which he represented. The same consideration holds good in respect of his mental ill-health. If it was only as one who was mentally ill that he was capable of this representation, or conversely, if he became mentally disordered in the course of it, the question who was really deranged amongst them may be seriously asked in relation to many who were perhaps healthy in mind, or seemed to be so, only because they did not or would not see that to be a consistent champion and representative of this humanity is necessarily to be or to become mentally sick. The current affirmation and accusation are so serious that there is every reason to hesitate before making them.

We now turn to the other saying: "Am I understood—Dionysus against the Crucified."

---

^{EN40} great lord

At a first glance, it does not seem as if the book will finally lead to this antithesis, or that Nietzsche all the time wishes it to be taken in the sense of this antithesis. Prior to the last five pages of the *Ecce homo* we are not directly prepared for it even by the occasional flashes which anticipate this conclusion. Its pregnancy and violence do not seem to stand in any real relationship to the polemic of the book or of the life-work of Nietzsche summed up in it. Nietz-

[237] sche was an indefatigable fighter. Proclaiming that existence on high, he could hardly be otherwise. He was always against what others were for. "I am the anti-donkey *par excellence*, and therefore a monster in world history." The continuation is, of course, as follows: "In Greek, and not only in Greek, I am the Antichrist." And under this title Nietzsche wrote a whole book in 1886. Yet we cannot conclude from the book that this was more than one of the many fronts on which he was active as "anti-donkey." Nietzsche attacked the philosophy, morals, art, science and civilisation of his own and most earlier times, and in none of these spheres did he fail to leave dead and wounded behind him. Often rather sketchily in detail, but always with a sure intuition for essentials, for true correspondence and opposition, he attempted with equal taste and ruthlessness in all these fields a "transvaluation of all values" in the light of the superman and his will to power. It was only natural, therefore, that he should also attack Christianity. But that as "anti-donkey" he should supremely and decisively be "Antichrist," that everything should finally become a formal crusade against the cross, is not immediately apparent, but has to be learned and noted from a reading of Nietzsche. Yet it must be learned and noted if we are to understand him. The strange culmination in the *Ecce homo* is no mere freak. For the book about Antichrist was not just one among many. Nietzsche did not fight on all fronts in all his books. And yet there is not a single one of them, so far as I can see, in which he did not have whole sections or notable individual statements devoted to Christianity and directed in more or less violent polemic against it. And the polemic gained in weight and severity with the passage of time. We might describe this conflict as a swelling base accompanying the others and finally overwhelming and taking them up into itself, until finally there is only the one theme: "Dionysius against the Crucified."

But a second point has also to be learned and noted. The Antichrist has a definite and concrete sense. If he opposes Dionysius to the Crucified, according to the last five pages of the *Ecce homo* this means that he opposes him, or rather himself, to what he calls Christian morality. Already in the sphere of morals as such it might have been said that this was not just one of Nietzsche's foes but like Christianity itself the great enemy which he always had in view when he fought the philosophy, art, science and civilisation of his time. From the very outset Nietzsche was concerned about ethics, and it was for this reason and in this sense that he was an "immoralist." And morality and Christianity finally coalesced for him in a single detestable form, so that wherever he encountered morality he thought that he could see and deplore and attack Christianity. The last five pages of the *Ecce homo* begin with the words: "But in a very different sense as well I have chosen the word immoralist as my banner, my badge of honour; I am proud to have this word as a mark of distinction from humanity. For no one previously has experienced Christian morality as something beneath him. For this there was required a hardness, a perspective, a hitherto unheard-of psychological depth and radicalness. Christian morality has previously been the Circe of all thinkers—they stood in its service. Who before me has descended to the depths from which there gushes out the poison of this kind of ideal—of world-renunciation?" (p. 428). And then he continues: "Am I understood?—What separates and marks me off from the rest of humanity is that I have discovered Christian morality." Discovered it as that which has corrupted humanity! "Not to have seen this before seems to me to be the greatest stain which humanity has on its conscience ... an almost criminal counterfeiting *in psychologicis*[EN41]. Blindness in face of Chris-

---

EN41 in matters of the spirit

tianity is the crime *par excellence*, a crime against life itself .... Millennia and nations, first and last, philosophers and old wives—apart from five or six moments of history, and myself as the seventh—have all been equally guilty in this respect" (p. 429). And again: "Am I understood? ... The discovery of Christian morality is an event without parallel, a veritable catastrophe. Whoever sheds light on it is a *force majeure*[EN42], a destiny, breaking the history of humanity into two parts. One either lives before him or after him .... The lightning of truth shatters that which formerly stood completely secure. Let him who understands what is destroyed see to it whether he has anything still in his hands" (p. 432). Nietzsche means that which must now be destroyed (it is not yet destroyed) on the basis of this epoch-making discovery. He thus concludes with Voltaire: *Ecrasez l' infame*[EN43]. And this is what leads him to his final word: "Am I understood?—Dionysius against the Crucified." [238]

It is not self-evident that Nietzsche's general offensive should finally be against Christianity in this sense and under this sign. Again, in the *Ecce homo* itself and the earlier writings there seems at first to be a certain discrepancy of polemical standpoint. The offence of modern man is primarily at the incredible fact of the past reaching from remote ages into the present in the form of Christianity. "When on a Sunday morning we hear the old bells sounding, we ask ourselves: Is it really possible? This all has to do with a crucified Jew of two thousand years ago who said that he was the Son of God" (*M. allzu M.*, 126). The Greek in him is offended at the "non-Greek element in Christianity" (*ib.*, 127). The philologist is offended at the exegetical and historical methods of the apostle Paul: "All these holy epileptics and seers did not possess a thousandth particle of the integrity of self-criticism with which a modern philologist reads a text or tests the truth of a historical event .... In comparison with us, they are moral cretins" (*W. z. Macht*, 123). He is also incensed at the imprudence, impatience and crudity of modern Christian theologians which drive the philologist in him almost to frenzy (*Antichrist*, 280; *W. z. Macht*, 152). Again, the aesthete in him experiences "a kind of inexpressible aversion at contact with the New Testament": little, bad-mannered bigots who quite uncalled-for try to speak about the deepest problems; a quite undistinguished type of man with the swelling claim to have more and indeed all value; something of *foeda superstitio*[EN44]; something from which we withdraw our hands in case of defilement (*ib.*, 141). "We would no more choose to be 'early Christians' than Polish Jews .... They have a nasty smell. I have looked in vain even for one redeeming feature in the New Testament. It does not contain anything free or generous or open or sincere. Humanity has not even made its first beginning at this point" (*Antichrist*, 269). Arguments are also used which show that it was not for nothing that Nietzsche was the friend of F. Overbeck. The greatest witness against Christianity is the pitiable figure of the everyday Christian, whose complacency—he has no thought of seeking his salvation with fear and trembling—is a clear demonstration that the decisive assertions of Christianity are of no importance (*M. allzu M.*, 128). It is the Church, which is the very thing against which Jesus preached and taught His disciples to fight, embodying the triumph of that which is anti-Christian no less than the modern state and modern nationalism (*W. zur Macht*, 131, 145). It is to be noted that the fact that Nietzsche will have nothing to do with God is so self-evident that it plays no part at all in his arguments against Christianity. In the *Ecce homo* he said that he knew atheism neither as an experience nor as an event, but by instinct. "God is dead"—there is no need for heat or polemics. But is he quite so sure about this? The Dionysius-dithyrambs of 1888 show that he must have had some misgivings on the point. An "unknown God" obtrudes his obviously dangerous being in the speeches of a curious opponent of Zarathustra, and he is not a

---

[EN42] superior force
[EN43] Crush the infamy
[EN44] vile superstition

complete stranger to Nietzsche himself, this hunter, thief, robber, bandit, this great enemy, this executioner-God etc., who tries to penetrate into his heart, his most secret thoughts (p. 457). But we need not pursue this aspect. Nietzsche's heart was not in contesting the existence of God, or in the other arguments to which we have referred. His central attack, into which he flung himself with all his force, was upon what he called Christian morality. All his other assaults upon Christianity derive their secret strength, and are initiated and directed, from this point. Even in the *Antichrist* this motif has become the *cantus firmus*[EN45], suppressing all the others.

[239]

But what is the absolutely intolerable and unequivocally perverted element which Nietzsche thinks that he has discovered, and must fight to the death, in Christian morality, and in this as the secret essence of all morality? Why is it that he must finally act in this matter as if there were no other foe upon earth, and no more urgent task than to vanquish it? The answer is given by Nietzsche himself with a hundred variations and nuances the complicated pattern of which we cannot follow, but the content of which is perfectly clear. It is because Christianity is not really a faith, and is not really "bound to any of its shameless dogmas," and does not basically need either metaphysics, asceticism, or "Christian" natural science, but is at root a practice, and is always possible as such, and in the strict sense has its "God" in this practice (*Antichrist*, 249, *W. z. Macht*. 155), that Nietzsche encounters it as the last enemy on his own true field. For he himself is finally concerned about a definite practice; he is decisively an ethicist. And he encounters it as an enemy because it opposes to Zarathustra or Dionysius, the lonely, noble, strong, proud, natural, healthy, wise, outstanding, splendid man, the superman, a type which is the very reverse, and so far has managed to do this successfully with its blatant claim that the only true man is the man who is little, poor and sick, the man who is weak and not strong, who does not evoke admiration but sympathy, who is not solitary but gregarious—the mass-man. It goes so far as to speak of a crucified God, and therefore to identify God Himself with this human type, and consequently to demand of all men not merely sympathy with others but that they themselves should be those who excite sympathy and not admiration. "The neighbour is transfigured into a God ... Jesus is the neighbour transposed into divinity, into a cause awakening emotion" (*W. z. Macht*, 142). "The absurd residuum of Christianity, its fables, concept-spinning and theology, do not concern us; they could be a thousand times more absurd, and we should not lift a finger against them. But this ideal we contest" (*ib.*, 154). Nietzsche contests it as the greatest misfortune of the human race thus far. For it was the practical victory of a religion and morality of slaves, of failures, of those who go under, of the colourless, the mistaken, the worthless, the underworld, the ghetto, the variegated mass of abjects and rejects, those who creep and crawl on the earth revolting against all that is lofty (*Antichrist*, 124, 229, 263, 278f.). It was "typically Socialist teaching." "What I do not like at all about this Jesus of Nazareth and His apostle Paul is that they put so many things into the heads of little people, as though their modest virtues were of some value. The price was too high; for they have brought into disrepute the far more valuable qualities of virtue and manhood, opposing a bad conscience to the self-esteem of the excellent soul, and betraying even to self-destruction the noble, generous, bold, excessive inclinations of the strong" (*W. z. Macht*, 142f.). And this pernicious ideal is Christianity both in kernel and in substance right up to the present day. It has been able to insinuate itself into the whole of Western culture, philosophy and morality to their great detriment, namely, at the price of the surrender of their Greek inheritance and their surreptitious and flagrant barbarisation. And apart from six or seven upright figures no one has ever even noticed the fact right up to the present time. "God has chosen what is weak and foolish and ignoble and despised in the eyes of the world, is how the formula ran, and

---

[EN45] bass line

36

2. *The Basic Form of Humanity*

décadence conquered *in hoc signo*[EN46]. God on the cross—do we still not understand the terrible background significance of this symbol?—Everything that suffers, everything that hangs on the cross, is divine. We all hang on the cross and therefore we are all divine .... We alone are divine .... Christianity was a victory, and a more excellent way went down before it—Christianity is the greatest misfortune of the human race thus far" (*Antichrist* 279).

This was what Nietzsche discovered as Christian morality, and this was his attack against it: [240] the attack in which all his onslaughts on Christianity finally have both their origin and issue; the attack which finally emerged in *Ecce homo* as the common denominator of his whole Dionysian offensive. What happened to the man that he had finally to burst out in this frenzied way and to give to his whole life-work the stamp of this outburst: Dionysius against the Crucified?

If we are to understand what took place, we must again draw some comparisons. Goethe, too, had no great time for Christianity. Nor did he merely repudiate the enthusiasm of his friend Lavater and similar contemporary manifestations of Christianity, but there lived and reverberated in him something of the Greek to whom the cross is foolishness, and we may even suspect that he was personally a far more obstinate pagan than Nietzsche. But his repudiation remained cool and good-tempered and mild. For what are the occasional slights which he allowed himself, as in his famous juxtaposition of the four annoyances, "tobacco-smoke, bugs, garlic and †"? As he was content to be Apollo or preferably Zeus, as he did not think of dramatising himself and his Hellenism in the form of Dionysius (he finally rejected this possibility in his Tasso, who is certainly no Dionysius), so he never even dreamed of compromising himself by explicitly and passionately opposing Christianity as Nietzsche did. And the same is true of the great philosophical Idealists of the time, of Kant, Fichte, Schelling and Hegel. If they could not make much of the Christianity of the New Testament, they were restrained and cautious and sparing in their criticisms, trying to interpret it as positively as possible within the framework of their systems, within the limits of their own understanding. They did not oppose to it any Zarathustra. Among them there was indeed a Herder and a Schleiermacher, with their strange but subjectively quite seriously meant attachment to Christianity and the Church. It is a little different with the heirs and disciples of this classical period. We undoubtedly have to say of a Feuerbach or a Strauss that—more akin to Nietzsche—they suffered all their lives from Christianity, and made it their main task to combat it. But on poor Strauss Nietzsche looked down as from a tower and laughed. He did not even remotely see himself as in the same class. And he was right. What was their critical philosophy and philosophy of religion to him, their biblical and dogmatic criticism, their contesting of Christianity in the name of modern reason and the modern view of things? Strauss certainly could not have introduced a Dionysius-Zarathustra (any more than Martin Werner in our own day), and certainly not the friend of nature, Feuerbach.

The new thing in Nietzsche was the fact that the development of humanity without the fellow-man, which secretly had been the humanity of the Olympian Goethe and other classical figures as well as the more mediocre, reached in him a much more advanced, explosive, dangerous and yet also vulnerable stage—possibly its last. The new thing in Nietzsche was the man of "azure isolation," six thousand feet above time and man; the man to whom a fellow-creature drinking at the same well is quite dreadful and insufferable; the man who is utterly inaccessible to others, having no friends and despising women; the man who is at home only with the eagles and strong winds; the man whose only possible environment is desert and wintry landscape; the man beyond good and evil, who can exist only as a consuming fire. And so the new thing in Nietzsche's relationship to Christianity necessarily consisted in the fact that this pressed and embarrassed him in a way which the others had not

---

[EN46] under this banner

37

seen, or at most had only sensed. On this view Christianity seemed to be so incomparably dreadful and harassing, presenting such a Medusa aspect, that he immediately dropped all the other polemics which he needed to proclaim his Zarathustra in favour of the necessary battle against this newly discovered side of Christianity, and all the other attacks on it, whether in the form of the dignified rejection of Goethe, the speculative reinterpretation of the classical Idealists, or the rational objections of their successors, necessarily seemed to him to be irrelevant, stupid and even—and especially—frivolous. These predecessors had not seen how serious the matter was or how much was at stake. They could not do so, because on the positive side they did not go far enough and were not consistent enough. At bottom, they really knew nothing of the "azure isolation" of the superman. They had been left far, far behind by Zarathustra. They still crept along the ground, having only an inkling of the proximity of the eagles and strong winds in which alone real man can breathe. How could they see the true danger in Christianity? How could they fail either to reach a frivolous compromise with this enemy, or, if they knew and attacked it as such, to commit the serious error of leaving it intact where it was really dangerous? Nietzsche, however, was consistent on this positive side. He trod the way of humanity without the fellow-man to the bitter end. And this enabled him, and him alone, to see the true danger at this point.

[241]

And the true danger in Christianity, which he alone saw at the climax of that tradition, and on account of which he had to attack it with unprecedented resolution and passion—and with all the greater resolution and passion because he was alone—was that Christianity—what he called Christian morality—confronts real man, the superman, this necessary, supreme and mature fruit of the whole development of true humanity, with a form of man which necessarily questions and disturbs and destroys and kills him at the very root. That is to say, it confronts him with the figure of suffering man. It demands that he should see this man, that he should accept his presence, that he should not be man without him but with him, that he must drink with him at the same source. Christianity places before the superman the Crucified, Jesus, as the Neighbour, and in the person of Jesus a whole host of others who are wholly and utterly ignoble and despised in the eyes of the world (of the world of Zarathustra, the true world of men), the hungry and thirsty and naked and sick and captive, a whole ocean of human meanness and painfulness. Nor does it merely place the Crucified and His host before his eyes. It does not merely will that he see Him and them. It wills that he should recognise in them his neighbours and himself. It aims to bring him down from his height, to put him in the ranks which begin with the Crucified, in the midst of His host. Dionysius-Zarathustra, it says, is not a God but a man, and therefore under the cross of the Crucified and one of His host. Nor can Dionysius-Zarathustra redeem himself, but the Crucified alone can be his Redeemer. Dionysius-Zarathustra is thus called to live for others and not himself. Here are his brothers and sisters who belong to him and to whom he belongs. In this Crucified, and therefore in fellowship with this mean and painful host of His people, he has thus to see his salvation, and his true humanity in the fact that he belongs to Him and therefore to them. This Crucified is God Himself, and therefore God Himself is only for those who belong to His host. They are then the elect of God. And Dionysius-Zarathustra can be an elect of God only if he belongs to them, Away, then, the six thousand feet, the azure, the isolation, the drinking from a lonely well! Everything is back to disturb and destroy the isolation. The fellow-man has returned whom Zarathustra had escaped or to whom he merely wanted to be a hammer, and he has returned in a form which makes escape impossible (because it embodies something which even Zarathustra cannot escape) and which makes all hammering futile (because in this form of suffering man there is nothing really to hammer).

This was the new thing which Nietzsche saw in Christianity and which he had to combat because he found it so intolerable, wounding and dangerous. It was for this reason that in the last resort his "anti-donkey" meant Antichrist. And it was only perhaps a relic of the frivolity of which he accused others that sometimes he could act as if Christianity were mere donkey-dom and he could meet it with the corresponding attitudes and measures. We might well ask how it was that all their life long even Strauss and Feuerbach found it necessary to keep hammering away at what they declared to be so bankrupt a thing as Christianity, especially in a century when it no longer cut a very imposing figure outwardly, and the battle against it had long since ceased to be a heroic war of liberation. But we have certainly to ask why Nietzsche was guilty of the Donquixotry of acting in the age of Bismarck as if the Christian morality of 1 Cor. 1 constituted the great danger by which humanity necessarily found itself most severely imperilled at every turn. Yet the fact remains that Nietzsche, did take up arms against Christianity, and especially the Christianity of 1 Cor. 1, as if it were a serious threat and no mere folly. And he had to do so. We cannot explain this necessity in purely historical terms, which in this context means psychological and psycho-pathological. That Nietzsche became deranged in this attack, or that he was deranged to undertake it, merely throws light on the fact; it does not alter the necessity. The one who as the heir, disciple and prophet of the Renaissance and its progeny discovered the superman was quite unable— irrespective of historical and psychological circumstances—to overlook the fact that in Western culture, in face of every repudiation, reinterpretation or assault, persisting in spite of every evacuation, there existed at least in the form of the Greek New Testament such a thing as Christianity, so that from the pages of the New Testament he was inevitably confronted by that figure, and could only recognise in that figure the direct opposite of his own ideal and that of the tradition which culminated in him, and was forced to protest and fight against it with the resolution and passion which we find in Nietzsche, not as against asininity, but with the final resolution which is reserved for a mortal threat.

[242]

Naturally there is an element of caricature in his depiction. Those who try to fight the Gospel always make caricatures, and they are then forced to fight these caricatures. Nietzsche's caricature consists in his (not very original) historical derivation of Christianity from a revolt on the part of slaves or the proletariat, for which Paul and other mischievous priests provided a metaphysical foundation and super-structure, and which thus became an incubus on the unhappy West. We all grasp at such aids as are available. And the 19th century had tried to bolster up Christianity with historical interpretations of this kind. Nietzsche was undoubtedly conditioned by his age when he thought that he could regard Christianity as typical Socialist teaching and contest it as such; for there did not lack those who in his own time thought that they should praise and commend it as typical Socialist teaching, or at least find a positive place for it as a transitional stage. At this point Nietzsche was perhaps loyally and sincerely a little class-conditioned. According to the Marxist analysis, he belonged to the middle-class, although in a form worthy of Zarathustra. In this respect he was at one with D. F. Strauss, to whom the moderate Social Democratic teaching of the period was as a red rag to a bull. But this is not really essential. The caricature which he served up was itself an element in his resistance and attack. And of this attack we have to say that it was well aimed, that it centred on the point which was vital for Nietzsche as the most consistent champion and prophet of humanity without the fellow-man. It is another matter, and one that objectively considered is to the praise of Nietzsche, that he thus hurled himself against the strongest and not the weakest point in the opposing front. With his discovery of the Crucified and His host he discovered the Gospel itself in a form which was missed even by the majority of its champions, let alone its opponents, in the 19th century. And by having to attack it in this form, he has done us the good office of bringing before us the fact that we have to keep to this form as unconditionally as he rejected it, in self-evident antithesis not only to him, but to the whole tradition on behalf of which he made this final hopeless sally.

[243]   We now know against what orientation of research and representation of humanity we are warned *a limine*[EN47] by the humanity of Jesus Christ, and having secured our rear we can look in the direction to which we are positively directed by this fact. The humanity of Jesus consists in His being for man. From the fact that this example is binding in humanity generally there follows the broad definition that humanity absolutely, the humanity of each and every man, consists in the determination of man's being as a being with others, or rather with the other man. It is not as he is for himself but with others, not in loneliness but in fellowship, that he is genuinely human, that he achieves true humanity, that he corresponds to his determination to be God's covenant-partner, that he is the being for which the man Jesus is, and therefore real man. If we overlook the fact of his being in fellowship, and see him for himself, constructing him in terms of an abstract "I am" in which others are not yet or no longer included, everything collapses, and in respect of the concept of the human we are betrayed into an obscurity in which it is no longer possible to make any real distinction between what may be called humanity and inhumanity. We must avoid this path. We must press straight on from the fact that the humanity of man consists in the determination of his being as a being with the other.

Before we move on from this point, we must try to clarify three of the terms employed in this definition.

1. We describe humanity as a determination of human being. Man is, as he is created by God for God, as this creature of God for covenant-partnership with God. But this being is a wholly definite being. It corresponds in its own way to its particular creation and to the meaning and goal of the particularity of its creation. The manner of its being is a likeness of its purpose and therefore of the fact that it is created by God for God. This parabolic determination of human being, this correspondence and similarity of its nature in relation to its being as such, is humanity.

2. We describe humanity as a being of man with others. With this cautious expression we distinguish humanity generally from the humanity of Jesus. There is also a being for others in the relation of man to man. But only the humanity of Jesus can be absolutely exhaustively and exclusively described as a being for man. There can be no question of a total being for others as the determination of any other men but Jesus. And to the humanity of other men there necessarily belongs reciprocity. Others are for them as they are for others. This reciprocity cannot arise in the humanity of Jesus with its irreversible "for." We are thus satisfied to describe the humanity generally with which we are now dealing as a being of the one with the other, and we shall have to show to what extent this includes a certain being of the one for the other.

3. We describe humanity as a being of the one man with the other. Funda-

---

[EN47] from the outset

mentally we speak on both sides in the singular and not in the plural. We are [244] not thinking here in terms of individualism. But the basic form of humanity, the determination of humanity, according to its creation, in the light of the humanity of Jesus—and it is of this that we speak—is a being of the one man with the other. And where one is with many, or many with one, or many with many, the humanity consists in the fact that in truth, in the basic form of this occurrence, one is always with another, and this basic form persists. Humanity is not in isolation, and it is in pluralities only when these are constituted by genuine duality, by the singular on both sides.

The singular, not alone but in this duality, is the presupposition without which there can never be humanity in the plural.

We may now move forward, and for the sake of clarity we shall begin with an analysis of the statement "I am," which we have so far understood only as the axiom of humanity without the fellow-man, but which will help us to a true understanding and exposition once we appreciate its true significance. The statement "I am" is ultimately a confession—and perhaps *the* confession—of the man Jesus; He therefore permits and requires of us an interpretation on which, as at least a corresponding and similar if not an equal confession in the mouth of others, it has a human and not an inhuman form; an interpretation which does not point us in the direction which we cannot take, but in the opposite and right direction, the being of one man with the other.

What is meant by "I?" I pronounce the word, and in so doing, even if I only do so mentally or to myself, I make a distinction, but also a connexion. In thinking and speaking this word, I do not remain in isolation. I distinguish myself from another who is not I and yet also not It, not an object, but one who can receive and estimate and understand my declaration "I" because he can make a similar declaration to me. In making this distinction, I presuppose, accept and make, as far as I am able, a connexion with him as one who is like me. Addressing this object as I, I distinguish him not only from myself but from all other objects, from every It, placing myself on the same level or in the same sphere with him, acknowledging that I am not without him in my sphere, that this sphere is not just mine but also his. The mere fact that I say "I" means that I describe and distinguish the object to which I say it as something like myself; in other words, that with my "I" I also address him as "Thou." By saying "I," I implicitly address and treat him as "Thou." Not, be it noted, as "He" or "She." So long and so far as he is only He or She, he is really It, an object like others, in a different sphere from mine, unlike myself; and my distinction from him and connexion with him are not yet human. But in this case I do not speak to him; I speak about him. And the word "I" is meaningful in relation to the one with whom I speak about him. It has no reference to himself. If I speak to him and not about him, he is neither It, He nor She, but Thou. I then make [245] the distinction and connexion in relation to him in the specific form of a demarcation in virtue of which my sphere is no longer my own but his, and he is like me. But there is more to it than this. For when I say "I" and therefore

"Thou" to someone else, I empower and invite and summon him to say "Thou" to me in return. The declaration "I" in what I say is the declaration of my expectation that the other being to which I declare myself in this way will respond and treat and describe and distinguish me as something like himself. When he accepts my "I"—and in turning to him I count on it that he is able to do so—he cannot possibly regard me as an It or a mere He or She, but I am distinguished from all other objects for him as he is for me, and distinguished from and connected to me as I am from and to him. And it can only be a matter of fulfilment that he for his part should admit his recognition of this fact by pronouncing the word "Thou" and thus proclaim himself not merely as something like an I but actually as an I. Thus the word "Thou," although it is a very different word, is immanent to "I." It is not a word which is radically alien, but one which belongs to it. The word "I" with which I think and declare my humanity implies as such humanity with and not without the fellow-man. I cannot say "I," even to myself, without also saying "Thou," without making that distinction and connexion in relation to another. And only as I think and say "I" in this way, only as I make this specific distinction and connexion with this word, can I expect to be recognised and acknowledged by others as a "Thou," as something like an "I," and more than that as a real "I," and therefore to be confirmed in the human determination of my being, and regarded, treated and addressed as a human being.

On this basis, what is meant by "I am?" It certainly means that I posit myself: myself as this being in the cosmos; myself in all the freedom and necessity of my being; myself in the totality of the movement of my distinctions and con-nexions in relation to what is for me the outside world; myself in my desire and ability to project myself into this world. There can be no objection to this for-mal description of "I am." But what does all this mean if I cannot say "I" with-out also saying "Thou," and being a Thou for this "Thou," and only in this way receiving confirmation that I am? What does "I am" mean on this presuppos-ition? Who and what am I myself as I confirm my being in this way? What kind of a being is it in the freedom and necessity of which I posit myself, distinguish-ing and connecting myself, projecting myself outwards? One thing at least is certain. A pure, absolute and self-sufficient I is an illusion, for as an I, even as I think and express this I, I am not alone or self-sufficient, but am distinguished from and connected with a Thou in which I find a being like my own, so that there is no place for an interpretation of the "I am" which means isolation and [246] necessarily consists in a description of the sovereign self-positing of an empty subject by eruptions of its pure, absolute and self-sufficient abyss. The I is not pure, absolute or self-sufficient. But this means that it is not empty. It is not an abyss. And so the being of the I cannot consist in the eruption, history and myth of an abyss. On the contrary, as I am—the genuine I—I am in distinction and connexion to the other which in the fact that I am is Thou, my Thou, and for which I am a Thou in return, thus receiving confirmation of my own being, of the "I am." "I am" is not an empty but a filled reality. As I am, the other is like me. I am as I am in a relation. And this means that as I posit myself—I should not be myself if it were otherwise—I at once come up against the fact that there takes place a corresponding self-positing and being on the part of the one whom I must see and treat as Thou as I think and declare myself as I. With this self-positing and being of his he comes towards me, or rather the Thou comes (for that is what he is as I am I in relation to him), and comes in such a way that I cannot evade him, since he is like myself and therefore Thou as surely as I am I, and therefore my sphere is not mine alone but his as well. What I am and posit as myself, I am and posit in relation to his positing and being, in distinction from and connexion with this alien happening which is characterised by the fact that I can see and recognise and accept this alien being and positing as one which corresponds to my own. This alien being and positing does not belong, therefore, to the general mass of happenings in the external world. In face of it I cannot refer back to myself, asserting and developing myself from myself as from a neutral point quite apart from it. The being and positing of this Thou reaches and affects me, for it is not that of an It, but of the Thou without which I should not be I. In its decisive content as a work of the Thou it is not the outside world which I can leave to itself, avoid or control. The work of the Thou cannot be indifferent to me, nor can I evade or master it. I cannot do this because as I do my own work, as I art myself and posit myself, I am necessarily claimed by and occupied with the being and positing of the Thou. My own being and positing takes place in and with the fact that I am claimed by that of the other and occupied with it. That of the other sets limits to my own. It indicates its problems. It poses questions which must be answered. And there are answers for which it asks. I am in encounter with the other who is in the same way as I am. I am under the conditions imposed by this encounter. I am as either well or badly I fulfil the conditions imposed by this encounter. Even if I fulfil them badly, I am as measured by these conditions. I have no being apart from them. I cannot posit myself without coming up against the self-positing of the other. I have no line of retreat to a place where he does not come up against me with his self-positing. If I had, it could only be that of a return to the inhumanity of a being without the being of the other, of the "I am" of an empty subject, of an I which cannot be more than an illusion. And here, too, we must consider the matter from the other side. As I myself am, and posit myself, I confront the other no less than he does me with his being and positing. He is my Thou, and therefore something like myself, in the sphere which is my own. My being and positing is for him more than the external world. Hence he cannot retreat before me into himself, and in this way exist without me. Since I am not an It, but an I and therefore a Thou, he is reached and affected by me no less than I am by him. He, too, is unable to leave aside or to evade or control my work. He, too, is claimed by and occupied with my being and positing. He, too, stands under the conditions which I create for him. I am his encounter as he is mine. In being myself, I cannot help being what I am for him. In this sense, too, there is no line of

[247]

43

retreat to a place where I exist neutrally for him, where I do not affect him, where I do not owe him anything, where I with my being and positing do not have to take any account of his. The only line of retreat is again that of a retreat to inhumanity—to the inhumanity of a being without the Thou in relation to which I can be alone, to the "I am" of an empty subject which cannot find fulfilment or really be a human subject, but is always, or always becomes again, an illusion.

"I am"—the true and filled "I am"—may thus be paraphrased: "I am in encounter." Nor am I in encounter before or after, incidentally, secondarily or subsequently, while primarily and properly I am alone in an inner world in which I am not in this encounter, but alongside which there is an outer world in which amongst other things I certainly come up against being, against the being of the Thou, and have to reckon with it, but in such sort that this is not at all essential, since essentially I am always outside this encounter, and can always retreat into this world apart. No, at the very root of my being and from the very first I am in encounter with the being of the Thou, under his claim and with my own being constituting a claim upon him. And the humanity of human being is this total determination as being in encounter with the being of the Thou, as being with the fellow-man, as fellow-humanity. To this extent we must oppose humanity without the fellow-man. This is the reach of the likeness in unlikeness, of the correspondence and similarity between the man Jesus and us other men. The minimal definition of our humanity, of humanity generally, must be that it is the being of man in encounter, and in this sense the determination of man as a being with the other man. We cannot go back on this. We cannot be content with anything less or weaker. We cannot accept any compromise or admixture with the opposite conception which would have it that at bottom—in the far depths of that abyss of an empty subject—man can be a man without the fellow-man, an I without the Thou.

[248]   But we must be more precise. Being with means encounter. Hence being with the other man means encounter with him. Hence humanity is the determination of our being as a being in encounter with the other man. We shall now try to understand the content of this encounter.

The basic formula to describe it must be as follows: "I am as Thou art." Naturally the word "as" does not imply that the "Thou art" is the cause, even the instrumental cause, or the true substance of the "I am." In this respect an excess of zeal in conflict with the idealistic concept of humanity has sometimes led to the emptying out of the baby with the bath-water. Man has been constructed wholly in the light of the fellow-man, and the "I am" has formally disappeared in the "Thou art." The word "as" does not tell us where human being is created—for this we can turn only to God the Creator—but how. It tells us that every "I am" is qualified, marked and determined by the "Thou art." Owing it to God the Creator that I am, I am only as Thou art; as, created by the same God, Thou art with me. Neither the I am nor the Thou art loses its own meaning and force. I do not become Thou, nor Thou I, in this co-existence. On the contrary, as I and Thou are together, their being acquires the character, the human style, of always being I for the self and Thou for the other. As we are in this encounter we are thus distinguished. On both sides— we shall return to this—the being has its own validity, dignity and self-certainty. Nor is this human being static, but dynamic and active. It is not an *esse*[EN48] but an *existere*[EN49]. To say man is to say history. On a false understanding no less than a true we are forced to put the statement "I am" in the form of a little history, describing it as that self-positing. Similarly, the statement "Thou art" denotes a history. Therefore in our formula: "I am as Thou art," we do not describe the relationship between two static complexes of being, but between two which are dynamic, which move out from themselves, which exist, and which meet or encounter each other in their existence. The "I am" and the "Thou art" encounter each other as two histories. It is to be noted that they do not just do this subsequently, as though there were one history here and another there which at a certain point became a common history; as though there were an "I am" here and a "Thou art" there which in the continuation of their two-sided movement came together and became a partnership. But in and with their creation, and therefore in and with the two-sided beginning of their movement and history, they are in encounter: I am as Thou art, and Thou art as I am. To say man is to say history, and this is to speak of the encounter between I and Thou. Thus the formula: "I am as Thou art," tells us that the encounter between I and Thou is not arbitrary or accidental, that it is not incidentally but essentially proper to the concept of man. It tells us noologically that this concept would at once be empty if the view basic to it were that of a pure subject and not of the subject in this encounter. And it tells us ontologically that we have to do with real man only when his existence takes place in this encounter, only in the form of man with his fellowman. [249]

On this basis we shall now try to see what are the categories, the constant, decisive and necessary elements in this history or encounter, and to that extent what are the categories of the distinctively human. Great caution is needed at this point. Things which might be said about man without his fellow, qualities and characteristics of that empty subject, are out of place here, because they have no "categorical" significance in the description of humanity, i.e., they tell us nothing about being in encounter and therefore about that which is properly and essentially human. Thus the fact that I am born and die; that I eat and drink and sleep; that I develop and maintain myself; that beyond this I assert myself in face of others, and even physically propagate my species; that I enjoy and work and play and fashion and possess; that I acquire and have and exercise powers; that I take part in all the works of the race either accomplished or in process of accomplishment; that in all this I satisfy religious needs and can realise religious possibilities; and that in it all I fulfil my aptitudes as an

---

[EN48] passive being
[EN49] active existing

understanding and thinking, willing and feeling being—all this as such is not my humanity. In it I can be either human or inhuman. In it I am only asked whether I am human or inhuman. In it all I must first answer the question whether I will affirm or deny my humanity. It is only the field on which human being either takes place or does not take place as history, as the encounter of I and Thou; the field on which it is revealed or obscured that "I am as Thou art." That I exist on this field, and do so in a particular way, does not of itself mean that I am human. But as I exist on this field and in this way, in this restriction or development, poverty or wealth, impotence or intensity, it has to become true and actual that I am human and not inhuman in my existence. There is no reason why in the realisation of my vital, natural and intellectual aptitudes and potentialities, in my life-act as such, and my participation in scholarship and art, politics and economics, civilisation and culture, I should not actualise and reveal that "I am as Thou art." But it may well be that in and with all this I deny it. It may well be that in all this I am only man without my fellow-man, and therefore not really human at all. Nothing of all this is in itself and as such the glory of my humanity.

For example, it is not the case that motherhood or work ennoble as such. It is also not the case that an accomplishment or achievement in any of these spheres ennobles as such. It can all be supremely inhuman. And there can be supreme humanity where it is all absent. Self-evidently, of course, it is equally untrue to try to seek nobility in the absence of distinction on this field, e.g., with a certain perverseness in sickness or poverty or insignificance or the lack of culture. It is rather the case that on this whole field both the positive and the negative only acquire a positive or negative meaning in respect of their relationship to humanity—and have to acquire it in the fulfilment of that history.

[250]

The question of the humanity of human being is independent of everything which takes place or does not take place on this field. Or conversely, this whole field with all that takes place or does not take place on it is an empty page on which there has still to be written the answer to the question of the humanity of human being. And this answer is written with the enactment of the history, the realisation of the encounter, in which "I am as Thou art." Hence as the constant, decisive and necessary categories, marks and criteria of humanity we can take into account only the elements which characterise this encounter constantly in all the circumstances which may arise on this field, decisively in face of all circumstances, and necessarily in the midst of all possibilities; the forms in which there takes place: "I am as Thou art."

Being in encounter is (1) a being in which one man looks the other in the eye. The human significance of the eye is that we see one another eye to eye. It is man who is seen in this way, not things, or the cosmos, but at the heart of things and the cosmos man, and man not after the manner of things or the cosmos, but in his distinction and particularity as man within the cosmos. It is man who is visible to man, and therefore as the other, as the one who is thus distinct from the one who sees him. This one cannot see himself, but he can and must see the other. That this should take place, that the other should be

46

visible to and seen by him as man, is the human significance of the eye and all seeing. Seeing is inhuman if it does not include this seeing, if it is not first and supremely, primarily and conclusively, this seeing—the seeing of the fellow-man. But this is only the one half. When one man looks the other in the eye, it takes place automatically that he lets the other look him in the eye. And it is a necessary part of the human meaning of the eye that man himself should be visible to the other: not an outward form, a something which might be like the rest of the cosmos; but man himself, the man who as such is particular and distinct within the cosmos. This one is visible in the seeing eye of the one for the other who comes to see him even as he is seen by him. To see the other thus means directly to let oneself be seen by him. If I do not do this, I do not see him. Conversely, as I do it, as I let him look me in the eye, I see him. The two together constitute the full human significance of the eye and its seeing. All seeing is inhuman in which the one who sees hides himself, refusing to be seen by the fellow-man whom he sees. The point is not unimportant that it is always two men, and therefore a real I and Thou, who look themselves in the eye and can thus see one another and be seen by one another. But we may now put the same thing rather more generally and say that being in encounter is a being in the openness of the one to the other with a view to and on behalf of the other. "I am as Thou art" is basically fulfilled in the fact that I am not closed   [251] to thee but open. I am not Thou, and thy being is not mine nor mine thine. But I with all that I am encounter thee with all that Thou art, and similarly Thou dost encounter me, and if this is the encounter of two men and not the collision of two things it means that Thou and what Thou art are not closed to me, and that I for my part do not remain closed to thee and what Thou art. As I am and Thou art we are open to one another. I know thee as a man, as something like myself, and I make it possible for thee to know me in the same way. We give each other something in our duality, and this is that I and Thou are men. We give each other an insight into our being. And as we do this, I am not for myself, but for thee, and Thou for me, so that we have a share and interest in one another. This two-sided openness is the first element of humanity. Where it lacks, and to the extent that it lacks, humanity does not occur. To the extent that we withhold and conceal ourselves, and therefore do not move or move any more out of ourselves to know others and to let ourselves be known by them, our existence is inhuman, even though in all other respects we exist at the highest level of humanity. The isolation in which we try to persist, the lack of participation which we show in relation to others and thus thrust upon others in relation to ourselves, is inhumanity. The expression: "That is no concern of mine," or: "That is no concern of yours," is almost always wrong, because it almost always means that the being of this or that man is nothing to me and my being nothing to him; that I will neither see him nor let myself be seen by him; that my eyes are too good for him and I am too good for his eyes; that my openness reaches its limit in him. But conversely, where openness obtains, humanity begins to occur. To the extent that we move out of ourselves, not refusing to know others or being afraid to be known by them, our existence is human, even though in all other respects we may exist at the very lowest level of humanity. (It is not necessarily the case, but seems to be a fact of experience, that where we think that in other respects we are nearer the depths than the heights of humanity we are generally much more open with and for one another, and to that extent, in spite of all appearances to the contrary, much more human than on the supposed heights.) The duality into which we enter when we encounter one another directly and not indirectly, revealed and not concealed as man with man; the participation which we grant one another by the very fact that we see and do not not see one another, and let ourselves be seen and not unseen by one another, these are the first and indispensable steps in humanity, without which the later ones cannot be taken, and which cannot be replaced by the exercise of any human capacity or virtue, however highly rated this may rightly or wrongly be. It is a great and solemn and incomparable moment when two men look themselves in the eye and [252] discover one another. This moment, this mutual look, is in some sense the root-formation of all humanity without which the rest is impossible. But it is to be noted again that in the strict sense it can take place only in duality, as I and Thou look one another in the eye. Where a man thinks he sees and knows a group, or a group a man, or one group another group, ambiguity always arises. After all, it might be only a matter of psychology and not the other man, of pedagogics and not the child, of sociological statistics and systematisation and not the individual, of the general and not the particular, which is the only thing that really counts in this respect. This is the dangerous—and usually more than dangerous—limit of all planning and philanthropy, but also of all doctrine and instruction, of all politics, and especially of all socialism. Whether on the one side or the other or both there is maintained or broken a closed and blind existence, thinking and speaking in the group, whether the one concrete man is invisible or visible to the other concrete man, is what decides whether there is humanity in all this or not.

Bureaucracy is the form in which man participates with his fellows when this first step into mutual openness is not taken, and not taken because duality is evaded for the sake of the simplicity of a general consideration and a general programme. Bureaucracy is the encounter of the blind with those whom they treat as blind. A bureau is a place where men are grouped in certain classes and treated, dismissed or doctored according to specified plans, principles and regulations. This may very well have the result that the men themselves, both those who act and those who are acted upon, are invisible to one another. A bureau does not have to be an office. Many a man unwittingly sits and acts all his life in a private bureau from which he considers how to treat and dismiss men according to his private plans, and in the process he may never see the real men and always be invisible to them. Certainly, there can and must be the bureau, both public and private. Bureaucracy does not hold sway in every bureau. But every bureau is situated hard by the frontier beyond which bureaucracy raises its head, and with it inhumanity, even on the presupposition of the most altruistic of intentions. It is not the man who works in a bureau, for to some extent we all have to do this, but the bureaucrat who is always inhuman. In this whole matter we may perhaps refer to the parable of the eye in Mt. 6$^{22f.}$: "The light of the body is the eye: if therefore thine eye be single (ἁπλοῦς), thy whole body shall be full of light. But if thine eye be evil (πονηρός), thy whole body shall be full of darkness." With this human picture of the good or bad eye the parable refers to the open or closed relationship of man to the imminent kingdom of God. "If therefore the light that is in thee be darkness, how great is that darkness!" But it is no accident that this particular picture, that of the clear or clouded eye, is chosen to illustrate this relationship.

Being in encounter consists (2) in the fact that there is mutual speech and hearing. The matter sounds simple, and yet it again consists in a complex action: I and Thou must both speak and hear, and speak with one another and hear one another. No element must be lacking. This is the human significance of speech. At this point we are on a higher level than the first. It is a good thing to see and to be seen. But there is a good deal more to humanity than that. The openness of encounter is excellent and indeed indispensable as a first step. But encounter is not exhausted in openness. Openness alone is no guarantee that I reach thee and Thou me, that there is thus a real encounter. Openness, seeing and being seen, is always a receptive and not a spontaneous happening. By mere seeing we either do not know one another at all or only imperfectly, for on the plane of mere seeing the one has no opportunity of putting himself before the other, i.e., of interpreting himself, of declaring who and what he is, what his person and being are according to his own understanding of himself. On the plane of mere seeing the one who sees has to form his own picture of the other, understanding the man himself and what he is and does from his own standpoint, and measuring and judging him by his own standards. The other has not contributed anything of his own to make himself knowable. To know him, he is thrown back entirely upon his own resources. And this limitation is a burden to the one who is seen as well. So long as he is known only by sight, he is compelled to exist for the one who sees him in the picture which he has formed of him. He is no more than what he seems to be in his eyes and according to his standards. He has not been able to do anything to give a different and perhaps better and more truthful representation. With his own self-interpretation he still stands impotently before the interpretation which the other has adopted from mere sight, wondering, no doubt, whether he has any real insight into him at all. And if in the encounter of I and Thou there is to be not merely mutual consideration but a mutual contact and intersection of being and activity, if there is to be a field of common life in which the I and Thou not only see themselves but continually have themselves and continually have to take each other into practical account, surely something more is demanded to secure the required intercourse than the pictures mutually formed and the arbitrary notions conceived on both sides? These pictures in which alone they exist for one another may well hamper instead of helping the intercourse, making it impossible rather than possible. So long as these pictures are normative, it may well be that both parties are only acted upon instead of acting. The extreme case is not excluded that seeing and being seen

[253]

do not prevent the one or the other or both from entering into this intercourse as a man without his fellow-man, and thus being a genuine and perhaps quite immovable obstacle to true intercourse, leading inevitably to conflict instead of co-operation. What is needed at this point is speech—the human use of the mouth and ears. Humanity as encounter must become the event of speech. And speech means comprehensively reciprocal expression and its reciprocal reception, reciprocal address and its reciprocal reception. All these four elements are vital. Man speaks and hears a good deal. But the line on which he is human in speaking and hearing is a fine one, and there must not be the slightest deviation from it either on the one side or the other.

[254] The I has thus to express itself to the Thou. A word spoken by me is my active self-declaration to the Thou, my spontaneous crossing of the necessary frontier of mere visibility in relation to the other. As I take to words, I testify that I am not leaving the interpretation of myself to the Thou, but am going to help him by at least adding my self-interpretation. As I speak, I set the other in a position to compare his own picture of me with my own, with my own conception of myself. I help him to answer the immediate question whether his picture of me is correct. That I express myself does not mean in the first instance—and from my standpoint it ought not to mean—that I aim to relieve, defend or justify myself against the wrong which I am done or might be done by the picture which the other has of me. My self-expression may later acquire this sense. But this cannot be its primary intention on my part. The real meaning of the fact that I express myself to the other is that I owe him this assistance. Thus my self-expression, if it is genuinely human, has nothing whatever to do with the fear of being misunderstood or the desire to give a better portrait of myself and vindicate myself before him. It is not for nothing that when this intention lurks behind self-expression it usually fails to attain its end. My word as self-declaration is human only when, in seizing the opportunity of making myself clear and understandable, I have before me the necessary concern of the other not only to see but also to understand me, to escape the uncertainty of the view which he has of me, and the embarrassment caused by this uncertainty. I can help him in this respect only as I tell him who I am, what I think of it, what my view is, with whom and what he has to do in me and my whole being according to the insight gained according to the best of my own knowledge and conscience. I can help him in this way with my word. Only when I speak with him with this purpose in view—not for my own sake but for his—do I express myself honestly and genuinely to him. Words are not genuine self-expression when in some respect I keep back myself, not representing or displaying myself. Words are not genuine self-expression when I represent myself in another guise than that in which I know myself to the best of my information and conscience. Nor are they genuine self-expression when they are perhaps a mask—*la parole est donnée a l'homme pour déguiser sa pensée*[EN50]—by means

---

[EN50] human beings were given language to conceal their thoughts

of which I try to prevent the other from understanding me, and thus do not really intend to express myself at all. How can I take the Thou seriously as a Thou if I express myself to him but do not really intend to express myself at all? How can I then be in true encounter with him? How can my speech be human speech or my mouth a human mouth? To take the Thou seriously is to be concerned for the Thou in self-expression and self-declaration; to have regard in my self-representation for this other who necessarily has to do with me for good or ill; to do my best not to leave him to his own devices in the unavoidable task of making something of me. Only on this presupposition will my self-expression in relation to him be true and not false. [255]

But the I has also to receive the expression of the other. A word heard by me is the active self-declaration of the Thou to me. The other, too, aims to cross the frontier of mere visibility. He, too, does not leave me to the picture which I have formed of him. He, too, tries to represent himself, inviting me to compare my picture of him with what he himself has to contribute. He, too, aims to help me. For this reason and with this intention he speaks with me. To receive or accept him in this sense is to listen to him. I do not hear him if I assume that he is only concerned about himself, either to commend himself to me or to gain my interest, and that he makes himself conspicuous and understandable, forcing himself and his being upon me, only for this reason. When he speaks to me, I must not be affected by the fact that in innumerable instances in which men express themselves to me this might actually be the case or appear to be so. What matters now is the humanity of my hearing, and this is conditioned negatively by the fact that at least I do not hear this other with suspicion, and positively by the fact that I presuppose that he is trying to come to my help with his self-expression and self-declaration. In relation to him I am in the uncertainty and therefore the embarrassment of knowing him only by sight and therefore equivoccally; of knowing him, and with whom or what I have to do in him, only from my own standpoint. This is where the word comes in. He is now trying to fill in or correct my conception of him by his own. He is trying to the best of his ability to help me over the difficulty in which I find myself, giving me by his word the opportunity to verify my view of him. My hearing is human, i.e., I have open ears for the other, only when I listen to him on this presupposition. Only then do I find a place for his self-declaration. If I do not accept the fact that my view is incomplete and needs to be supplemented and corrected, that it may indeed be wholly distorted; if I do not suffer from the embarrassment caused by the Thou so long as I have to interpret him from myself and his self-declaration is withheld; if I do not see and deplore the obvious lacuna at this point, there can be no place for the word of the Thou. However loudly it beats against my ear, I cannot hear; my ear is not in any sense a human ear, and I do not take seriously the Thou of the fellow-man unhesitatingly subordinated to myself. To take the Thou seriously and therefore to have a human ear is to move towards the self-declaration of the other and to welcome it as an event which for my own sake must take place between him and me. It is necessary for me that the other should represent and display himself to me no matter what this may involve or entail. I am not a true I and do not genuinely exist without him. I am only an empty subject if I do not escape that difficulty in relation to him. How can I help thanking him for the favour which he does me by expressing himself? Whatever he may have in view, whatever he may want of me, however sincere or insincere he may be in what he does, the point at issue, the objective significance of the event of his self-expression to me, is that now at least this supreme favour is done me. Hearing on this pre-supposition is human hearing of the self-expression of the fellow-man.

But there is another side to the matter. The I is not merely concerned to express itself, but also to address the Thou. The word spoken by me is my impartation to the Thou. Self-declaration to the other cannot be an end in itself. What is the point of crossing that frontier of mere visibility, what inconvenience it may cause the other that I represent myself to him, how little it may genuinely concern him, if the point between us is not that in my self-expression I have something objective to offer and impart for his appropriation! Why do I necessarily try to make myself clear and explain myself to him? We have given as our reason the fact that he cannot fulfil the task of knowing me by sight alone. But why does he have to know me at all? He has to know me, we must now continue, because I am for him the sum of something objective which he needs as a subject but which is in the first instance unattainable, being concealed in me. We remember that I am not Thou, nor Thou I. Hence what the other comes to see in me is something new and strange and different. I am outside for him, an unknown being, near and yet remote. But when he sees and encounters me, I cannot remain strange. Being so near, I cannot continue to be remote. Since there has to be intercourse between us, I cannot be merely external, a self-enclosed object. In this form I am a vital need to him so long as no bridge is built or way found from him to me. His difficulty so long as he knows me only by sight is that he has no way to me; that he cannot appropriate the new and strange and different thing in me, and therefore cannot have intercourse with me. For this reason he has to know me. And for this reason I have an obligation to make myself known. I have something to say to him, i.e., I have to entrust to him what would remain unknown so long as he knew me only by sight, the new and different thing in me. This is the meaning of the word of address from the one to the other. The word of address is necessary as a kind of penetration from the sphere of the one into the sphere of another being. As I address another, whether in the form of exposition, question, petition or demand, but always with the request to be heard, I ask that he should not remain in isolation but be there for me; that he should not be concerned only with himself but with me too; in other words, that he should hear. Address is coming to another with one's being, and knocking and asking to be admitted. As I address him, I allow myself to unsettle and disturb him by drawing attention to the fact that I am there too. In certain cases this may well be a thankless task. For we cannot take it for granted that he is conscious of [257] needing the objective thing which I can offer and impart; that he wants the new and strange and different thing which I am for him; that he thinks it a vital matter that there is no bridge or way between him and me and therefore he cannot have intercourse with me; that he is willing and ready to accept that penetration from my sphere to his, to be told something by me. On the contrary, it is far more likely that the conscious wish of the other will be that I should leave him in peace. But we must not allow this fact to obscure the real point at issue. It merely reminds us that in the genuine address of the I to the Thou we have to do with the imparting of something objective, with the disclosure of a particular side of the great matter of the life to be lived in common by the I and the Thou. The words with which I turn to the other, seeking him out and perhaps reaching him, are human when the new and strange and different thing with which I knock and demand entrance as I address him is directed at himself, when it penetrates to him as a vital element which constrains and is important and indispensable for him. It is thus a human address when in my claim to be heard by the other I have something decisive for himself to give him. Basically, however, there can be no doubt that one man needs another, and particularly in respect of that in which the other is unknown to him; that one man has something decisive to give another; that so long as one man does not know another this is a vital need which waits to be satisfied. And because this is the case, nothing can basically compromise the human duty and obligation of addressing the other. We cannot consider the matter merely from the standpoint of the personal need of the one. It is obvious that personal need, when it arises, may just as well constrain to silence as to speech, leading to isolation rather than to fellowship, and therefore not to the addressing of another. What have I to say and offer and impart with my words? How can I expect that the other will want to listen to me? Why I cannot be silent but am required to speak is that I necessarily abandon him and leave him to his own devices if I spare myself what is perhaps the thankless venture, and him the unwelcome penetration of his sphere, and withhold from him that which he definitely ought to know, but cannot know until I tell him. I cannot withhold it, because he encounters me as a man, and I should not take him seriously as a man if I did not seriously try to find the way from me to him. No matter what the results, I cannot refrain from knocking. The humanity of the encounter between I and Thou demands that I should not merely make a few tentative efforts in this direction, but do my utmost. Speaking on this presupposition, not for one's own sake but for that of the needy other, is human speaking.

But again the I has to receive the address of the Thou. The words of the Thou heard by me are his impartation to the I. The other has not represented himself to me merely that I should consider him from without. He has not [258] expressed himself to me that he should remain for me a mere object. I have not heard him if the distance between him and me remains. As he speaks with

53

me, his aim is to be known by me, i.e., to seek me out in his own new and strange and different being, and therefore to be seen and grasped from within. This time it is he who comes to me, trying to find a bridge, a way, an open door. It is he who wills to be in me. This is the purpose of his speaking, expounding, questioning and requesting, of his concern, of his claim and the requirement imposed by it. It may appear to me that he wants something from me. In spite of appearance, do I see what is really at stake? It is really a matter of myself. I cannot be I without accepting this claim of the other, without letting him come to me, and therefore without hearing him. It is a matter of satisfying my vital need, in which I should necessarily sink if I remained alone, if the other and the objective thing with which he knocks on my door and seeks admission were to remain objective, if I did not make it my own. I am in encounter with him, and what is to become of me, how can I be in encounter with him, if he is merely external, an unknown object of consideration, remote even in his proximity? The question may be raised whether I have any room for him; whether I can make anything of him; whether he will really be helped and served by my hearing him and allowing him to come to me. What can it mean for him if I allow this penetration into my sphere, as though he were definitely in good hands with me? Surely the claim of the fellow-man, however modest, demands far too much for me ever to dream of meeting it. Far too much stands behind the words of others for me ever to hope, even with the best will in the world, to do them justice. Each fellow-man is a whole world, and the request which he makes of me is not merely that I should know this or that about him, but the man himself, and therefore this whole world. It is tempting—and might even seem to be an act of humility in face of too great a task—not to listen too much or too seriously to what is said by the other. Might it not be too presumptuous, and awaken false hopes, to open the door too wide and not just a little? Is it not too much to demand that I should really and seriously know the man himself? But the first question is not what we can achieve in this matter, or what it can mean for the other. The first question is what is to become of us if we do not listen to him, if we refuse to allow this penetration into our sphere either as a whole or in part. Whatever may happen to him, whether he is helped or not, or much or little, there he is and there I am: he in his new and strange and different form, so impenetrable and yet so near that I cannot escape him but have to see and have him, speaking to me and expecting to be admitted; and I in my intolerable isolation (intolerable because it is threatened by his presence), in the seclusion in which I cannot maintain [259] myself now that the encounter with him has taken place, hearing in my ears the words with which he is trying to impart himself to me. Even for my own sake, to save myself like the unjust judge, what option have I but to listen to what the other has to say to me, and therefore to open up myself and receive what he has to give? So long as I do not stand under this compulsion, so long as I have not grasped that it is not just a matter of the other but of myself, so long as I can think that I can avoid hearing the other without harm to myself, I do not give a human hearing, even though humility may demand a thousand times that I hear only in part or not at all. Human hearing of the other takes place on the presupposition that I am affected myself if I do not hear him, and do so in all seriousness.

Drawing the various aspects together, we again emphasise that the human significance of speech, of the human mouth and human ear, depends absolutely upon the fact that man and his fellow speak to one another and listen to one another; that the expression and address between I and Thou are reciprocal. As we can look past people, we can also talk past them and hear past them. When this happens, it always means that we are not in encounter and therefore inhuman. But we talk and hear past them when there is no reciprocity. Two men can talk together openly, exhaustively and earnestly. But if their words serve only their own needs, it may well be that as they talk together each is only trying to assure and help himself, so that they do not reach one another or speak to mutual advantage, but merely talk past one another. How can it be otherwise, how can they find each other, when they are not sought by one another, but each is merely speaking for himself and not for the other? Two monologues do not constitute a dialogue. A dialogue, and therefore the humanity of the encounter of I and Thou, begins only when the spoken word becomes a means to seek and help the other in the difficulty which each entails for the other. On this presupposition the two do not merely speak together, in a commonly produced sound of words, but they genuinely talk with and to one another in human words. The converse is true in hearing. Two men may listen very openly and attentively and tensely to one another, but if there is not in both a genuine need to listen, if they merely listen but not honestly for their own sake, the words mutually spoken will not reach their goal, but their ears will be closed so that they hear past one another. This is inevitable. As hearers, we can find only what we seek. From this standpoint, a dialogue begins only when the hearers are concerned about themselves, about the removal of their own difficulty in respect of the other, so that the words of the other are received and welcomed as a help in this embarrassment. Without this presupposition, hearing is merely a common endurance of a commonly produced sound of words. Only on this presupposition is it mutual hearing, a hearing in which not only the words are human, but also the ears for which they are destined.

No specific proof is required to show that there is much practical justification for suspicion in relation to human words as such. Only words! Nothing but words! Empty words! Words are "sound and fury." There is good cause for the disillusionment expressed in these phrases. Most of the words which we speak and hear obviously have nothing whatever to do with conversation between I and Thou, with the encounter of man and man, with the attempt to speak with one another and listen to one another, and therefore with humanity. Most of our words, spoken or heard, are an inhuman and barbaric affair because we will not speak or listen to one another. We speak them without wanting to seek or help. And we listen to them without letting ourselves be found or helped. This is the case not only in private

[260]

conversation but in sermons, lectures and discussions, in books and articles. This is how we both hear and read. What we speak and write and hear and read is propaganda. And the result is that our words are emptied and devalued and become mere words. We live in a constant deflation of the word. Yet we have to realise that suspicion and disillusionment are not the way to improve things either here or anywhere. It is not the words that are really empty. It is men themselves when they speak and hear empty words. It is the I which is empty in relation to the Thou, one empty subject confronting another. What is not yet or no longer grasped is that neither I nor Thou can be human in isolation, but only in encounter, and that the word spoken and heard, which leads them both beyond a mere reciprocal view and notion, can be the means in the use of which they can both become human. As we speak with one another and listen to one another, we at least have the possibility for being in encounter, and thus stand on the threshold of humanity. So long as we can speak and hear, there is no compelling force to keep us without, no obstacle to the word spoken and heard finding its fulfilment in a proper use. With suspicion and disillusionment in relation to the word we basically turn our back on humanity. For this reason, although suspicion and disillusionment are no doubt justified in practice, we must not in any circumstances allow them house-room.

Being in encounter consists (3) in the fact that we render mutual assistance in the act of being. We now climb a step higher. There is a being for one another, however limited, even in the relationship of man and man in general. And human being is not human if it does not include this being for one another. As openness between the I and the Thou, their reciprocal visibility, is only a preparatory stage to their mutual expression and address, so the latter cannot be an end, but only the means to something higher, to fellowship in which the one is not only knowable by the other, but is there for him, at his disposal within the necessary limits. Perhaps being in encounter, humanity, is very restricted and broken at the lower levels; perhaps so little is known in practice about saving openness and therefore real speaking and hearing between one man and another, because even at the lower levels it is a matter of the way to this higher. We see that it is this higher which claims us. We must see and be seen, speak and listen, because to be human we must be prepared to be there for the other, to be at his disposal. We thus hesitate. We are afraid. This is too much to ask. And because this is too much, everything that leads to it is too much: sincere seeing and letting oneself be seen; sincere speech between man and man. There is indeed a necessary connexion at this point. If I and Thou [261] really see each other and speak with one another and listen to one another, inevitably they mutually summon each other to action. At this higher level it is a matter of the human significance of human activity. If our activity is to be human, this is not guaranteed merely by the fact that it is determined in form by human understanding and volition, art or technique. No degree of perfection which it may have in these respects can ensure that it is not an empty subject which is at work, the man who, because he is without his fellow-man, has not become human, who has not discovered the relationship of I and Thou and therefore himself, who has not become a real I. He may be engaged in the most forceful action both intensively and extensively, and yet he lacks everything for true humanity if he lacks the one thing—that he is not in encounter, and is not therefore human, and has no real part in humanity. Action in encounter is action in correspondence with the summons which the Thou issues to the I when it encounters it, and therefore (for everything is reciprocal in this matter) in correspondence with the summons which the I for its part issues to the Thou in this encounter. The humanity of my activity includes both the fact that I act as one who has received the call of the other and also the fact that I do so as one who has called and must continually call the other. The distinction between human activity and inhuman is not the same as that between altruistic and egoistic. Egoistic activity—for there is a healthy egoism—can be thoroughly human if, without denying itself as such, it is placed at the service of the summons issued by the Thou to the I. And altruistic activity—for there is an unhealthy altruism—can be supremely inhuman if it does not derive from the summons of the one to the other, but the one acts under the illusion that he does not need the other just as much as the other now seems to need him. Action, and therefore being in encounter, and therefore human action, carries with it the twofold correspondence that the other has summoned me and I him; that he really needs me and I him; that I act as one who is called but who also calls. This is the higher thing which is decisive beyond mere reciprocal sight and speech and hearing; the fellowship to which these preliminary stages necessarily lead. It consists in the fact that the one is at the disposal of the other in his activity, and *vice versa*. It is this fellowship— and there is still, of course, a good deal more to be said concerning it—which leads the encounter of I and Thou to its goal and makes human being human. It is actualised concretely in the fact that we render mutual assistance in the act of our being. View and concept are necessarily limited. We cannot replace one another. I cannot be Thou, nor canst Thou live my life. I cannot accept thy responsibility, nor Thou mine. For I and Thou are not inter-changeable. I and Thou are ultimate creaturely reality in their distinction as well as their relationship. If the man Jesus, even though He is Himself, is for us in the strictest sense, living for us, accepting responsibility for us, in this respect, acting as the [262] Son of God in the power of the Creator, He differs from us. This is His prerogative, and no other man can be compared with Him. Correspondence to His being and action consists in the more limited fact that we render mutual assistance. This correspondence is, of course, necessary. Measured by the man Jesus, humanity cannot be less than this for any of us. If our action is human, this means that it is an action in which we give and receive assistance. An action in which assistance is either withheld or rejected is inhuman. For either way it means isolation and persistence in isolation. Only the empty subject can be guilty of such isolation, refusing either to give assistance or to accept it. Only the action of the empty subject and not real man can be autarchic. The more autarchy there is, the more dangerously we skirt the frontier of inhumanity. The more humanity there is, the more the autarchy of our action is pierced. Assistance is actively standing by the other. It is standing so close by him that one's own action means help or support for his. It thus means not to leave him to his own being and action, but in and with one's own to take part in the question and anxiety and burden of his, accepting concern for his life, even though it must always be his and we cannot represent him. Assistance means to live with the other. As we see one another and speak and listen to one another, we call to one another for assistance. As man, as the creature of God, man needs this assistance, and can only call for it. And as man, as the creature of God, he is able and ordained to render assistance to his fellow-man and to receive it from him. God alone, and the man Jesus as the Son of God, has no need of assistance, and is thus able to render far more than assistance to man, namely, to represent him. For us, however, humanity consists in the fact that we need and are capable of mutual assistance. In the very fact that he lives, man calls to his fellow not to leave him alone or to his own devices. He knows well enough that he has to live his own life and bear responsibility for it. But he also knows that he cannot do this if his fellow does not spring to his side and give him his hand and actively stand by him. He cannot be for him in the strict sense. This is possible only for God. But he can be at his disposal. He can be so near to him that his being supports though it does not carry him; that he gives him comfort and encouragement though not victory and triumph; that he alleviates though he does not liberate. In the very fact that he lives, man calls for this help that only his fellow-man can give—the being which is in the same position, which can know him, which can enter into his situation and prescribe and offer the help required. No other being can come so near as to offer what is needed in the way of help. No other can know him so well, or see him as he is, or speak with him and listen to him. And so—in so far as he calls for assistance and not for that which God alone can give—he calls to his fellow-man. An

[263] action is human in which a man, even as he tries to help himself, also summons the help of his fellow, reaching out for the support which he alone can give. His action might seem to be very noble but it is not human if he really thinks that he can be self-sufficient and refuses to ask for help. In this very likeness to God he becomes inhuman. In this apparent nobility he falls into the abyss. Nor is this because there is no one to help. This might sometimes be the case, and it only goes to show how much that help is needed. But primarily it is because he betrays and denies his own being with his pretended self-sufficiency. Turning his back on the helping Thou he cannot be an I. He is transformed and dissolved into an empty subject. And he is thus plunged into misery even though in spite of his perversion a hundred helping hands are stretched out to him on all sides. If we will not let ourselves be helped, others cannot help us however much they would like to do so. My humanity depends upon the fact that I am always aware, and my action is determined by the awareness, that I need the assistance of others as a fish needs water. It depends upon my not being content with what I can do for myself, but calling for the Thou to give me the benefit of his action as well.

The other aspect of the same situation follows a similar pattern. In the very fact that he lives a man is summoned by his fellow-man. The latter does not wish to be left alone or to his own devices in his action. I cannot represent him. I cannot make his life-task my own. He cannot expect this from me. He must not confuse me with God. And he will certainly have no reason to do so. I must try to help myself, and he will have to do the same. But as he tries to do so, he has the right to expect that I shall be there for him as well as myself, that I shall not ignore him but live with him, that my life will be a support for his, that it will mean comfort, encouragement and alleviation for him. This is what he requests. His whole action is always this call for my assistance. And as I act for my part, I always stand under this expectation; this cry for help always reaches me. Perhaps I will not look him too straight in the eye, or let him look too straight into mine; perhaps I will not speak too sincerely with him, or listen too sincerely to him, because to look straight and speak sincerely is at once—and the more sincerely the more compellingly—to accept this cry for help. I may do so willingly or unwillingly, well or badly, but the cry goes out and somehow reaches me. I am not a thing, nor is my fellow. But as a man I have a direct awareness that my fellow—in the same position as myself—stretches out his hand to me and seeks my support. I know that he too is not God and cannot therefore be self-sufficient. And I also know that what he expects of me— namely, a little support—does not exceed my powers, that this little assistance is not in any sense a divine but a very human work which may rightly be expected, that I am able to render it, and under an obligation to do so. I can- not evade my fellow who asks for it. I must stand by him and help him. I become inhuman if I resist this awareness or try to escape the limited but [264] definite service I can render. The humanity of my action is again at stake, and therefore I myself. An action is human when a man who must help himself either well or badly also accepts the call for help issued by another and gives his need a place in the determination of his own action. My action is human when the outstretched hand of the other does not grope in the void but finds in mine the support which is asked. It is inhuman if I am content merely to help myself. It is to be noted that I do not plunge the other but myself into perdition, namely, inhumanity, if I refuse him my support and do not do the modest thing which I could do. If he has called and claimed me, he has done what he can for the humanity of his action. It is I who am affected if I withhold my help. As much as in him lies, he is in encounter. But I am not. I am without the Thou. And therefore I cannot be an I. I transform myself on this side into an empty subject. I am in misery. I am the void in which the other gropes. I am thus a futile being, however perfect may be the help which I give myself, thus satisfying my own needs. If we will not help others, there is no help even in the most perfect self-help. My humanity depends upon the fact that I am always aware, and my action is determined by the awareness, that I need to give my assistance to the Thou as a fish needs water. It depends upon my answering the call of the other, and acting on his behalf, even in and with what I do for myself.

For an understanding of this third step, which is as it were the goal of all that we have so far said, it is to be noted that humanity is not an ideal nor its exercise a virtue. We do not speak of man imagined on the basis of a hypothesis, whose picture we have to fill out, and yet can always escape with the excuse that real man is very different. We are not guilty of idealisation when we say of man that he is created and ordained to receive help from his fellow-man and to give help to his fellow-man. We are speaking of real man. And we are speaking of him realistically, whereas all the descriptions of man in which the presupposition is normative of an empty subject isolated from the fellow-man can only be called idealistic in the wrong sense. For in them, in more or less consistent approximation to Zarathustra, the reference is to a man who does not and cannot exist, but can only be the vision of a maniac. The counterpart of the man Jesus; the picture of man who, although he is not God, is adopted by God in the man Jesus; the picture of the man whom God is for as He is for the man Jesus; the picture of this man is the realistic picture of real man. No optimistic law or lofty aim is given us on this view, but the primitive factuality of our situation as it is—that man is not alone, but with his fellow-man, needing his help and pledged to help him. Is there anything extraordinary in this demand? Is there any real demand at all? Can there be any virtue merely in accepting our true situation? The only extraordinary thing, the only demand, would be the madness and folly of leaving this situation, of ceasing to be human. To be human, and therefore to act accordingly, confessing both the need of assistance and the willingness to render it, is supremely natural and not unnatural. It is the most obvious thing to do, whereas the opposite is by far the most artificial. What is demanded is simply that man should not wander away but be himself in the best sense of the term, keeping to the determination which he has been [265] given as a man. It is to be noted that at the place and in the form in which Christian anthropology sees him man cannot make the favourite excuse that too much is expected of him, that he is given too high and holy a destiny. On the contrary, all that he has to do is simply to see himself in the situation in which he actually finds himself, keeping to this situation, and not trying to adapt himself to any other.

But being in encounter consists (4) in the fact that all the occurrence which we have so far described as the basic form of humanity stands under the sign that it is done on both sides with gladness. We gladly see and are seen; we gladly speak and listen; we gladly receive and offer assistance. This can be called the last and final step of humanity. Or, we might equally well say, this is the secret of the whole, and therefore of the three preceding stages. Our description of the three preceding stages still lacks a certain dimension without the underscoring of which we still fall short of the human as such. All that we have so far said about the relationship of I and Thou, and therefore the basic form of humanity, however realistic outwardly the picture of real man, might seem to be no more than the description of a fairly complicated mechanism, or, more organically, of a perfect flower unfortunately detached from its roots. I see the Thou and am pleased to be seen by him. I speak with him and hear as he speaks with me. I need him, and see that he needs me. But all this may take place and be understood and yet leave a great unseen lacuna which must be filled if there is to be true and serious humanity. It may all be merely an inhuman description of the human. It may all lack a decisive, all-animating and motivating dynamic, and therefore the real substance or soul of the human without which all the humanity of our being, however perfect externally, is only external, but internally and properly and essentially is inhuman. In conclusion, therefore, we shall try to incorporate this true and inward element into our picture of real man, of human man, expressly asking concerning the dynamic, the substance or soul of it all, and therefore the secret of humanity.

There must be no confusion. We ask concerning the secret of humanity as such. We presuppose that it is the humanity of the man whose determination is to be the covenant-partner of God. It is the great secret of man that he belongs to God, that God is for him, and for him in the person of the man Jesus. We do not now speak of this great mystery, but of the lesser yet not inconsiderable secret of his humanity, of his human nature, as this is fashioned in correspondence with his determination for covenant-partnership with God. It would not correspond to this determination if it did not contain within itself as such a secret. Because it corresponds to the determination of man, and therefore to the great secret, we must ask concerning its own lesser and in some sense immanent secret. There is no sense in trying to dispute this secret. We do not really honour the great secret of man, which consists in his relationship to God, by ignoring the fact that the man who enters into this relationship to God is fashioned by the same God in such a way that even in his creaturely mode of existence as such, and therefore in his humanity, he is not without mystery, but the bearer, executor and guardian of a secret which is not inconsiderable in its own place and manner.

We cannot solve the mystery as such. That is to say, we can only show that it is [266] a secret by our attempt to describe it. But after all, has not all that we have said concerning humanity been more in the nature of indication than direct description? Has not all that we have finally said concerning the human significance of the eye and mouth and ear and action pointed beyond itself to something decisive which is itself concealed, so that although we can point to it we cannot pinpoint it? If, then, we turn to consider this decisive thing as such, this can only mean that we admit that in our whole description of humanity we can only denote and indicate its final derivation and true essence. With all that we can say we merely point to something inward and hidden which is the meaning and power of its describable exterior. We everywhere point to its secret. And we must now do this expressly, and therefore in the form of a particular discussion, and to that extent in relation to a final and supreme level of the concept of humanity.

The obvious lacuna in our description of humanity consists, however, in the fact that we have not explicitly affirmed that being in encounter, in which we have seen the basic form of humanity, is a being which is gladly actualised by man. I think that this unpretentious word "gladly," while it does not penetrate the secret before which we stand, does at least indicate it correctly as the *conditio sine qua non*[EN51] of humanity.

The alternative to "gladly" is not "reluctantly" but "neutrally"—which means that I am free to choose between "gladly" and "reluctantly." Do I really have the choice of actualising being in the encounter between I and Thou either gladly or reluctantly? Am I in some sense free to do justice either gladly or reluctantly

---

[EN51] necessary condition

to the human significance of eyes and mouth and ear and action, and therefore of my whole relationship to the Thou, of which we have been considering the positive content? Can I in some way have both possibilities at my disposal, reserving them both for myself? If we describe the humanity of man in terms such as these, even though we may have had a true perception of the earlier stages, and have portrayed them correctly, we have obviously not taken it seriously as a determination of the true being of man, of man himself. We are still (or again) looking past real man, who is not capable of this reservation and control.

For what would this neutrality between gladly and reluctantly really mean? It would mean that the being of man in encounter is a real fact, the actual situation in which he finds himself and cannot outwardly escape without self-alienation. If he is to do justice to his situation, and therefore to himself, he has thus no option but to keep to the fact, with all that it involves, that the I is ordered in relation to the Thou and the Thou to the I, and that this order [267] must be realised. He thus subjects himself to this order as to an ineluctable law of nature. He actualises the reciprocal openness, the reciprocal self-expression and address, the reciprocal assistance, and therefore the whole concept of humanity to the best of his knowledge and conscience, well aware that he has no real option. But he does have one option, and may leave it open, namely, whether he does it all gladly or reluctantly. In his innermost being, or—to use the popular, and biblical, and very expressive phrase—in his heart, he remains at a point above the gladly or reluctantly, from which he can decide either for the one or the other; either for or against a spontaneous acceptance of this encounter; either for or against a willing participation in the Thou; either for or against an inner Yes as the motive of this participation. The law is thus binding, but only externally. Basically and properly it is not binding. He can affirm and fulfil it as a law which is not his own but an alien law, not established by himself but laid upon him and prescribed for him.

If we accept this view, at the last hour we take a decision which compromises all that we have said and apparently secured. For the unavoidable implication is that the mutual relationship of I and Thou is only an accidental *fact* of human existence, although inescapable and to be respected only as such, but that it does not finally effect the essence of man, man himself, since it is alien to his innermost being. In his essence, his innermost being, his heart, he is only what he is gladly. If we do not speak primarily of what he is gladly, we do not speak of his essence, of himself. If it is an open question whether he is human and engaged in the encounter of I and Thou gladly or reluctantly, this means no more and no less than that it does not belong to his essence as man to be human. He is it in fact, because he has no option in the unavoidable presence of his fellow-man. But in himself he might not be. At bottom, in the innermost recesses of his proper self, he is not. Humanity is alien to him. It is a kind of hat which he can put on and take off. It is not intrinsic to him. It is not the law which he prescribes for himself as a man. It is not the freedom in which he draws his first breath. His first and true freedom is the strange freedom of choice in which he can satisfy the law laid upon him from without either gladly or reluctantly. He breathes first in this freedom, not in the freedom to do justice to his humanity gladly. And this means that, even if he does justice to his humanity, and does it gladly, it is without root, without dynamic, without substance, without soul.

The secret of his humanity, however, is that in his being in the encounter of I and Thou we do not have to do with a determination which is accidental and later imposed from without, but with a self-determination which is free and intrinsic to his essence. He is not a man first, and then has his fellow-man alongside him, and is gladly or reluctantly human, i.e., in encounter with him. He is a man as he is human, and gladly in the sense that there can be no question of a "reluctantly." He is unequivocally and radically human. He fol- [268] lows the voice and impulse of his own heart when he is human, when he looks the other in the eye, when he speaks with him and listens to him, when he receives and offers assistance. There are no secret hiding-places or recesses, no dark forest-depths, where deep down he wills or can will anything else. He himself is human. He himself, in the sense described in those three stages, is not without but with his fellow-man. He would not be a man if he were without and not with his fellow-man. This is the great lacuna in our previous exposition which we must now fill to the best of our ability. This is the dimension which we must now especially and expressly indicate.

That man is not without his fellow-man is not an accident which overtakes him. It is no mere contingent fact. It is not a given factor with which he must arbitrarily wrestle and to which he must somehow adjust himself. From the very outset, as man, he is not without but with his fellow-man. Nor is he one essence with his fellow-man. He is with him in the sense that he is one being and his fellow-man another. We have always had occasion, and have so now, to remember that I am I and Thou Thou; that Thou art Thou and not I. In humanity it is not a question of the removal and dissolution but the confirmation and exercise of duality as such. At this point, as in the relationship with God, identity-mysticism is not the way to do justice to the facts. Man and fellow-man, I and Thou—this means mutual limitation. But in this relationship, which is not a relationship of things but the very different relationship of people, limitation means mutual determination. And this determination is inward as well as outward. It is not therefore added to his essence, to the man himself, as though it were originally and properly alien to him and he to it, and at some level of his being he were not determined by it. He is not free in relation to it, but as he is determined by it. He is himself in this determination. The externality of the different fellow-man who encounters me has this in common with the very different externality of the God distinct from me—that it is also inward to me; inward in the sense that this external thing, the other man, is inward and intrinsic to me even in his otherness. Man is not the fellow-man, but he is with him. I am not Thou, but I am with Thee. Humanity is the realisation of this "with." As two men look one another in the eye, and speak with one another and listen to one another, and render mutual assistance, they are together. But everything depends on whether they are not merely together under a law imposed from without, or merely accepting an unavoidable situation. To be sure, there is a law here—the law of the Creator imposed as such on the creature. And there is a situation in which man finds himself—created by the fact that he is not alone, but the fellow-man is present with him. But that law of God is given him as his own law, the law which he himself has set up, the law of his own freedom. Only as such is its validity genuine according to the intention of its Giver. Valid in any other way, it would be obeyed by man, but only as an alien law imposed from without and not as his own law. It would not, therefore, be obeyed gladly. Man would know the other possibility of either not obeying it at all or doing so reluctantly because he himself wills or can will something very different. It would not, then, be valid or known at all. But if he does not really know it, this means that he does not know himself. He is not himself but lost outside himself. For he is himself as he stands under this law as the law of his own freedom. When he is obedient to it in this way, as to the law of his own freedom, he realises that "with"—with the fellow-man, with the Thou—by inner as well as outer necessity, and therefore gladly and spontaneously. Being together thus acquires the character of something absolutely spontaneous. The fellow-man is not merely imposed or thrust upon man, or the Thou upon the I, so that the encounter has almost the instinctive form of a "falling-out," i.e., of a secret or open reversal of encounter, or movement of retreat, in which a hasty greeting is exchanged and then the one seeks safety as quickly as possible from the other, withdrawing into himself for fear of violation and in the interest of self-assertion. On the contrary, the fellow-man belongs to man, the Thou to the I, and is therefore welcome, even in his otherness and particularity. I have waited for Thee. I sought Thee before Thou didst encounter me. I had Thee in view even before I knew Thee. The encounter with Thee is not, therefore, the encounter with something strange which disturbs me, but with a counterpart which I have lacked and without which I would be empty and futile. The situation between man and man is genuinely inescapable, and I do real justice to it, only if it is not subject to my caprice even in the sense that I am not free inwardly to accept or reject it, but can only accept it, knowing that it is only and exclusively in this situation that I am myself, and can act as such. Humanity is the realisation of this togetherness of man and man grounded in human freedom and necessary in this freedom.

We have to safeguard this statement against two misunderstandings. The first in this. Humanity in the highest sense cannot consist in the fact that the one loses himself in the other, surrendering or forgetting or neglecting his own life and task and responsibility, making himself a mere copy of the other, and the life and task and responsibility of the other a framework for his own life. Man is bound to his fellow-man, but he cannot belong to him, i.e., he cannot be his property. This is impossible because if he did he would not see and recognise in him what he is to him, namely, the other. In paying him what seems to be so great an honour, he would pay him too little. In asking what is apparently so complete a self-sacrifice, he would withhold himself. He would encroach too much upon him by changing the encounter with him into a union. He would force himself upon him, and thus become a burden com-   [270] mensurate neither with the dignity nor powers of the other. We cannot subject ourselves to a fellow-man without doing him the deepest injury. For what he can expect of me as another cannot be that I should cease to be his Thou, and therefore to stand before him in my distinction from him. What he gladly and in freedom desires of me is that I should be with him. But I escape him if I lose myself in him, ceasing to be for him a genuine counterpart. He intends and seeks me in my uniqueness and irreplaceability, as a being standing and moving on its own feet. He has no use for a mere adaptation to himself, existing only in dependence on him. I thus escape my fellow-man if I depend on him. He cannot accept this gladly. And the result will be that, unable to use me, he will repulse me, startled by this encounter which is no true encounter, and withdrawing into himself or even turning against me. Make no mistake, there is an excessive relationship to the fellow-man in which the very relationship in which humanity ought to be attained is supremely inhuman because it is not realised that it can arise and persist only in two-sided freedom, and not in the bondage of the one for the sake of the freedom of the other. To belong to another is man's bondage. If I am his property, I am no longer with him gladly. Our being together has become a constraint to which I myself am subject and which I seek to lay on the other. But in this togetherness of mutual constraint I can only at bottom despise myself and cause myself to be despised by the other, having first despised the other by encroaching too much upon him. Humanity is thus the realisation of this togetherness only when I do not lose but maintain myself in it, living my own life with the other, accepting my own task and responsibility, and thus keeping and not overrunning the proper distance between us.

The second misunderstanding is the direct opposite. Humanity in the highest sense cannot consist in the fact that the one only intends and seeks in the other himself, and thus uses the encounter with him to extend and enrich and deepen and confirm and secure his own being. Being in encounter is no more active subjection than passive. It has nothing whatever to do with a campaign of conquest as in cheap love-stories. If I want the other for myself, I do better to stay at home. For there can be no worse self-deception than to desire to be with the other in order to find myself in him. In so doing, do I not forget even my own uniqueness and irreplaceability? I cannot find myself in the other, nor is this what I can intend and seek and strive after gladly and in the necessity of my own freedom. If in the other I seek myself at a higher or deeper level, the Thou is for me merely my extended I. I do not respect it as a being which does not belong to me but must be true to itself and not violated. And in these circumstances I experience something which I can experience only reluctantly,

[271]   namely, that I am really quite alone even with this Thou which I have supposedly conquered and appropriated and made my own. Moreover, I have missed the opportunity of experiencing what I might have experienced gladly. In violating the freedom of the other, I have forfeited my own. I have despised him, and in so doing I have basically despised myself. The fellow-man is bound to me only in the sense that he does not belong to me. If I treat him as though he were my own property, he is no longer bound to me. And I need not then be surprised if the supposed and false coming together is really a falling-out, and the encounter between us sooner or later becomes a mutual attack or a mutual withdrawal. Because the relationship has an excessive form, it is wrong from the very first, and the attempt to realise it is bound to end in failure.

   The way of humanity, and therefore the way to realise the togetherness of man grounded in human freedom and necessary in this freedom, does not lie between these two misunderstandings but above them. In a togetherness which is accepted gladly and in freedom man is neither a slave nor a tyrant, and the fellow-man is neither a slave nor tyrant, but both are companions, associates, comrades, fellows and helpmates. As such they are indispensable to one another. As such they intend and expect and seek one another. As such they cannot be without one another. As such they look one another in the eye, and speak and listen to one another, and render mutual assistance. All this is impossible if they meet as tyrant and slave. Between tyrant and slave there is no genuine encounter, and even genuine encounter ceases to be genuine to the extent that it is understood and actualised on the one side or the other as the encounter of tyrant and slave. Only in the atmosphere of freedom can it be genuine. Companions are free. So are associates. So are comrades. So are fellows. So are helpmates. Only what takes place between such as these is humanity.

   What we indicate in this way is really the *secret* of humanity. For here we have to do with an element in the concept which, in contrast to those previously mentioned, cannot be described or at any rate grounded or deduced from elsewhere, but can only be affirmed as the living centre of the whole. At a pinch we can describe, and have tried to do so, how the encounter takes place between men who meet gladly and in freedom, how they open up themselves to one another, and speak with one another, and listen to one another, and help one another. But in so doing we presuppose as the living centre of the whole the decisive point that they meet gladly and in freedom, not as tyrants and slaves, but as companions, associates, comrades, fellows and helpmates. But how are we to describe this decisive thing? We can say of what takes place between men only something to the following effect—that there is a discovery, the mutual recognition that each is essential to the other. There is thus enacted the paradox that the one is unique and irreplaceable for the other.

[272]   But this means that there is also an electing and election. Each can affirm the other as the being with which he wants to be and cannot be without. But this leads to mutual joy, each in the existence of the other and both in the fact that

they can exist together. For in these circumstances even the co-existence is joy. The fact remains that common existence is still something posited and given, but this givenness is now clear and vital in an active willing of this fellowship, a willing which derives quite simply from the fact that each has received a gift which he necessarily desires to reciprocate to the best of his ability. And if it is asked in what this gift consists, the answer must be that the one has quite simply been given the other, and that what he for his part has to give is again himself. It is in this being given and giving that there consists the electing and election, the mutual acceptance, the common joy, and therefore the freedom of this encounter—the freedom in which there is no room for those misunderstandings, in which both can breathe as they let breathe, in which both keep their distance because they are so close, and are so close because they can keep their distance. But what else is the discovery but the discovery how great and unfathomable and inexpressible is the secret that this may be so. The fact that it may be so, the why and wherefore of it, is never understood. It is simply effected without disclosing itself. It is a pure fact, inward as well as outward. It is the truth of the situation, not only of an outward but also of an inward and mutually recognised or established situation. Thus all words fail at the decisive point. And they fail at the point where we have to describe how and why each man has his own creaturely existence, and is this particular man in fulfilment of it, and continually rediscovers himself as such. Even what is to be discovered at this point is a riddle to which there is no key apart from faith in God the Creator. Nor do we have here two points, two discoveries, two mysteries. For that which cannot be fathomed or expressed, but only established in the fulfilment of our existence, is the one secret of humanity. Man discovers the uniqueness and irreplaceability of the other man in his actuality as the companion, associate, comrade, fellow and helpmate which he is given, and in this way and this way alone, in all the necessity of the presence of this other, he discovers his own uniqueness and irreplaceability, and therefore his own being and actuality as a man. Or conversely, he discovers himself as this particular man existing for himself, and in this way and this way alone, in all the necessity of his own existence, he discovers the other man as the being which is with him and to which he for his part has to give himself as a companion, associate, comrade, fellow and helpmate. Humanity lives and moves and has its being in this freedom to be oneself with the other, and oneself to be with the other.

At this fourth stage we are really speaking of the *conditio sine qua non*[EN52] of humanity, just because we can only talk around the subject, and cannot describe anything, but only point to something hidden. What we have here is not just an optional addition to the whole, a beautiful crown finally adorning humanity but not indispensable. No, if humanity does not consist first and last in this freedom, it does not exist at all. All true openness, and reciprocal speech and hearing, and mutual assistance, has its basis and stability in this [273]

[EN52] necessary condition

dynamic thing, and all that can be described in this indescribable. If the encounter of I and Thou lacked the secret of this freedom, if its whole realisation were merely external and in some sense hollow, how could it be genuine and effective? From the very outset we have tried to represent it in its genuineness and force, and not as a mere mechanism or empty form which might have another content than true humanity. We must now expressly add that the presupposition, if we have not described an empty form, is that which we have finally indicated with our reference to freedom as the secret of being in encounter and therefore the secret of humanity. What we have described—openness, and speech and hearing, and mutual assistance—can be real only when there is also this discovery between man and man, and the necessity of this "gladly," this freedom, rules in their seeing and being seen, their speech and hearing, their reciprocal help. This is not merely the crown of humanity, but its root.

But this means that if we are to embrace human nature as such, as created and given by God, then we must grasp as its motivating element the decisive point that man is essentially determined to be with his fellow-man gladly, in the indicated freedom of the heart. By nature he has no possibility or point of departure for any other choice. If we have to maintain that he has this choice in fact, it does not derive from his nature. For we cannot make God his Creator responsible for this fatal possibility. And it is even worse if we praise the Creator for obviously giving man the possibility of a different choice. For this is to praise Him for allowing and enabling man to choose in his heart inhumanity as well as humanity, and therefore to be in his heart inhuman as well as human, or both perhaps alternately. And we then ascribe to human nature the strange distinction of a freedom for its own denial and destruction. We should not call this freedom nature, but sin. And we should not connect it with God the Creator or the creaturely essence of man, but with man's irrational and inexplicable apostasy from God and from himself. It is the man who has fallen away from God and from himself who thinks that he can find his essence in that false freedom and therefore himself in an original isolation from which he emerges either gladly or reluctantly to be with his fellow-man. Real man as God created him is not in the waste of isolation. He does not have this choice. He does not need to emerge from this waste. It is not just subsequently, and therefore not with final seriousness, that he is with his fellow-man. His free-

[274] dom consists from the very outset in his intending and seeking this other, not to be his tyrant or slave, but his companion, associate, comrade, fellow and helpmate, and that the other may be the same to him. As we call this humanity, and say that everything which belongs to humanity has both its culmination and root in this one thing, we must call this human nature. Human nature is man himself. But man is what he is freely and from the heart. And freely and from the heart he is what he is in the secret of the encounter with his fellow-man in which the latter is welcome and he is with him gladly.

2. *The Basic Form of Humanity*

We have now reached a provisional conclusion in our investigation. What we shall have to say in our third sub-section will not add anything material to it. All that we can do is to establish a definite and unequivocal form of being in the encounter of I and Thou, namely, being in the encounter of man and woman. But first, in relation to our present theme, we must fill out what we have said on the fourth and final level of humanity by a critical observation. At this final level of the concept of humanity we have not been speaking about Christian love.

In the light of the Word of God and on the presupposition of the given divine reality of revelation, i.e., of the humanity of the man Jesus, we have been speaking about the creaturely essence of man, human nature. On this basis, we could not say anything other or less of man than that by nature he is determined for his fellow-man, to be with him gladly. It would be inadmissible to describe man as a being to which this determination does not radically belong but is alien. A being to which it was alien would be different by nature from the man Jesus. If man were a being of this kind, we should either have to say that only the man Jesus was real man as God created him, or that Jesus was not a real man at all, but a being of a different order. If, however, there is similarity as well as dissimilarity between him and us, to His being *for* others there must correspond as at least a minimum on our side the fact that our human being is at root a free being *with* others. This is what we have maintained as the secret of humanity.

We do not associate ourselves, therefore, with the common theological practice of depreciating human nature as much as possible in order to oppose to it the more effectively what may be made of man by divine grace. Orientation by the picture of the man Jesus shows us a very definite way from which we must not be frightened by the danger of meeting the false propositions of Roman Catholicism, humanism or natural theology. If we accept this orientation, what we think and say cannot be false. But it may well be so if we arbitrarily try to avoid certain conclusions. That there is a human nature created by God and therefore good and not evil must be accepted as we see man against the background of the man Jesus. It is not by nature, but by its denial and misuse, that man is as alien and opposed to the grace of God as we see him to be in fact. But rightly to appreciate this corruption brought about by man, and therefore the sin of man, we must quietly consider what is corrupted, and calmly maintain that all the corruption of man cannot make evil by nature the good work of God. It is because the secret of humanity remains even when it is shamed by man that sin is always such an inconceivable revolt, and never loses the character of a crime, or becomes a kind of second natural state which is excusable as such. But this enables us to see and understand why the mercy of God to man is not an act of caprice but has its sure basis in the fact that man is not a stranger or lost to his Creator even as a sinner, but in respect of his nature, of the secret of his humanity, still confronts him as he was created. Becoming a sinner, he has not vanished as a man, or changed into a different being, but still stands before God as the being [275] as which he was created, and therefore as the being whose nature consists in that freedom. And as God makes Himself his Deliverer, He merely exercises His faithfulness as the Creator to His creature, which has not become different or been lost to Him by its fall into sin. This does not mean that by ascribing to man this secret of his humanity as an indestructible determination of his nature we concede to him a power to save himself or even to co-operate in his salvation. This is where the false propositions of Roman Catholicism and humanism arise, and we must be on our guard against them. How can it save a man, or what can it contribute to his salvation, that even as a sinner he is a man, and therefore has the manner of a man? God alone saves and pardons and renews him, and He does so in free mercy. Yet we have still to point to the fact that that secret is proper to man as an indestructible determination of his nature, for to deny this truth would be to deny the continuity of the human subject as a creature, a sinner, and a sinner saved by grace. Our Christological starting-point gives us no reason to make this denial. In what we have said, we do not ascribe to man more than belongs to him on this basis. To contest what is proper to him on this basis is hardly to magnify the glory of God and His grace.

But we have not been speaking of Christian love. New Testament ἀγάπη EN53 is not a determination of human nature as such. It is the action and attitude of the man who only becomes real and can only be understood in the course of his history with God. Love is the new gratitude of those who have come to know God the Creator as the merciful Deliverer. As such it is the gracious gift of the Holy Ghost shed abroad in the hearts of Christians convicted of sin against God and outrage against themselves, and to that extent lost, but assured of their justification and preservation in faith in Jesus Christ (Rom. 5⁵). In love they respond to the revelation of the covenant fulfilled in Jesus Christ, in which God comes to them as their merciful Father, Lord and Judge, and they see their fellow-men as brothers and sisters, i.e., as those who have sinned with them and found grace with them. It is thus the turning to them of this particular love of God which in Christian love binds and keeps men together in common life and action. Christian love is humility before Him, obedience to Him, hope in Him, the commonly received freedom of those who know that they are born and created anew as His children and are called as His community to the common proclamation of His name. It is another matter that in love that freedom of the human creature and therefore the secret of humanity is also honoured. But the honour which it receives is a completely new one. In it, it is like a brand plucked from the burning. And it is seen in an unexpected and completely new light which has fallen upon it from above, from the God who has dealings with man, when it was previously wrapped in darkness through the sin of man. Christian love is the determination of the man who in the fulfilled covenant of God is snatched from the depth of his guilt and the misery of his consequent isolation from his fellow-man and exalted to life in fellowship with Jesus Christ as his Saviour and therefore to fellowship with his fellow-man. Love itself, and in love man, lives with his fellow-man on the basis of the revelation and knowledge of what God has done for His human creature; on the basis of the forgiveness declared to and received by him, and his sanctification as it takes place in this justification. But it is not of this Christian love that we have been speaking.

On the contrary, we have been speaking of the nature of the human creature. The same man who in the course of his history with God, in the fulfilment of his fellowship with Jesus Christ, will also participate in and be capable of Christian love for God and his fellow-men as brothers, is as such this creature whose manner is that which we have come to know as humanity. Humanity, even as we finally spoke of it in the secret of that free co-existence of man and man, is not Christian love, but only the natural exercise and actualisation of human nature—something which formally is on the same level as the corresponding vital functions and natural determinations of other beings which are not men. The fact that a stone is a stone involves a definite nexus of chemical, physical and mathematical conditions and determinations. The fact that a plant is a plant involves a specific organic process. The fact that an animal is an animal involves a particular consciousness and spontaneity in this vital process. But the fact that a man is a man involves freedom in the co-existence of man and man in which the one may be, and will be, the companion, associate, comrade, fellow and helpmate of the other. This is human nature, humanity. Down below, in and for himself, the man who is determined from above as the covenant-partner of God is the creature fashioned and determined and existing in this way. For all the differences in detail, he always lives with varying degrees of consistency and perfection the life characterised by this nature. It is to be expressly noted that we do not have here a gracious gift of the Holy Ghost for the possession of which he must be a Christian, or an operation of the Word of God directly proclaimed to

[276]

EN53 love

man and directly received and believed by him. What we have called humanity can be present and known in varying degrees of perfection or imperfection even where there can be no question of a direct revelation and knowledge of Jesus Christ. This reality of human nature and its recognition are not, therefore, restricted to the Christian community, to the "children" of light, but, as we are told in Lk. 16[8], the "children of this world" may in this respect be wiser than the children of light, being more human, and knowing more about humanity, than the often very inhuman and therefore foolish Christians. Of course, there is no reason why Christians too should not be human and know about humanity. But this is not what necessarily distinguishes them from other men. In this respect they may be at a disadvantage as compared with other men. At bottom, they are at one with them in this. Hence the totality which we have described as humanity is the determination of human being as such irrespective of what may become of man in the course of his history with God. We cannot, therefore, expect to hear about Christian love when the reference is to humanity in the Christian doctrine of the creature.

"Love never faileth" (1 Cor. 13[8]). It is the life of those who after the fall are restored by the grace of God, and as such a life which cannot be destroyed again, and is not threatened even by death and the end of the world. This is something which cannot be said of humanity and that secret of humanity. Humanity might fail. When man sins, his humanity does not disappear, but it is sick and blurred and perverted and destroyed and unrecognisable. And when man falls victim to death, a term is put even to his life in that freedom. If there were no deliverance from sin and death, if God would not acknowledge the creature in His mercy and keep it from destruction, the end of man would inevitably entail the end of his life in that secret and therefore the extirpation of that freedom. Only as love is shed abroad in our hearts as the love of God can humanity as the nature of man receive new honour and acquire a new stability. As it participates in love, it can and will never fail. We have not, therefore, spoken of that which in itself and as such, as the determination of man, is eternally secure even though man and the world perish. In the history of the covenant between God and man there are two determinations of man which do not belong at all to his creatureliness and therefore to his nature. The one is his determination by the inconceivable act of his own sin, and the other is his determination by the even more inconceivable act of the divine mercy. In his humanity as such there is to be found neither the reality nor even the possibility of his sin, and neither the reality nor even the possibility of divine grace. Hence even in the deepest secret of humanity to which we must continually point there cannot be ascribed to it what may be ascribed only to love.

Yet we must not cease to point to this secret. And it would be highly inappropriate if, to make the distinction between humanity and Christian love even clearer, we adopted a perverse standpoint in defining the concept of numanity, making no use of the Christian judgment, and therefore describing humanity perhaps in the sense of Idealism as humanity without the fellow-man, or as a mere co-existence of man and fellow-man, and therefore excluding from the concept that freedom of the heart in which man and fellow-man are together gladly, as though this freedom could arise only in the sphere of Christian love. To do this is not honest dealing. For how can we fail to see that even outwith the Christian sphere and quite apart from the concept of Christian love humanity is not necessarily present in that perverse and unfounded way, but for all the perverse and unfounded interpretations it is genuinely there, and is to be sought and found in the direction which we have taken. It would fare ill with theological anthropology if it were to fail to keep pace with attempts at something better as they have actually been made outside the sphere of the Church altogether; if in its anxiety not to depreciate grace and Christian love it were to propose a concept of humanity the falsity and untenability of which were immediately apparent even to the decided non-Christian. Surely nothing but the best and most securely

[277]

grounded is good enough to describe the nature which God Himself has given to man. There is no reason for surprise that in the light of the divine grace shown in the existence of the man Jesus there has to be ascribed to human nature as much as we have actually ascribed to it in the development of our doctrine of humanity. Half-measures are obviously illegitimate at this point, and we are justified least of all by anxiety lest too little will remain for divine grace if we concede too much to human nature. In this respect theological anthropology has to go its own way, and as it pursues it resolutely to the end it is led to statements which are very similar to those in which humanity is described from a very different angle (e.g., by the pagan Confucius, the atheist L. Feuerbach and the Jew M. Buber). But does this constitute any good reason why we should not make them? Of course, if we look carefully, there can be no question of an exact correspondence and coincidence between the Christian statements and these others which rest on very different foundations. We need not be surprised that there are approximations and similarities. Indeed, in this very fact we may even see a certain confirmation of our results—a confirmation which we do not need and which will not cause us any particular excitement, but of which, in view of its occurrence, we shall not be ashamed. Why should there not be confirmations of this kind? In this context we are not speaking of the Christian in particular but of man in general, and therefore of something which has been the object of all kinds of "worldly," i.e., non-Christian wisdom. And surely it need not be, and is not actually, the case, that this worldly wisdom with its very different criteria has always been mistaken, always seeking humanity in the direction of Idealism and finally of Nietzsche, and therefore establishing and describing it as humanity without the fellow-man, the humanity of man in isolation. It would be far more strange if not the slightest trace had ever been found of fellow-humanity, of the humanity of I and Thou. Since we ourselves have reached the conclusion that the nature of man in himself and in general is to be found in this conception of humanity, we shall not take offence, but quietly see an indirect confirmation of our assertion, if we find that a certain knowledge of this conception was and is possible to man in general, even to the pagan, atheist and Jew, and that as *figura*[EN54] shows it has actually been represented outwith Christian theology. Even with his natural knowledge of himself the natural man is still in the sphere of divine grace; in the sphere in which Jesus too was man. How, then, can he lack a certain ability to have some better knowledge of himself as well as a good deal worse? But theological anthropology has the advantage over this better knowledge of the natural man that it possesses a criterion—its knowledge of divine grace and the man Jesus—which allows and commands it from the very outset and with final resoluteness and clarity to turn its back on that worse knowledge and

[278] ignorance, and from the very first and necessarily and therefore with final consistency to move in the direction of the conception of humanity and therefore of human nature according to which man as such and radically is not without but with the fellow-man, and his humanity at its deepest and highest level consists in the freedom of his heart for the other. As we quietly rejoice in the fact that in the general direction of our investigation and presentation we find ourselves in a certain agreement with the wisest of the wise of this world, we can equally quietly leave it undecided whether and to what extent they for their part follow us even to the final and decisive consequences of this conception, namely, to that "gladly," to that freedom of the heart between man and man as the root and crown of the concept of humanity. If they did not do this, as they surely seem to do in the case of Confucius, Feuerbach and Buber, it would certainly be made clear that *duo cum faciunt idem non est idem*[EN55]. The difference between a Christian and every other anthropology would then emerge in the fact that even in respect of human nature we finally and decisively reach different conclu-

---

[EN54] a figure
[EN55] when two people do the same thing, it is not the same

sions. But we do not insist that this is necessarily so. We should not and do not take offence—
"Is thine eye evil, because I am good?"—if Confucius, Feuerbach and Buber finally had in
view this freedom of the heart, and only failed by accident to tread it to its ultimate consequences, and thus to come to this final conclusion. What else can they have meant, or what
other goal had in view, once they had taken the right direction of human duality? At any
rate, we have no reason not to welcome the proximity to some of the wiser of the wise of this
world in which we in some degree find ourselves in this respect, and therefore we have no
reason to allow this proximity to deflect us from the consistent pursuit of our own way.

But this brings me to the real point of this final critical observation. The Christian
Church, Christianity, has every reason to take note of the reality which we have discovered in
treading our own way of theological anthropology consistently to the end. Properly and at its
deepest level, which is also its highest, human nature is not isolated but dual. It does not
consist in thefreedom of a heart closed to the fellow-man, but in that of a heart open to the
fellow-man. It does not consist in the refusal of man to see the fellow-man and to be seen by
him, to speak with him and listen to him, to receive his assistance and to render assistance to
him. It does not consist in an indifference in which he might just as well be disposed for
these things as not. But it consists in an unequivocal inclination for them. Man is human in
the fact that he is with his fellow-man gladly. But in Christianity there is an inveterate and
tenacious tendency to ignore or not to accept this; not to know, or not to want to know, this
reality of humanity. The reason is obvious, and has been mentioned already. It is thought
that the grace of God will be magnified if man is represented as a blotted or best an empty
page. But in the light of grace itself, of the connexion between the humanity of Jesus and
humanity generally, this representation cannot be sustained. Man cannot be depicted as a
blotted or empty page. The fatal consequence of this representation which we have seen to
be theologically untenable is that real man as he is and is sometimes known to himself is not
known in the Church, but in preaching, instruction and the cure of souls a picture of man is
used which does not correspond to the reality, but to an erroneous figment of the imagination. And the consequence of this consequence is that real man cannot normally be
reached from the Christian side either with what has to be said to him concerning the grace
of God or with what has to be said concerning his own sin, because he simply does not
recognise himself in the portrait held up to him on the Christian side. And then in what is
said about the grace of God and especially Christian love there will probably be brought in
that which was ignored and unrecognised as an attribute of human nature. That is to say,
under the title of divine grace and Christian love there will probably be proclaimed the
humanity which has to come in somewhere, and which will do so all the more forcefully if it
is ignored and suppressed at the point where it ought to be mentioned. And the final result [279]
will be that the man addressed will conclude that he does not need the Christian Church
and its message to know this, because he can know it of himself, or learn it from some of the
wiser of the wise of this world. He will then either not hear at all the new and different thing
which he ought to be told as that which is Christian, or he will not receive it as such, and
either way he cannot take up the corresponding attitude in relation to it. It is no doubt right
and good and even necessary that the Church should call him at least to humanity, but in so
doing it does not discharge its real task. And it does not do this because it has failed to see
that there is a humanity common to the Christian and non-Christian to which it must relate
itself, which it must presuppose, which it must take into account in its message, with which it
must contrast its message, and which it must above all know and take seriously as such. And if
this humanity is overlooked or denied, when reference is made to sin man is probably
accused at a point where he knows that he is fallible and imperfect but cannot honestly see
himself as truly and radically evil in the Christian sense of sin. It may then be overlooked that
even evil man in the Christian sense, the sinner, is capable of humanity in the sense of that

freedom of the heart for others, and in a way which puts many Christians to shame, and that he does not really need to be shown from the Christian pulpit that he finds too little place for this freedom. Or it may happen, as it does, that from the pulpit an attempt is made to blacken even that which is human in him for all his wickedness, and with a more or less clear awareness of the truth he is forced to resist this attack. How can he accept a serious accusation in this respect, as the message of the Christian Church seems to demand? He will rightly defend himself against what he is told. He will not be convicted of his sin if he is uncharitably—and falsely—addressed concerning his humanity. Just because humanity even at its root and crown is not identical with Christian love, and yet has its own different reality with this root and crown, Christianity has every reason to seek and tread other paths in this respect, and, in order to be able to do so, not to close its eyes any longer to the necessary insights.

I shall try to make this clear by reference to a point which has played a certain role in recent theological discussion and which is of supreme significance in relation to what has here been called the root and crown of humanity, namely, that "gladly," that freedom of the heart between man and man. No inconsiderable literature is now available on the contrast between *eros* and *agape*. The two can easily be played off the one against the other in history. In Greek religion, mysticism and philosophy, and above all in the ancient Greek feeling for life (cf. for what follows the article ἀγαπάω in *TWBzNT*), eros was the sum of the human fulfilment and exaltation of life, the experience, depicted and magnified with awe and rapture, of the end and beginning of all choice and volition, of being in transcendence of human being, of that which can take place in sensual or sexual (and thus in the narrower sense erotic) intoxication, but also in an inner spiritual encounter with the suprasensual and suprarational, with the incomprehensible yet present origin of all being and knowledge, in the encounter with the Godhead and union with it. *Eros* is humanity as dæmonism in both the lowest and the highest sense, and as such it is a kind of supreme divinity. According to Euripides it is the τύραννος θεῶν τε κἀνθρώπων EN56 According to Aristotle it is the power of attraction by which the original principle of all being is maintained in order and in motion. That is to say, it moves all being as it is itself that which is moved by it, the ἐρώμενον EN57. Eros is the "universal love seeking satisfaction now at one point, now at another." It is the indefinite impulse, with no taint of decision or act, for an indefinite object, now one thing and now another. In its purest form it is an impulse from below upwards, from man to what is above him, to the divine. In any case, however, it is not a turning to the other for the other's sake, but the satisfying of the vital hunger of the one who loves, for whom the beloved, whether a thing, a man or the divine, is only as it were consumer goods, the means to an end. It needs little wit to see, or skill to prove, that this *eros* is very different from Christian love. That the realities denoted by the two terms are to be sought at very different levels emerges at once from the fact that the words ἔρως and ἐρᾶν EN58 are never used at all in the New Testament. We need not pursue this point in the present context. But because the insight and proof are easy, we are ill-advised to make the contrast a reason for not pressing on to a deeper knowledge of human nature or a more true and valid definition of the essence of humanity. From the fact that *agape* is not to be defined as *eros* it does not follow that humanity, the manner of the natural man, is to be defined as *eros* in this historical sense of the term. This is the conclusion on the basis of which there has been set up on the Christian side a picture of man which has nothing whatever to do with the reality of the natural man, and in which the latter finds it impossible to recognise himself. If Christian love

[280]

EN56 tyrant over gods and human beings
EN57 desired
EN58 Desire ... to desire

cannot be seen in *eros*, it is also difficult—we naturally have to use a more cautious expression—to see humanity in it. In this *eros* of the Greeks there thrusts unmistakeably into the forefront of the picture Dionysius-Zarathustra, the superman, the man without his fellow-man, the great solitary, who at the peak of his aspiration must inevitably make the mistake of regarding himself as God and thus forfeit his humanity. In him, of course, the supreme freedom of man has already become tyranny and therefore slavery. According to our deliberations, a definition of humanity on the basis of its identification with this *eros* could only be called a bad definition. We make a bad start if we accept this bad definition, equating the being of natural man with this dæmonic form, and in this form contrasting it very rigidly but also very unprofitably with Christian love. Even natural man is not yet the Christian man, the man renewed by love as the gracious gift of the Holy Ghost. But does this mean that he is necessarily the man of this Greek *eros*? As we have seen, *tertium datur*[EN59]. The real natural man is the man who in the freedom of his heart is with his fellow-man. It is bad to be fascinated and transfixed as it were by the picture of erotic man in the Greek sense to which the picture of Christian man can be so easily—indeed, far too easily—opposed. The remarkable consequence of this far too simple opposition has been that in whole spheres of Christendom Christian love has been far too unthinkingly accepted merely as an antithesis to Greek *eros* and thus unconsciously depicted and extolled in the contours and colours of the original. At a first glance it is not easy to tell which of the two figures in Titian's famous painting is supposed to be heavenly love and which earthly. For the two sisters are so much alike. And in whole spheres of meditation and speculation on the part of Christian mystics, who have made so liberal a use of Plato and Plotinus, do we not have to ask seriously whether what is called *agape* is not really a spiritualised, idealised, sublimated and pious form of *eros*, an *eros* which was unacceptable in its original form, but from which it was impossible to break free, and which asserted itself all the more strongly? In face of this repressed eroticism we do well to remember that there is a third factor, something which is neither *agape* nor *eros*, from which there can be a genuine reference to *agape*, and yet in the light of which there can also be done to *eros*, even to the *eros* of the Greeks, the justice which is surely due to so powerful a historical phenomenon, and of which it is not perhaps altogether unworthy, even in substance.

We shall first try to draw an upward line from the concept of humanity discovered and indicated by us, namely, in the direction of Christian *agape*. Humanity as the freedom of the heart for the fellow-man is certainly not Christian love. Man can indeed, not on the basis of a possibility of his nature, but in its inconceivable perversion, fall from God and become sinful man. This does not rob him of his humanity. But what, then, becomes of this humanity, of the freedom of his heart? What does it mean that even in this state essentially, properly and [281] inwardly he is still undeniably with the other "gladly," and still uses as the vital and indispensable element in his life the mutual vision, speech, hearing and assistance of man and man? What is man—still and perhaps for the first time genuinely in the freedom of his heart—if his heart, not by nature or divine creation, but in evil factuality, is evil from his youth up? What does it really mean that he is "gladly" with his fellow-man? What takes place in this free co-existence? This state of real man is the one with which we have actually to reckon and in which he really exists in his history with God. He exists against his nature in this state, this state of sin, which is not really a standing but a falling against which he has no safeguard in his nature, but in which his nature develops, so that his nature becomes a fallen nature. He exists under the negative sign of his antithesis to God, and this is also to be said of his humanity. If he is held, upheld in his fall, and thus kept from plunging into the abyss, this is by the fact that God His Creator intervenes for him in Jesus Christ, making his cause His

---

[EN59] there is a third possibility

own, and thus being gracious to him afresh. And if his nature, his humanity, now acquires a positive sign and content, if the freedom of his heart for the fellow-man is for himself and the other a saving, upbuilding, beneficial and helpful freedom, if he is together with his fellow-man not just with a formal "gladly," but gladly in the good sense, i.e., in common thankfulness, in praising the divine mercy, this is not due to himself or his human nature, but this fulfilment of the natural is the gracious gift of the Holy Ghost, and Christian love. God as his Saviour from sin and death has said a new Yes to him in his humanity, a Yes which was not spoken in the fact that he was created in his humanity and therefore in that freedom of the heart, and which he, man, could not speak of himself in his humanity. If he lives in Christian love, he lives in the power of this new divine Yes which frees and saves himself and his humanity from sin and death. He owes it to the faithfulness and constancy of the covenant which God made with the creature if his heart is not merely free for this or that togetherness with the other, but free in the peace and joy and holiness and righteousness of a commonly obligatory service to be together with him in the community of those who may live by the forgiveness of sins and therefore for the magnifying of this grace. Hence humanity and Christian love are two very different things. We may thus speak quite calmly of a gulf between them. But even though the gulf cannot be bridged (except by God alone), there is also an unmistakeable connexion. In humanity, even as it falls through human sin and is thus perverted and brought under that negative sign, it is still a matter of the freedom of one man for another. It was in this freedom, even if in its corruption, that the first men sinned. It is in the wickedness of our heart, which as such, as our own true and essential human being, is still determined for this freedom, in an evil use of this freedom which is not instrinsically evil, that we are evil. Even if we mean it wrongly, we still like to be, and are in fact, with the other "gladly." Highly unnaturally and artificially, we pervert the "gladly" into a "reluctantly." And this "reluctantly" is set aside by Christian love, in which human freedom finds its true exercise. This perversion is reversed in Christian love, in the knowledge of the forgiveness of sins, and in the summons to gratitude by the gracious gift of the Holy Ghost. But it must also be said of Christian love that in it and it alone is it a question of the freedom of the one for the other. This is the new co-existence of man and man which is not merely formal but filled out with positive content. In it, then, humanity is not shamed but honoured. The faithfulness and constancy of the covenant, to which man owes wholly and exclusively the gracious gift of the Holy Ghost, is simply the faithfulness and the constancy of God the Creator acknowledging His work by saving it, and by renewing it as its Saviour. It is again a matter of the heart of man, of his true and essential human being, of his own heart, though new in relation to his evil and corrupt heart, even in the Christian love in which man loves God [282] instead of hating Him and may thus love his neighbour instead of hating him (and thus denying his own nature). What would Christian love be if in it there did not become true and actual what man cannot make true and actual of himself even though his nature is determined for it, namely, a co-existence of man and fellow-man "gladly" fulfilled in freedom. What would be the good to the Christian of all his knowledge of forgiveness and the necessity to be thankful for it, of all the holiness and righteousness of his restored and reconstituted life, of all his praise of God and zeal in His service, if he lacked this element of humanity, and he were not present gladly and in freedom, which means concretely in the freedom of the one man for the other, in the freedom of the heart for the fellow-man? Where in Christian faith and hope there is no awakening, i.e., no positive fulfilment of humanity, there is no real faith or hope, and certainly no Christian love, however great may be its inward and outward works. And if I am without love I am nothing. For love alone—the love in which there is an awakening and positive fulfilment of humanity, and the Christian is displayed and revealed as real man—is the fulfilment of the Law, because this human and therefore Christian love, the love which includes humanity, is the life of man in the power of the new and saving divine Yes to the creature. This is the connexion between humanity and Christian love.

But now the question seriously arises whether it is not possible and necessary that there should also be a downward connexion in the direction of the world of Greek *eros*, thus enabling us to find a calmer and more objective solution to the dilemma of *eros* and Christian *agape* than that to which Christians far too hastily rush, but without the power to work it out to the extent that it is justified. We perhaps safeguard ourselves better against the danger of slipping back into *eros* (possibly in the most refined of ways), if we refrain from representing it as the one form of sin, and contrasting it as such with *agape*. When we understand humanity as a third thing between the two, we can be more perspicacious and just in relation to *eros*. It is obvious enough that in the historical form of this reality we have a form of sin, i.e., of the corruption of man occasioned and conditioned by his fall from God. It is perhaps the greatness of this historical phenomenon that it can be called a classical representation of human sin. It was understandable and right that the early Christians should first turn their backs on the whole world of Greek *eros* with horror and relief. Where man seeks his self-fulfilment in a self-transcending attempt to have the divinity, the fellow-man and all things as consumer goods for himself, where his vital hunger leads him to be himself the one in all things, we have to do unequivocally with the evil which can only have its wages in death. It would have been far better if Christianity had not so often had the idea of interpreting Christian love as the true form of this hunger and fulfilment. As we have already said, Greek *eros* is ill-adapted to be a definition of humanity. But in all this we must not overlook the point that for all its obvious sinfulness, and the obscurity, confusion and corruption in which it represents humanity, *eros* contains an element which in its visible form and even in its essence is not evil or reprehensible, but of decisive (and not merely incidental and non-essential) importance for the concept of humanity, and therefore indirectly for that of Christian love. For where else but in the world of ancient Hellenism filled and controlled by this *eros* does there emerge with such vitality and consolation, for all the sinful corruption, that which we have seen and described as the *conditio sine qua non*[EN60] of humanity, that "gladly," as the true and original motive of human existence, preceding all the choice and volition of man, and limiting and determining all human choice and volition? Is it a mere accident that the Gospel of Jesus Christ, this seed of Israel, took root in the perishing world of Hellenism? Has it been a misfortune that this origin has haunted its whole subsequent career? Is it merely in culpable self-will that we seek in soul the land of the Greeks, and cannot refrain from doing so even to-day, when we see so clearly that the necessary reformation of the Church cannot be the [283] same thing as a renaissance of Greek antiquity? Is there not here something obligatory, which it is better to see and accept than to ignore and deny, if we are ready and anxious to understand the Gospel of Jesus Christ in the full range of its content? And is not this factor to be found in the "gladly" which incontestably has a basic significance for the Christian concept of man and his humanity (and therefore indirectly for that of Christian *agape*)? We see the whole distortion of this "gladly" in Greek eroticism. The freedom of this highly-extolled man-god is only too easily seen and stated to be tyranny. It recognised itself to be such—to be a daemonism. But there is more to it than that. We cannot ignore it merely because it originally and properly maintains and actualises in a way which is still unmistakeable the tyranny of freedom. It is not finally for nothing that it was in the atmosphere of Greek *eros* that for the first time in the West, and perhaps over the whole earth, human freedom in the co-existence of man and man attained a noteworthy and unforgettable form for every age and place. This does not mean that we can despise the barbarians who knew nothing of this freedom. Paul mentioned them together with the Greeks (Rom. 1[14]), and declared that he was under a

---

[EN60] necessary condition

similar obligation to both. But this can hardly mean that as Christians we have to champion the barbarians against the Greeks, or that we should ignore the superiority of the latter to the former. The Early Church certainly did not do this, for all its differentiation of itself from Hellenism. We might almost wish that it had done so more, and that its differentiation had been more radical. But again this cannot mean that we can or should fail to see what is so clearly to be seen. The violence displayed against Hellenism in recent theology is not a good thing, and its continuation can only mean that in a short time we shall again be exposed to the Greek danger. The Greeks with their *eros*—and it was no inconsiderable but a very real achievement—grasped the fact that the being of man is free, radically open, willing, spontaneous, joyful, cheerful and gregarious. The shadow of conflict and suffering, of resignation, pain and death, of tragedy, must and does always fall on them as they can give it only the form of a basically erroneous yearning for an object and a radically capricious and finally disillusioning wandering from one object to another, being unable to realise it except in the daemonism and hybris of psychical and physical, ideal and only too real intoxication. The imagination which created the Homeric Olympus and its inhabitants is one of the strongest proofs of the fact that the heart of man is evil from his youth. Yet for all that the Greeks were able to reveal the human heart, to show what humanity is in itself and as such even in a state of distortion and corruption, to bring out the enduring factor in humanity which persists in spite of distortion and corruption, in a way which cannot be said of any other ancient people (and especially Israel, the people of God), and which can to some extent be said of the peoples of later Western history only as and because they have learned concerning *eros* from the ancient Greeks. How these Greeks knew how to see themselves as men, to speak with one another, to live together in freedom, as friends, as teachers and scholars, and above all as citizens! To be sure, even apart from perversion and corruption, they did so only to a certain degree, but in such a way that this emerged so clearly as the secret centre of their reflection and volition, as the measure of all their virtues, and even as the secret of their obvious mistakes and defects and vices, that other peoples which came in contact with them could not forget it, and even the community of Jesus Christ had to see and take note of it. The Greeks with their *eros* could not be for it a fact of salvation or divine revelation. If it let them be this, it soon found itself on bypaths. The Christian love proclaimed by Paul did not come from the school of the Greeks. And the Christian community could not and cannot learn from them even what humanity is. We ourselves have not gained our understanding of the concept from them. But even though we gain our understanding of the concept of humanity

[284] elsewhere, from the one true fact of salvation and divine revelation, yet we cannot fail to acknowledge—and this was and is the basis of the legitimate relationship between Christianity and Hellenism—that our understanding finds in the Greek with his *eros* a confirmation which we have every reason to remember and by which we have good cause to orientate ourselves when it is a matter of understanding Christian love as the awakening and fulfilment of humanity, of the distorted and perverted but not forfeited manner of the natural man, i.e., of man as God created him. The theology of Paul and his proclamation of Christian love derives neither from the Greeks nor the barbarians but from Israel. But when he portrays the Christian living in this love he never uses barbarian or Israelitish colours and contours, but he undoubtedly makes use of Greek, thus betraying the fact that he both saw and took note of the Greeks and their *eros*. Otherwise he could not have added quite so directly to the great saying: "The peace of God which passeth all understanding, shall keep your hearts and minds through Christ Jesus," the remarkable verse which follows: "Finally, brethren, whatsoever things are true, whatsoever things are honest ($\sigma\epsilon\mu\nu\acute{a}$), whatsoever things are just, whatsoever things are pure ($\acute{a}\gamma\nu\acute{a}$), whatsoever things are lovely ($\pi\rho\sigma\phi\iota\lambda\hat{\eta}$), whatsoever things are of good report ($\epsilon\check{v}\phi\eta\mu\alpha$); if there be any virtue ($\acute{a}\rho\epsilon\tau\acute{\eta}$), and if there be any praise ($\check{\epsilon}\pi\alpha\iota\nu\sigma$), think on these things" (Phil. 4^{7-8}). Otherwise he could not have

written Philippians with its dominating χαίρετε^{EN61} or even the great hymn to *agape* in 1 Cor. 13. As love itself primarily and from within itself, as the gracious gift of the Holy Ghost, is an open, willing, spontaneous, joyful, cheerful and gregarious being and action, and all this newly awakened and filled, in a good sense and not in a bad, it is obviously ready and willing to recognise itself and its humanity in everything human as in the good gift of God the Creator, even though it may be actual and recognisable only in that distortion and perversion in the man who is without love. Surely we may and must apply to its relationship to the Greek man and his *eros* the unforgettable words of 1 Cor. 13 ^{4–6}: "Love suffereth long (μακροθυμεῖ), and is kind (χρηστεύεται); love envieth not (οὐ ζηλοῖ); love vaunteth not itself (οὐ περπερεύεται), is not puffed up (οὐ φυσιοῦται), doth not behave itself unseemly (οὐκ ἀσχημονεῖ), seeketh not her own, is not easily provoked (οὐ παροξύνεται), thinketh no evil; rejoiceth not in iniquity, but rejoiceth in the truth (συγχάρει δὲ τῇ ἀληθείᾳ)"? It would partly do and partly leave undone all the things said of it if there were no way from it to man, even sinful man, refusing to him the humanity which is also its own instead of recognising, welcoming, acknowledging and respecting it, and declaring its solidarity with it, even where it appears in its most alien garb. It could not be the joy referred to in Philippians if it were unable or unwilling to rejoice in the truth even when it encounters it in sinners, and therefore to "rejoice with them that do rejoice" (Rom. 12¹⁵). It says No to the sin of these χαίροντες^{EN62} but it says Yes to their χαίρειν^{EN63} as such, because it is not as such something inhuman, but that which is human in all their inhumanity. Love is itself a life in the "gladly," in the holy, righteous and pure "gladly" of the gratitude which binds together brothers and sisters in Christ, and therefore of the supreme "gladly." How, then, can it fail to penetrate to the depths of the fellow-man who is not yet awakened to this thankfulness but still held by the intoxication of *eros*, thus being both permitted and commanded to find and accept even in his foolish, confused and evil "gladly" that which is genuinely creaturely and human? How can the Christian fail to see that in this respect and on this level too, with the natural bond of the "gladly," he is bound to the non-Christian, with whom he knows that he is primarily connected in a very different way by the judgment and grace of God in Jesus Christ? And let him finally see to it that the non-Christian finds the same in him—humanity, and therefore this "gladly"! "Let your moderation (ἐπιεικές) be known unto all men" (Phil. 4⁵, cf. Tit. 3²). It is, of course, quite normal that Christian love should seem strange and foolish to those who are without, just as the way in which those who are without live to their *eros* necessarily seems alien and nonsensical from the standpoint of Christian love. But it would be quite abnormal if those who are without did not find in Christian love at least the humanity which is their own; if they did not perceive in Christians at least that life in the "gladly"; if this did not speak to them and bind Christians to them. The *agape* of the Christians would perhaps not be all that it professes to be if the Greek man with his *eros* could not see that even in the Christian he has to do with a man and therefore with a being with which he can at least feel and proclaim solidarity in respect of that root of his *eros*. If this were not the case, the love of the supposed Christian would surely be a very loveless love. If it is genuine, in this respect and on this human level at least he will be no less perceptible and understandable to the non-Christian that the non-Christian must be to him. The non-Christian may say No or shake his head in face of what makes the Christian a Christian, but there should be no reason in the Christian why he should not at least say Yes to his χαίρειν^{EN64} as such, because this as such is the human element in him too. This downward

[285]

---

^{EN61} rejoice
^{EN62} rejoicing people
^{EN63} rejoicing
^{EN64} rejoicing

79

connexion of love by way of humanity to the *eros* of the Greeks was obviously present in New Testament times for all the differentiation of the spheres, and it is hard to see why the connexion cannot and should not be seen, respected and used in our own day as well. What we have here is a relationship between the Church and the world without which the Church cannot discharge its function in the world because without it it would not be the Church, the Church of Christian love.

3. HUMANITY AS LIKENESS AND HOPE

In its basic form humanity is fellow-humanity. Everything else which is to be described as human nature and essence stands under this sign to the extent that it is human. If it is not fellow-human, if it is not in some way an approximation to being in the encounter of I and Thou, it is not human. But provision is made that man should not break loose from this human factor. He can forget it. He can misconstrue it. He can despise it. He can scorn and dishonour it. But he cannot slough it off or break free from it. Humanity is not an ideal which he can accept or discard, or a virtue which he can practise or not practise. Humanity is one of the determinations with which we have to do in theological anthropology. It is an inviolable constant of human existence as such. An anthropology which ignored or denied this basic form of humanity would be explicable in terms of the practical corruption and perversion of man. But it would fly in face of a fact which the practical corruption and perversion of man cannot alter, let alone a theoretical judgment based upon it and therefore false. Man is in fact fellow-human. He is in fact in the encounter of I and Thou. This is true even though he may contradict it both in theory and in practice; even though he may pretend to be man in isolation and produce anthropologies to match. In so doing he merely proves that he is contradicting [286] himself, not that he can divest himself of this basic form of humanity. He has no choice to be fellow-human or something else. His being has this basic form.

That this is the case it is brought before us by the fact that we cannot say man without having to say male or female and also male and female. Man exists in this differentiation, in this duality. It is to be noted at once that this is the only structural differentiation in which he exists. The so-called races of mankind are only variations of one and the same structure, allowing at any time the practical intermingling of the one with the other and consisting only in fleeting transitions from the one to the other, so that they cannot be fixed and differentiated with any precision but only very approximately, and certainly cannot be compared with the distinct species and sub-species of the animal kingdom. In the distinction of man and woman, however, we have a structural differentiation of human existence. Man has this sexual differentiation in common with animals of all species and sub-species. This is the unavoidable sign and reminder that he exists in proximity to them and therefore within the context of creation as a whole; within and not above the boundary of the creature. But his creatureliness is to be male or female, male and female, and human in this distinction and connexion. He certainly exists in other essential and non-essential differentiations. He is necessarily a child, and this individual as opposed to others. But these distinctions as such are not structural in character. On the other hand, he does not need to be father or mother, brother or sister, young or old, gifted or not gifted, endowed in this way or that, a man of this or that particular time or sphere or race. Even if he is, it is again not on the basis of structural distinction. In all these essential and non-essential but secondary relationships and distinctions, however, he is primarily male or female, male and female. And the necessity with which he is a child, and a son or daughter, and this or that particular individual, is bound up with the fact that he is male or female, and the one or the other on the basis of structural differentiation. In and with his existence as man, and as this particular man, he is male or female, male and female. And in and with all the other essential and non-essential distinctions and connexions, this is decisive and in a sense exemplary because this alone is structural and runs through all the others, maintaining, expressing and revealing itself in them. In all the common and opposing features of human existence, there is no man in isolation, but only man or woman, man and woman. In the whole reach of human life there is no abstractly human but only concretely masculine or feminine being, feeling, willing, thinking, speaking, conduct and action, and only concretely masculine and feminine co-existence and co-operation in all these things. There is conflict and fellowship, there is encounter between men and therefore human being, only on the presupposition and under the sign and conditions of this one and distinctive differentiation. These things are present only in the [287] encounter of man and woman, but they are present at once, and with particular force, where this takes place as the necessary limitation and determination, whether to the furtherance or the detriment, of the actuality of their co-existence and co-operation. They are present, too, where man encounters man or woman woman, for man remains what he is, and therefore a being which intends and seeks his true partner in woman and not in man, and woman remains what she is, and therefore a being whose true counterpart cannot be found in woman but only in man. And because fundamentally— even though it cannot attain any corresponding form externally, and the counterpart is either absent or unrecognised—human being is a being in encounter, even human being which is temporarily isolated will definitely bear and in some way reveal the character of this one particular distinction and connexion.

Our present concern is not with the physiology and psychology of the sexes, and we shall not attempt to describe their distinctive structure. But we may perhaps be permitted to issue the following warning in respect of the involved psychological question—that it is much better if we avoid such generalised pronouncements as that man's interests are more outward and objective and woman's inward and subjective; that man is more disposed to freedom and woman to dependence; that man is more concerned with conquest and construction and woman with adornment; that man is more inclined to wander and woman to stay at home. Statements such as these may sometimes be ventured as hypotheses, but cannot be represented as knowledge or dogma because real man and real woman are far too complex and contradictory to be summed up in portrayals of this nature. It cannot be contested that both physiologically and biblically a certain strength and corresponding precedence are a very general characteristic of man, and a weakness and corresponding subsequence of woman. But in what the strength and precedence consists on the one side, and the weakness and subsequence on the other, what it means that man is the head of woman and not *vice versa*, is something which is better left unresolved in a general statement, and value-judgments must certainly be resisted. Man speaks against himself if he assesses and treats woman as an inferior being, for without her weakness and subsequence he could not be man. And woman speaks against herself if she envies that which is proper to man, for his strength and precedence are the reality without which she could not be woman. What distinguishes man from woman and woman from man even in this relationship of super- and subordination is more easily discovered, perceived, respected and valued in the encounter between them than it is defined. It is to be constantly experienced in their mutual exchanges and co-existence. Provision is made that it will be experienced here in supreme reality, not in theory, but in the practice of human existence as a being in encounter.

[288]   There can be no question that man is to woman and woman to man supremely the other, the fellow-man, to see and to be seen by whom, to speak with and to listen to whom, to receive from and to render assistance to whom is necessarily a supreme human need and problem and fulfilment, so that whatever may take place between man and man and woman and woman is only as it were a preliminary and accompaniment for this true encounter between man and fellow-man, for this true being in fellow-humanity. Why is this the case? Obviously because, however we may describe and represent man and woman phenomenologically, it is only here, where they are structural, that the antitheses between man and man are so great and estranging and yet stimulating that the encounter between them carries with it the possibility of a supreme difficulty otherwise absent, and yet in all these antitheses their relatedness, their power of mutual attraction and their reciprocal reference the one to the other are so great and illuminating and imperative that the possibility also emerges at least of a supreme interest otherwise absent. It is to be noted that the sphere of this special difficulty and interest, of this play and counterplay of the sexes, is much greater than the circle of what is usually understood more narrowly as sexual love in more or less close connexion with the problem of marriage. In the wider circle around the narrower it is to be found in the relationship of fathers and daughters, mothers and sons, brothers and sisters, and in similar relationships it plays its fruitful but perhaps disturbing and even

dangerous role in the whole sphere of education and instruction, and the life of churches of all confessions. Indeed, it is the subterranean motive, which has to be taken seriously into account, in all possible forms of fellowship between man and woman, whether in society, industry or life, among which we have to remember, not with malice but with all honour, the innumerable ways in which it finds compensation or sublimation in friendship between man and man or woman and woman. Yet it is obvious that the encounter between man and woman is fully and properly achieved only where there is the special connexion of one man loving this woman and one woman loving this man in free choice and with a view to a full life-partnership; a connexion which is on both sides so clear and strong as to make their marriage both possible and necessary as a unique and definitive attachment. This is naturally the true element of particularity in this intrinsically particular sphere, and constitutes its centre. There takes place here what can only be indicated and prepared in the wider circle, the female becoming to the male, and the male to the female, the other, the fellow-man, which man cannot and will not be without. Here all that we have described as humanity has its proper locus, the home from which it must continually go out and to which it must continually return. Here there is fulfilled first and perfectly the fact that man and man may be companions, associates, comrades, fellows and helpmates. Here this is all moved and sustained [289] from within by the clear-cut and simple fact that two human beings love each other, and that in small things and great alike they may will and have the same thing, each other. This capacity, the freedom of the heart for the other, and therefore that "gladly," has here its simplest and yet its strongest form. May it not be that this particular place is attended, at least in the so-called civilised nations, by so much interest and curiosity, but also so much reticence and anxiety, so much phantasy, poetry, morality and immorality, and so much empty talk and sighing and sniggering on the part of the inexperienced, because there are so few who realise that they have to do here with the centre of the human, with the basic form of primal humanity? But whatever we may realise or not realise, in this sphere, with which we gladly reckon the preliminary as well as the inner circle, and therefore the whole field of sexual encounter, we do actually stand before the primary form of all that has occupied us as humanity. To know nothing of this sphere is to know nothing of the I and Thou and their encounter, and therefore of the human. For where else can a man know it if he does not know it here, if he is a man to whom woman as woman (or a woman to whom man as man) is neutral and indifferent, to whom this structurally different counterpart presents neither difficulty nor interest, who does not stand in some relationship to it, however distorted or repressed, clumsy or unfortunate? Provision is made that no men are excluded from this centre of the human. To be sure, there are only a few who can see clearly and calmly at this point, and therefore live comparatively clearly and calmly, whether in marriage or outside it. There are innumerable men and women who theoretically and practically are walking blindly in a mist, and never see what they have missed, whether in marriage or outside it. But there is none who can escape the fact that he is man or woman and therefore in some sense man and woman. There is none who can escape this whole sphere. Man cannot escape his existence, and his existence as such stands under this determination. In the light of this we said at the very outset that man is fellow-human, that he is in the encounter of I and Thou, that humanity is not an ideal or virtue but an inviolable constant of human existence. In the fact of the duality of male and female, which cannot be resolved in a higher synthesis, we have this constant so clearly before us that we can only live it out, however well or badly. There can be no question of setting this fact aside, or overlooking it in practice. There is no being of man above the being of male and female.

[290]

Is not this fact a subsequent confirmation of the decided and apparently "dogmatic" precaution which we took, at the beginning of the previous subsection, of taking up the historically important anthropology of man in isolation only in the form of a delimitation from it *a limine*[EN65], and therefore of an outright rejection? We took this path because Christology left us no option, but compelled us to decide for the opposite path. And now we can only add that we were right, and that a little more of the readiness for real life which is so often lacking in the studies of philosophers and theologians would necessarily lead their occupants to the same result. That it has not done so is perhaps due to the fact that for so many centuries the philosophical and theological study of the West was the cloister-cell, from whose distinctive I-speculation in the absence of the Thou it has been difficult to break free even outside the cloister. Nietzsche did not live in a cell. But it is hard to decide where he was most at home, as a prophet of humanity without the fellow-man, in his repudiation of Christianity or in his almost brutal contempt for women (which fortunately was only literary in form). There is a necessary connexion between the two. This ought to have been remembered in the monastic cells where humanity without the fellow-man was not discovered but forcefully advanced and practised. No veneration of Mary or love for God could fill the terrible vacuum in which it was desired to live and a good deal of life was actually lived to the detriment of the Church and the world. But the vacuum is not filled merely by leaving the cloister, just as the external cloister does not necessarily entail the vacuum. It is very possible even for external life in the cloister to be in fact a being in encounter. And it is equally evident that even a flood of love for women such as that which filled the life of Goethe is not strong enough to make impossible a humanity without the fellow-man, or to actualise with certainty a being in encounter. At any rate, it did not prevent Goethe from becoming, if not the prophet, at least the high-priest of this humanity. And when he broke off his deepest and finest love-affair to study Greek antiquity in Italy, there was revealed the fact that his repudiation of humanity was coincident with a repudiation of this nervous centre of humanity, and he gave conclusive proof of an attitude to woman, confirmed rather than altered by his marriage with Christiana Vulpius, which, while it cannot be compared with the scorn of Nietzsche, can only be described as that of the man who is finally emancipated from women. He too, and especially, was finally captured by the secularised cloister. And behind all this there stands the fact that we have here the profoundest symptom of sickness in the world of the Greeks and their *eros* (which only too fully enslaved the West both in real and secularised cloisters). For all the eroticism of theory and practice, it was a man's world in which there was no real place for woman; and for this reason it was necessarily a world of the I without the Thou, and therefore a world of the I wandering without limit or object, a daemonic and tyrannical world. It is

---

[EN65] from the outset

not surprising, then, that the discovery or the many re-discoveries of the humanity of the free heart present and not absolutely concealed in the Greek world of *eros* were overtaken by such disasters in the narrower and wider Christian sphere, in real and secularised cloisters. The only safeguard against these disasters is Christology, and a little knowledge of life. By a little knowledge of life we mean a placid and cheerful and sure knowledge of the duality of human existence, of the original form of the I and Thou in the continuity of human being as the being of male or female, of male and female. Where Christianity is genuine in the sense that it is not merely theoretical but living wisdom (the biblical *ḥokma* or σοφία), it unavoidably carries with it a little knowledge of life. This was forgotten in the mediaeval cloister, and it has been forgotten in all other studies where its supposedly Christian but inhuman tradition has been continued. But to attain a little knowledge of life Christology must not be despised as has been the case, with equally inhuman results, in secularised, untheological and non-Christian cells, e.g., that of Goethe or Nietzsche. The Christian community, receiving and proclaiming Christian love and Christian theology with its doctrine of man, ought to be secured against those disasters and to be able to pass triumphantly through every cloister, knowing the man Jesus as the man who is for His fellow-man, and therefore knowing man generally, knowing his humanity as fellow-humanity, and this fellow-humanity at the point [291] where it is most concretely and incontestably a fact, in the antithesis and connexion of man and woman. But the test of this twofold and at bottom unitary knowledge is whether it can be ruthless enough to turn its back at once and absolutely on the error of the humanity of man without the fellow-man.

The Old Testament Magna Carta of humanity is the J saga which tells us how God completed the creation of man by giving him woman as a companion (Gen. 2^{18-25}). We have already expounded this text in *C.D.* III, I, 288f., and to establish our present point reference must be made both generally and in detail to this exposition.

The main point may be briefly recapitulated. In Gen. 2 (like Gen. 1), the account of the creation of man as male and female is the climax of the whole history of creation. In both cases it is solemnly emphasised and introduced by the mention of special reflection on the part of the Creator. In this case, the reference is as follows: "It is not good that the man should be alone; I will make him an help meet for him." In this saying there is a radical rejection of the picture of man in isolation. And the point of the whole text is to say and tell—for it has the form of a story—who and what is the man who is created good by God— good as the partner of God in the history which is the meaning and purpose of creation. This man created good by God must have a partner like himself, and must therefore be a partner to a being like himself; to a being in which he can recognise himself, and yet not himself but another, seeing it is not only like him but also different from him; in other words, a "help meet." This helpmeet is woman. With her he is the man created good by God, the complete human creature. He would not be this alone. That he is not alone, but complete in this duality, he owes to the grace of his Creator. But the intention of this grace is as revealed in this completion. And according to the fine declaration of the text its intention is not merely that he should acquire this duality, woman, but, acquiring her from God, recognise and confess her by his own choice and decision as a helpmeet. God the Creator knows and ordains, but He leaves it to man to discover, that only woman and not animals can be this helpmeet. Thus the climax of the history of creation coincides with this first act of human freedom. Man sees all kinds of animals. He exercises his superiority over them by giving them names. But he does not find in them a being like himself, a helpmeet. He is thus alone with them (even in his superiority), and therefore not good, not yet complete as man. In the first instance, then, he exercises his human freedom, his humanity, negatively. He remains free for the being which the Creator will give him as a partner. He waits for woman, and can do so. He must not grasp after a false completion. But who and what is woman? That man obviously waits for her does not mean that he knows her in advance. She is not his postulate, or ideal, let alone his creation. Like himself, she is the thought and work of God. "And (he) brought her unto the man." She is not merely there to be arbitrarily and accidentally discovered and accepted by man. As God creates both man and woman, He also creates their relationship, and brings them together. But this divinely created relationship—which is not just any kind of relationship, but the distinctive human relationship—has to be recognised and affirmed by man himself. This takes place when he cries triumphantly: "This is now bone of my bones, and flesh of my flesh." Here we have the second and positive step in the act of freedom, in the venture of free thought and speech, of man exercising his humanity in this freedom. At the heart of his humanity he is free in and for the fact that he may recognise and accept the woman whom he himself has not imagined and conjured up by his desire, but

[292]   whom God has created and brought. With this choice he confirms who and what he is within creation, his own election, the particularity of his creation. He is man in this negative and positive relationship. Human being becomes the being in encounter in which alone it can be good. His last objective assertion concerning another being becomes his subjective confession (as a male) of this other being, this fellow-man, the woman who has her own equal but proper and independent honour and dignity in the fact that she can be his helpmeet, without whose participation in his life he could not be a man, and without whose honour and dignity it would be all up with his own. "Therefore shall a man leave his father and his mother, and shall cleave unto his wife" means that because woman is so utterly from man he must be utterly to her; because she is so utterly for him he must be utterly for her; because she can only follow him in order that he should not be alone he must also follow her not to be alone; because he the first and stronger can only be one and strong in relationship to her he must accept and treat her, the second and weaker, as his first and stronger. It is in this inversion that the possibility of the human, the natural supremacy of the I over the Thou, is developed in reality. It is in this way that the genuinely human declares its possibility. It is in this form that there exists the possibility of man in isolation, but also of all androcracy and gynocracy. "And they were both naked, the man and his wife, and were not ashamed." The human is the male and female in its differentiation but also its connexion. Hence there is no humiliation or shame. The human cannot be a burden or reproach. It is not an occasion for unrest or embarrassment. It does not need to be concealed and hidden. There can be no shame in respect of the human. In the work of God—which is what the human is—there is nothing offensive and therefore no *pudendum*[EN66]. The work of God is without spot, pure, holy and innocent. Hence man does not need to be ashamed of his humanity, the male of his masculinity or the female of her femininity. There is no need of justification. To be the creature of God is self-justification. Only sin, the fall from God, can shame the human, i.e., the masculine and the feminine, and thus make it an object of shame. And the awful genius of sin is nowhere more plainly revealed than in the fact that it shames man at this centre of his humanity, so that he is necessarily ashamed of his humanity, his masculinity and femininity, before God and men, and every attempt to escape this shame, every self-justification, or concretely every denial and suppression of sexuality can only confirm and increase the shame. It is to be noted carefully that this is the climax of this text, and therefore of the whole biblical history of creation.

The whole of Gen. $2^{18f.}$ points to the man who is fellow-human as such, as

---

[EN66] embarrassment

the creature of God, in his divinely given nature, and therefore originally and not secondarily. And it speaks of the co-existence of man and woman as the original and proper form of this fellow-humanity. It singles out this among all other possible relationships as the one which belongs to the creation-history preceding all others, and which alone can come into question when it is a matter of describing the nature which man has been given by God. At this point the reference cannot be to parents and children, to brothers and sisters and other relatives, to friends, to Europeans and Asiatics, to Semites and Aryans, to old and young, to gifted and ungifted, to rulers and subjects, teachers and scholars, rich and poor, or even the basic distinction of individual and individual. Or rather, this basic distinction, the differentiation and connexion of I and Thou, must be explained as coincident with that of male and female. All other relationships are involved in this as the original relationship. All other humanity is included in this centre. In this connexion, particular attention must be paid to the fact that in Genesis 2 the reference is to man and woman in their relationship as such, and therefore not to fatherhood and motherhood or the establishment of the family. It is true that in the rest of the Old Testament the relationship is seen almost exclusively from the latter aspect, in the light of the question of progeny, and with the main interest in the conception and birth of children, especially the son. But it is equally true that this is not the case in the present passage. No mention is here made of child or family. The relationship of man and woman has its own reality and dignity. As such it is the basic relationship involving all others. At this point the Bible thinks and speaks far more seriously "erotically" than all Hellenism. In the light of this text it cannot be called arbitrary if, having sketched the basic form of humanity in general terms, we make the reference to this particular relationship the climax of our presentation, and without the usual expansion or restriction that when it is a question of man and woman we are inevitably led to father and mother and therefore child as the third thing proceeding from the other two. If the Old Testament is a commentary on the New, and decisive account has to be taken of an important passage like Genesis 2, we can only say that this weakens and obscures the true situation and is thus to be rejected. But this means that the encounter of man and woman as such is being in encounter and therefore the centre of humanity, so that before we proceed to consider the circumference of this centre it is worth pausing at this encounter, since otherwise we shall probably misinterpret all other encounters, even that of parents and children. For it is here first and decisively that we have to see and learn what is meant by freedom of heart for the other, and therefore what constitutes the humanity of all other encounters. Genesis 2 is imperious in this respect. If it is objected that it is isolated in its reference to man and woman, the answer is that creation is isolated in relation to the rest of the creature's history, and the divinely given nature of man in relation to what this became at the hands of man. But our present question concerns creation

[293]

87

and the creaturely nature of man, and we have every reason to put this question even to understand the history of the human creature and man in his corruption as a sinner. If we are to find an answer, we must read this passage in Genesis 2 without subtraction or addition, as we have tried to do. And we must therefore learn from it that man is first and unquestionably and generally man and woman, and only then all kinds of other things, including perhaps father and mother.

[294]

And in any case Genesis 2 is not absolutely isolated in the Old Testament. We might almost speak of a second Magna Carta of humanity in this connexion when we remember that at a rather curious point in the Old Testament Canon a place is found for the Song of Songs. We should not wish that this book were not in the Canon. We should not treat it as if it were outside. And we should not spiritualise it, as if what is in the Canon can have only a spiritualised significance. As all honest exposition must admit, and as ought to be recognised gladly rather than with hesitation and embarrassment, it is a collection of genuine love-songs in the primitive sense, in which there is no reference to the child, but only to man and woman in their differentiation and connexion, in their being in encounter. At this point the most natural exegesis might well prove to be the most profound.

It is to be noted that in this second text we hear a voice which is lacking in the first. This is the voice of the woman, to whom the man looks and moves with no less pain and joy than she to him, and who finds him with no less freedom—only the "This" of Genesis is lacking—than she is found. Implicitly, of course, this voice is to be heard in Genesis as well. But it now finds expression in words. And what words! "Set me as a seal upon thine heart, as a seal upon thine arm: for love is strong as death; jealousy is cruel as the grave: the coals thereof are coals of fire, which hath a most vehement flame. Many waters cannot quench love, neither can the floods drown it: if a man would give all the substance of his house for love, it would utterly be contemned" (8⁶ᶠ·). And so everything is more luminous if not more strong, more direct if not more unequivocal. And all that takes place is sketched and depicted against a background of day and night, of the passing seasons, of the plants and animals of the Palestinian scene. And this is what the Old Testament calls the song of all songs. Again, it is an isolated text, and in its theological assessment we must take the same line as in Genesis 2, except that now we are obviously at the other end of the line, the end and not the beginning. That this song belongs to the so-called Solomonic literature, being attached to Proverbs and Ecclesiastes, reminds us that Solomon the builder of the temple, and his kingdom, glory and wisdom, represent the figure of the King of the last day and His glory. This is how the expected son of David appeared and his kingdom—so powerful, resplendent and wise, and finally so human. And so we must understand eschatologically the songs ascribed to him when we take seriously their very concrete content. On the long line from creation to the last day the Old Testament speaks very differently of man and woman. The dominating question is that of children. The "erotic" notes are few. Everything is controlled by the Law, and especially the danger and prohibition of adultery. In this respect, too, we are in the world of sin and infamy and shame, in which the love-song must always have a rather dubious sound, and the original of the covenant between man and woman, the covenant between Yahweh and Israel, is continually broken on the part of Israel, and has still to be properly constituted. But the beginning and end, the origin and goal, both between Yahweh and Israel and between man and woman, are as depicted in Genesis 2 and the Song of Songs. In retrospect of creation and prospect of the new creation of the last time, we can and may and must speak of man and woman as is done in these texts.

Hence both these passages justify us in speaking of man in this way when we ask concerning his creaturely nature.

In the light of the theological significance of the Song of Songs this is perhaps the point to elucidate an eschatological question which at a first glance might cause considerable difficulty. We read in Gal. 3²⁶ᶠ: "For ye are all the children of God by faith in Christ Jesus. For as [295] many of you as have been baptised into Christ have put on Christ. There is neither Jew nor Greek, there is neither bond nor free, there is neither male nor female: for ye are all one in Christ Jesus. And if ye be Christ's, then are ye Abraham's seed, and heirs according to the promise." What Paul is saying, and not saying, is quite clear. He is saying that the being of Christians on the basis of the grace of God commonly directed to them and commonly received by them in faith, their being as children of God, the seed of Abraham and heirs according to the promise, their being in correspondence with their baptism, is one which makes impossible any exaltation of the one over the other or hostility of the one to the other, so that in the Christian community there can be no assertion of natural and historical antitheses. For in this community all are one in Christ Jesus in the sense that all live thankfully by the grace which is manifested equally to each of them as mercy. But Paul is not saying that the antitheses are simply set aside and done away by the being of Christians in Christ. *Cest ordre là est inviolable et nostre Seigneur Jésus Christ n'est pas venu au monde pour faire une telle confusion que ce qui est establi de Dieu son Père soit aboli*ᴱᴺ⁶⁷. (Calvin, *C.R.* 28, 568). Thus the fact that male and female are one in Christ does not mean that they are no longer male and female. Yet it might be asked whether this is the last word. Does it not apply only so long as Christians still share in this present aeon which passes? In their life which according to Col. 3³ is hidden with Christ in God, and especially in its future manifestation in the resurrection of the dead, will it not perhaps be the case that they are no longer male or female, but a third thing which is higher and better. The question is an obvious one in view of Mk. 12¹⁸⁻²⁷ and *par.*, where in answer to the question of the Sadducees which of the seven brothers should have the woman to wife in the resurrection Jesus said: "For when they shall rise from the dead, they neither marry, nor are given in marriage; but are as the angels which are in heaven." Does this mean that they will no longer be male and female? Is A. Oepke right (*TWBzNT,* 1, 785) when he says that by proposing for man in the perfected lordship of God a sexless being similar to that of the angels Jesus lifts from woman particularly the curse of her sex and sets her at the side of man as no less justifiably the child of God? Yet it does not actually say that man and woman will be ἄγγελοι ᴱᴺ⁶⁸, but ὡς ἄγγελοι ᴱᴺ⁶⁹ (ἰσάγγελοι ᴱᴺ⁷⁰, Lk. 20³⁶), i.e., those who according to 1 Cor. 13¹² no longer see God, themselves and all things in a glass darkly but face to face, and are thus liberated from the problematical, burdensome and complicated nature of their existence in the form which they now know (through a glass darkly). To this form there belongs marrying and giving in marriage with such implicated questions as that raised by the Sadducees on the basis of Deut. 25⁵ᶠ, and the overriding concern for children. It is not from the insights of the world of the Song of Songs that the Sadducees ask concerning the solution of such complicated matters in the future

---

ᴱᴺ⁶⁷ That order is inviolable, and our Lord Jesus Christ did not come into the world to create the kind of confusion that would follow if that which was established by God his Father were destroyed

ᴱᴺ⁶⁸ angels

ᴱᴺ⁶⁹ as the angels

ᴱᴺ⁷⁰ like angels

aeon, and the stern rebuke which Jesus gives them is fully justified: "Do ye not therefore err, because ye know not the Scriptures, neither the power of God?" This, whole concern for marrying and giving in marriage and the raising up of children, says Jesus, can no longer occupy men in the resurrection when according to Lk. 20^{36} they cannot "die any more." God is the God of Abraham, Isaac and Jacob, and therefore the God of the living ($\theta\epsilon\grave{o}\varsigma$ $\zeta\acute{\omega}\nu\tau\omega\nu$) and not the dead; the God for whom, and before whose eyes which span the centuries, all men (or they all, Lk. 20^{38}) are alive in their time. As such they will be revealed in the resurrection, and with their death the necessary cares which now lie like a cover over their lives will be lifted and left behind. Thus the fact that that woman had belonged to seven successive husbands, and must still belong to them according to the law of marriage, could cast no shadow on her temporal life as disclosed in the resurrection, nor on the life of the seven

[296] men. For the fact that she married and was married will then be a past event with many other happenings and finally with the death of those concerned. The only thing that will count is that like Abraham, Isaac and Jacob they have lived in their time for God, the God of the living, and therefore live eternally. To that extent they will be as the angels of heaven, not in heaven, but on the new earth under the new heaven—new because the cosmos will then be revealed in the form in which there will be no more possibility or place for tears and death and sorrow and crying and pain (Rev. 21^4). They will thus be as the angels of heaven because this is how it is already with the angels. But there is no reference here, and cannot be, to an abolition of the sexes or cessation of the being of man as male and female. It is worth noting that even Augustine, who must have been tempted to this thought, expressly repudiated it (*De civ. Dei*, XXII, 17). He met it in the distinctive variation that from the saying in Rom. 8^{29} about our being conformed to the image of God's Son, and the saying in Eph. 4^{13} about our coming unto a $\grave{\alpha}\nu\grave{\eta}\rho$ $\tau\acute{\epsilon}\lambda\epsilon\iota o\varsigma$^{EN71}, it follows that woman will rise after the fashion of the male and not the female. But as against this Augustine prefers the view of those *qui utrumque sexum resurrecturum esse non dubitant*^{EN72}. What is to be set aside in the resurrection is not nature itself, but the violation of nature. But the female sex belongs in its particularity to nature. And so he maintains the opinion: *qui utrumque sexum instituit, utrumque restituet*^{EN73}. Thus in this Synoptic passage Jesus certainly tells us that there will be no continuation of marriage but not that woman will not be woman in the resurrection. By His very negation He presupposes that men will still be men and women women. It cannot be otherwise. In the *Syn. Theol. Leiden* (1624, *Disp.* 51, 37) it is rightly observed that this is also demanded by the identity of the human subject in the two aeons. The determination as man or woman is not the least important of the *conditiones individuantes*^{EN74} of the human subject, so that if it were to lack in the resurrection the subject would no longer be this subject, and man would no longer be man. And in this case it would no longer be $\tau\grave{o}$ $\phi\theta\alpha\rho\tau\grave{o}\nu$ $\tau o\hat{v}\tau o$^{EN75} which in the resurrection puts on $\grave{\alpha}\phi\theta\alpha\rho\sigma\acute{\iota}\alpha$^{EN76}, nor $\tau\grave{o}$ $\theta\nu\eta\tau\grave{o}\nu$ $\tau o\hat{v}\tau o$^{EN77} which puts on $\grave{\alpha}\theta\alpha\nu\alpha\sigma\acute{\iota}\alpha$^{EN78} (1 Cor. 15$^{53f.}$). Man would not be man if he were no longer male or female, if his humanity did not consist in this concrete fellow-humanity, in this distinction and connexion. He has lived in no other way in time, and he can live in no other way in eternity. This is something which he cannot lose. For by it there stands or falls his creatureliness. In relation to the goal of our existence in the future aeon we have thus no cause to doubt a statement which we formu-

---

EN71 perfect man
EN72 who do not doubt that both sexes will rise
EN73 he who established each sex will restore each sex
EN74 individuating conditions
EN75 this perishible body
EN76 incorruption
EN77 this mortal body
EN78 immortality

lated in relation to creation as its beginning. We have no cause not to see together the picture of Genesis 2 and that of the Song of Songs.

Why does it have to be as we have stated on the primary basis of these passages? Why do Genesis 2 and the Song of Songs give us this particular picture of man and his humanity? Our statement would seem at least to be rather fortuitous if we simply appealed to this Magna Carta in its twofold form, accepting the fact that this is what is actually written and not something else. Why do we read particularly that man is male or female, male and female? In fact, there is nothing fortuitous about it. It belongs to the very centre of Holy Scripture. It is necessarily grounded in the decisive content of the Word of God. We can thus see, and if we are to have a proper understanding we must see, that there can be no question of anything but what is actually there, and that we cannot possibly adopt any other view than that which we have actually adopted. We must now try to show why this is the case.

As concerns the Old Testament, we have already sketched our answer. [297] Behind the relationship of man and woman as we meet it in the picture of Genesis 2 and the Song of Songs there stands the controlling original of the relationship between the God Yahweh-Elohim and His people Israel. Behind these passages there stands Old Testament prophecy. And according to the insight which continually breaks through, the sum of all truth and actuality, which is thus also the beginning and end of all things, the secret of creation and its consummation, is the very different duality merely reflected in the nature of man—that of God and man in their co-existence in the concrete form of the covenant established by God between Himself and His people Israel. This duality, the covenant, is the centre of the Old Testament. And it is the original of which the essence of the human as the being of man and woman can only be the reflection and copy. Man is primarily and properly Yahweh, and woman primarily and properly Israel. That is why it is necessary, and the Old Testament poets of creation and the consummation are compelled to describe the human as they have actually done. That is why what they say belongs as it stands to the Canon of Holy Scripture. That is why we have to do here with God's Word concerning man, so that we cannot deviate on either side from what is said. We note that Old Testament prophecy everywhere presupposes the sin of man, Israel's apostasy and therefore the Law and judgment of God, but also and more particularly the faithfulness of God. It thus speaks in the light of the shattering of the original on the side of man. It speaks of the covenant broken by Israel, and therefore of the unfaithful wife who has forfeited her rights and dignity. But in contrast it also speaks of the kindness and mercy of the Husband whom she has left and injured but who does not abandon her. It thus speaks with reference to the long period between creation and the end. But with this reference it speaks concerning this relationship. And it counts on the fact that in and in spite of its disruption it is not ended but persists. The covenant remains. Yahweh is faithful to Israel. His betrothal and marriage continue. His love also remains. And because everything remains on His side, this means that there is also an indestructible continuity in the being of Israel. Even in its apostasy and the rejection and abandonment which it entails it is still the people which Yahweh has marked out and sought and loved, and with which He has entered into covenant. And the end and goal of its history will prove this continuity which exists from the beginning. The hope of Israel is that its continuation in the covenant (not in virtue of its own goodness, but of that of Yahweh) will finally be revealed. This immutable covenant relationship between Yahweh and Israel, and therefore the centre of the Old Testament witness, stands dominatingly behind Genesis 2 and the Song of Songs. As this original confronts them, shattered in the middle of the line, but [298] also in its totality at the beginning and the end, the poets dare to speak of man and woman as they do. We must be clear that they were not just speaking symbolically or allegorically; they were speaking directly and concretely of man and woman and their relationship. But they could do as they did because they had before them as a model and final basis of the form of humanity of which they wrote the relationship of Yahweh and Israel. It was an unattainable model of humanity because love such as that of Yahweh for Israel is beyond the reach of a human husband in relation to his wife. On the one hand we have a covenant between Creator and creature; on the other only a covenant between creature and creature. But the latter covenant rests on the former. Because even God, God Himself, the Lord and King of the heavenly and earthly space created by Him, did not will to be alone, but to have His concrete counterpart in the people Israel, man was not to be alone, but to have his helpmeet or counterpart in woman. Hence it is not at all impossible to find the outlines of the covenant of grace between Yahweh and Israel even in the details of the story of the creation of man as male and female. Because this is the case, it is not by chance that this story has its present form in the Old Testament, and there is good reason to claim it as the Magna Carta of a concept of humanity in which the basic relationship of man and woman receives due honour.

But the final and decisive step has still to be taken to establish it on a biblical foundation. A last appearance of fortuitousness might still cling to it so long as we move only in the sphere of Old Testament promise and not of New Testament fulfilment.

The Old Testament shows an amazing knowledge in this whole matter. Without a knowledge of the true and final meaning of the relationship of man and woman it would be quite intolerable to see this intra-creaturely relationship in the holy relationship between Yahweh and Israel. Again, without a knowledge of the menacing and shattering of the relationship between man and woman the Old Testament could not have such a terribly plastic view of the devastation of the relationship between Yahweh and Israel. On the other hand, without the hope of the last time with its divine fulfilment of the covenant with Israel it would be impossible to see the covenant of man and woman with the freedom of Genesis 2 and the Song of Songs. Again, without the strictly eschatological character of this hope it would be hard to understand why this view of man and woman is the exception to the normal rule of the Old Testament, which is not to consider man and woman as such, in their mutual relationship of husband and wife, but as father and mother in the light of their destiny to have descendants. Thus the knowledge displayed by the Old Testament is strikingly unanimous and yet strikingly contradictory. Why does it include the primary statements ? How does it know the dignity of the relationship of the sexes? And yet how does it also know that it is menaced and shattered? How does it know of the eschatological fulfilment of the covenant of grace with Israel? And how does it know that this fulfilment is not to be sought in the sphere of vision of the Israelite, but beyond his sphere of vision, as an eschatological event? It cannot be contested that the Old Testament does know this. But it is also incontestable that in this respect it rests on a secret which is nowhere revealed and never even takes concrete shape in its own sphere. Thus if we were restricted to this sphere alone we should have to accept that a certain fortuitousness and uncertainty clings to our statement. We could [299] maintain that things are as we have seen them in the Old Testament. But it could not be said or proved that we for our part are forced to see them in this way.

But why should we be restricted to this sphere? The secret on which the unanimous but contradictory knowledge of the Old Testament rests may well be visible and therefore disclosed outwith the witness of the Old Testament if not within it. The witness of the New Testament tells us that this is the case. If we are to take it seriously we are forced to say that the New Testament tells us what the Old for all its knowledge does not know and therefore cannot tell us. It tells us where this Old Testament knowledge of man derives, where it has objectively its origin and basis, and on what grounds things can be only as indicated in the Old Testament. *Vetus testamentum in novo patet*[EN79]. It is indeed the case that the New Testament reaches back behind the Old, revealing and disclosing the secret presupposed but nowhere revealed or disclosed in the Old, and thus proving what the Old in itself and as such can never prove—that in all its parts it is right and speaks the truth in a way which is normative for us. We can grasp this if we take our previous questions one by one.

How does the Old Testament know the dignity of the relationship between the sexes? How does it have the knowledge which permits and commands it to see this intra-creaturely relationship in the holy relationship between Yahweh and Israel? The New Testament answers that the covenant between Jesus Christ and His community was in the beginning, the first and proper object of the divine will and plan and election, and the internal basis of creation. This covenant is the original of the Old Testament original, the relationship between Yahweh and Israel, and therefore the original of the relationship between man and woman. It is on the basis of this original that the intra-creaturely relationship has its dignity and necessity, and that the Old Testament finds it essential to see this intra-creaturely relationship at the central point in its witness, in the covenant between God and the people.

But again, how does the Old Testament know that the relationship of the sexes is menaced and shattered? How does it have the knowledge which gives to its complaint against Israel its distinctively sharp and drastic quality as an accusation of adultery? The New Testament answers that the covenant

---

EN79 The Old Testament is disclosed in the New

between Jesus Christ and His community, which is the secret of creation, is of such a kind that its Lord, Jesus Christ, is the One who for His community—a gathering of sinners who have fallen victim to the wrath of God and their own perdition—gives Himself up to death in order to win it as His own possession. The history of the covenant between Yahweh and Israel must culminate in the crucifixion of the King for the people because it is grounded in this earlier

[300]   covenant, the covenant of the Holy with the unholy. On the basis of this earlier covenant Israel throughout the history of the covenant between Yahweh and itself has the form of the ungrateful, faithless and adulterous wife. And on this basis the relationship of the sexes is necessarily seen under the shadow which always falls on it in the Old Testament.

How does the Old Testament know of the eschatological fulfilment of the covenant of grace with Israel? How does it have the knowledge which permits and commands it at least occasionally in these supreme passages to see the relationship of man and woman with this great freedom? The New Testament answers that in the covenant between Jesus Christ and His community it takes place that man's apostasy from God is finally cancelled and made good, that fidelity and love between God and man are made reciprocal by the gift of the Holy Spirit, and that the accusation against man, and therefore the Law which accuses, drop away. On the basis of this covenant the hope of Israel is ineluctably necessary and sure, as constantly depicted in the Old Testament. And on this basis it is possible and necessary to give to the covenant between man and woman—this intra-creaturely covenant as such, and quite apart from any question of progeny—the dignity and honour which are ascribed to it in Genesis 2 and the Song of Songs.

But how does the Old Testament know that the fulfilment of the covenant of grace with Israel is a strictly eschatological reality, and therefore to be sought outside the sphere of the Israelite? How does it have the knowledge which compels the Old Testament normally to speak otherwise of man and woman than in Genesis 2 and the Song of Songs, necessarily putting the fatherhood of the man and motherhood of the woman into the forefront of the picture? The New Testament answers that it is in the covenant between Jesus Christ and His community that the divine will and plan and election have their proper object and thus find their fulfilment. This covenant is the goal even of the covenant between Yahweh and Israel as a promise and preparation. The history of Israel as the history of this covenant has its meaning in the appearance of the Son of God and Son of Man as the Head of a people holy by Him and in Him. And on the basis of this first and proper covenant the Old Testament throughout the middle stretch between creation and the end must display that sober interest in man and woman in their quality as father and mother. This is necessary because in Israel, in the whole sequence of its generations, it is a question only of this promise and preparation, which means finally of the miraculous conception and natural birth of the Son and His people gathered from Jews and Gentiles. Thus the picture of man and woman given in Genesis 2 and the Song of Songs could stand only on the margin of the Old Testament witness, but on this margin it had a place which was not just possible but necessary.

Thus the New Testament witness reaches back behind the Old. It reveals the   [301] source of the knowledge displayed in the Old Testament. It indicates and discloses the secret which does not emerge and is certainly not revealed in the Old Testament. It proves point by point that the Old Testament is right and speaks the truth in a way which is normative for us, and that it does not therefore say fortuitously of humanity that it consists in the co-existence of male and female.

It is only fitting that at this point we should consider the decisive statements of the New Testament independently and in their own context.

We must first remember the general truth that when the New Testament speaks of Jesus Christ and His community it really speaks of the goal (and therefore of the origin and beginning) of all earthly things. Jesus Christ and His community is not an additional promise given to men. The existence and history of Israel in covenant with Yahweh was a promise. The reality of Jesus Christ and His community does not continue this history. It is not a further stage in actualisation of the divine will and plan and election which are the purpose of creation. It concludes this process. It is the complete fulfilment of the promise. It is the goal and end of all the ways of God. It is *the* eschatological reality. It cannot be surpassed, deepened or enriched by anything still to come. It is followed only by its proclamation to all nations and all creation as the task laid upon the community. But the community has not to proclaim a new offer or promise and its law. It has to proclaim the accomplishment of the divine decree as it has already taken place in the appearance of Jesus Christ, in His death and resurrection, and in the outpouring of the Holy Ghost. All that is outstanding is its manifestation as the light of the cosmos which does not yet know it—its manifestation by Jesus Christ Himself. But as the Head of His community He is already the Head of the cosmos (Col. 1$^{17f.}$). Hence His return cannot alter or improve anything, let alone introduce anything new. "If any man be in Christ, he *is* a new creature" (2 Cor. 5^{17}). What is to be proclaimed by the ministry of His community, and finally revealed by Himself, is simply the fact that this is the case. He is a new creature. For God has given Jesus Christ to be the κεφαλὴ ὑπὲρ πάντα[EN80] to the community which is His body and in which He has His own divine fulness and His whole divine fulfilment (Eph. 1$^{22f.}$). This completed fact is still to be shown to the cosmos. This completed fact must be revealed as the meaning of the whole cosmos. But it is already a completed fact. There is no salvation which has not already come to the world in the death and resurrection of Jesus Christ and the existence of the community which He has purchased by His blood and has gathered and still gathers by His Holy Spirit.

It was on the basis of this insight that Paul treated his communities, and each of them as *the* community of Jesus Christ. A Christian community is not a religious experiment. It is not a fellowship of faith and hope with a more or less distant and exalted goal to which it is directed and towards which it strives as an ideal. It is this as little as Jesus Christ is a prophet pointing to the future and prophesying something which is not yet real. The people Israel waits for the Son. Its whole history is the history of this expectation. But the community of Jews and Gentiles founded by the apostle derives from the Son. It has its history in the fact that it is in Christ and therefore lives in the fulfilment which has taken place in this Head. It belongs to Him, and what belongs to Him belongs as His gift to it. As the apostle proclaimed

---

[EN80] head over all things

to it the Word concerning Him, and it received this Word in faith, as Christians were baptised in the name of Jesus Christ, they were united to Him, and with Him they constitute the eschatological reality and the end of all God's ways, so that they can will only that the glory in which they participate in Him and by Him should be revealed among them and through them to others, and they can expect only that Jesus Christ Himself will finally confess them and manifest the glory with which He has already invested them to their own eyes and those of others, in order that the whole world may be radiant and full of the glory of God in this revelation. It is on this basis that Paul addresses the Christian communities, and always in the light of the fact that the fulfilment has taken place in Jesus Christ alone, but in Jesus Christ for them. All the instruction, consolation and admonition which he imparts to them are references back to this completed fact, to the portion which they have in Jesus Christ and therefore in the fulfilment which has taken place in Him. Any deviation from this line, any return to the situation of the people Israel, i.e., to that of the unfulfilled promise, any re-establishment of the Israelitish Law, but also any legalistic demand for faith and hope, would necessarily mean that Jesus Christ Himself is called in question. But someone in whom everything is not fulfilled would not be Jesus Christ. We know how passionately Paul avoided this kind of Christ. And he was not guilty of any such deviation or compromise. The warfare against sin, error and disorder which he waged in the Christian community was conducted solely on the basis of the fact that Jesus Christ and His community in their interconnexion are the reality of the last time beyond which we cannot expect any other, or any other insights, possibilities or powers, but in which God has reached with man the end for which He created heaven and earth and all that therein is. And the whole warfare of the spirit against the flesh, the good fight of faith, to which Paul summons the community and all its members, can only be the battle to maintain the position which has already been captured and allotted to them by the act of God in Jesus Christ, and from which no one and nothing can ever drive them.

It is on this presupposition that Paul addresses the Corinthians, for example, when he writes in 2 Cor. 11[2f.]: "For I am jealous over you with godly jealousy: for I have espoused you to one husband, that I may present you as a chaste virgin to Christ. But I fear, lest by any means, as the serpent beguiled Eve through his subtilty, so your minds should be corrupted from sincerity towards Christ." We do not know in detail against whom or what Paul was jealous. The only thing which is clear (v. 4) is that an attempt had been made in Corinth to preach another Jesus than the One whom Paul had preached. But in relation to the preaching of Paul another Jesus can only be one in whom we can and must believe without living with him in the fulfilment, or finding consolation in the fulfilment, or fighting the battles which have still to be fought on the basis of the fulfilment as it has been accomplished in him. From Paul's standpoint another Jesus can only be a Jesus who is a mere prophet or the mere bearer of a further promise. If Paul says that in this matter he is "jealous with a godly jealousy" for the Corinthians, and the maintenance of fellowship with them, and the constancy of the faith which he has proclaimed to them, it is obvious that this is not the jealousy of an Elijah or any other Old Testament figure for the fidelity of Israel and in face of its infidelity to the promise and the law of the promise which it has been given. It is the jealousy of God which Paul must make his own as the apostle of Jesus Christ; the jealousy of the God who has brought the history of the covenant to its goal, and who cannot possibly allow what He has done to be reversed even in the name of another Jesus, in the very name of the One in whom it has reached its goal. The true Jesus Himself stands in question. That is why Paul is jealous with a godly jealousy for the Corinthians. For the true Jesus is not alone. They, too, belong to Him, the One who has fulfilled the work of God. For the apostolic word has been heard by them, and received by them in faith. Something irrevocable has thus taken place for them and to them. The death and resurrection of Jesus Christ are the reality which not only refers to them (as to the whole world) but which also embraces them and in which they have their life. To the extent that they are the Christian community, they are absolutely from [303] Him and to Him, and therefore they are determined in what they are and do and refrain from doing by the fact that there is accomplished in Him that which God intended for man from the very first. He, Paul, is the witness of this. For he has attested to them the real Jesus as their Lord, and even the witness of their faith belongs to him. He thus knows that in this matter he is responsible both to God for them and to them for God. He cannot be content merely with the fact that they are Christians and accept Jesus as a good man in whom they somehow have dealings with God but concerning whose significance they have another view which has to be tolerated side by side with that of Paul. No, says Paul, this is not another view of Jesus. It is another Jesus. And this we cannot in any circumstances or in any sense admit. Between the real Jesus and the Corinthians something has taken place, a decision has been made, which cannot be reversed. And he, Paul, was present when this decision was made. As the messenger of the Gospel he was the man who sought and brought them from afar (as Eliezer brought Rebekah to Isaac in Gen. 24$^{1f.}$). Indeed, we might almost say that as God brought Eve and showed her to Adam, he brought and showed them to the real Jesus as the one Husband, betrothing them to Him as His bride. Between this one Husband Christ and them there is a legal relationship created by His Word and Spirit and therefore solidly established. He, Paul, can testify that everything has been in order in the establishment of this relationship. He has not brought the community to any other husband. The Christ proclaimed by him was the One in whom everything was accomplished for them, for He is the Head over all things, and there cannot possibly be any other. And He has brought them to this Husband as a chaste virgin. He knew that when he brought them to this Husband their past and its sins would not be remembered; that as the elect and beloved of this One they could come to Him absolutely pure and righteous and holy; that their faith in this One was genuine and sincere; and that their baptism was not merely water-baptism but the baptism of the Spirit (so that there could be no question of this One later repulsing them as unworthy). The relationship between the one Husband Christ and His bride is a definitive relationship which no power in heaven or earth can alter, let alone a change of opinion which they have allowed themselves in the meantime. It is to be noted that the distinctness with which Paul speaks of the definitive character of this relationship is not denied even by what follows. He fears for them. He fears that their thoughts might be led away from sincerity towards Christ, and therefore corrupted. He fears that something might happen to them analogous to what took place between the treacherous serpent and Eve who was so terribly deceived. He starts back from the possibility that they might go this ruinous way even in thought; that even in thought they might try to play the Eve. But he obviously does not believe that he cannot appeal to their sincerity towards Christ as their true position. "Sincerity (ἁπλότης) towards Christ" is the basic knowledge in which, without glancing aside to the right hand or the left, they are content with Christ because all things are given them in Him. He sees the possibility that their thoughts might go astray in spite of this knowledge, as the thoughts of the community of Jesus Christ have often played the Eve in spite of it, and thus been betrayed into error. But even in this danger he still sees it as the community of Jesus Christ which cannot move away from its basis in Jesus Christ, which cannot separate itself from this Head, which cannot be shaken in this basic knowledge. He is not referring to the legal relationship at the establishment of which he was a witness and assistant. He does not question the continuance of this relationship. He would contradict himself if he did. He would be reckoning with another Jesus; with a Christ whose work could be incomplete or futile like that of so many of the prophets; with a covenant to which one would rather be unfaithful after entering into it. The Christ with whom Paul reckons is the One who has acted and spoken conclusively in the [304] name of God, and therefore united Himself conclusively with His community, however dangerously its thoughts concerning Him may oscillate, so that even though its fidelity may seem to stand in jeopardy we can always appeal to its sincerity towards Christ, and the threat to its fidelity is most effectively met by this appeal. This appeal can and may and must be made, not because we can trust Christians as those who are united with Him, but because we can be confident that the Lord whose possession they are has not given them His Spirit in vain. We maintain that Paul regarded it as right in elucidation of this thesis to recall the encounter of bridegroom and bride and therefore the primitive form of humanity as being in encounter.

On the same presupposition he declared in Rom. 7^{1-6} that Christians are those who in virtue of the death and resurrection of Jesus Christ really have the situation of Israel behind them, who are really liberated from the Law which finally can only accuse and condemn them by confirming that they are sinners. For our present purposes the decisive verses are 3 and 4: "So then if, while her husband liveth, she shall be married to another man, she shall be called an adulteress: but if her husband be dead she is freed from that law; so that she is no adulteress, though she be married to another man. Wherefore, my brethren, ye also are become dead to the law by the body (the physical slaying) of Christ; that ye should be married to another, even to him who is raised from the dead." It is to be noted that in this passage the purity of the bride brought to Christ in 2 Cor. 11^2 is interpreted in the sense in which we understood it in the previous reference. It is not intrinsic but is acquired as she is brought to this Husband. As we are now told explicitly, she had previously belonged to another. This other, her first husband, was none other than the man of the first aeon; the man of the world standing under the dominion of the sin of Adam and Eve. This man was under the Law which accused and condemned him, which confirmed the fact that he was a sinner, and in this way provoked and quickened his sin, so that the fruit which he produced (v. 5), the reward which he earned (6^{23}), could only be death. This man was the first husband of Christians. He was their old man under whose law they had necessarily to stand. So long as he lived! Only his death could free them from his law and therefore from the fact that they were accused and condemned as sinners. Every attempt made prior to the death of this man to escape his law, to disregard its accusation and condemnation, to act in an arbitrarily gained or imagined freedom in respect of him, to pretend to be elsewhere than on the fatal middle stretch between creation and the consummation, could only make them genuinely guilty and worthy of death. So long as our old man lives, what can we accomplish in this direction but what the Old Testament calls the adultery of Israel against its God, the service of alien gods and the corresponding practical alienation from the true God, the sin which does not drive out sin but merely reveals it in its true colours? At this point only the intervention of a higher power can save us. Freedom can be legitimately and effectively established only by the death of the old man and the loosing of our connexion with him. And it is on this basis that Christians rest. They no longer belong to the first man because he is no longer alive. He was put to death on Golgotha in the self-offering of the body of Christ. He was crucified and died in and with the slain body of Christ. And with him their sin was also crucified and died (Rom. $6^{3f.}$). The man of the old aeon was there and then destroyed with his aeon. Thus the law of this man, which was binding so long as he was alive, has lost its validity. He cannot accuse or condemn them any more. He cannot confirm or increase their sin. They are free, not with the illusory and evil freedom of adulterous Israel, but genuinely free. They have not accomplished this themselves. They could have won for themselves only that adulterous freedom. But there and then, in the death of Jesus Christ who alone could do it, they have become genuinely free: free to be the wife of this Other, their Liberator, Jesus Christ risen from the dead; and therefore free for life under His law, which according to Rom. $8^{2f.}$, is the "Law of the Spirit of Life." "There is therefore now no condemnation to them which are in Christ Jesus" (Rom. 8^1). The community may thus be absolutely pure and

[305]

righteous and holy as His bride and help meet. It is a creature, but a new creature by His death and resurrection and in the power of His Spirit. Thus man and wife again confront one another as man and fellow-man and need not be ashamed—the original of humanity.

But Paul also spoke on the same presupposition in the passages in which he looked at things from the opposite angle. In 2 Cor. 11²ᶠ· and Rom. 7¹ᶠ· he was obviously considering the relationship between Christ and His community in the light of various aspects of that of the relationship of husband and wife, Jesus Christ being the Bridegroom to whom the community was legally brought as a bride, or the other man by whom and for whom the community is legally free although previously married to another. But there are passages in Paul, understandably better known and more frequently cited, in which he is dealing with some form of the reality of the relationship between husband and wife, and in his interpretation of this reality recalls the relationship between Jesus Christ and the community, explaining the former by the latter. Even and especially in these passages it is obvious that in this relationship, in the act of God which took place on Good Friday, Easter Day and Pentecost, he sees the fulfilment and completion of all things, the dawn of the last time which makes quite impossible any return to the economy of the Old Testament.

In 1 Cor. 6¹²⁻²⁰ we have a clear warning against $\pi o \rho \nu \epsilon i a$ ᴱᴺ⁸¹, or sexual intercourse with a $\pi \acute{o} \rho \nu \eta$ ᴱᴺ⁸², i.e., the kind of intercourse in which man turns to woman merely for the satisfaction of his carnal needs and woman is only an occasion and means to provide this satisfaction. The decisive positive statements which serve as the basis of the warning are as follows (vv. 16b–17): "For two, saith he, shall be one flesh. But he that is joined unto the Lord is one spirit." From what we are told by the second statement, i.e., from the relationship between Jesus Christ and His community, Paul looks back and down on the relationship between man and woman to which the first statement refers. That the Christian is one body with his wife can take place only in correspondence with the fact that he himself is one spirit with the Lord. But in the kind of sexual intercourse referred to there is no such correspondence and therefore it is impossible. It would be wrong to say that it is forbidden. It is not forbidden; it is intrinsically impossible. The whole purpose of Paul in this passage is to recall to Christians the impossibility. "Know ye not?" is his insistent question in v. 15, v. 16 and v. 19. It would be wrong to speak of a Pauline prohibition because at the beginning of the passage (v. 12) there stands the impressive and twofold $\pi \acute{a} \nu \tau a$ $\mu o \iota$ $\acute{\epsilon} \xi \epsilon \sigma \tau \iota \nu$ ᴱᴺ⁸³: "I have power over all things." Behind this passage, too, there stands the Pauline message of the liberation of man in Jesus Christ from the law of sin and death, and if we do not understand this we cannot understand his warning. We certainly cannot understand how categorical it is. For it is the freedom created by Jesus Christ and given to His community which has the power of decision of which the Pauline warning speaks. The "know ye not?" is a reminder of this freedom. It is the freedom to choose that which helps ($\sigma \upsilon \mu \phi \acute{\epsilon} \rho \epsilon \iota$) the Christian and to repudiate that which would bring him under the domination of an alien power, involving an $\acute{\epsilon} \xi o \upsilon \sigma \iota \acute{a} \zeta \epsilon \sigma \theta a \iota$ $\acute{\upsilon} \pi \acute{o}$ $\tau \iota \nu o s$ ᴱᴺ⁸⁴, and thus limiting and even destroying his freedom. Not everything is a help to him. Having power over all things, he has the freedom to reject that which does not help him. And many things would bring him under an alien domination. Having power over all things, he has the freedom to reject them. The connexion between freedom and decision is seen in a different light in 1 Cor. 10²³: $\pi \acute{a} \nu \tau a$ $\acute{\epsilon} \xi \epsilon \sigma \tau \iota \nu$, $\acute{a} \lambda \lambda$' $o \dot{\upsilon}$ $\pi \acute{a} \nu \tau a$ $o \dot{\iota} \kappa o \delta o \mu \epsilon \hat{\iota}$ ᴱᴺ⁸⁵. We have to remember here too that the freedom of the Christian is

---

ᴱᴺ⁸¹ fornication
ᴱᴺ⁸² prostitute
ᴱᴺ⁸³ all things are lawful to me
ᴱᴺ⁸⁴ be brought under the power of something
ᴱᴺ⁸⁵ all things are lawful for me, but all things are not expedient

[306]   the freedom to play his part in the upbuilding of the community. Who is the Christian? He is a man who "is joined unto the Lord" (κολλώμενος in v. 17 is the same term as that which the LXX uses in Gen. 2²⁴ᶠ· for the cleaving of a wife to her husband). The Christian is dearly bought (v. 20). At the supreme cost of the self-offering of the Son of God he is freed from the powers which determine a whole world which is now past for him. According to Col. 1¹³ he is translated by God into the kingdom of His dear Son. He has thus become His possession. He shares His lordship over these powers. And his freedom rests in this fact. As he lives in this freedom, he lives in the Spirit. And as he lives in the Spirit, he is one with the Lord. The Christian is thus a man who does not belong to himself but to this Lord (v. 19). He is joined to Him. It is not something abstract which is joined to Him (his soul perhaps), but something very concrete, he himself as the soul of his body. He in his totality, and therefore in his corporeality, does not belong to himself but to the Lord. He is a member of Christ, of His body, of His community (v. 15), and thus participates in His lordship and is free for what is helpful to him as a Christian, free from all alien dominion, and free for the edification of the community. The order under which he stands as this concrete being in his corporeality is, however, that "God hath both raised up the Lord, and will also raise up us by his own power" (v. 14). The Lord took to Himself concrete human being, corporeality. He suffered and died in the body. He accomplished that self-offering in the body. And He was also raised from the dead in the body. In this context the last is the decisive point. As certainly as Christ was raised from the dead in the body the Christian is not subject to death in the body. Jesus Christ has drawn him as His member even in his corporeality after and towards Himself to a new life. In his corporeality he is already determined, disposed and organised for this new life as "the temple of the Holy Ghost, which ye have of God" (v. 19). He is thus summoned to glorify God in his corporeality (v. 20). This is how it stands with the Christian. He is free for what is necessary for him in the light of the resurrection of Jesus Christ; for what helps him in his being on this basis (as the temple of the Holy Ghost and for the glorifying of God); for what confirms and increases his freedom from the powers of the old aeon; for what edifies the community. He is also free to refrain from the opposite of all these things. He would not be what he is if he had a freedom which could be defined in any other way: the freedom to do the latter and not to do the former; the freedom to do what does not help him but brings him into captivity and destroys the community. But in this being of the Christian—and Paul thinks it quite impossible that the Corinthians should not know this, or that he should have to do more than give them an interrogative reminder—the decision is already taken what is intrinsically possible and what is intrinsically impossible for the Christian in this matter of sexual intercourse. In the first instance, there is a pre-decision concerning the significance of his action as such. In sexual intercourse it is not merely a question—as some at Corinth obviously seem to have thought (v. 13)—of the satisfaction of a physical and in this case sexual need, which can be met without any particular question of the means, like the need of the stomach by eating. In sexual intercourse we do not move within this kind of physical cycle: "meats for the belly, and the belly for meats"; a need which cries out for satisfaction, and the satisfaction which answers to the need. Ὁ δὲ θεὸς καὶ ταύτην καὶ ταῦτα καταργήσει ᴱᴺ⁸⁶. When the time of man is up, God will destroy this physical cycle. It belongs to his corporeality, and therefore to himself. Of course, as Paul himself obviously presupposes a few verses later (7¹ᶠ·), even in sexual intercourse there is a question of this kind of cycle of need and satisfaction belonging to the corporeality of man and therefore to himself. But in sexual intercourse it is also a matter of the body itself and as such, and therefore of man in his corporeality. For sexual intercourse means that at the climax and in the comple-

---

ᴱᴺ⁸⁶ But God shall destroy both it [the belly] and them [meats]

tion of their encounter they become one body, belonging wholly to one another in their [307] corporeality, and mutually attesting and guaranteeing their humanity. In this completion the man no longer belongs to himself, but to the woman; and the woman no longer belongs to herself, but to the man. In this completion there takes place between them something final and irrevocable. They are both what they became in this completion—a being belonging to this other. This is not, then, a neutral sphere or indifferent occurrence. There is decided here to whom man belongs as in this completion he belongs to another. For the Christian this decision has been made. Belonging to a woman, he cannot contradict but must correspond to the fact that he belongs to Christ. But he would contradict this if he belonged to a harlot and became one body with her. But why is this so total a contradiction? Why does the "one spirit" with Christ exclude in this way the "one body" with a harlot? Obviously because Christ is the faithfulness of God in person, whereas the harlot personifies human unfaithfulness against God. He cannot will to become one body with a harlot, or actually become this, in the freedom which is created for and given to him by Christ. In so doing he who is one spirit with the Lord would become something which would not help him, in which he would not be the temple of the Holy Ghost, or glorify God, or edify the community, but merely return to the bondage from which he has been so dearly and definitively ransomed. In sexual intercourse with a harlot there can be only a sorry distortion of the completion between man and woman. For what kind of a completion is it? The completion of fellowship? No, it can be only the completion of self-satisfaction, and therefore at the climax of the encounter the denial of any real encounter; fellowship in the form of the betrayal of fellowship. For in this intercourse man does not seek woman in the totality of her corporeality. He seeks only the sexual being as an occasion and means to the satisfaction of his own corresponding need. He forgets, and wills to forget, that in woman as herself a human being he has to do with the fellow-man; that as an I he has to do in her with a Thou. He thus denies the humanity of woman, treating her as an It. And the woman does not expect man as a man, or in the totality of his corporeality. He is for her too an It and not a Thou. She does not seek a true and serious and genuine connexion. She merely answers to his sexual impulse, shaming not only her own womanhood but his manhood too. Let there be no mistake—even in this distortion the completion is real enough. There takes place a mutual self-offering. Male and female become one flesh as stated in Gen. 2²⁴. They belong together. Although as betrayers of their humanity, they mutually determine and shame each other. If a Christian seeks intercourse with a harlot, this is not a neutral happening which does not affect the man himself in his being as a Christian. What happens is that he "takes" ($\mathring{a}\rho\alpha\varsigma$) his body, i.e., himself in his corporeality, as though it belonged to himself and he could do this with it, and makes it (himself) the member of a harlot (v. 15), thus giving it (himself) a part in that betrayal. His being as a man is thus brought into contradiction with his being as a Christian. He thus sins against his own body (v. 18). That is to say, he does not merely pervert and corrupt something extraneous, but decisively he perverts and corrupts himself. And he perverts and corrupts himself wholly and utterly, and therefore in his relationship to God and his fellow-man. He who in his corporeality is a member of Christ and as such moves forward to the raising of the dead by the power of God pronounces sentence of death upon himself. For if he belongs to a harlot—and this is what intercourse with her means—he can only die totally and with no hope of life. I take it that in the difficult v. 18 Paul is speaking of a sin of which only the Christian is really capable. $\mu\mathring{\eta}\ \gamma\acute{\epsilon}\nu o\iota\tau o$ EN87, he says to this sin (v. 15), and this is an expression which he usually reserves for the rebuttal of a possibility which is radically excluded. He thinks through this possibility logically and to the bitter end. But he definitely tells the Corinthians that this is a way which cannot be entered.

EN87 may it never be!

[308] It must be remembered that immediately prior to this passage he had written (6¹¹): "But ye are washed (in baptism), but ye are sanctified, but ye are justified in the name of the Lord Jesus, and by the Spirit of our God." This "ye are" is like a barrier blocking the way. This is what they know according to vv. 15, 16 and 19. This is what Paul has only to remind them in order to say something which is far more powerful than any prohibition. It is the same absolute obstacle to which Jesus Himself referred in Mt. 6²⁴: "No man can serve two masters .... Ye cannot serve God and mammon." Paul takes the same line. He does not need to present any law or morality. He has only to show what they can and cannot do. They cannot place themselves afresh under forces which they have once and for all escaped as they belong to Christ in their corporeality. Conversely, they cannot escape the service in which they have been placed once and for all as they belong to Christ in their corporeality. They cannot exist in their corporeality as only the victims of death can exist. They have the risen Christ behind them and before. They cannot make the temple of God a den of thieves. They cannot blaspheme God; they can only glorify Him. They cannot compromise Jesus Christ, with whom they are one spirit, as though He Himself to whom they are joined—in this case they would indeed belong to another Jesus—were one of the powers of the old world and He Himself invited them to do so. They cannot be guilty of that contradiction. For they know perfectly well that that contradiction is itself contradicted, and that it is contradicted victoriously and definitively, so that no option remains. Hence they cannot either seek woman in the form of a harlot, or accept her advances in this form. It is to be noted that this does not merely apply to what is called extramarital intercourse. They cannot make woman a harlot, or accept her as such, either outside marriage or within it. They cannot affirm πορνεία EN88 and the πόρνη EN89 in any form. They cannot do this because their being excludes this affirmation of the harlot in any form. They can only really do what Paul commands in v. 18: φεύγετε τὴν πορνείαν EN90. Turn your back on it with the firmness and totality which are the only possibility when we have to do with the impossible. What is intrinsically possible to the man who is one spirit with Christ in the relationship of man and woman and therefore in the completion of this relationship can only be, as an exercise of his freedom and therefore his participation in the lordship of Christ, and in his obedience to "the law of the Spirit of life," the intercourse which beyond all need and its satisfaction is the completion of the encounter of man and fellow-man and the fulfilment of full and serious and genuine fellowship. There is thus possible for him only the becoming "one body" in which there is clearly and unequivocally reflected the full and serious and genuine fellowship of Jesus Christ with His community and each of its individual members. There is possible only the becoming "one body" of which he does not need to be ashamed in face of the fact that he is "one spirit" with Jesus Christ, and in respect of which the man and woman have no cause for mutual shame but for rejoicing as in a reflection of light from above. It is on the basis of this positive recognition that the decision goes against πορνεία EN91. At this critical point, therefore, Paul set the anthropological question as that of man's humanity in the light of Christology, and answered it accordingly. All that remains for us is simply to state that this is what happens in the passage. Paul brings the concrete form of the fellow-humanity of man and woman, and sexual intercourse as its most concrete form, into connexion with the relationship between Jesus Christ and His community, and derives his normative concept of the human—not without express reference to Gen. 2—from this basic norm. The necessary stringency is not lacking. But there is none of the papistical severity which is so often encountered in this

---

EN88 fornication
EN89 prostitute
EN90 flee fornication
EN91 fornication

sphere. Paul knew how to give a categorical and effective warning on the basis of the whole Gospel, and his warning is far more categorical and effective than that of many who before and after him have tackled the problem purely from the standpoint of the Law.

In 1 Cor. 7^{1-10} and then again in 7^{25-40} Paul took up the question of marriage and celibacy. [309] In 7^{10-17} he dealt with divorce. In 14^{33-38} and 1 Tim. 2^{8-12} he discussed the question of women speaking, or rather being silent, in the $\dot{\epsilon}\kappa\kappa\lambda\eta\sigma\dot{\iota}\alpha$[EN92]. We shall not take up these problems here because in these passages (as distinct from 1 Cor. 6^{12-20}) there is no explicit reference to the connexion between man and woman on the one side and Christ and His community on the other. To understand these passages we can hardly avoid making this connexion in their exposition. But our present question is not where it can and must be made, but where it is actually made in the New Testament.

The second passage in which this is indisputably the case is 1 Cor. 11^{1-16}. As a text for this whole section we might well take vv. 11–12: "Nevertheless neither is the man without the woman, neither the woman without the man, in the Lord. For as the woman is of the man, even so is the man also by the woman; but all things of God." Man and woman are here considered in relation to a question of liturgical order. It is a small, external and peripheral question. But Paul regards the decision made in its solution as so great, internal and central that he does not hesitate to devote 16 verses to it and to make again the connexion which is our present concern. His aim is to show that because in the Lord and "of God" the woman is not without the man or the man without the woman, a definite course has to be adopted in relation to this peripheral question of order. What was the point at issue? An enthusiastic attempt was being made to introduce equality where previously the custom had been both at Corinth and in other Christian communities that in their gatherings for worship the men should be uncovered and the women covered. We may well imagine that Gal. 3^{28} ("neither male nor female") provided either verbally or materially the main argument in favour of abolishing this outward distinction and therefore against Paul, who had given this dictum but now favoured the keeping of the tradition (v. 2). There can be little doubt, as we gather from the earlier chapters of the Epistle, that an attempt of this kind was being made at Corinth, and that it was directed generally against the recognition of the specific authority and office and word of the apostle. Must the freedom won in Christ acquiesce in the irreversibility of the relationship of order and ministry between the apostle and the community? We learn from 4^8 that the Corinthians were very largely of the opinion that they were full and rich, and had thus attained to a $\beta\alpha\sigma\iota\lambda\epsilon\dot{\upsilon}\epsilon\iota\nu$[EN93] independent of the apostle. And it may be gathered from 12^{29} that the slogan "We are all apostles" was only just round the corner. It is certainly no accident that Paul refers briefly to this basic question in vv. 1–2, and even vv. 3–16 with their presentation of the relationship between man and woman (perhaps this is one of the reasons why they are so definite) are to be understood as an indirect elucidation of the relationship between the apostle and the community. The latter is a decisively important derivative of the relationship between Christ and the community. Because it was a matter of the absolute and incomparable authority of the crucified Jesus, Paul as His witness could not yield an inch in the question of his own relative and human authority as an apostle. Without Christ's commission and Spirit there was no apostolic word, but without the apostolic word there was no Christian hearing, no hearing of the Word of Christ, no life in the Holy Spirit. And it was also a question of the relationship between absolute and relative, directly divine and indirectly human order in the problem of man and woman discussed in vv. 3–16. Paul tells us plainly enough in vv. 11–12 that he does not retract anything that he has said in Gal. 3^{28}. In the Lord, "of God," it is just as true that the woman is of the man and

---

[EN92] church
[EN93] reigning

[310] the man by the woman. Both are told us by Gen. 2. Woman is taken out of man, but man is man only by the woman taken out of him. Yet only an inattentive enthusiasm could deduce from this that man and woman are absolutely alike, that there can be no question of super- and subordination between them, and that it is both legitimate and obligatory to abolish the distinction between the uncovered and the covered head in divine service. It was the same inattentive enthusiasm which concluded from the fulness of spiritual gifts of which there was evidently no lack in Corinth that there was no further need for the teaching, exhortation and admonition of the apostle. In both cases, as in many other respects, it was forgotten that God (14³³) is not a God of ἀκαταστασία EN94 but of peace. But there is peace only if distinctions are observed in the fellowship: in the fellowship, so that the antitheses caused by their misunderstanding and misuse are overcome; but genuinely observed, so that there is true super- and subordination, and it is seen that we are dealing with two different things and not one and the same when we are told by Gen. 2 that woman is from the man and by Gen. 2 again that man is by the woman. The demonstration of this peace, and therefore of these distinctions in the fellowship of man and woman, is the theme of the present passage. Paul is trying to show that the observance of this relative, indirect and human order is necessary because it rests on an absolute, direct and divine order, so that the denial of the one means the denial of the other. The curious saying about the angels in v. 10 is most simply explained as follows. The angels are generally the bearers and representatives of the relative principles necessarily posited with the work of God, and they are specifically the bearers and representatives of the indirect human orders necessarily posited with the divine work of salvation. They cannot, therefore, see these orders violated without sorrow. This is something which should not happen. Hence διὰ τοὺς ἀγγέλους EN95 the woman must bear on her head in divine service an ἐξουσία EN96 (a sign of her recognition of the ἐξουσία EN97 of the man which she does not possess). But what is the connexion between the divine work of salvation and the order in question? The decisive statement in this regard is undoubtedly to be found in v. 3: κεφαλὴ δὲ γυναικὸς ὁ ἀνήρ EN98. If this is accepted as a justifiable assertion, we maintain that it proves both the point and even the necessity of the custom. The uncovered head of the man is the sign that in divine service, in his participation in the act of προσεύχεσθαι EN99 and προφητεύειν EN100, he has no κεφαλή EN101 over him because he is himself κεφαλή EN102. But the covering of the head of the woman is a sign that in the worship of the community, in her participation in the act of προσεύχεσθαι EN103 and προφητεύειν EN104, she has a κεφαλή EN105 over her and is not therefore herself κεφαλή EN106. The conclusion is drawn in vv. 4–6 that in the light of v. 3b any other practice dishonours both the head of man and that of woman. The particular honour of both demands this custom. Verse 10 underlines this conclusion by referring to the angels, and vv. 12–15 add that it corresponds to natural sensibility. But the whole argument depends on v. 3b and therefore on whether this assertion is justified. What is its basis? We might refer to the

---

EN 94 confusion
EN 95 because of the angels
EN 96 authority
EN 97 authority
EN 98 the head of the woman is the man
EN 99 praying
EN100 prophesying
EN101 head
EN102 head
EN103 praying
EN104 prophesying
EN105 head
EN106 head

passage in Eph. 5²²⁻²³, where this assertion is reversed and explained in v. 23: ἀνήρ ἐστιν κεφαλὴ τῆς γυναικὸς ὡς καὶ ὁ Χριστὸς κεφαλὴ τῆς ἐκκλησίας ᴱᴺ¹⁰⁷. On this basis we could argue that the whole point of the statement is that man in his relationship to woman represents Christ in His relationship to the community, and that woman in her relationship to man represents the community in its relationship to Christ, as developed in the Ephesian passage. But in the first instance the assertion in 1 Cor. 11³ᵇ should be evaluated in its own context. It is immediately preceded by 3a: παντὸς ἀνδρὸς ἡ κεφαλὴ ὁ χριστός ἐστιν ᴱᴺ¹⁰⁸, and followed by 3c: κεφαλὴ δὲ τοῦ χριστοῦ ὁ θεός ᴱᴺ¹⁰⁹. On the basis of these three statements in their interconnexion Paul then goes on to say: "But I would have you know ...." It is to be noted that he does not ask here as in 1 Cor. 6⁹: "Know ye not?" It is obviously presupposed that they ought to know, but it emerges more plainly at this point that they need the apostle to proclaim and interpret what they might basically know of themselves. Above all, the order of the statements is to be noted. They are not arranged as a demand for perspicuity might suggest: 3c, that God is the Head of Christ; 3a, that Christ is the Head of man; and 3b that man is the head of woman. Nor do they take the opposite course—3b, 3a, 3c. [311] They are necessarily arranged as in the text. They contain neither deduction from above downwards nor induction from below upwards. They are not a scale. They have often been understood in this way, with the absurd result that man is taken to be for woman what Christ is for him and God for Christ, so that it is only indirectly and by way of man that woman is in relationship to Christ and therefore to God. The remarkable position of 3b warns us against this interpretation. Telling us that man is set above woman, it is preceded by the statement that Christ is set above him. And telling us of the subordination of woman, it is followed by a statement which speaks of a subordination of Christ to God. Thus it is grounded and explained in Christ whether it speaks of the superordination of man or the subordination of woman. Both superordination and subordination are primarily and properly in Christ. According to Col. 2¹⁰ He is ἡ κεφαλὴ πάσης ἀρχῆς καὶ ἐξουσίας ᴱᴺ¹¹⁰. According to Eph. 1¹⁰ it was the good-pleasure of God ἀνακεφαλαιώσασθαι τὰ πάντα ᴱᴺ¹¹¹ in Him." πᾶσα ἐξουσία ᴱᴺ¹¹² is given unto me in heaven and in earth" (Mt. 28¹⁸, cf. also Col. 1¹⁶, Eph. 1²⁰ and 1 Pet. 3²²). He, then, is the Head of every man. That is to say, He is the sum of all superordination, and He stands relatively much higher than man behind his majesty. Whatever may be the ἐξουσία ᴱᴺ¹¹³ of man in relation to woman, it is legitimate and effective only to the extent that primarily and properly it does not belong to him but to Christ, and can therefore only be attested and represented by man. Conversely, Christ is the sum of all humility before God, of all the obedient fulfilment of His will. He is the One who according to Phil. 2⁶ᶠ·, although He was in the form of God, did not count it His prey to be equal with God, but emptied Himself, and took the form of a servant, and made Himself equal to man ... and humbled Himself. He thus enters on His lordship by becoming the slave of God and man. God has made Him—we must not forget this supreme statement—to be sin for us (2 Cor. 5²¹). Could He stoop any lower before God than this? He is thus the sum of all subordination, and stands relatively much lower than woman under man. And whatever may be her relationship to the ἐξουσία ᴱᴺ¹¹⁴ of man which she lacks, it is sanctified, ennobled and glorified by the fact that her subordination is primarily and properly that of Christ and can only

---

ᴱᴺ¹⁰⁷ for the husband is the head of the wife, even as Christ is the head of the church
ᴱᴺ¹⁰⁸ the head of every man is Christ
ᴱᴺ¹⁰⁹ and the head of Christ is God
ᴱᴺ¹¹⁰ the head of all principality and power
ᴱᴺ¹¹¹ to gather together in one all things
ᴱᴺ¹¹² all authority
ᴱᴺ¹¹³ authority
ᴱᴺ¹¹⁴ authority

be attested and represented by her. Thus it can really be said between the height and the depth, the lordship and service, the divinity and humanity of Christ: "The head of the woman is the man." So little does this ascribe to man or refer to woman! So sharply and clearly is it determined and limited on both sides by what is primarily and properly the affair of Christ! His is the superordination and His the subordination. His is the place of man, and His the place of woman. And what place is there to speak of little or much? There is assigned to each that which is helpful and right and worthy. If it is no little thing for man to be $\kappa\epsilon\phi\alpha\lambda\acute{\eta}$ EN115 in relation to woman, i.e., the one who has precedence, initiative and authority, the representative of the order which embraces them both, it is no little thing for woman to take the place which she is assigned in relation to man and therefore not to be $\kappa\epsilon\phi\alpha\lambda\acute{\eta}$ EN116 but to be led by him, to accept his authority, to recognise the order which claims them both as it is represented by him. In vv. 7–9 Paul refers explicitly to Gen. 2. The determination and limitation of the relationship of man and woman as established in Christ emerge already in the work of creation. Woman is fashioned out of man and for the sake of man. She is not created as he is out of the dust of the earth but (more humanly, we might almost say) out of man himself, in order that he should not be alone but have a helpmeet (vv. 8–9). Thus he is the "image and glory of God," yet not alone or without or against the woman, but together with the woman who is his glory (v. 7). This basic order of the human established by God's creation is not accidental or contingent. It cannot be overlooked or ironed out. We cannot arbitrarily go behind it. It is solidly and necessarily grounded in Christ, with a view to whom heaven and earth and finally man were created. It is so solidly grounded in the lordship and service, the divinity and humanity of Christ that there can be no occasion either for the exaltation of man or the oppression of woman. "If any man be in Christ, he is a new creature." It is the life of this new creature which Paul describes with the saying that the head of the woman is the man. Gal. 3^{28} is still valid, in spite of shortsighted exegetes, like the Corinthians themselves, who shake their heads and think they can claim a contradiction. The mutuality of the relationship still obtains, as described in vv. 11–12. To that extent there is an equality of man and woman $\dot{\epsilon}\nu$ $\kappa\nu\rho\acute{\iota}\omega$ EN117 in the order in which the one God has with equal directness assigned this place to man and that to woman. Where is there any real knowledge of differentiation and mutuality, and where are the exaltation of man and the oppression of woman radically excluded, except in the community of Jesus Christ, in which His lordship and service are the final word, and the Creator of all things is found and recognised in the baby in the crib, and in the baby in the crib the Creator of all things, no contradiction being seen between majesty and humility, superordination and subordination, lordship and service? Is not the community of Jesus Christ itself and as such, as adduced in Eph. 5, the model of the woman who has her $\kappa\epsilon\phi\alpha\lambda\acute{\eta}$ EN118 in the man, and cannot really exist except in subordination to this $\kappa\epsilon\phi\alpha\lambda\acute{\eta}$ EN119, but in this way, determined and limited in Him, is exalted above all heavens by His majesty and lowliness, in fellowship with this Head? It is for this reason that this order cannot be broken in the community; that the relationship of man and woman established in creation, and the distinctions which it entails, cannot be regarded as transitory and accidental and abolished in Christ, as though Christ were not their meaning and origin. In the community this relationship cannot imperil either man or woman. It can only be their honour and joy and blessing. There is thus no cause to deny or abolish it as though it were a mere convention. On the contrary, dishon-

[312]

EN115 head
EN116 head
EN117 in the Lord
EN118 head
EN119 head

our and harm are done both to man and to woman if this clear relationship is abolished. It is quite ridiculous to think that progressiveness should be played off against conservatism in the matter of this relationship. If there is anything which is inwardly necessary and no mere convention, it is this relationship. Progress beyond it can only be regress to the old aeon. It is only in the world of the old aeon that the feminist question can arise. And for this reason the Corinthians should accept the custom. It is a symbolic recognition of the relationship, and therefore of the basis, determination and limitation which it has been given in Christ. This recognition may not be withheld. Self-evidently it might have taken a different form in a different age and place. But in Corinth and all the Christian communities of the time (v. 16) it took this form. And as it was called in question in this form it had to be protected and defended in this form, not for the sake of the form, but for the sake of what was at issue in this form. The fact that it also conformed to natural sensibility, to φύσις EN120 (v. 14), was an additional recommendation as Paul saw it. But this statement was only incidental. The decisive point was that the enthusiasm for equality which outran the form was not particularly Christian, but that the custom should be accepted in Christ. We cannot say more than that it should be, for Paul was not arguing from the Law, but centrally from the Gospel. It was not the one who called the Corinthians to order who was thinking legalistically, but the Corinthians themselves, who, armed with a general, liberal, non-Christological concept of humanity, thought it their duty to attack this relative and indirectly human order, as though they were all apostles, and as though an apostle were a genius. It was as well for them that they had in Paul a real apostle able to maintain an unruffled front against their impulsive genius; and they were well-advised to accept his summons to be imitators of him as he himself tried to be of Christ (v. 1).

Our final passage is Eph. 5²²⁻²³, the *locus classicus*EN121 for the point at issue. No other passage makes the connexion so emphatically. No other is so primarily concerned to make it. No other is so complete in its exposition of the two relationships. And no other refers so $\quad$ [313] solemnly to Gen. 2. From it we can survey the whole landscape which we have traversed: the New Testament relationship of man and woman in the light of the relationship between Christ and the community, and conversely the elucidation of the relationship between Christ and His people by reference to the man-woman relationship; the Old Testament marriage between Yahweh and Israel and its reflection in the man and woman of the Song of Songs; and finally our starting-point in Genesis 2, the natural being of man as fellow-humanity, as being in the encounter of I and Thou. Should we really have the courage or find it necessary to consider all these things not only in detail but in their manifold relationships if they were not set before us so authoritatively and perspicuously in Eph. 5? But this is an idle question. This passage does in fact make everything clear. And we have only to apply ourselves directly to this text in which everything is set out directly and verbally in an exegetical norm for all other texts. It forms the introduction to the so-called "house-table" of Ephesians, a list of specific admonitions to wives, husbands, children, fathers, slaves and masters among the members of the community, all of which stand under the overriding injunction "Be filled with the Spirit; speaking to yourselves in psalms and hymns and spiritual songs, singing and making melody in your heart to the Lord; giving thanks always for all things in the name of our Lord Jesus Christ; submitting yourselves one to another in the fear of God" (vv. 18–21). This basic note must be remembered if we are to understand the ensuing injunctions, and especially the first and lengthy admonition addressed to husbands and wives. Be filled with the Spirit, speaking to one another in praise of God, not only with your lips but in your hearts, not ceasing to give thanks, and subordinating yourselves to one

---

EN120 nature
EN121 standard reference

another as you are engaged in this thanksgiving to God. Humanity in the New Testament thus derives directly from the practical experience of the Gospel. And we must certainly not forget the negative beginning to this general exhortation: "Be not drunk with wine." We recall from 1 Cor. 11 that the knowledge of the true relationship between man and wife established and determined and limited by the knowledge of Jesus Christ stands in contrast to an enthusiasm for equality which will not accept the fact that they are both allotted to their distinctive place and way in the peace of God. Where it is not a matter of this intoxication but of the fulness of the Spirit, not of the boasting and defiance of man but of the praise of God, not of the establishment of one's own right by one's own might but of constant thanksgiving, there flows from the Gospel the necessity of the reciprocal subordination in which each gives to the other that which is proper to him. This is the meaning of the house-table: *Suum cuique*^{EN122}. It has nothing really to do with patriarchalism, or with a hierarchy of domestic and civil values and powers. It does not give one control over the other, or put anyone under the dominion of the other. The ὑποτασσόμενοι^{EN123} of v. 21 applies equally to all, each in his own place and in respect of his own way. What it demands is ὑποτασσόμενοι ἀλλήλοις ἐν φόβῳ χριστοῦ^{EN124}; mutual subordination in respect before the Lord. He is the Exalted but also the Lowly, the Lowly but also the Exalted, who causes each to share in His glory but also His burden, His sovereignty but also His service. And here there is only mutual subordination in full reciprocity. In this way order is created within the creaturely sphere, and humanity established. It is, of course, no accident that more than half of the table is devoted to the relationship of man and woman, and particularly their relationship in marriage. This relationship is typical or exemplary for the whole relationship which has to be estimated in the fear of Christ. In good or evil alike all other relations between the sexes have their fulfilment and norm in the fact that this man finds this woman and this woman this man and therefore man the fellow-man to whom he is referred and with whom he is united. We stated at the outset that expression is given to fellow-humanity as one man looks the other in the eyes and lets himself be seen by the other. The meaning and promise of marriage is that this should take place between man and woman, that one woman should encounter one man as his, and one man one woman as hers. Where it takes place we have a good marriage; the marriage which can only be monogamous. It is from this height that the whole field is surveyed. Again, it is no accident that the list of admonitions opens with that to the wife and not to the husband (v. 22). That the participle clause ὑποτασσόμενοι^{EN125} is naturally continued in this way, and general mutual subordination has its first concrete form in the wife, is explained at once in v. 23 by the comparison: "For the husband is the head of the wife (a statement taken from 1 Cor. 11³), even as Christ is the head of the church: and he is the saviour of the body." Because her subordination stands under this comparison, the woman must see to it that it is not broken but maintained. And therefore the subordination of woman to man is the first and most interesting problem which arises in this field. Not man but woman represents the reality which embraces all those who are addressed, whether they be wives or husbands, old or young, slaves or masters, which claims even the apostle himself in his peculiar position, and from which he thinks and speaks and admonishes them to think and act. They are all the community which has in Jesus Christ its Head. They are all set in this place and called and gathered to this community by baptism. For none of them can there be any question of a higher or better place. None of them can ever think of escaping from or trying to climb above it. In the fulness of the Spirit they can only wish to remain at this place,

[314]

---

^{EN122} To each his own
^{EN123} submitting
^{EN124} submitting one to another in the fear of Christ
^{EN125} submitting

listening, obedient and therefore subordinate to the One from whom and for whose sake the whole community exists, and without whom it could not continue for a single moment or in any respect, since it is the body which is snatched and rescued from the fire of perdition only in virtue of its union with this Head. The advantage of the wife, her birthright, is that it is she and not the man who, in relation to her husband and subordination to him, may reflect, represent and attest this reality of the community. The exhortation specifically addressed to her is simply a particular form of the basic admonition which applies to all. She is subordinated to her husband as the whole community is to Christ. The whole community can only take up the position in relation to Christ which is proper to the wife in relation to her husband. Even husbands and masters must take up the same position in relation to Christ as the wife in relation to her husband. This is what makes the admonition to the wife so urgent and inescapable. And this is what characterises it as a peculiar distinction for the wife. If she does not break but respects the true relationship to her husband, the wife is not less but greater than her husband in the community. She is not the second but the first. In a qualified sense she is the community. The husband has no option but to order himself by the wife as she is subordinate in this way. The curious wish of Schleiermacher that he had been a woman is not so foolish when it is seen against this background. It is striking that the final statement of the whole passage (v. 33b) repeats the admonition to the wife: "And the wife see that she reverence her husband." Whatever is said to the husband stands within the framework of what has to be said to the wife as wife. She and not her husband is the type of the community listening to Christ and the apostolic admonition. She must be mentioned both first and last, for she may first and last take this admonition to heart, all hearing and obedience being represented in her hearing and obedience. On the other hand, the greater part of the passage (vv. 25–33) is devoted to the particular admonition to husbands. This emphasis is significant. What is meant by the mutual subordination in the fear of Christ expected of all (v. 21) is demonstrated in the attitude of the husband, who in his relationship to his wife is the $\kappa\epsilon\phi\alpha\lambda\acute{\eta}$ EN126, the superior, the first, the leader, the bearer of primary responsibility. In this respect he is the type of the $\kappa\epsilon\phi\alpha\lambda\acute{\eta}$ EN127 of the whole, of the Author and Lord of the community, of the Saviour of the body (v. 23). In the being and action of the husband in relation to the wife there is thus decided whether the hearing and obedience of the wife take place in the sense in which they are established; whether she is really subordinated to him $\dot{\omega}_S$ $\tau\hat{\omega}$ $\kappa\upsilon\rho\acute{\iota}\omega$ EN128 and therefore necessarily and not merely in the sense of an androcracy which might easily become a gynocracy. As men in their being and action towards the wife reflect the being and action of the $\kappa\epsilon\phi\alpha\lambda\acute{\eta}$ EN129 Christ, the community is the community and not merely seems to be or would like to be. How could it be the body of this Head without this reflection? And it is the particular calling of husbands to produce this reflection. More has to be said to them than to wives because in respect of the life of the community more has to be said about the being and action of Christ than the being and action of the men concerned. There can be no question of anything more than reflection. Men are not the authors, lords and saviours of women any more than they can be their own authors, lords and saviours. Christ stands equally above both husbands and wives as He stands equally below them. But the reflection of His majesty and lowliness in relation to them and their wives, to the whole community, is the particular responsibility of the men. It consists in the fact that they love their wives. For Christ loved the community—it was in this that He became its Author, Lord and Saviour. He gave Himself for it (v. 25). And in this self-

[315]

EN126 head
EN127 head
EN128 as to the Lord
EN129 head

giving He made it His community. It did not make itself His community. It did not even make itself ready to be this. He Himself sanctioned it when it was unholy and purified it when it was unclean. He gives it a part in His own Word and Spirit. He invested it with His own glory, and thus made it the counterpart from which He had taken away every spot of reproach or occasion for blame. He Himself prepared it for Himself. He thus made it His own (vv. 26–27). It owes itself to Him and Him alone. This is the love of Christ for His community. This is the original form of the majesty and humility in which He stands in relation to it, and to both husbands and wives within it. There can be no question of repeating the original of this love of Christ. It is unique and once-for-all. But even less can there be any question of living in the light of this original without accepting the summons to a relative imitation and reflection of this original. This once-for-all and unique light does not shine into the void but into a sphere of men and therefore of males and females, i.e., into the sphere described in Gen. 2, where it is decided that it is not good for man to be alone, where he is to recognise himself in another and another in himself, where humanity relentlessly means fellow-humanity, where the body or existence of woman is the same to man as his own body or existence, where the I is not just unreal but impossible without the Thou, and where all the willing and longing of the I—on the far side of all egoism or altruism—must be the willing and longing of the Thou. This is the humanity of man which in the community is set in the unique and once-for-all light of the love of Christ. What else can this mean but that place is found for this fellow-humanity (which is what is meant by the imitation of that image); that man (who is the first to be summoned) takes seriously the "This now" of Gen. 2^{23}; that he loves the woman which God has given him as himself, i.e., that he deals with her as with the fellow-man without whom he could not be himself, in whose person he constantly has to do with himself, in whose person he does good or evil to himself, exalting or abasing himself, and whose existence gives humanity to his own. This is what Paul describes as the particular responsibility of men in vv. 28–29a. They may and should and must precede women by accepting and affirming them in such a way that they do what man did at the climax of his creation in Gen. 2. For, as the decisive passage vv. 29b-32 goes on to tell us, what man did at the climax of his creation; this humanity as the fellow-humanity of male and female; the purely creaturely happening that a man leaves his father and mother and cleaves to his wife and they become one flesh—this is not a primary thing, the original, but a secondary, the copy. We have to do here with the great mystery and not just the small (v. 32). For the creation of man and for this climax, for this form of humanity, the normative pattern, the basic decree and the plan of all the plans of God is "Christ and the community." This stands inaccessibly before and above the copy of man and woman. Thus in the little copy, between man and woman, there can be no question of the self-offering of the one for the other, of the one making the other a worthy counterpart by self-offering, and of the other owing itself and all that it is and has to it. Man cannot be the Creator and Saviour of men, or the man of the woman. On the other hand, it belongs to the very essence of the copy modelled on this pattern that the man should be with the woman, that he should not will to be without her, and that he should therefore love her as himself. And that this may and must take place is the admonition which must be given and heard where the light of this original falls into the human sphere, i.e., in the community created by baptism and the Word of Jesus Christ. And it is to the men first that this admonition must be given, and by them that it must first be heard: "Let every one of you in particular so love his wife even as himself" (v. 33), willing and affirming her existence together with his own, and her honour and welfare with and as his own, willing himself only as he wills her too. Wives must and will hear this also. We remember that this inversion takes place in the Song of Songs. There is a love of the community for Christ as well as a love of Christ for the community. But as the love of Christ precedes the answering love of the community, so the love of the husband precedes that of the wife. In

[316]

imitation of the attitude of Christ the husband may and should precede at this point as the wife may and should precede him in representing the community in its absolute subordination to Christ. But it is to subordination that the husband himself is summoned. That he should love his wife is his particular part or function in the mutual subordination demanded in v. 21.

"This is a great mystery" (Eph. 5^{32}). The saying refers to Gen. $2^{18f.}$. But in Gen. $2^{18f.}$ it is a matter of the creation of man as male and female, and therefore of the basic form of being in the encounter of I and Thou, of humanity as fellow-humanity. In the New Testament a mystery ($\mu\nu\sigma\tau\acute{\eta}\rho\iota\sigma\nu$) is a reality which carries with it a definite message and does so in such a way that it is both concealed and declared. Where the revelation of God does not take place in and with this reality, and in such a way that it evokes the faith of man, and in his faith knowledge, the message is concealed and the mystery undisclosed. It is received, but not revealed. But where in and with it the revelation of God takes place and faith is evoked, it speaks and discloses itself; it is an open secret. The humanity of man is a reality of this kind. "But I speak," says Paul in Eph. 5^{32}, "concerning Christ and the Church." If we read Gen. $2^{18f.}$ in the context of the Old Testament "Yahweh and Israel" is the message contained in this matter and both concealed and declared. The New Testament does not exclude but includes this interpretation. But it reaches above and behind the whole of the Old Testament as such. It sees the same reality, the creation and being of man as male and female, his humanity as fellow-humanity. It also sees the "Yahweh and Israel" contained and both concealed and declared in it. But it sees further and deeper. For it even the "Yahweh and Israel," and the whole Old Testament message grouped around this word of the covenant, is itself a mystery [317] which has still to be disclosed, a prophecy which has still to be fulfilled, a preliminary history which has still to be followed by the true history. The disclosure, the fulfilment, the true history is "Christ and the community." The New Testament knows that before all time, and in the beginning of time posited by the act of creation, and in the perishing time which stands under the sign of the fall and its penalty, and finally in the new time of freedom which has dawned, the resolve and will of God was and is and will be: "Christ and the community." And for this reason it says of the humanity of man that it is *this* mystery; that it is the concealed and declared content, undisclosed without the Word and the Spirit and faith but disclosed by the Word, in the Spirit and for faith, of the reality "Christ and the community."

This is the biblical confirmation of the presupposition with which we took up this theme at the beginning of the section. We described the humanity of man as a mystery of faith. We had to deal with it accordingly. We had thus to ask first concerning the humanity of the man Jesus. In answer to this question we found that Jesus is the man who is *for* His fellows. We descended from this height to the lower question of humanity generally, and we found that man is the man who is *with* his fellows, the I with the Thou, the male with the female. We could not say more than "with." To say "for" would be to make the false assertion of a general anthropology. It would be to say too much. It can and must be said of the man Jesus, but of Him alone. Yet on the other hand we could not say less. For man without the fellow-man would be a creature which has nothing in common with the man Jesus, and with which the man Jesus has nothing in common. We had to turn our back resolutely on the idea of a man without the fellow-man and the ensuing anthropology. Setting our aim neither too high nor too low, we had thus to interpret humanity simply as fellow-humanity. And we had finally to realise that in this fellow-humanity we are not dealing with an ideal or law or anything of that kind, but with the normative and natural determination of man. For in the co-existence of man and woman at least we have a difference and fellowship given to man in and with his exist-ence, so that in it he is fellow-human quite apart from his own thought or volition. This I-Thou relationship in its distinctive factuality and necessity is thus characteristic of his whole being, controlling it and giving it its character as fellow-humanity. We also saw that in this fellow-humanity, and at the very point where it emerges unequivocally as a natural fact of creation, i.e., in the co-existence of man and woman, the New Testament finds a great mystery. And the New Testament explanation of this mystery is as follows. What is con-tained and both concealed and declared in this reality, what everyone can receive but not everyone can know because its recognition is conditioned by [318] God's revelation and the obedient faith which it evokes, is "Christ and His community." It is obvious that this brings us back to the starting-point and beginning of our whole investigation and presentation. We have here a con-firmation of the fact that to understand what humanity is we had to look first at the man Jesus, the man *for* the fellow-man, and that on this basis we could come to see in man generally only man *with* his fellow-man. According to the main passage in Ephesians 5, but finally in all the relevant New Testament texts, Christ *and* the community means quite unequivocally Christ *for* the com-munity. This dualism stands in clear distinction to that of man and woman and every human I and Thou denoted and controlled by that of man and woman. For the One who takes the place of man—and in this He differs from every other man or I—does not exist and act for Himself or for His own sake, but absolutely for others, for those who are united with Him as His community. He is their Head and Saviour. He is the One who takes away their sins and con-quers their death. He is the One who lifts from them the yoke of the corres-ponding and confirmatory law of their sin and death. He is the One who brings and guarantees their freedom. He is the pledge of the eternal life prom-ised to them. He is wholly for them and not for Himself; Jesus, the man for His fellows. And the co-existence of man and woman, humanity as fellow-humanity, is a great mystery because it contains and both conceals and dis-closes this fact that Jesus is the man for His fellows, both hiding and disclosing it, so that it can be received by everyone but not known by everyone. In this reality we have the witness of the creature itself to this truth. The Old Testa-ment plainly attests it with its Yahweh and Israel. In the fact that it does so it is itself a mystery, prophecy and preliminary history, which must speak of man exactly but exclusively in the way in which it actually does in Genesis 2 and the Song of Songs. If, then, humanity as such, as a purely natural and creaturely determination of man, is this mystery, this real witness, disclosed and received or concealed and rejected, to this first and final element in the will and decree of God, it must be seen as we have tried to see it, and we have no option but to resist any idea of man without his fellow-man, and to understand humanity as fellow-humanity. As fellow-humanity, in the form of the co-existence of man and woman, it is this real witness. The general "with" corresponds to the unique "for" of Jesus from which all the plans and ways and works of God proceed and to which they move. If we accept Ephesians 5 and the New Testament view of this matter, we see that the circle closes at this point, that this is the end, and that we could not begin at any other point than that at which we did, or move forward from that point in any other way. Against this background the basic thesis of theological anthropology, that human being is a being in encounter, loses every shred of similarity with a mere hypothetical assertion. It acquires an axiomatic and dogmatic quality. In the Christian   [319] Church we have no option but to interpret humanity as fellow-humanity. And *si quis dixerit hominem esse solitarium, anathema sit*[EN130]. We can now regard this as secured and demonstrated. And the future history of humanity may well depend to some extent upon whether the Christian Church can agree to recognise this as secured and demonstrated, and thereafter assert that anathema with a stringency for which it has so far lacked both the perception and the resolution. It is to be noted, however, that this is possible only on the basis of Ephesians 5.

We have still to draw a concluding line. It is no accident that in this whole sphere we have had to make such ready use of terms like image, original, copy, correspondence, analogy, parity, likeness, similarity, and finally mystery. The title which we have given to the whole section is: "Man in his Determination as the Covenant-partner of God." Our starting-point was that man is determined in and with his creation and existence to be the covenant-partner of God. Our problem was how far he is this; how far his creation and existence, his nature, must correspond to this determination. Our interest has been focused upon man below, in his reality distinct from God, in his creaturely nature in relation to that for which he was created, and may exist, and is summoned to exist from above. We have thus been concerned with the inner relationship between this being and his destiny. We have seen that this relationship is not one of contradiction but of correspondence. Man is orientated towards that for which he is determined. Even when he sins, he can deny and conceal but he cannot remove or destroy the fact that he is orientated in this way. Even as a sinner he remains the creature of God and therefore the being whose orientation is to be the covenant-partner of God. He can give himself up for lost. But he cannot

---

EN130 if anyone should say that the human being is solitary, let him be anathema

escape God, or lose his being as the creature of God, or the nature of this being. He can trifle with the grace of God, but he cannot make himself wholly unworthy to be in covenant with God. He does this too. But he is found and rescued by the free and totally undeserved grace of God as the creature which even when it gave itself up for lost did not escape God, but whose being in all its perversion and corruption remained a being in correspondence with its determination as the covenant-partner of God. God is faithful. God acknowledges and confesses Himself the Creator by reconciling the world to Himself in Christ, in the One for whom and with a view to whom He created it. He thus proves true that which we contested but which did not in any way cease to be the truth because we did so, but was always the truth even in the form of our lie, namely, that our orientation is to be the covenant-partners of God.

And now we have investigated and described what we are, what our humanity is, in what way we are orientated to be God's covenant-partners in spite of

[320]

our perversion and corruption, in what our correspondence to this determination consists. Our corresponding being is a being in the encounter of man and fellow-man. In this being we are covenant-partners by nature. This does not mean that we are the covenant-partners of God by nature. This is the determination under which we are created and exist. This is the particular plan and will of God operative and executed in our creation. This is the gracious meaning of our existence and nature. But it is not a human attribute. It does not belong to us in virtue of the fact that as men we are the creatures of God. We are not created the covenant-partners of God, but to be His covenant-partners, to be His partners in the history which is the goal of His creation and in which His work as Creator finds its continuation and fulfilment. That this is achieved, that we fulfil this determination, that this history is in train and moves steadily to its goal, is a matter of the free grace with which God deals in sovereignty with His creature, of the Word and Spirit with which He has intercourse with His creature, of His good-pleasure which we cannot control but must always acknowledge that we do not deserve. Yet the fact remains—and this is something which belongs to us as the creatures of God, which is part of our human essence, which can rightly be called a human and even the typically human attribute—that we are covenant-partners by nature and in our mutual dealings, the man with the fellow-man, the I with the Thou, the man with the woman. This is something which is our own, and is inviolable and indestructible. This constitutes the unbroken continuity of human existence. In this we correspond to our determination, and cannot cease to do so. In this there is a positive relationship between our being and our destiny. In this we ourselves, whether we know and accept the fact or not, are in sheer fact a sign and witness of our determination. We are created as mutual partners. And this leaves open the further possibility that we are created to be the partners of God. The latter statement speaks of the free grace of God in relation to man created with a specific nature. But it does undoubtedly speak of this human nature as such.

And the content of the two statements makes it clear that the first is a reflection of the second, its truth being a likeness of that of the second.

It is to be noted that the *tertium comparationis*[EN131], the feature common to both likeness and reality, to both copy and original, consists in both cases, between man and his fellow-man on the one hand and God and man on the other, in an indestructible connexion and fellowship between two subjects which are indestructibly distinct. The only point of comparison is that on both sides there is a firm and genuine covenant. A covenant means co-existence for better for worse. It is genuine if it is between two partners who are obviously not identical. And it is sure if there is no question of the dissolution of the relationship between the two partners. More than this cannot be said. For apart from this common feature everything is different. On the one side we have a union of creature with creature in virtue of the creaturely nature which they do not owe to themselves but to their Creator; on the other we have a union of the Creator and His creature, in which the Creator is the free Lord of the covenant, and His mercy is its basis and goal, His wisdom the power of its initiation and execution. His faithfulness the guarantee of its continuance, and finally His own person its fulfilment. On the one side we have reciprocity, the giving and receiving of two partners of equal essence and dignity; on the other everything is one-sided—the authority, the rule and the judgment, the plan and the work, being all of God, and His, too, the gift which makes it possible for the human partner to have a part in the covenant. On the one side man is with man; on the other, God is with man but also for him in a way in which man can never be for God. On the one side there is an obvious and necessarily two-sided need; on the other all the need is on the side of man but on God's side there is the sheer sovereignty of a grace which knows neither internal nor external compulsion but is wholly free, its address to man being an overflow of the inconceivable goodness of God. In our consideration of the man and woman on the one side and Christ and the community on the other, we have seen how great are the differences between the two relationships. But we have to remember that even the autonomy of the two partners is different in the two cases. In the one case it is only the relative and parallel autonomy of two creatures, but in the other we have the absolute autonomy of God on the one side and the relative autonomy of the creature on the other. And we have to remember that the firmness of the covenant differs in the two cases. In the one case it is that of the factuality which man cannot escape because he has this nature and no other; but in the other it is that of the constancy of God which cannot turn from man because it is the free mercy of God which will not let go of man. It is, therefore, with this disparity that the being of man corresponds to the fact that man is ordained to be the covenant-partner of God. And this means that the correspondence of his nature does not give him any right or claim, any power to decide either to be or not to be the covenant-partner of

[321]

[EN131] basis of comparison

God. It is no merit if he is ready to become this. He can only magnify the grace of God if he may do so. For it is only the grace of God if he is called and enabled to do so. It thus follows that natural theology cannot find here a point of contact for the proclamation of the grace and revelation of God. For if it is true that man in his humanity is himself a purely factual sign and witness of his determination, this can only mean that he is himself a mystery, a reality which encloses the declaration of his ordination to be with God, but only encloses it, and therefore conceals no less than discloses it, and discloses it only when it is expressed by the grace and revelation of God, and in the knowledge of faith thereby awakened. If this does not happen, it is of no help to man that he is himself a sign and witness. He is dumb even in relation to himself. The declaration of his determination takes place—he is in fact a man with the fellow-man—but he does not receive it. It does not tell him that God is with him and for him; that he is not merely the covenant-partner of the fellow-man, but of God. This is something which man cannot tell himself. He cannot even prepare himself to receive it. Only the Word and Spirit of God can tell it to him. Only subsequently can the proclamation of the grace and revelation of God draw his attention to the fact that it cannot be anything strange or unnatural for him to be called and set in covenant with God and gathered to the people of God.

[322]

And this is the positive thing which results from the fact that for all the dissimilarity there is similarity. This is the firm and genuine covenant in which man finds himself by nature in virtue of the fact that his humanity as such is fellow-humanity—corresponding to the firm and genuine covenant with God to which he, the creature to whom this nature is intrinsic, is summoned by the grace and revelation of God. If this takes place, this calling, this actualisation of his determination, finds him in the deepest sense at home. The Word of God really applies to him, this creature. The Spirit of God really speaks to his spirit. For as God discloses Himself to him, there is also disclosed to him the mystery of his own human reality, the meaning of the fact that he is man with his fellow-man, man with woman. If God comes to man, He comes to His possession which He has already marked as such in creating it. And what man may discover by the Word and Spirit of God as God comes to him is that God has not created him as a being alien to Himself, but as His neighbour and confidant. He has marked his nature, himself in his humanity, with the mark of one who is His neighbour and confidant. Man bears the sign of the firm and genuine covenant in which he may find and have his fellow-man, the I the Thou and man woman. He may recognise and find confirmed in this sign the fact that God really intends and seeks him when He calls him to covenant with Himself, to this covenant which is firm and genuine in a different way because grounded in and maintained by His grace. This sign and likeness, this reality full of declaration, the mystery of his own reality, is no longer dumb but eloquent. His humanity can no longer be a mere fact—a matter of accident or caprice. As the reflection of the light of grace which lay on it even when he did not know it, marking his existence as such, his humanity becomes the task and problem and content of his own action. Now that the meaning of his being is no longer unknown or obscure, he will now will, and will to practise and actualise, what he is by nature. In order that the fact of the human nature of man may be actualised, there is needed the grace and revelation of the covenant which God has concluded with the man created for this purpose. On the side of man there is needed his hearing of the Word of God, his calling by His [323] Spirit, his awakening to faith, his accepting and occupying his place and status as God's partner in this covenant. There is thus needed for the human willing and actualising of humanity the fact that this humanity, which in the first instance is a mere fact and as such a mystery, should be inwardly illumined and made transparent by the free act of God from above. There is needed what takes place in Ephesians 5—that the relationship of husband and wife should be lit up by that of Christ and His community. "In thy light shall we see light." But humanity, the human and natural relationship which is made clear and transparent in this way, itself becomes light. It is the fact of humanity which, giving light and speaking as a sign and mystery, becomes the task and problem and content of human action and therefore, as in Ephesians 5, the theme of Christian admonition. And conversely this fact presupposed in all human action and grounded in the nature of man is as such the sign and witness that as man lives in the human covenant he is obedient to his calling to be the covenant-partner of God and thus participates in this covenant-fellowship. That the covenant between God and man is the original of that between man and man means, therefore, on the one side that the latter covenant may and should be lived out in human action; and it means on the other side that in its actual existence it is the hope that may also live in covenant with God and live this out too in his own action. This sign given him in and with his own nature tells and assures him that he is the neighbour and confidant of God, that he has not slipped from Him, that marked in this way he has always been regarded by God as His own, and always will be. It tells him that in this nature of his he who stands in this temporal covenant is also called to the eternal, that he may take comfort in and hold to the fact that he is called in this way, and that the Creator is faithful by whom he is called.

It must be pointed out in conclusion that if the being of man in encounter is a being in correspondence to his determination as the covenant-partner of God, the statement is unavoidable that it is a being in correspondence to God Himself, to the being of His Creator. The Initiator, Lord and Sustainer of the covenant between God and man is God Himself, and He alone. If man is ordained to be God's partner in this covenant, and if his nature is a likeness corresponding to this ordination, necessarily it corresponds in this respect to the nature of God Himself. God has created him in this correspondence, as a reflection of Himself. Man is the image of God. This is not an arbitrarily invented statement. In relation to the man Jesus, by whom we are impelled already to this conclusion, it is clear and necessary as a final definition. But in

[324]

Gen. 1²⁶ᶠ· he Old Testament also makes it in relation to man generally. I refer to my discussion of this text in *C.D.* III, 1, 191f., and believe that the present train of thought yields exactly the same results. Man generally, the man with the fellow-man, has indeed a part in the divine likeness of the man Jesus, the man for the fellow-man. As man generally is modelled on the man Jesus and His being for others, and as the man Jesus is modelled on God, it has to be said of man generally that he is created in the image of God. He is in his humanity, and therefore in his fellow-humanity. God created him in His own image in the fact that He did not create him alone but in this connexion and fellowship. For in God's action as the Lord of the covenant, and even further back in His action as the Creator of a reality distinct from Himself, it is proved that God Himself is not solitary, that although He is one in essence He is not alone, but that primarily and properly He is in connexion and fellowship. It is inevitable that we should recall the triune being of God at this point. God exists in relationship and fellowship. As the Father of the Son and the Son of the Father He is Himself I and Thou, confronting Himself and yet always one and the same in the Holy Ghost. God created man in His own image, in correspondence with His own being and essence. He created Him in the image which emerges even in His work as the Creator and Lord of the covenant. Because He is not solitary in Himself, and therefore does not will to be so *ad extra*, it is not good for man to be alone, and God created him in His own image, as male and female. This is what is emphatically said by Gen. 1²⁷, and all other explanations of the *imago Dei*ᴱᴺ¹³² suffer from the fact that they do not do justice to this decisive statement. We need not waste words on the dissimilarity in the similarity of the similitude. Quite obviously we do not have here more than an analogy, i.e., similarity in dissimilarity. We merely repeat that there can be no question of an analogy of being, but of relationship. God is in relationship, and so too is the man created by Him. This is his divine likeness. When we view it in this way, the dispute whether it is lost by sin finds a self-evident solution. It is not lost. But more important is the fact that what man is indestructibly as he is man with the fellow-man, he is in hope of the being and action of the One who is his original in this relationship.

ᴱᴺ¹³² image of God

MAN AS SOUL AND BODY

Through the Spirit of God, man is the subject, form and life of a substantial organism, the soul of his body—wholly and simultaneously both, in effaceable difference, inseparable unity, and indestructible order.

1. JESUS, WHOLE MAN

So far it has been man's being in itself and as such that has occupied us. We have learned to know it as being in covenant with God and in encounter with fellow-men. The anthropology of traditional Christian dogmatics has usually omitted to lay this foundation and addressed itself immediately to the problem to which we turn only now. This is the problem of the constitution of this being, the problem of man's existence and nature. These problems were dealt with in the traditional doctrine of the human soul, which was strongly emphasised, and of the human body, which was almost always emphatically disregarded. Man's being exists, and is therefore soul; and it exists in a certain form, and is therefore body. This is the simplest description of the being of soul and body and their relationship. Man is soul and body—this is in brief the constitution of his being. For this reason, we have now to clarify this being of man in itself and as such. Man's being is being with God and therefore being with fellow-men. With this recognition as our starting point, we too can and must reckon with the fact that this being has an existence and a nature, and therefore with the question concerning body and soul as the constituents of man's being. Thus we have the advantage over the older dogmatics of having firm ground under our feet and of occupying a point of vantage from which the scope of this new problem can really be observed. It is probable that, starting from this point, we shall avoid a certain one-sidedness, exaggeration and vulnerability more easily than could the older dogmatics which did not trouble to lay this foundation.

Advance into the region of new insights and conceptions which we now enter has its own difficulties. For one thing, we come at this point very close to the propositions of all kinds of non-theological studies of mankind, among which one can very easily go astray, especially as they always arouse at this point the burning interest which powerful inner contradictions always bring to light. The danger is all the more acute in view of the fact that the primitive and New Testament witnesses to revelation apparently took no very great interest in the [326] questions here to be answered, but took up their position towards them only incidentally and with a certain carefree inexactness, thus giving the impression that they were to be regarded rather as formal. Hence we must be circumspect if on the one hand we are not to be burdened with the relevant non-theological inquiries and theories, and on the other hand we are to see and think at this point too from an adequately biblical and exegetical ground and thus reach an understanding, and a Christian understanding, in the matter. But we shall affirm that we may still be taught by the revealed Word of God, and that in no circumstances can we interrupt our investigation and presentation at this point. A gap at this point would be intolerable, would have the most fatal consequences, and would give free entrance to the most varied ambiguities and errors.

In this section, we have to prove that man is to be understood as "soul and body," that this constitutes his being; and we have to show how far this is the case. It will serve to illumine the problem if at the same time we state the other pairs of concepts which more or less exactly express the same truth and might therefore be considered as alternative headings: "Man as spirit and substantial organism," as "rational and sensuous," "inner and outer," "invisible and visible," "inapprehensible and apprehensible," "intelligible and empirical," and even as "heavenly and earthly"—these are certainly not excluded as possible designations of the same thing. What these other pairs of ideas express or indicate must certainly come under discussion under the title "Man as Soul and Body." Of all other possibilities, we choose the latter because they keep us closest to the language of the Bible, and because in their popular simplicity they indicate not only most unpretentiously but also, for all the problems which they involve, most unambiguously, concretely, and comprehensively the questions which are here to be asked and answered.

The presupposition that the constitution of man is to be understood under one of the pairs of ideas that point in this direction, is a theological truth requiring theological foundation and explanation. We cannot, of course, overlook the fact that in themselves the words "soul" and "body," which in combination can be interpreted in so many different ways, indicate a very real problem—or rather a whole complex of problems—concerning man's general understanding of himself. Inevitably in interpretation of this complex of problems we must not only negatively but also positively deal with many an old and new presentation attempted in the course of man's general understanding of himself. But here again we go our own way on our own responsibility. That is, we inquire concerning the nature of man as he is in the Word of God and as he considers and is responsible to himself on the basis of the call of God. By the constitution of this man, the man of whom "thou art mindful" and whom "thou regardest," we understand the true constitution of man. And of [327] the constitution of this man, we say that it is to be understood as soul and body (or at least in terms of one of the pairs of ideas that point in this direction). Thus we do not work with a borrowing from another kind of discipline when we employ these two words and their combination ; and we reserve to ourselves the freedom, irrespective of parallel or divergent presentations in other disciplines, to interpret and use them in accordance with the theological inquiry and discipline.

Here too, then, we first go back to the source of understanding which alone can be authentic and normative for the theological doctrine of man's nature. We find our bearings and our instruction as we look to the constitution of the humanity of Jesus. With the clarity and certainty that we gain here, we can then set out the propositions in which the Christian understanding of the constitution of all men generally may be expressed and comprehended.

Rather surprisingly, the first and decisive impression gained when we address our questions to the man Jesus of the New Testament is that the pairs of ideas with which we provisionally designated the problem are insufficient in His case. The differentiation in the constitution of man which they suggest has in His case only a provisional and relative and not an ultimate and absolute meaning. What is there in Him which is only inner and not outer, sensuous and not rational? What does soul or body mean for Him to the extent that either implies an importance and function of its own, different from and opposed to the other?

The Jesus of the New Testament is supremely true man in the very fact that He does not conform to the later definition, and far from existing as the union of two parts or two "substances," He is one whole man, embodied soul and besouled body: the one in the other and never merely beside it; the one never without the other but only with it, and in it present, active and significant; the one with all its attributes always to be taken as seriously as the other. As this one whole man, and therefore as true man, the Jesus of the New Testament is born and lives and suffers and dies and is raised again. Between His death and His resurrection there is a transformation, but no alteration, division or least of all subtraction. The body does not remain behind, nor does the soul depart. As the same whole man, soul and body, He rises as He died, and sits at the right hand of God, and will come again. And He is one whole man in His relation to others, in what He does for them, what He gives them, what He asks of them, what He is for them and for the whole cosmos. He does not fulfil His office and His work from His miraculous annunciation to His fulfilment in such a way that we can separate His outer form from His inner or His inner form from His outer. Everything is the revelation of an inner, invisible, spiritual plane of life. But it is almost more striking and characteristic that everything has an outer, visible, bodily form. There is no logic here which is not as such physics, no cure [328] of souls which is not as such bound up with cure of bodies. The man who is called by Him and who takes part in His way and work as a recipient and fellow-worker does not only receive something to consider and to will and to feel; he enters into bodily contact and fellowship. The man who comes to hear of the kingdom of God comes also to taste it. He comes to eat and to drink bodily, so that it again becomes apparent that in this bodily eating and drinking he has to do with nothing less than the hidden—in our terminology, "inner" or "spiritual"—savouring and tasting of the heavenly bread and the powers of the world to come. To believe on Him is to be on the way to the same whole manhood which is His own mystery. To serve Him is not only to speak to others, but also to give these others to eat and to drink. And it is again this one whole manhood which is revealed in His person as wide as the future and the hope not only of His community but of the whole cosmos.

This can be illustrated linguistically from the decisive section of the New Testament witness to Christ. In Gal. 1⁴ we read that Jesus Christ gave Himself (ἑαυτόν) up for our sins. The same ἑαυτόν [EN1] is found in the same expression in Gal. 2²⁰ and Eph. 5² ²⁵ But compare Mt. 20²⁸ and *par.*: the Son of man is come to give His soul (ψυχὴν αὐτοῦ) a ransom for many. Similarly 1 Jn. 3¹⁶: His ψυχή [EN2] for us; Jn. 10¹¹ ¹⁵: the Good Shepherd gives His ψυχή for His sheep; Jn. 15¹³: his ψυχή for his friends. But again compare Lk. 22¹⁹: This is my body (τὸ σῶμά μου) which is given for you; Heb. 10¹⁰: we are sanctified by the sacrifice of the σῶμα Ἰησοῦ χριστοῦ; Rom. 7⁴: through the σῶμα τοῦ χριστοῦ [EN3] you are dead to the law; Col. 1²²: He has reconciled you ἐν τῷ σώματι τῆς σαρκὸς αὐτοῦ [EN4] by His death; 1 Pet. 2²⁴: He bore our sins ἐν τῷ σώματι αὐτοῦ [EN5] on the tree. The action of which all these passages speak is the same, as are also its consequence and significance, its subject, and obviously and above all its object, which is materially identical with the subject. But this object can be designated sometimes as ἑαυτός [EN6], sometimes as ψυχὴ αὐτοῦ [EN7], sometimes as σῶμα αὐτοῦ [EN8]. The difference in usage is not, of course, unpremeditated; yet obviously the one term could always be used in place of the others. Jesus, He Himself, is His soul and His body, and it is this one whole man who died on the cross and thus made our sin inoperative and completed our reconciliation.

That the New Testament really points to this unity is shown by the fact that the passages which especially mention the soul (or even "spirit") and the body of the man Jesus are comparatively rare in appearance and parsimonious in content. The reader is led to note clearly only the fact that in Jesus we are concerned with the unity of two realms or aspects and thus undoubtedly—and this emphatically prevents all Docetism—with a real man.

In the Fourth Gospel we hear repeatedly of a "troubling" (ταράσσεσθαι) of the soul of Jesus (or of His "spirit,") which in 11³³ ³⁸ (in face of the lamentation over Lazarus) has the character of indignation (ἐνεβριμήσατο τῷ πνεύματι [EN9]), in 12²⁷ (at the thought of the approaching "hour") of fright, and in 13²¹ (in face of the traitor Judas) of amazement. According to Lk. 12⁵⁰, He is straitened (συνέχομαι) as He awaits the coming of the baptism with which He is to be baptised. We read in Mk. 8¹² that, at the question: Why does this generation seek after a sign? Jesus "sighed deeply in his spirit" (ἀναστενάξας τῷ πνεύματι). We read in Mt. 26³⁷ᶠ, in the description of the scene in Gethsemane: He "began to be sorrowful (λυπεῖσθαι) and very heavy (ἀδημονεῖν). Then saith he unto them, My soul is exceeding sorrowful, even unto death (περίλυπος ... ἕως θανάτου: the saying is a citation

---

[EN1] himself
[EN2] soul
[EN3] body of Jesus Christ
[EN4] in the body of his flesh
[EN5] in his body
[EN6] himself
[EN7] his soul
[EN8] his body
[EN9] he groaned in the spirit

from Ps. 42$^{6-12}$ and 43^5, where the original has "cast down"): tarry ye here and watch with [329] me." Relevant, too, is Lk. 22^{44}: "And being in ἀγωνία^{EN10} he prayed more earnestly"; and also Heb. 5^7: "Who in the days of his flesh, when he had offered up prayers and supplications, with strong crying and tears unto him that was able to save him from death." From Lk. 19^{41}, again, we hear how Jesus wept over Jerusalem, and almost more impressive are the sentences in the story of Lazarus in Jn. 11$^{34ff.}$: He "said, Where have ye laid him? They said unto him, Lord, come and see. ἐδάκρυσεν ὁ Ἰησοῦς^{EN11}. Then said the Jews, Behold how he loved him!" According to the context Jesus was called to Bethany: "Lord, behold, he whom thou lovest is sick" (v. 3). And v. 5 (heightening the contrast of the fact that Jesus for two days gave no heed to the summons) records: "Now Jesus loved Martha, and her sister, and Lazarus." That Jesus "loved" individual persons appears elsewhere in the Fourth Gospel only in the person of the mysterious disciple (ὃν ἠγάπα ὁ Ἰησοῦς^{EN12} 13^{23}, 19^{26}, 20^2, 21^7 ^{20}), and in the rest of the New Testament only in Mk. 10^{21} where the rich young man is deliberately described in this way. From what is said in Jn. 15$^{13-15}$ the relation of Jesus to His disciples is certainly not to be thought of in terms of what we understand by "friendship." And it is striking that the general expression that Jesus loved His own (Jn. 13^1; 15$^{9-12}$; Gal. 2^{20}; Eph. 5$^{2\ 25\ 28}$; Rev. 1^5) occurs much more seldom than one would expect. The saying in Lk. 10^{21} is strangely isolated when it tells us that "in the spirit" Jesus breaks into a rapturous cry of jubilation (ἠγαλλιάσατο) in praise of God and of the mystery of the divine election He apprehends in the calling of His disciples to see and hear the revelation which takes place in Him.

What we thus learn of the inner life of Jesus is certainly not little, but it is definitely not very much, and it falls far short of all that we should like to know. Nowhere do we hear of Jesus meditating, deciding, rejoicing or laughing. Of course, we are not told that He did not do these things. There is obviously no attempt at a full portrait or even a characterisation; and certainly not the exhibition of an inner development. It is customary to take it that Lk. 2^{52}, with its reference to the growth (προκόπτειν) of the child Jesus in wisdom and stature and in favour with God and man, is a hint in this direction. Similar hints have also been found in Heb. 5^8 (ἔμαθεν ... ὑπακοήν^{EN13}), and of course indirectly in the story of the temptation. But it cannot be overlooked how unfruitful these indications are, if indeed they are indications at all. By all these passages we are only made aware that Jesus had a really human inner life. But we are given no guidance for reflection concerning it, and for forming a picture of this matter we are in fact offered no material at all.

The same indigence characterises the statements about His physical life. It is made unambiguously and emphatically clear that we have to do with a real man. That Jesus is "born of a woman" is the self-evident presupposition of all the New Testament writers; but its underlining by Paul in Gal. 4^4 is not gratuitous. All four Gospels speak of Jesus' mother and His brethren. It is, of course, noteworthy that the Second and Fourth Evangelists did not consider it necessary to start with an account of the birth of Jesus or even with a note about it, but begin forthwith *in mediis rebus*^{EN14}. Even Mt. 1^{25} regards His birth only as a future event, and Mt. 2^1 as a past event. But its reality could not be more powerfully attested than with the ὁ λόγος σὰρξ ἐγένετο^{EN15} (Jn. 1^{14}) And Luke, the companion of Paul, gives us in 2$^{1ff.}$ a detailed account, as he also records the saying of that woman of the people (11^{27}): "Blessed is the womb that bare thee, and the paps which thou hast sucked." The authenticity of the

---

^{EN10} agony
^{EN11} Jesus wept
^{EN12} whom Jesus loved
^{EN13} he learned ... obedience
^{EN14} in the middle of things
^{EN15} the Word was made flesh

message of the apostles "of the word of life" is expressly based (1 Jn. 1¹) on the fact that they deal not only with what they know and understand, or what they have merely heard and seen and observed with their eyes, but with what "our hands have handled." This physical contact with Jesus is regarded as decisive, not only in the story of the healing of the issue of blood (Mk. 5²⁵ and *par.*), but also in several general reports of His healing works (Mt. 14³⁶; Lk. 6¹⁹). That doubting Thomas (Jn. 20²⁴ᶠ·) wished to see the marks of the nails in the hands of Jesus, and to put his hand in His side, was not really doubt. This was the normal way, the way recognised and even demanded by the risen Jesus, in which as a disciple he should come to believe, and therefore become an apostle. Even the risen Jesus will and must be recognised as true man by His first witnesses through physical sight and bodily apprehension. In Luke's account of the meeting of the eleven with the Resurrected (Lk. 24³⁶ᶠ·), it is expressly said: "Why are ye troubled? and why do thoughts arise in your hearts? Behold my hands and feet, ὅτι ἐγώ εἰμι αὐτός EN16: handle me, and see; for a spirit hath not flesh and bones, as ye see me have." So we read in Mt. 4² of Jesus' hunger in the desert, in Jn. 19²⁸ of His thirst on the cross, in Jn. 4⁶ that He grew tired on the journey, in Lk. 22⁴⁴ that in Gethsemane His sweat was like drops of blood falling to the ground, and in Mt. 8²⁴ that He slept in the ship. In Mt. 11¹⁹ Jesus Himself tells us: "The Son of man came eating and drinking, and they say, Behold a man gluttonous, and a winebibber"; and in Lk. 15² there is the emphatic accusation: "This man receiveth sinners, and eateth with them." Again, in the story of the resurrection (Lk. 24⁴¹ᶠ·; Jn. 21⁵ᶠ·, cf. also Lk. 24³⁰ᶠ·) we read that Jesus comes to the disciples, that He asks to eat, and that He is recognised by them in His taking a meal with them. On this side, too, we learn more than a little; and what we are told cannot be ignored. But on this side, again, we are not given a complete, much less a concrete, picture. It is clearly no concern of ours whether Jesus was ever sick. An impenetrable veil of silence lies over the fact that He was a male (Jn. 4²⁷). The noteworthy thing is the absence of both positive and negative information on both points. No attention is paid to the health or to the celibacy of Jesus, nor are these things even mentioned. The fact of His corporeality is crucially important. The substance and nature of this fact, which are so desirable and even necessary to a biographer, remain fundamentally hidden, and can be supplied only by an imagination whose methods have nothing in common with what the New Testament has to say to us.

Clearly, then, the New Testament points consciously and effectively to the one whole man Jesus. On both sides He is seen only in the fact of His wholeness, and this alone is important. To ask concerning the manner, raising questions prompted by biographical curiosity, can only divert attention from what the apostles saw and wanted to attest, obscuring rather than illuminating the oneness and wholeness in which the constitution of man is visible in this man. It is in the palpable poverty of this picture that its richness consists and may be discerned. Its richness is Jesus Himself, in His physical life, as soul and body, both wholly real, and neither in a form of its own nor important only for itself. The soul is real and important only as *His* shocked and grieved and angered but also loving and rejoicing soul; the body, on the other hand, is real and important only as *His* humiliated but also exalted body. It is always He as both, but in both and also over both the κύριος EN17 even and already in this aspect.

We have now to set alongside this another well-known consideration. According to the New Testament authors, and the so-called harmony of the Gospels and Acts, the outline of the life of Jesus is consciously and expressly conceived and presented as a combination or fusion of word and deed, of acts of oral proclamation, of preaching and teaching and of mighty works which are objectively verifiable and effective. "Jesus not only speaks; He also

[330]

EN16 that it is I myself
EN17 Lord

acts" (K. L. Schmidt, article *"Jesus Christus," RGG³*, III, 142). Neither of these two moments of the New Testament Gospel is dispensable; neither may be overlooked to the advantage of the other, or regarded as less important than the other. The oneness and wholeness of Jesus' human person is reflected in the works of this person. Against the powerful and too spiritualised conception of the picture of Jesus in the 18th and 19th centuries, it was and is necessary to draw attention to this, especially in relation to the bodily aspect and the whole range [331] of the mighty works of the New Testament. According to the Synoptic and Pauline accounts of the Last Supper, as well as to Jn. 6⁵¹ᶠ, it is the body (or flesh) and blood of Jesus which in the New Testament is the essence of the fellowship guaranteed by Jesus to the others and of all the gifts to be had from Him in this fellowship. After the crucifixion of Jesus, the burning question concerned (Mt. 27⁵⁸ᶠ and *par*; Jn. 2²¹, 19³⁸ᶠ, 20¹²) the slain body of the Lord, and it is as bodily resurrection that the resurrection on the third day is given as the answer to this question. The community founded on the calling of the twelve apostles and their witness is called the σῶμα τοῦ χριστοῦ EN18 which builds itself up and coheres and lives in its many members in dependence on its Head. Phil. 3²¹ describes the essence of the Christian hope as waiting for the Lord Jesus Christ from heaven, "who shall change our vile bodies" into likeness with σῶμα τῆς δόξης αὐτοῦ EN19. And in Col. 2¹⁷, the irruption of the reality of the kingdom of God (τὰ μέλλοντα EN20) is again compared, in distinction from the shadow world of outward legal observances, with the σῶμα τοῦ χριστοῦ. In all this, the spirit is not wronged but honoured. But it is clear that, according to the New Testament understanding, the pneumatic characteristically reckons with the somatic, that apart from this it neither has form nor is it active, and that abstracted from it is no longer the pneumatic. From this point of view, we cannot ignore how prominently, even in those communal traditions—cf. Mt. 4²³⁻²⁵ or Mt. 11²ᶠ—the element of the corporeal and therefore of the acts of Jesus stands in the foreground of the picture of His life and activity which the disciples witnessed and the New Testament offers us. The acts of Jesus do not merely accompany His reported words. It is clear that in the view of the New Testament writers the reported bodily acts of Jesus are to be understood as the decisive indication, declaration and attestation of the speaking Subject and therefore of His words, so that they cannot in any sense be regarded as mere incidentals and accessories. "Another teacher or prophet might also have spoken some or all the words; but here spoke One equipped with unique authority." And it must be added at once: "Another miracle worker might have done some or all the acts; but here One operates who stood at the dawn of the kingdom of God actualised in Him and who in virtue of this forgave sins" (K. L. Schmidt, *op. cit.*, 118). But the first contrast is of equal weight with the second: Jesus not only announced the forgiveness of sins but really effected it; He met the physically sick not only with sympathy and words of comfort, not only as a skilful doctor, but as the One who makes whole. He is the man He is precisely in the unity of His work as it is apprehensible in this second moment. The "Christian science" which isolates the Jesus of this second apprehensible moment, and in the Saviour sees only the Healer, evidently constructs an abstraction as remote from the text and as illegitimate as the Liberal theology which clings only to Jesus the Teacher and at most to His personal life. The person of the Messiah and the ἐξουσία EN21 of the Messianic work of the New Testament Jesus, the kingdom or better the kingly rule of God which is operative and evident in this man, comprises these two moments. They are not two parts in Him. They are not two parallels in Him, or two intersecting lines,

---

EN18 body of Christ
EN19 his glorious body
EN20 the things to come
EN21 authority

or two agreeing or concurring functions. They permit no choice. They cannot be considered independently. In and with one another they are the oneness and wholeness of this life.

This oneness and wholeness, then, is the first thing to be noted in consideration of the human nature of Jesus. It is in no sense arbitrary to ask whether there could be any problem of the inner contradictions in human nature if we had to do only with this man. And it may already be seen from afar—since the problem does arise in relation to all other men—in what direction we must look for an answer if in Jesus we have to do with true man.

[332]

A second point to be noted is that the oneness and wholeness of this human life is fashioned, structured and determined from within, and therefore necessary and of lasting significance. The interconnexion of the soul and body and Word and act of Jesus is not a chaos but a cosmos, a formed and ordered totality. There is in it a higher and a lower, a first and a second, a dominating and a dominated. But the man Jesus Himself is both. He is not only the higher, the first, the dominating, nor is He both in such a way that the lower, the second, the dominated is associated with him only externally or accidentally. This would again imply the destruction of that oneness and wholeness. He is also the lower, the second, the dominated. He is not only His soul but also His body. But He is both soul and body in an ordered oneness and wholeness. His being is orderly and not disorderly. Nor is He this in such a way that the order is accidental and imposed from without. He is it in an order which derives from Himself. He Himself and from Himself is both the higher and the lower, the first and the second, the dominant and dominated. He Himself is in both cases His own principle. The meaning, plan and intention, the logos of His life is thus not exterior and accidental. It is no foreign law to which He binds Himself but which comes from elsewhere and is established over Him. Rather He is His own law, and He is subject to it in a free obedience arising in Himself and proceeding from Himself. Jesus wills and fulfils Himself. He is His own ground and His own intention. He lives in such a way that command and obedience, ordination and subordination, plan and execution, goal and aim proceed from Himself and thus partake of an equal inward necessity. He lives truly because He does not live secondarily, or in such a way that He as soul and body partakes of a common life which is originally alien to Himself, which is always distinguishable from His own, which must accrue to Him and can be lost again by Him. He lives in sovereignty. His life of soul and body is really His life. He has full authority over it. Thus He can give it and impart it; He can live it for many others and in many others; He can make it the life of many others without its ceasing to belong to Him and to be His life, without its being diminished or lost to Him. On the contrary, He can gain it only as He gives and imparts it, living it for many others and in them. He can possess it only by losing it. This is how the New Testament writers describe the oneness and wholeness of this human life.

1. Jesus, Whole Man

Our best starting-point in this respect is the decisive statement in which they bring the human person of Jesus into an absolutely unique relation with the Holy Spirit. It is to be noted in advance that this statement is not quite identical with the statement that He is the Messiah of Israel and the Son of God. The latter statement is basic but must be excluded for the sake of clarity. It is connected with the former to the extent that it is essential for a man who as such really is the Messiah and the Son of God to stand in this unique relationship to the Holy Spirit. But it is not this special relationship to the Holy Spirit which makes this man the Messiah and the Son of God. On the contrary, it is because this man is the Messiah and the Son of God that He stands to the Holy Spirit in this special relationship. We have here to regard this relationship as the particular determination of the human constitution of Jesus. [333]

The New Testament writers see in the existence of the man Jesus the fulfilment of the central prophecy of the coming son of David in Is. $11^{1f.}$. We read in this passage that "there shall come forth a rod out of the stem of Jesse, and a Branch shall grow out of his roots: And the spirit of the Lord shall rest upon him, the spirit of wisdom and understanding, the spirit of counsel and might, the spirit of knowledge and of the fear of the Lord." In a word, it is the Spirit of the true king that will be the Spirit of this man—of the king that Solomon desired to be according to his prayer (1 K. $3^{6f.}$), and that according to the continuation of this passage and the rest of the Old Testament tradition he actually was, at least in outline, likeness and prototype. But according to Is. 11, this kingly Spirit is to rest on the Messiah (in contrast to Solomon, to David himself, and to all who in greater or less measure partake of his line). He is to be a man who is pervasively and constantly, intensively and totally filled and governed by this kingly Spirit. Hence Jn. 1^{32}: "And John bare record, saying, I saw the Spirit descending from heaven like a dove, and it abode on him" (καὶ ἔμεινεν ἐπ᾽ αὐτόν); Lk. 4^1: "And Jesus being full of the Holy Ghost (πλήρης πνεύματος ἁγίου) returned from Jordan"; Mt. 12^{18} (quoting from Is. 42^1): "I have put my Spirit upon him (θήσω τὸ πνεῦμά μου ἐπ᾽ αὐτόν): he shall bring forth judgment to the Gentiles"; Lk. 4^{18} (quoting from Is. 61^1): "The Spirit of the Lord is upon me (πνεῦμα κυρίου ἐπ᾽ ἐμέ), because he hath anointed me"; Jn. 3^{34}: "For he whom God hath sent speaketh the words of God: for God giveth not the Spirit by measure unto him" (οὐ γὰρ ἐκ μέτρου δίδωσιν τὸ πνεῦμα); and Jn. 6^{63}: "The words that I speak unto you, they are spirit, and they are life." Similarly Rom. $1^{3f.}$ and 1 Pet. 3^{18} tell us that Jesus' resurrection from the dead is grounded on the fact that over against His determination κατὰ σάρκα EN22 as the son of David (the determination under which He could be and was slain) stands His determination κατὰ πνεῦμα EN23 under which His resurrection from the dead was a divine necessity. Similarly, 2 Cor. 3^{17} can venture the identification: ὁ δὲ κύριος τὸ πνεῦμα ἐστιν EN24; and 1 Cor. 15^{45}: ἐγένετο ... ὁ ἔσχατος Ἀδὰμ εἰς πνεῦμα ζωοποιοῦν EN25. The most fundamental New Testament statement concerning this relationship is that concerning the conception of Jesus by the Holy Spirit (cf. C.D., I, 2, 172 ff.) as the miraculous sign of the mystery of His Messiahship and divine Sonship. Thus in Lk. 1^{35} we have the annunciation of the angel to Mary: "The Holy Ghost shall come upon thee, and the power of the Highest shall overshadow thee: Therefore also that holy thing which shall be born of thee shall be called the Son of God." Again, we read in Mt. 1^{18}: "When as his mother Mary was espoused to Joseph, before they came together, she was found with child of the Holy Ghost." Again, in Mt. 1^{20} the angel says to Joseph: "Fear not to take unto thee Mary thy wife: for that which is conceived in her is of the Holy Ghost." These passages do not say that

---

EN22 according to the flesh
EN23 according to the spirit
EN24 the Lord is the Spirit
EN25 the last Adam was made a quickening spirit

the man Jesus is the Son of the Holy Spirit and that the Holy Spirit is thus His Father, but simply that this conception—which is no miracle as conception in the womb of a woman—is nevertheless a pure miracle in so far as this man has no physical father, and that in the event of His conception God deals with His mother as Creator to the exclusion of male volition and action. The relationship of this man to the Holy Spirit is so close and special that He owes no more and no less than His existence itself and as such to the Holy Spirit. But in the Old and New Testaments the Holy Spirit is God Himself in His creative movement to His creation. It is God who breathes specially upon man (Gen. 2⁷), thus living for him, allowing him to partake of His own life, and therefore making him on his side a living being. From the standpoint of man, He is thus his possibility of being a "living soul" (Gen. 2⁷, ψυχὴ ζῶσα, 1 Cor. 15⁴⁵), and as such a body. That this Spirit rests on man, is laid on Him and remains over him, that man is full of the Spirit and his being and doing are consequently spiritual, and he himself is spirit because created by the Spirit—these biblical statements are not anthropological but exclusively Messianic. That man in general lives, he owes of course to the Holy Ghost. Hence it can also be said of man in general that the Holy Spirit is given to him, that he receives Him, that he lives by and from the Spirit, that he has the Spirit and is of a spiritual or intellectual nature. But there is this difference. Of man in general, this can be said only in virtue of a special operation of God and of specific events in which God turns towards him and enables him. From the general anthropological standpoint, however, possession of the Spirit is not a human state according to the Bible. In those events, the Spirit is imparted only "by measure" (Jn. 3³⁴). The events can cease. The Holy Spirit does not dwell lastingly in men; He comes to them. Thus life is given to them from time to time, but if God intermits His gift of the Spirit, if the last of those events lies behind them, they can no longer live but only die. In view of these transitory and partial bestowals of the Spirit, the Bible can speak in general of the spirit (*ruah*, πνεῦμα) of man. In practice, this means nothing else but the soul living through the Spirit (*nephesh*, ψυχή). Occasionally the New Testament speaks of the soul of Jesus in this sense. When Jesus sighs or is moved or angered or troubled in spirit, when He commends His spirit into the hands of God (Lk. 23⁴⁶), and when He gives up the spirit (Mt. 27⁵⁰, Jn. 19³⁰), the word "spirit" is used in a general anthropological sense for the word "soul" and does not refer at all (or only indirectly) to the Holy Spirit. For Jesus does not have the Holy Spirit in the way in which it can be said of any man that he has the Spirit. He does not have Him only in virtue of an occasional, transitory and partial bestowal. He could not be without Him, and would thus be subject to death and corruption. Jesus has the Holy Spirit lastingly and totally. He is the man to whom the creative movement of God has come primarily, originally and therefore definitively, who derives in His existence as soul and body from this movement, and for whom to be the "living soul" of an earthly body and earthly body of a "living soul" is not a mere possibility but a most proper reality. He breathes lastingly and totally in the air of the "life-giving Spirit." He not only has the Spirit, but primarily and basically He is Spirit as He is soul and body. For this reason and in this way He lives. This is His absolutely unique relationship to the Holy Spirit.

In the Holy Spirit, God does of course move towards all His creatures in the fulness of His own life. The fact that they live depends upon this movement. In so far as they live at all, they live by the Spirit. For the manner and measure of their life corresponds to the manner and measure in which this movement of God is of benefit to them. It could be of benefit to man as such in the most perfect manner and measure. But of man as we know him it must be said that in fact it is of only transitory and partial benefit to him. Hence his life is only transitory and partial: transitory, since it comes only to go; partial, since death and corruption are always near it. But in Jesus the Evangelists and apostles discovered the new man. That is, they rediscovered the true nature of man. They discovered the man upon whom the Spirit not only descends intermittently and partially but on whom He rests, who does not merely live from the Spirit but in the Spirit. They discovered the spirit of man in which life dwells with the fulness with which it is addressed by God to the creature. In other words, they discovered the man who lives in sovereignty, who has power of Himself to live in likeness to God, from whose life they saw life transmitted to themselves and others—a great limitless world of others—while the source remained quite inexhaustible, for it was the fulness of life which [335] they saw poured out in the middle of the creaturely and human world. Correlative to the affirmation about Jesus the perfect Recipient and Bearer of the Holy Spirit, there is a whole series of New Testament statements which are simply intensive or extensive variations of Jn. 1⁴: "In him (it is the man Jesus to whom the Prologue of the Fourth Gospel also refers) was life." "The life was manifested" (ἐφανερώθη), is how 1 Jn. 1² summarises what the apostles have seen and heard and handled. According to Heb. 7³, Jesus is the prototype of Melchisedec in that He has "neither beginning of days nor end of life"; and according to Heb. 7¹⁶, He is priest "after the power of an endless life" (ζωῆς ἀκαταλύτου). What Jn. 5²⁶ says is specially important in this connexion: "For as the Father hath life in himself (ἐν ἑαυτῷ); so hath he given to the Son to have life in himself " (ἐν ἑαυτῷ). In virtue of this ἐν ἑαυτῷ EN26, we twice have (Jn. 11²⁵; 14⁶) the clear-cut declaration: "I am … the life." Of Him it is said "that God sent his only begotten Son into the world, that we might live through him" (1 Jn. 4⁹); and according to 1 Jn. 5¹², to "have the Son" is equivalent to "have life," and not to have the Son of God is not to have life. For He is the ἀρχηγός EN27 of life (Ac. 3¹⁵). "I am the bread of life" (Jn. 6³⁵). "I live and ye shall live also" (Jn. 14¹⁹). It is especially in the Fourth Gospel that this theme is developed: "I am come that they might have life, and that they might have it more abundantly (καὶ περισσόν, Jn. 10¹⁰). But it is also the general declaration of Paul that "we shall be saved by his life" (Rom. 5¹⁰). Again, it is the personal hope of Paul that the life of the Lord Jesus might be manifested in his body (2 Cor. 4¹⁰). And it is Paul who in this matter coins the strongest metaphor: "Your life is hid with Christ in God. When Christ, who is our life shall appear, then shall ye also appear with him in glory" (Col. 3³); and again, with supreme directness: "For to me to live is Christ" (Phil, 1²¹), and "Christ liveth in me" (Gal. 2²⁰).

From this can be seen what may be called the meaning, the logic and the rationale of the human existence of Jesus. Since according to the New Testament He is as Messiah and Son of God the perfect Recipient and Bearer of the Spirit, and therefore is and has life in its fulness, His life as soul and body is a personal life, permeated and determined by His I, by Himself. The life Which rests on Him is the life which corresponds to that kingly Spirit. It is the life in which the divine βασιλεία EN28 itself is present in creaturely form. It is meaningful for this reason. The saying of Jn. 1¹⁴: "The Word was made flesh, and dwelt among us, and we beheld his glory," must be assessed from this side. What the apostles here found in fulness in a man was significance, meaning, will, purpose, plan and rule. All this in its fulness became flesh. We must not disregard the paradox of this statement on the anthropological side. The word "flesh" is frequently and primarily used in the Bible in the general and neutral sense of human existence or the human mode of being. It can often indicate man or mankind as such. But it undoubtedly has also an evil connotation. It indicates the condition of man in contradiction, in disorder and in consequent sickness, man after Adam's fall, the man who lives a fleeting life in the neighbourhood of death and corruption. Flesh is man, or soul and body, without the Logos. But the New Testament lays weight on the statement that the Logos became flesh. According to 1 Jn. 4¹ᶠ· one recognises the Spirit of God in a Christian and therefore the authenticity of his Christian confession in the very fact that he confesses that

---

EN26 in himself
EN27 author
EN28 kingdom

Jesus Christ is come "in the flesh," while (cf. 2 Jn. 7) in him who denies this there speaks not only an imperfectly Christian spirit but the spirit of Antichrist. Thus the confessional hymn cited in 1 Tim. 3^{16} begins with the words: ὅς ἐφανερώθη ἐν σαρκί^{EN29}. Again, according to Rom. 8^3 God sent His Son—the One who brings life because He Himself is and has it—not in another and better human form but in our own familiar human form and therefore in the

[336] likeness (ἐν ὁμοιώματι) of sinful flesh (σαρκὸς ἁμαρτίας). Again, according to 1 Pet. 4^1 He suffered in the flesh. Again, according to Col. 1^{22} He reconciled us "in the body of his flesh" through His death. Again, according to Eph. 2^{14} He is in His flesh our peace, who made both one and broke down the middle wall of partition, the natural opposition between Israel and the Gentiles. Again, according to Heb. 10^{20} He is in His flesh the parted veil to holiness. Again, according to Lk. 24^{39} He is not a pure spirit even in His resurrection, nor is He merely soul and body, but "flesh and bone"; and in the remarkable statement of Eph. 5^{30} we too, as members of His body, are "of his flesh, and of his bones." This is the case, even though according to 1 Cor. 15^{50} flesh and blood cannot inherit the kingdom of God. Again, according to the particularly impressive passage Jn. 6$^{51f.}$, the true food, the bread of life, which Jesus gives, is His flesh. His flesh must be eaten and His blood drunk by those who are to live through and with Him. This is the case even though according to Jn. 6^{63} it is the Spirit that quickens, while the flesh "profiteth nothing." It is quite evident in all these passages that something happens to the flesh and therefore to the intrinsically more than dubious being of man when the Logos becomes flesh and the human person of Jesus is constituted in this way. Something happens to it here of which otherwise and in itself it is incapable. In the flesh—as He is in the flesh like all of us—something happens for and in the flesh. The flesh, which in itself is disobedient, becomes obedient. The flesh, which in itself profits nothing, becomes a purposeful instrument. The flesh, which in itself is lost, attains a determination and a hope. The flesh, which in itself is illogical and irrational, becomes logical and rational. As the Logos becomes flesh and Jesus is flesh, it is shown that this man has and is spirit and life, and the flesh itself becomes quickening and living and meaningful. In the flesh and for the flesh, words can and must be said and deeds done—words and deeds in which the divine βασιλεία^{EN30} is not only announced but present and effective in the arena of human history: ἐντὸς ὑμῖν^{EN31} (Lk. 17$^{20f.}$), so that every pointer in this or that direction ("lo here! or lo there!") is completely superfluous. In the flesh, defiance is made and an end is put to the contingency, diffusion, emptiness and lostness which are otherwise hopelessly characteristic of the flesh. In the flesh, victory is won, or in positive terms the transformation of the fleshly nature achieved. The flesh now becomes the object and subject of saving passion and action. In the flesh the reconciliation of the flesh is completed. This is the triumph of the meaning of the human existence of Jesus.

And from this standpoint it may be seen and understood how this man as soul and body is a whole, shaped and ordered by and of Himself, and therefore not a chaos but a cosmos. The analogy which inevitably suggests itself here is the event of creation. The logicalising and rationalising, and therefore the formation and ordering, which come on the flesh when the Logos becomes flesh and the Spirit rests upon this man, is and creates something quite new in and out of the flesh. The new subject which flesh now becomes suspends its old predicates and demands and supplies new predicates. And this is just the formation and ordering, of the soul and the body of the man Jesus accomplished by and of itself, the passing of the old and the coming into being of a new form in the flesh. The human existence of Jesus is in its totality the event of this formation and ordering and therefore this conquest and renewal of

---

^{EN29} who was manifest in the flesh
^{EN30} kingdom
^{EN31} in your midst

the flesh, its slaying and displacement in the old form and its quickening and coming to life in a new. The totality of the human existence of Jesus is here concerned. The New Testament knows nothing of a part of the person of Jesus which does not take part in this event. Even His soul, whose various affections we have mentioned, does not live outside this event but in the middle of it. Nor does the New Testament know of a time in Jesus' life when this event is not yet, or as yet only partially, in progress, or when it is visible perhaps only on its negative side. In retrospect the Evangelists took care to show that the "breath of the resurrection" (J. A. Bengel) filled and penetrated the life, words and acts of Jesus even before His resur- [337] rection, and that from the earliest beginnings the quickening and coming to life of the flesh were in full train. The resurrection of Jesus adds nothing new to what happened from the beginning. It only crowns this event as its disclosure and revelation. According to Lk. 24$^{13-35}$, it merely brings the disciples to the point where their sluggish hearts may and must believe and their eyes open upon the totality of the event whose blind witnesses they have hitherto been. It is the totality of the passion and action of which the clarity and glory now overwhelm and are realised by the disciples. This passion and action must be understood in the flesh, as a real event, yet not as a single event or as many single events, but as the totality of the event of the existence of Jesus. It is shown that the Spirit rests upon this man, and that He has and is life in sovereignty, by the fact that through the whole course of His life He is engaged in that passion and action in the flesh. That the Spirit rests upon Him is, of course, His possession and status; it is proper to Him as the Messiah of Israel and Son of God. But even this implies in practice that His whole being consists in the event in which soul and body come into formation and order, in which chaos is left behind and cosmos is realised, and in which the flesh is slain in its old form and is quickened and comes alive in its new—and all this by and from out of itself. Of the incarnation of the Word of God we may truly say both that in the conception of Jesus by the Holy Spirit and His birth of the Virgin Mary it was a completed and perfect fact, yet also that it was continually worked out in His whole existence and is not therefore exhausted in any sense in the special event of Christmas with which it began. The truth conveyed by the first conception is that the formation and ordering of the flesh in the flesh is represented in the New Testament as a procedure which unfolded itself as it did with a necessity originally imposed upon Jesus. "I have meat to eat that ye know not of …. My meat is to do the will of him that sent me, and to finish his work" (Jn. 4$^{32f.}$). "Wist ye not that I must be about my Father's business?" (Lk. 2^{49}). He must work the works of Him that sent Him, while it is day (Jn. 9^4). He must be lifted up from the earth (Jn. 3^{14}; 12^{34}). He must go to Jerusalem, to suffer many things, and be killed, and rise again, as the Synoptic predictions of the passion repeatedly say. This is the necessity of His action given at the beginning in the person of Jesus—the incarnation as an already completed fact. But alongside this we have to set what is said about His freedom: "Therefore doth my Father love me, because I lay down my life, that I might take it again. No man taketh it from me, but I lay it down of myself ($\dot{\alpha}\phi$' $\dot{\epsilon}\mu\alpha\upsilon\tau o\hat{\upsilon}$). I have power ($\dot{\epsilon}\xi o\upsilon\sigma\dot{\iota}\alpha\nu$) to lay it down, and I have power to take it again" (Jn. 10$^{17f.}$). Alongside this we have to set the intentionally revealed and not concealed drama of the temptation at the beginning and Gethsemane at the end of the Synoptic presentation, together with the insufficiently noticed commentary on the latter in Heb. 5$^{7f.}$: "Who in the days of his flesh, when he had offered up prayers and supplications with strong crying and tears unto him that was able to save him from death, and was heard in that he feared; though he were a Son ($\kappa\alpha\dot{\iota}\pi\epsilon\rho$ $\ddot{\omega}\nu$ $\upsilon\dot{\iota}\dot{o}\varsigma$), yet learned he obedience by the things which he suffered ($\ddot{\epsilon}\mu\alpha\theta\epsilon\nu$ $\dot{\alpha}\phi$' $\ddot{\omega}\nu$ $\ddot{\epsilon}\pi\alpha\theta\epsilon\nu$); and being made perfect ($\tau\epsilon\lambda\epsilon\iota\omega\theta\epsilon\dot{\iota}\varsigma$), he became the author of eternal salvation unto all them that obey him." This is clearly the incarnation freely executed. It is to be noted that this aspect is also to be found in the Fourth Gospel, which begins with the ὁ λόγος σὰρξ ἐγένετο[EN32], and that it lays upon Jesus, after He has thirsted and drunk of the hyssop, the final word τετέλεσται[EN33] (Jn. 19³⁰).

We must everywhere reckon with the two dimensions in which this matter is represented in the New Testament. But either way, both in its perfection and its execution, it is a formation accomplished in the flesh and therefore in human nature as it is forfeited and delivered over to death. It is the establishment of an order which is not otherwise proper to this flesh but has been lost in all other men; of an order opposed to the disorder by which human nature in all other men is degraded to mere "flesh." The fact that the Spirit—that kingly Spirit—rests upon Jesus, that He has and is life and that in Him the Logos became flesh, results in a quite specific relationship of His being as soul and body. The oneness and wholeness of His being is not amorphous, nor is it the victim of arbitrariness and contingency. The meeting of "willing spirit" and "weak flesh" (Mt. 26⁴¹) pursues here a victorious course in favour of the Spirit. And this means that the tempter and his temptation to act as the "flesh" or psycho-physical man without the Logos usually does are vanquished by Jesus (Mt. 4³ᶠ·). His food is to do the will of Him that sent Him. He is supremely assaulted in His psycho-physical humanity and therefore as Bearer of our flesh no less at the end than at the beginning of His way. But his prayer concludes, according to Mt. 26³⁹, with the acknowledgment: "Not as I will, but as thou wilt." In the fidelity of the Son towards the Father and therefore in necessary obedience to His own most proper being and therefore in supreme freedom, He gave up Himself according to the passages already quoted, and therefore He gave up His soul and also His body, giving Himself to the service of the mercy of God towards men, and therefore to the cause of the men to whom God in His mercy wished to make Himself serviceable. It is thus that He is in the flesh. It is thus that He is man as soul and body. But the exaltation of the flesh and of the psycho-physical man which takes place in Him means that in Him there is completed an ordering of the relationship of these two moments of His human existence. These two moments are not in opposition. That the soul is opposed to the body and the body to the soul is due to the flesh, to human nature without the Spirit or lacking the Logos, not only in the case where the body triumphs over the soul but also where the soul successfully—or apparently successfully—resists the body. The New Testament contains not the slightest hint of an emancipation of the bodily life of Jesus from the soul nor of an ascetic conflict of the soul of Jesus against the body. The Spirit resting upon Him clearly makes the one impossible and the other superfluous. The exaltation, the logicalising and rationalising of the flesh, which is the mystery of His humanity, does not permit His body to become the enemy and conqueror of His soul; nor does it consist in the soul masquerading as the enemy or conqueror of the body. These two possibilities, all too current amongst us, would presuppose something like the parallelism and rivalry of independent substances contingently and unessentially united into a whole. The flesh that is without the Spirit and stranger to the Logos has, of course, only the choice between these two possibilities. But the spiritual man, Jesus who is life, and the Logos becoming and exalting flesh in Him, is not faced by this choice. And the oneness and wholeness of His humanity forbids us to understand Him from the dualistic standpoint of these alternatives. On the contrary we are confronted by the picture of peace between these two moments of human existence.

This freedom, however, is of such a kind that it contains a first and a second, an upper and a lower, a command and therefore that which controls, an obedience and therefore that which is controlled. The soul is the first and the body the second in this peace—this is the order in this relationship. It presupposes no original separation, and includes not even the most hidden conflict. The superiority of the soul of Jesus is entirely without any flavour of

[338]

[EN32] the Word was made flesh
[EN33] it is finished

pride, scorn or even hidden apprehension or anxiety concerning the body. Hence the inferiority of His body does not mean that it is subjugated and oppressed and therefore engaged in hidden rebellion in which it is necessarily opposed to His soul. We have here no commanding tyrant nor obeying slave, no triumphing conqueror nor sighing victim. There is super- and subordination, but it is an order of peace in which both moments, each in its own place and function, have equal share in the dignity of the whole, which means the dignity of the one man Jesus and therefore in the fulness of the Spirit that rests upon Him and the glory of the Logos incarnate in Him. Yet as this order of peace, it does include superior and [339] inferior. The equal dignity which soul and body have in this man does not exclude but necessarily includes the inequality of position and function. It is not to be forgotten that before publicly entering upon His Messianic office Jesus fasted forty days and nights in the desert (Mt. $4^{1f.}$), though it must be added that He obviously did not repeat this fast and that it was after this fast that the tempter met Him, and not at the marriage at Cana or when He ate and drank with publicans and sinners or even with the scribes and Pharisees. This fast from which Jesus comes in His later course shows manifestly that there is here that which controls and that which is controlled, and not a man who first eats and drinks and then has also all kinds of good things to say and do. There is here a man who has something to say and do and who then and for that reason may and will eat and drink. The incident of Mary and Martha (Lk. $10^{38f.}$), which of course has other dimensions, must be considered here. Mary indeed chose "the good part" because in contrast to Martha she met the real requirement of her guest, not with bodily service, but by sitting listening at His feet. This is the irreversible order within the oneness and wholeness of the man Jesus. His body is the body of His soul, not *vice versa*. His body is in His soul—we have to say this before we can say with right understanding that His soul is in His body. It is thus that He is soul and body. It is thus that He is organised and disposed by the Spirit that rests upon Him. This is life; the life which God breathed into man here now in its original form and fulness; and therefore bodily life. In the being of Jesus presented by the New Testament we look in vain for a moment when His corporeality plays a special and independent role. It is never wanting; it is always present; it is the companion, helper and servant of all His words and acts. In their depiction it is never hidden, but often enough intentionally displayed. He is not His soul alone; nor does He speak and act in a medium indifferent and strange. He is also—as is expressly stated in the accounts of the Last Supper—His body, His flesh and His blood. But His body never plays an independent role, nor does the depiction ever direct special attention upon it. It does not occur to the first or even the second generation of the Church to wish to have a bodily picture of Jesus, though the Evangelist Luke is supposed to have been an artist as well as physician and though Paul himself seems to come very near to the thought when he says that he has painted Jesus Christ the Crucified "before the eyes" of the Galatians (3^1). Jesus spoke and acted and suffered 'in obedience and omnipotence in and not without His body, so that He was also wholly this body. Yet His action and passion are first, *a parte potiori*[EN34], those of His soul, and in that way and on that basis of His body. His body is used and governed by Him for the purpose of a specific and conscious speech and action and suffering. It serves Him in the execution of this purpose. It is impregnated with soul, i.e., a body filled with this consciousness; but we obviously cannot say that his soul is impregnated with body, i.e., a soul filled by the needs and desires of His bodily life. This is the distinction and inequality to be noted within the oneness and the wholeness. The fulfilment, the willing and the execution and therefore the true movement of this body occurs from above downwards, from soul to body and not *vice versa*; not in two opposed lines running parallel and of equal originality; nor in the form of a competitive or even harmonious satisfaction of two different requirements;

[EN34] chiefly

nor in a rotation in which each requirement continuously supersedes and takes up the other. The movement of this life is rather of such a kind that the requirement of the soul, of the Spirit resting upon this man, according to His nature can only be first the requirement of the soul, then being made by the soul the requirement of the body as well, and joyfully and willingly accepted by the body. In this way the body, too, acquires its full and undiminished share in the Spirit that rests upon this man, in the life based on this Spirit, in the glory of the Logos in the flesh, in the dignity of the one man Jesus. All this must naturally be

[340]

applied also to the oneness and wholeness of the work of Jesus and therefore to the relationship between His words and acts. Here too, as we have seen, there is no dualism. The unity of the person of Jesus is reflected intact in the unity of His work also. But here too there is order—superiority and inferiority. The Word leads; the sign follows. The Word affirms; the sign confirms. The Word is the light; the sign its shining. The two cannot be separated; but they are to be seen in this relationship to one another. It was a serious if not perverse thing if people were always wanting a sign before they believed (Mt. 12^{39}; Jn. 4^{48} &c.); yet this is never said of those who wished to hear His word. Similarly, the account of Jesus' stay in Nazareth (Mt. 13^{58}), that He could not do many works there because of their unbelief, has no parallel in a corresponding statement concerning the proclamation of Jesus. It is never said that His mighty works were wholly suspended, but only that on occasion they could retire into the background, and apparently did so frequently. But His proclamation can neither cease nor retire. Jesus spoke even when He was silent before the high-priests (Mt. 26^{63}) and Pilate (Mt. 27^{14}), the high-priests and Pilate themselves involuntarily undertaking the task of expressing the truth. The Word is the proper revealing movement of His work, the act the confirmatory. The act never occurs alone and for itself or for its own sake. It can only be misunderstood, if considered, desired or admired for itself. It is produced by the power of the Word. Indirectly it is itself Word, *verbum visibile*[EN35]; and it wills to be accepted as such. But one could not say that Jesus' Word is the *signum audibile*[EN36]. Within the unity of His work, and without breaking the unity, there is a precedence, because it is an ordered unity. It is no chance that He who is at work here is called *a parte potiori*[EN37] the Logos and not the *dynamis* of God, though there can be no doubt that He is the latter as well. Here, too, the movement is from above to below, from the word to the act, and not *vice versa*. Similarly, the preaching and healing of Jesus are not two activities which, because they are both laudable and excellent, are contingently co-ordinated and harmonised in Him, though in themselves they have different origins and purposes. Here again there is a firm leading and following in which preaching leads and healing—inevitably and as necessary complement—follows, being comprised in the activity of the Prophet and Teacher Jesus, nourished from the origin of this work and serviceable to its purpose. In this order the work as well as the person of Jesus is fashioned into a whole.

Summarising, we may say that Jesus is true man in the sense that He is whole man, a meaningfully ordered unity of soul and body. That His human existence unfolds in these two moments—not in one only, but also in the other—is as visible in Him as it can possibly be. But there is lacking in Him all cleavage between the moments, and to that extent the problem of their relationship is resolved; so much so that one might miss the reality of their difference. Yet it must also be said that their difference is seen particularly in the person of Jesus in the sense that their relationship emerges in Him as a clarified relationship

---

[EN35] visible word
[EN36] audible sign
[EN37] chiefly

and human existence in these two moments as one which is cosmically fashioned.

All this cannot be stated without looking beyond this human existence as such. Guided by the New Testament, we must think of the Holy Spirit, and more especially of the presence and efficacy of the Holy Spirit, if we would give an account of the special constitution of this man. This immediately reminds us of the supreme particularity that this true man is primarily and at the same time the true God Himself. It is in this way, this higher unity of His existence with that of God Himself, that He is whole man, a meaningfully ordered unity of soul and body. Can we disregard or fail to note that the constitution of His being as man is a repetition, imitation and correlation of the relationship in which He is primarily and at the same time true God and as such also true man? Soul and body are clearly related to one another in the man Jesus, as His being as Son and Word of God the Creator is related to His creaturely constitution as soul and body of this man. It is with a relationship in absolute totality of these two moments that we have to do primarily and basically in this higher sphere by which the lower is transcended and enveloped. The two moments are indestructibly different even on this higher level, for it is a matter of divinity and humanity. But abstractions and separations are impossible. In the place of man stands the One who is God Himself in man; and in the place of God stands the same One who is man in Jesus. And in this wholeness and oneness the relationship of God and man, of man and God, in Jesus is itself a meaningfully ordered relation. Here already there manifestly operate superior and inferior, lordship and service, command and obedience, leadership and following—and this in a constant and irreversible relation. We can have no more than an analogy. The soul of Jesus is not His divinity, but only comparable with it in its function within His being as man. And His body is not His humanity, but only comparable with it (in His totality of soul and body) within His humanity. It is only in the same proportions that divinity and humanity confront one another on the higher and the soul and body of Jesus on the lower level. But the power and necessity in which Jesus is whole man are not grounded in themselves but in the fact that He is primarily and at the same time true God and true man. We have seen that they are the power and necessity of the Holy Spirit resting upon Him. It is because He is the Son and Word of God that the Holy Spirit rests upon Him, and that He exists in the fulness of the Holy Spirit, and that He is whole man in a meaningfully ordered unity of soul and body. This foundation, this relationship of Giver and gift, even of Creator and creature, is not reversible. Hence the disparity of the two relationships, and the fact that we cannot have here more than an analogy. But that there is an analogy may be neither overlooked nor denied. It shows us that in this question we do not stand on the periphery but in closest proximity to the theological centre.

We can realise that this is so at a second point of which we are just as immediately reminded by the special constitution of the human being of Jesus. The

[341]

relationship between soul and body in Jesus is also, and exegetically much more obviously, comparable with the relationship between Him and His community. It is no accident that Paul indicates and describes the community as [342] the "body" of Jesus and Jesus in His relationship to it as its "Head." If in the relationship between God and man in the person of Jesus we can speak of a comparison upwards, so here we can speak of a comparison downwards. The soul and body of Jesus are here primary, original and basic. Since He exists as man in that ordered wholeness, He anticipates in a measure in His person the relationship in which He is the Lord in the midst of His disciples and those who are called by them. Soul and body are related to one another in Him as He Himself as Prophet, Priest and King is related to the company of those who, in His person reconciled with God, are children of God for His sake, and by faith in Him are aware of this benefit and grateful for it, and have become His witnesses. Between Him and them, too, there is a complete relationship. But it is not accidental, dissoluble, nor amenable to abstractions. Jesus Christ exists in the founding and upbuilding of His community; His community exists as it is founded and built up by Him. A Christ without His community would be a figment of the imagination, and even more so a community without Christ. The one divine act of election is the election of this head and this body. As Jesus' soul and body are inseparably one, so are He and His people. And as order rules in the one case, so also in the other. The disciples cannot be above their Master, but the Master will be to all eternity above His disciples. The Head is always the Head. The body is always the body. Where Christ does not rule, the body is dead, just as the body without soul can only be dead. But where the body is alive it is obedient to Christ, just as the living body will necessarily serve the soul. Here, too, the relationship is irreversible. Christ is the primary form of this wholeness, Christendom the secondary, and not *vice versa*. Again, we have only an analogy. Perfect similarity is not to be expected between the relationships compared. As Paul named Him the "Head," so in the same fashion He may be regarded as the soul of His community. But this is preceded by the fact that in His own person He is soul and body. And the latter is the original and higher sphere. The one beloved Son of God, in whom men are the object of divine election, is first and foremost the man Jesus for Himself, and only then, through Him and in Him, others. And as the Holy Spirit rests upon Him, He will be directed and poured out upon them also, as the Holy Spirit of the community of the many towards whom God willed to reveal and direct His love in Him and through Him. That He is theirs and they His is primarily and basically effective and necessary in the fact that He is this whole man in the meaningfully ordered unity of His soul and His body. The whole meaning and soundness of the secondary and lower relationship depends on the existence and order of the primary and higher. To this extent there is here not only similarity but also dissimilarity. To this extent there is really only repe- [343] tition, imitation and correspondence. That this is so here too must not be overlooked or disregarded. We can and must look both upwards and down-

136

wards from the structure of the human existence of Jesus—upwards to the mystery of His being with God and downwards to the no less mystery of His being with men. It is no accident that here too, for all the other differences, the proportions are the same.

We refrain from any detailed account of the more distant analogies, some more and some less exact, which might be discerned on this basis. They need only be named. It is not impossible, and even in different degrees promising and fruitful, to ask whether the soul and body of Jesus might not be related to one another like heaven and earth in the totality of creation; or justification and sanctification in the atoning work of Christ; or Law and Gospel in the Word of God; or faith and works in the human response to God; or preaching and sacrament in the divine service of the community; or the confessional formula and the corresponding attitude and action in its confession; or Church and state in the inner articulation of the kingdom of Christ. The mere enumeration may arouse reflection. Since the revealed truth and reality of God and His covenant of grace is single, we cannot wonder if even formally its individual elements obviously stand in a certain connexion, as appears in these analogies. Again, we are certainly not required either to systematise this formal connexion or to discern it everywhere. There are important points of Christian knowledge where we cannot speak of such analogy and where only a combination of lack of taste and direct error would try to discover it. For example, there is no totality in which the Creator and the creature in general, or in which the freedom and initiative of God and of man, are so unified as are the soul and body of Jesus. Similarly, the meaningful order of these two elements in the existence of Jesus has no analogy in the relationship between the grace of God and the sin of man, since we can understand the latter only as the relationship of exclusive opposites. We have good reason, therefore, to refrain from an indiscriminate pursuit of analogies. And even where we may speak of real analogies to the constitution of the humanity of Jesus, in each case we must consider whether and how far the points concerned may be brought into mutual relationship, in cross connexions. At this point no certain conclusions result from logical possibilities alone. For theological truths and relationships of truth have in their own place and way their own worth and fulness, the light of which can be increased but may also be easily diminished when they are set in relation to others. In no case can they be treated as the implications of a single formal principle or brought under a single denominator. We content ourselves, therefore, with the two really close comparisons which we have unfolded. The soul and body of Jesus are mutually related to one another as are God and man in His person, and Himself and His community. These two [344] comparisons are important enough to show us what had to be shown, namely, that with our knowledge of Jesus as the whole man we find ourselves at the centre of all Christian knowledge.

The reason why we have taken trouble over the knowledge of the constitution of the human existence of Jesus is that for all theological knowledge of man as such we must begin with the picture of this man. It is here that the decision must be taken about the true constitution of man. Totality in the meaningful order of his humanity will certainly not be found in man in general and as such. But we do at any rate know in what direction we must look in the general question which occupies us. The only understanding possible for us is one in which this wholeness and its orderliness form the unchangeable standpoint. The picture of the man Jesus demands an understanding of man which is controlled from this standpoint. It protests against an understanding of man which leaves this standpoint out of account or neglected. Thus it is the norm with which we again approach our true task, the anthropological.

2. THE SPIRIT AS BASIS OF SOUL AND BODY

Man exists because he has spirit. That he has spirit means that he is grounded, constituted and maintained by God as the soul of his body. In the briefest formula, this is the basic anthropological insight with which we have to start.

Man is not God. God is the Creator of man. Man is God's creature. It is God's gift to man that he is man and not something else, and that he is and is not. Man owes it to God that he is man and not something else, and that he is and is not not. This distinction is for man irremovable. For God it is not irremovable. In the existence of the man Jesus, He has in fact removed it. He, the Creator, has become creature. But for man this distinction is irremovable. It is of his essence to be creature—the creature which as such can neither be nor become the Creator. It is of his essence not to be God. We must begin with this negative statement, with the affirmation of this limitation of man, if we are now to establish and describe his constitution.

The very basis of this negative statement compels us at once to formulate in provisionally negative form the supplementary statement that man is not without God. Since he owes it to God that he is and that he is man, how can he be without God who gives him both? The being of man is from its very origin and basis a being with God, because man is made and determined for covenant with God. But the statement that man is not without God belongs also to the [345] climax of our present description of the constitution of the being of man. When we say "man" or "soul and body," then wittingly or unwittingly we have first said "God." From our standpoint, in our attempt at theological anthropology, we have to know that we have first said God when we say man. There can thus be no question of revising or reducing our first statement that man is not God. God does not in any sense belong to the constitution of man. God is neither a part nor the whole of human nature. He is identical neither with one of the elements of which in unity and order we are composed, nor with us ourselves. But the whole which we are in this unity and order is not without

God. In abstraction from the fact that this being is not without God, we should not really know ourselves as the being which we thought we knew as a specific unity and ordering of soul and body, and we should be reckoning with a fanciful picture which would render us as such unknowable. That this being is no fanciful picture, that man really is, is ontically and therefore noetically dependent on the fact that he is not without God. Man without God is not; he has neither being nor existence. And man without God is not an object of knowledge. Again, the fact that he is not without God is not a supplementary, optional or purely historical determination of his constitution which might well be lacking according to his decision, or according to his positive or negative formulation of his relation to God, so that provisionally at least it might be disregarded in describing his constitution. That man is not without God has nothing to do with the religious convictions or behaviour in which he in some measure gives or does not give honour to God. Even the error of a theoretical, practical or methodical atheism in his self-knowledge can do nothing to alter the fact that he is not without God. This error can only mean that he unwittingly regards himself as not being, and therefore renders basically questionable not only his atheistic decision but also his self-knowledge. He may undertake and do this. Yet even so he is not without God. Man cannot escape God, because he always derives from Him. This is the negative form of the basic statement with which we must begin our description of the constitution of man. Man as soul and body is in no case so made that he is simply there, as though self-grounded, self-based, self-constituted and self-maintained. His constitution is in no case that of a first and last reality; nor is it one which enables and empowers him to understand himself by himself, or to hold the criteria of his own perception and thought, however he may define them, as standards by the help of which he can, secluded in himself, arrive at the core of the matter. As he is not without God, he cannot understand himself without God.

It is clear that we must here depart from the way taken by the anthropology which sets itself the aim of understanding man without God. It is of the essence of every non-theological anthropology to set itself some such aim. Of course, it is not essential that this aim be set absolutely and so be intended in the sense of atheistic dogma. It can be intended [346] only hypothetically. It can deliberately leave open the first and last question concerning the constitution of man. In some circumstances it can even work alongside theology with a more or less concealed or open affinity. But so far as it does not do this, but remains firmly on its own ground, it must seek to understand man primarily without God, as though he were a first and last reality, as though he were in a position to understand himself of himself, as though the criteria of human perception and thought were the standard with whose application alone a knowledge or an adequate knowledge can be founded. It is this "as though" that distinguishes the non-theological from the theological knowledge of man. We have neither to criticise nor to vindicate this non-theological understanding of man here. So far as it conceives its aim atheistically, it rests on a plain error which necessarily involves it in other errors; but this is a separate question. So far as it conceives it only relatively, it has in its restricted place its own right and responsibility, to which we can only desire that it may attend firmly and therefore, for the sake of assurance, without direct theological ties. But from the point of view of our responsibility we can neither accept this "as though" nor be content with the corresponding inquiry. We cannot try to understand man even hypothetically without God in order to find out whether the last word in the matter is an open question, or a statement borrowed from theology, or perhaps atheistic dogma. On the contrary, we must advance from the starting-point that man is not to be understood without God. If theological anthropology renounced this statement, it would surrender itself along with its object and theme; and when it later reverted to the question of God it would be of no interest to non-theological science. But in any case, whether we find the others interesting or not, we ourselves must follow our own way in this matter.

The negative formula "not without God" is not of course adequate in itself. We shall now state the same thing positively: Man exists as he is grounded, constituted and maintained by God. God is not, we remember, a higher or highest being with certain personal or impersonal physical and moral attributes and properties appropriate in our estimation and opinion to his eminence. God is He who has revealed Himself in His eternal Word in time as the true and merciful Lord of man. God is the Creator who has maintained and fulfilled His covenant with man by Himself becoming a human creature in Jesus Christ and giving Himself up for us. God is the God of Israel, besides whom is no other, and measured by whom every other is a trivial fabrication. Our first statement concerning the constitution of man is that he is not without this God who is true, not because we regard Him as such, but because He has proved and expressed and manifested Himself as such. And now we make the positive statement that man exists as he is grounded, constituted and maintained by this God. He is, i.e., he is this human being and has existence in this being, as he is from this God. There is no other possibility. This cannot be an open question, for we come from a beginning where the answer is that there are no possibilities. Man cannot even be of and by himself—our starting-point precludes this too. Again, he cannot derive from a high or highest being whose existence must be the basis of ours as we ourselves direct. Our starting-point, the human nature of Jesus, forbids us at this point to look to any kind of a [347] height selected and adorned by ourselves. Man is from the God whom the man Jesus called His Father and whose Son He called Himself.

"In him we live, and move, and have our being," and "we are also his offspring" (Ac. 17^{28}). In this verse Paul made use of heathen wisdom, but he immediately gave it a Christian sense and thus in a sense baptised it. He, whom Paul proclaimed to the Athenians in these words which had once been heathen, but in his mouth were so no longer, is undoubtedly neither the classical Zeus nor Hellenistic fate. He is rather the One who has disregarded the "times of ignorance" as a world of shadows, and who calls men to repentance by causing a day of judgment to dawn, setting a Judge upon the throne, and demanding faith in Him who is raised from the dead. He is the "unknown God" to whom in their ignorance they accorded their religious worship. He is the Creator of the cosmos. He is the Lord of human history, and His object is that they might "feel after and find" Him on the far side of all man's faith, heresy, superstition and unbelief. He, this God! This is the missionary message of Paul (Ac. $17^{22f.}$). It does not really link up with anything. It immediately sets up the new in the place of the old. But it sets this new as such immediately behind and above the man who is

140

imprisoned in the old. It releases him directly from this imprisonment and places him directly in freedom. It speaks of the God whom even in his imprisonment man did not and never will escape. It takes the imprisonment of man seriously only as his impotent attempt to escape this God, whom he can only confirm as his origin with this attempt.

Just as man is distinguished from the rest of the created world by the fact that, as the likeness and promise of the divine covenant of grace, he is called to responsibility before God, so his special constitution corresponding to this calling is determined by the fact that he owes it to the God who is the Lord of this covenant of grace. This God as such is also the Creator of man. This God as such gives him his creatureliness. This God as such establishes him as soul and body, constituting the unity and order of this being, and maintaining him in this being in its unity and order. Because He is this God in the constitution of man we have to do with an unshakeable but also a saving fact. Since his constitution derives from this God, from Him who is faithful and does not repent of His goodness, it is therefore unshakeable. It can, of course, be disturbed and perverted by human sin, but it cannot be destroyed or rendered nugatory. Hence man remains man even in his deepest fall, even in the last judgment of death; and even in death he is still man within the hand and power of God. In no case, therefore, does He become another being, a being which is deprived of the promise of the covenant of grace and cannot even in death and hell appeal to this covenant. And since the constitution of man is from God, it is a saving fact. For from its origin from God, like the being of man as man and woman, it has an inner relation to God's turning towards man and to the salvation which God intends for him; for man cannot be what he is, soul and body in ordered unity, without representing in himself—long before he understands it, and even when he will not understand it—the good intention of God towards him, without himself being guarantor for this good intention of God.

We must look closer at the matter. This God grounds, constitutes and main- [348] tains man's constitution. From Him man is, and his being and his existence are. When we say this, we do not describe a property of man. Otherwise the fact that he is from this God would be a kind of element in his constitution as such. But it is not "natural" to him in this sense. What we describe is a transcendental determination of the human constitution, an action and operation of the God who is free in relation to man. That man is from God and is grounded, constituted and maintained by Him, is an event which is willed, decided and effected by God. It is always on the basis of this act of God, and therefore not on the basis of a potency conceded to him by God, nor of a kind of fixed relation of God to him, that man is. He comes to be grounded, constituted and maintained. This must continually take place anew—every morning, every moment. This God is and acts in this way. He does it as the living God. Here, too, it is important not to interchange the God from whom man is with any high or highest being. What value would this have? For the determination of man by another supposed higher being would be described in the end only as a fixed relation and therefore ultimately only as a human property. But the God of Israel, the Father of Jesus Christ, is the Creator whose mercy is new every morning. That He has made man does not mean that He has ceased to make him. It means rather that God has made him the being who in an ever new act of divine creation is to be again based, again constituted and again maintained—the being over against whom, even when He ceases to do this and therefore in death, there stands the God who is able to do this and from whom such action is to be expected. Man is, as God is in this living way his active basis. And since God is this living and active basis of man, He is and always is the hope of man, even when He will no longer grant him his being. We cannot avoid considering at this point the possibility of human death. The idea of the living God from whom man is, and the idea of His action in which this becomes true, would otherwise be incomplete. This action of God is a free action. This alone distinguishes it from a continuing and fixed relation, and from the operations customarily ascribed to a superior being. God is not obliged to act in this way. It is His gift. It is grace which He shows to man but does not owe to man; grace by which He binds us but not Himself. This is revealed in human death. He is still the God from whom man is, even when He lets man die. Thus in death and above death, He is still the hope of man. He is the one hope of man, not only in his death—for death only discloses the fact— but in his life. Even in life, man is wholly dependent upon the living God causing His livingness to benefit him, upon this God willing him and thus newly confirming, newly basing, newly constituting, and newly maintaining him in his constitution as soul and body. He must and would perish immedi- [349] ately, hopelessly and eternally, if God ceased to be for him this living God, from whom he may expect that He will continually act on him accordingly.

Man lives and dies in the event of the livingness of God. In this event he is created. In this event he is what he is by nature: soul and body in ordered unity. In this event and not otherwise! He would not be created by and for the grace of God His Creator, if it were otherwise. He is, then, in virtue of the fact that God relates Himself to him in the event of this act. He lives, as the living God lives also and precisely for him, for his benefit and advantage. It is to be noted that we speak now of man's natural condition, of his human existence and of his being in this existence. Of this already, of this creatureliness of his, it must also be laid down that man is, as God is for him. The same thing can and must be said word for word of the historical standing of man in covenant with God which is grounded along with his being and his existence, of his being called by grace to gratitude. He is made for this historical standing. This is man's determination. And it cannot be otherwise than that his creatureliness in its fundamental determination must correspond to this historical standing of his. He will be in this standing only as God is for him. And this is how the matter stands already in the natural condition presupposed in the historical standing. It is of this we now speak. Already in it he is not apart from but by God's grace on the ground of this divine attitude to him. He is determined for this historical standing in his natural condition, and indeed in its determinative ground of his being or non-being. He is determined by the one grace, that of his creation, for the other grace, that of the covenant; and he is referred by the one to the other. As he is what he is, and as he is and is not not, he is on the way which has only this objective, which as he goes this way he cannot miss. This way is really his way, and this objective really his objective. No other way and no other objective is possible for him. The whence that is most properly his, his creatureliness, permits him no other whither.

We now take a further step. Man is, as he is grounded, constituted and maintained by God as soul of his body. With the expression "soul of his body," we affirm first of all that he is at all events one who also belongs to the visible, outward, earthly world of bodies. Like land and sea and plants and animals, he is also in space. He himself is also an individual being, distinguished from others and isolated in his particular space. He is also a visible form. He is also earthly and therefore material. To be man is not only to be soul in a particular spatial body, but to be soul of one such spatial body, and therefore to be wholly bound to it, to be one with it, and therefore to belong with it to the visible, outward, earthly world of bodies, to be with it in space, to be a being particularly limited in space, a being which with it is visibly shaped and material. He is soul of a material body. But we must be more precise and add at once that he is soul of a physical body. A physical body is also a material body. A physical body [350] is an organic material body, which as such, i.e., to make possible and to realise its organic being and existence, is dependent upon having life. Without life, it can only decay even as material body, necessarily losing its special being and existence over against the other material bodies with their being and their existence which surround it in space. Without life, it cannot begin to enter upon its special being and existence at all. Man is soul of such a material body—one which is organic in its being and exists organically, and is thus dependent upon the reception and possession of life.

To call man "soul" is simply to say in the first place that he is the life which is essentially necessary for his body. This is not to be understood as if first of all he were simply life for itself, which as such had a being and existence beside and outside his body and then entered it as its life, yet all the time continued its own being and existence as well and finally perhaps left it without losing this being and existence. No; man is the life of this body of his. This body itself is not any body, but his body. If it were not his body, the body whose life he is, it would not be body. It could then at once be only decaying material body; it could never achieve being and existence even as material body. What this material body is, and the fact that it is, depends on the fact that it is alive. Man is as his material body is *alive* and therefore physical body. The converse must also be viewed and stated—that he is, as his *material body* is alive. He is neither before nor beside nor after his material body. He is the life of his physical body, not a life in itself, and not a life hovering freely over his body or dwelling in it only incidentally. This is what we mean when we describe man as soul. This is all we can mean. The statement that "man is soul" would be without meaning if we did not immediately enlarge and expound it: Soul of one body, i.e., his body. He is soul as he is a body and this is his body. Hence he is not only soul that "has" a body which perhaps it might not have, but he is bodily soul, as he is also besouled body.

Both concepts are analytical. Soul would not be soul, if it were not bodily; and body would not be body, if it were not besouled. We are not free to make abstractions here, either on one side or the other. When we say that man is the life or soul of his body, this naturally means that he not only belongs to the material world and therefore that he is not only in space and himself spatial, that he not only partakes of earthly material being and an earthly material manner of existence. If he is life or soul—and he would not be body, unless he were life or soul—it is implied that he is essentially and existentially in time as well, that he is not only visible but also invisible, not only outward but also inward, not only earthly but also heavenly. When we use the latter term in this connexion, we remember that as it is used in the Bible "heavenly" does not [351] mean "divine," but merely refers to the higher, upper, inapprehensible side of the whole of created reality. "Soul" is a determination of earthly being. As it can only be the soul of a physical and therefore a material body, from which it cannot be parted, this settles the fact that man belongs to the earth and therefore to the lower side of created reality, but not in such a way that he does not in virtue of his decisive determination—he is *soul* of his body—partake of the invisibility of created reality in the midst of the visibility, and of the being of heaven even as a being which is wholly of earth. Since he is soul of his *body*, he is the earthly representation of that above and below of a world totality. That he is the *soul* of his body decides the fact that he cannot fall victim to his spatiality, visibility and materiality even though he is bound to it, and that the boundary they impose on him is not a prison but a significant and ordered economy. Since he is besouled body and bodily soul and no abstraction is possible, since he lives and partakes of the heavenly side of the cosmos, but also lives bodily and therefore has an indissoluble part in the bodily world, since as soul of his body he is that earthly representation of the whole of created reality, he necessarily stands even as body in clear relation to its higher, invisible and inner side. He could not be living body, or the connexion between body and life could not be indissoluble, if in its unity his body did not also stand in this relation to the upper cosmos—and this without ceasing to be material body. Naturally this could not be said if it were only material body. But in fact it can be material body only in such a way as to have life; and as physical body, and therefore living material body, it is not merely material body but besouled body. But if it is besouled, to that extent it too, and therefore the whole man, stands in that relation to the upper cosmos and is thus a representation of the whole cosmos.

We must develop and expound in even greater detail the view and concept: "man as soul of his body." And first our attention is claimed by the fact that it is by the free act of God that man is grounded, constituted and maintained as soul of his body. In and of himself he cannot be soul and body and soul of his body. That he is so is based upon God's free creative grace through which he is prepared and equipped for his historical standing in the covenant with Him and in which the grace of the covenant is reflected and announced. That man may be soul of his body, and therefore belong even to space and the material world, is above all God's free act of grace. We say expressly "may." Space and the material world are the outer and substantial and therefore the lower side of the cosmos, but this does not mean that they are a worse side. They do not mean bondage for the soul. It would be real bondage for the soul in the biblical sense to be in a condition in which there is no being in space and the material world, but it is left or becomes bodiless. In its way, earth is no less the [352] Lord's than heaven. That man is soul of his *body* is a divine favour which in its way is no less indispensable for the constitution of man as he is than the fact that he is the *soul* of his body. On this fact that he is soul of his body is dependent nothing less than the reality of his being and existence. If he were not body, he could be only a shadow and less than a shadow. That God has willed it otherwise is not at all to be regarded and construed as a kind of disadvantage or *pudendum*EN38 for human existence, for example in contrast to that of the angels. This would be to forget that God has set man high above the angels in the very fact that it is man and not the angels whom He has determined to be His covenant-partner. But in respect of his human constitution, it belongs to his covenant-partnership that man is a representation of the whole of created reality, so that he partakes fully and seriously of the material side, and therefore is not only soul but soul of a body. This is to be understood as God's free unmerited act of grace. He could and can withhold from him that which He bestows with it: He is under no obligation to will to have him and to prepare him as a covenent-partner. He could quite well be content to survey His heavenly and earthly cosmos without choosing and preparing man to represent the whole. No one has any claim to be this wonderful thing, man. And God could and can take back from man what He has given him by willing and making him soul of his body. What is death, if not at least the threat of a bodiless life, a life-negating life? It is at any rate the impressive reminder that even as body man does not belong to himself. Even as bodily, life is a matter which does not rest in our hands, but in the hand of God. This is applicable not only to material bodiliness, but also to physical bodiliness and therefore to living bodiliness. The benefit of creation consists in the fact that man may be the soul of his body, that as a living material body he is not restricted to space and the world of bodies, but may also be and exist temporally and belong to the invisible upper cosmos. He thus is in the twofold mystery that he lives as a bodily organism, and that his bodily organism is ordained to be the bearer and the expression of his life. He is, as he is material body in this invisible, inner, heavenly

---

EN38 embarrassment

145

relation. Even this he does not assume to himself; in this too we have the event of a created reality which is every moment wonderful. If it takes place he lives: not merely his bodily organism with its functions, but he himself in and with and yet independent of it and its functions; he himself as the subject and form of its inner and outer experiences; he himself as the subject and form of specific apprehensions, thoughts, sensations, feelings, purposes and endeavours which are more or less bound up with these experiences. If that event takes place, then he is in the bodily world and his own material body in such a way that, while identical with it, he also oversees, knows, uses and controls, in short,

[353] possesses it, so that he himself is superior to it and thus far to himself. Life is life of the body, and while it is this it is more than this. Life is to be subject and form; it is freedom, apprehension and control of the body. If man is the soul of his body, this does not mean that his soul belongs to a body, but that his body belongs to him, to his soul. As soul of his body, man is obviously heavenly as he is earthly.

But what do we mean when we say "he is" and "he lives"? That he "lives" his life obviously cannot mean that he takes and gives himself life from somewhere, or that he makes his material body and therefore himself living and besouled and thus a physical body, his own body supervised, known, used, controlled and possessed by him. That he is soul and therefore subject and form of a body, and thus belongs not only to the lower but also to the upper cosmos, is something which clearly demands an event over whose occurrence he has no control. The reality of his being and existence depends upon this event taking place; and on it there also depends the call of God and self-knowledge and response as His creature. In this event it becomes possible for him to meet the divine person as person, to be a covenant-partner, if God wills and institutes this covenant. But as this fundamental event of his quickening takes place, and therefore in every moment of his life before God, and indeed before the free unmerited act of grace of God the Creator, he is wholly and exclusively dependent on this act happening to him and on the living God being afresh his Quickener and dealing with him as such. As he really lives, and is thus soul of his body, he is always and immediately of God. If he were not of God, he would not be. And if God were to withdraw what He alone can and does give in this event, not only would his body sink back to the status of a purely material body, to rise and disintegrate even as a material body in the surrounding world of all other bodies, but he himself would necessarily become a shadow and less than a shadow, a departed soul which once was but now has been, an extinct life. He would then no longer be God's covenant-partner, nor see God's face, nor receive the grace of this covenant. And if then God should objectively cease to hear or see the one who no longer sees Him, if He should cease even to be his God, the God of this man who no longer exists (for it is also possible that He will not cease to be his God and so his hope), he would not only be lost, but lost eternally. To live and thus to be soul of his body means on this side of death to be warned against, and on the other side of death to be delivered from, this lostness. And it is God Himself and God alone who can both warn and deliver; for He alone is the source of life. His act alone is the event in which the reality of human being and human existence, the soul of the body, can arise and remain.

This is the statement with which our description of the constitution of man must begin and which is indispensable for all that follows. We have not yet [354] expressed it in the form in which it is recognisable as an anthropological statement and therefore useful as a presupposition for other anthropological statements. We repeat and expound all we have hitherto said if we introduce a concept which we earlier saw to be fundamental for an analysis of the human nature of Jesus—the concept of spirit. Man is not without God but by and from God—by and from the God of Israel and His ever new act of grace. In this way alone is he soul of his body. This can and must now be summarised in the single brief statement that man is as he has spirit. This is the form of expression which is now necessary: man *has* spirit. It is, of course, a form which itself requires explanation. We can and must say of man that he is soul; and from this we go on to say that he is body. But we cannot simply say that he is spirit. This would be to obscure the nature of the spirit as that of man. It would be to miss the very thing which we are trying to say when we describe the constitution of man in terms of spirit.

To call man spirit whether "created" or "ultimate," as modern theology likes to do, especially in the school of Hegel, always involves at least an indirect identification of man with God, or must sooner or later lead to such an identification. That man is spirit could be rightly said only in so far as he is soul and therefore also body in virtue of spirit, a spiritual soul and to that extent also a spiritual body. Man himself cannot be characterised as spirit because in the Bible spirit denotes what God Himself is and does for man, man himself being identified with the fact that he is soul (of his body).

Man has spirit. By putting it in this way we describe the spirit as something that comes to man, something not essentially his own but to be received and actually received by him, something that totally limits his constitution and thus totally determines it. As he is man and soul of his body, he has spirit. We must perhaps be more precise and say that he is, as the spirit has him. Man has spirit, as one who is possessed by it. Although it belongs to the constitution of man, it is not, like soul and body and as a third thing alongside them, a moment of his constitution as such. It belongs to his constitution in so far as it is its superior, determining and limiting basis.

It is to be noted that according to Mt. 27^{50} Jesus "yielded up" His spirit; that according to Lk. 23^{46} He commended it into His Father's hands; and that according to the passages adduced earlier He gives His soul or His body and either way Himself for others, but not His spirit. Here His spirit is not Himself; nor can it be at His disposal or be given for others. The body can be killed and die; and the soul can be committed to eternal loss in hell by the One whose right it is to do this, namely, God (Mt. 10^{28}); it can be "given in exchange" (Mt. 16^{26}); and it can be lost (Mt. 10^{39}). This happens to what man is. But it cannot happen to the spirit which man has as he is man. On the contrary, it is of the very essence of the spirit to prevent

[355]

this happening to man, so far and so long as man has it. This can happen to man only at the time and with the consequence that he ceases to have spirit. Death is equivalent to absence of spirit. As the spirit makes of man an embodied soul and a besouled body, so the absence of spirit makes of him a bodiless soul and a soulless body. The spirit is immortal. For this reason it can be identical neither with the man nor with a part of the being of man. The spirit is the basis and the determination of the limit of the whole man; and in so far it belongs to his constitution and is thus no third thing in man and no further moment of his constitution additional to soul and body.

We have thus to consent to the decision which the Early Church took against the so-called trichotomism espoused by Philo, by Apollinaris of Laodicea in the Christological conflict of the fourth century and by the Arab philosophers in the Middle Ages. It is another matter that there is no necessary reference to parts. We could not speak of three sides or moments of the one human reality. It is soul and it is body, but it is not spirit. Yet it is soul and body as spirit comes to it, as it receives and has spirit, as spirit has it and will not leave it, but grounds, determines and limits it. The only biblical passage which can be regarded as ambiguous in this regard is 1 Thess. 5²³: "And the very God of peace sanctify you wholly; and I pray God your whole spirit and soul and body be preserved blameless unto the coming of our Lord Jesus Christ." It must be admitted that this passage sounds difficult, because of the only slightly differentiated conjunction of the three ideas, and even more because of the circumstances that Paul seems to describe the spirit as also in need of preservation and therefore as not per se completely preserved. Calvin (*Comm. ad loc.*, C.R. 30, 179) is certainly right when in this connexion he declines to understand by "soul" the *motus vitalis*[EN39] (the natural movement of life), and by "spirit" the *pars hominis renovata: atqui tunc absurda esset Pauli precatio*[EN40]. His own view is that "spirit" here means the *ratio vel intelligentia*[EN41], and "soul" the *voluntas et omnes affectus*[EN42]. This yields good sense: *tunc enim purus et integer est homo, si nihil mente cogitat, nihil corde appetit, nihil corpore exsequitur, nisi quod probatur Deo*[EN43]. But we have to confess that neither in text nor context is there any support for this meaning. The slight differentiation of "spirit" in relation to soul and body must be regarded as decisive, for if "spirit" really denotes a third thing beside soul and body the passage is isolated not only in Paul but in the rest of the Old and New Testaments. For example, when Lk. 1⁴⁶ᶠ· says of Mary: "My soul doth magnify the Lord, and my spirit hath rejoiced in God my Saviour," we do not have a double statement but a *parallelismus membrorum*[EN44], in which the subjects, as often happens between "spirit" and "soul"—we shall come back to this—can be interchanged. And in the passage Heb. 4¹², which is often cited in this connexion, it is said that the Word of God is sharper than a two-edged sword and pierces to the dividing asunder ($\mu\epsilon\rho\iota\sigma\mu\acute{o}\varsigma$) of soul and spirit, and that from this point of division, and obviously in such a way that the spirit comes to stand on God's side and the soul on man's, it becomes the discerner of the thoughts and intents of the heart. Scripture never says "soul" where only "spirit" can be meant. But it often says "spirit" where "soul" is meant; and there is inner reason for this in the fact that the constitution of man as soul and body cannot be fully and exactly described without thinking first and foremost of the spirit as its proper basis. We are nowhere invited to think of three entities. Even Augustine, when he once gave the almost intolerably harsh

---

[EN39] vital force

[EN40] renewed part of the human being, otherwise Paul's prayer would be absurd

[EN41] reason or intellect

[EN42] will and all dispositions

[EN43] for then the individual is whole and pure, when she thinks nothing with the mind, desires nothing in the heart, and follows nothing in the body, unless it is approved by God

[EN44] parallelism of members (a poetic device)

formulation: *Tria, sunt, quibus homo constat: spiritus, anima et corpus*[EN45], immediately corrected himself: *quae rursus duo dicuntur, quia saepe anima simul cum spiritu nominatur*[EN46] (*De fide et symb.* 10, 23). Trichotomism must necessarily issue in the view and concept of two different souls and therefore in a splitting of man's being. This makes understandable the force with which it was condemned at the Fourth Council of Constantinople in A.D. 869–70 (Denz., *No.* 338).

We thus understand the statement that man has spirit and is thereby man as equivalent in content to our first statement, that he is man, and therefore soul [356] of his body, not without God but by God, i.e., by the ever new act of God. Spirit is, in the most general sense, the operation of God upon His creation, and especially the movement of God towards man. Spirit is thus the principle of man's relation to God, of man's fellowship with Him. This relation and fellowship cannot proceed from man himself, for God is his Creator and he His creature. He himself cannot be its principle. If this is indeed possible for him, and if he on his side realises it as movement from him towards God, this is because the movement of God towards him has preceded and because he may in his movement imitate it. This is what is meant when Scripture says of man that he has spirit or the Spirit, or that he has done this or that in the Spirit or through the Spirit, or has said or done or suffered from the Spirit. This never signifies a capacity or ability of his own nature, but always one originally foreign to his nature which has come to it from God and has thus been specially imparted to it in a special movement of God towards him. It thus describes man as one who on God's initiative stands in relation to and fellowship with God, in order to be what he is in the relation and fellowship, limitation and determination thus based. The Spirit, in so far as He not only comes but proceeds from God Himself, is identical with God.

This is not taken only from the familiar passage Jn. 4²⁴, where $\pi\nu\epsilon\hat{v}\mu\alpha$ and $\theta\epsilon\acute{o}s$[EN47] are expressly equated. It is implicitly stated in the fact that, in some passages in the Old Testament and then emphatically in the New, the Spirit is called the "Holy" Spirit. This has always to be taken into account where He is called the Spirit of God or the "spirit from on high" (Is. 32¹⁵), where it is said that He is "from God" or "proceeds" from Him, or that God gives Him, or sends or pours Him forth, or where divine predicates such as omnipresence (Ps. 139⁷), sovereignty (Is. 40¹³ᶠ), judicial eminence (Is. 34¹⁶) and the like, are attributed to Him. So, too, the fundamental meaning of the concepts *ruaḥ.*[EN48]; or *neshamah*[EN49] and $\pi\nu\epsilon\hat{v}\mu\alpha$[EN50], i.e., wind as breath, leads back of itself to a source in which breath is not to be distinguished from one who breathes. The Church was therefore right when it understood Him as the Holy Ghost, different from all creatures and of one essence with the Father and the Son.

[EN45] There are three things which define a human being: spirit, soul and body
[EN46] these may, on the other hand, be called two, since often the soul is named together with the spirit
[EN47] spirit … God
[EN48] wind
[EN49] breath
[EN50] wind

Apart from this origin, we can only say that the question whether the Spirit is God or creature cannot be answered because it is falsely put. Spirit in His being *ad extra*[EN51] is neither a divine nor a created something, but an action and attitude of the Creator in relation to His creation. We cannot say that Spirit is, but that He takes place as the divine basis of this relation and fellowship. Spirit is precisely the essence of God's operation in relation to His creature. Spirit is thus the powerful and exclusive meeting initiated by God between Creator and creature. It is of this that we have now to think for the understanding of the significance of Spirit for the grounding, constituting and maintaining of man as soul of his body.

[357] After what has been said, it cannot surprise us that we must affirm that by Spirit we have primarily and originally to understand the movement of God towards man and therefore the principle of human relation to him and fellowship with Him, in which we do not have to do with man's natural constitution but in some sense with his standing in covenant with God. The covenant is the inner basis of creation. And thus the historical standing of man in covenant with God, although it seems objectively to follow man's natural constitution, is in fact the original and model to which the natural constitution of man must succeed and correspond. Spirit in His fundamental significance is the element in virtue of which man is actively and passively introduced as a partner in the covenant of grace, in which he is installed in his position as God's partner in the particular stages and decisions of the history of this covenant and in which he is equipped for his function as such, in order that in this position and function he himself may begin to speak and act—he himself, not of himself, but out of the fact that God has first spoken to him and acted upon him. Hence it is as a recipient of the Spirit, as a charismatic, that, neither increased, reduced nor altered, but newly limited and therefore newly determined in his humanity or as a human subject, moving therefore in this alien element and placed on this new ground, he has to answer, to speak certain words, do certain deeds, and manifest a certain attitude. Whoever is given the Spirit by God becomes, as the man he is, another man—a man of God, the kind of man whom God uses, and who as he is used by God begins to live a new life.

To understand biblical anthropology, it is best to start with those passages and contexts in which the Spirit is described as the power through which certain human persons are pre-eminently equipped and supplied with their office and commission in the history of God with men. Passages such as Is. 59^{21}, where it is said of the people of Israel as such that the Spirit rests upon it, must be infrequent in the Old Testament. Even in this passage, the meaning is eschatological, and by Israel is to be understood the converted "remnant." The constant rule confirmed by this exception is that in the reception and possession of the Spirit the reference is to the election of individuals and not a communal possession. Only in the New Testament, where the community as the body of Christ is the object of election, is it otherwise; and even here individuals specially endowed with the Spirit are always rising above the common level. To be a receiver and bearer of the Spirit, a man in the Old Testa-

---

[EN51] outside of God

ment must be not only a member of the people of Israel, but be called Moses (Nu. 11$^{17\ 25\ 29}$), or Joshua (Nu. 27^{18}; Deut. 34^9), or Othniel, Gideon, Jephthah, Samson (Jud. 3^{10}, &c.), or Saul (1 Sam. 10^6), or David (2 Sam. 23^2), or Elijah (2 K. 2$^{9\ 15}$), or Micah (Mi. 3^8), or Ezekiel (Ezek. 11^5). And the bearer of the fulness of the Spirit, the man on whom the Spirit will rest, is the Messiah (Is. 11^2, 42^1). The saying in Neh. 9^{30} is to be noted, where the operation of the Spirit and the operation of the prophets are equated. In all these contexts, to have the Spirit is to have a commission from God and God's authorisation and power for its execution. This commission, authorisation and power can be withdrawn; the Spirit can abandon the man who is endowed with Him. This happened in the case of Samson and Saul, 1 K. 22^{24}, in the dialogue between the false and the true prophets, alludes to this. Of course He can be restored in certain circumstances to the one who is thus deprived, as happens in the case of Samson. God remains free to give, to take, and to give again. He shows Himself free in the fact that He can also give an evil spirit to a man—this too is a kind of commission imposed on [358] the man concerned—as again with Saul (1 Sam. 16$^{14f.}$, &c.) and in 2 K. 19^7 with the king of Assur; and it can again happen (1 Sam. 16^{23}) that this evil spirit too can depart from him. Even the "lying spirit in the mouth of all false prophets" is, as we are told in the remarkable passage in 1 K. 22$^{21f.}$, one of the spirits that surround the throne of Yahweh, and it is called and empowered by Yahweh Himself for the infatuation of Ahab. There are other passages (Is. 4^4, 40^7; Job 4^9) where the Spirit is the burning blast of the divine judgment, a power of destruction and extermination. Hence we cannot be surprised to hear in Job 20^3 of a spirit "without insight" (Zurich Bible), in Is. 29^{24} of an "erring spirit," in Zech. 13^2 of an "unclean spirit"; and even in the New Testament of a "spirit of bondage" (Rom. 8^{15}), of "another spirit" which presents another Jesus and another gospel (2 Cor. 11^4); and further, with a frequency which cannot be disregarded, of evil spirits, unclean spirits and spirits that cause sickness, with all the work of these spirits in and upon men. If God condemns a man and through him other men, He can give him such a spirit. He then falls, not without the active co-operation of God, whose Spirit leaves him, into the power of such an evil spirit. We must keep this before us because it makes it particularly clear that Spirit is God's free encounter with man. The work of the Spirit, according to Jn. 16^7, is twofold, the reproving of the world of sin and of righteousness, and comprehensively of the judgment in which God vindicates His lordship. In such a fulness. He rests upon the Messiah. Similarly (Ac. 2$^{3f.}$) He is poured forth from heaven in the form of tongues of fire upon the New Testament community. Similarly the community is receiver and possessor of the Spirit, first in the apostles and then in its whole membership (1 Cor. 2^{12}; Rom. 8^{15}, &c.). Similarly Christians are "led" by Him (Gal. 5^{18}; Rom. 8^{14}); they "live" in the Spirit (Gal. 5^{25}), and so can be commanded to "walk" in the Spirit (Gal. 5^{16}), to undertake the battle of the Spirit against the flesh (Gal. 5^{17}), to be "full" of the Spirit (Eph. 5^{18}). Similarly the community is constituted by His different gifts (1 Cor. 12$^{4f.}$), and it can and must be asked concerning His fruits (Gal. 5$^{22f.}$). By "Spirit" must always be understood the divine operation of grace in its full scope, as is most clearly comprehended in the idea of the righteous judgment of God. As Israel's Judge, God is already in the Old Testament Israel's Lord and Helper; even in the New the operation of God in the person of His Messiah is to be understood decisively as the act of the helpful, liberating God (Ac. 17^{31}). As man receives the Spirit, he comes to deal with God and therefore with his Judge, and he is justly judged by God. It is to be observed how the "new and right" spirit for which Ps. 51^{10} prays is in one and the selfsame breath called a joyful (v. 12) and an alarmed spirit (v. 17), and in Is. 66^2 a broken spirit. All this is included in the operation of the Spirit. God's election acts decisively, determining and limiting man; it decides not only this *or* that but this *and* that; so that this decision, no matter from which side it is seen, is to be understood as an event whose subject is God, but also one in which man, as is said of Saul in 1 Sam. 10^6, becomes "another man," or according to Jn. 3$^{3f.}$ is born anew from above (ἄνωθεν), being set in relation to God his Judge, subjected to His judgment and therefore in the best sense judged by Him. As such, possessing the Spirit (Rom. 8^{23}; 2 Cor. 1^{22}), he has the pledge (ἀπαρχή, ἀρραβών) of future glorification in participation of the glory of God, who, as He gave him the Spirit and became his Judge through the Spirit, entered into relationship with him. This is the meaning and function of the Spirit in the historical position which He occupies as a partner in the covenant of grace initiated in the existence of Israel and fulfilled and completed in the existence of the Messiah.

[359]   It is from this standpoint that the being and work of the Spirit are to be understood in the narrower anthropological sphere which now concerns us. As the elected and called and to that extent "new" man lives in the covenant by the fact that God gives him His Spirit, the natural man also lives in the same way. The same Spirit, who is there the principle of his renewal, is here the principle of his creaturely reality. Without Spirit, without the absolutely free encounter between God and man initiated by God, and outside the relation and fellowship based on this encounter, there can be no prophet or any other commissioned agent of God, and no living member of the body of Christ. But without the same Spirit man cannot in any sense be man, nor in any sense soul of his body. As he has the Spirit from God, he lives, he becomes and is soul, his material body becomes and is a physical body, and he is soul of this body. If he did not have the Spirit, he would not be able even to begin to live, he would not be soul, nor would his material body become a physical body. If he ceased to have the Spirit, he would no longer live, his soul would become a shadow of itself and his body a purely material body which as such could only dissolve in the world of bodies surrounding it. It is really the Spirit and He alone who quickens man, grounding, constituting and maintaining him as soul of his body. Man has no power over the Spirit; on the contrary, he is man as the Spirit has power over him. The Spirit belongs to God even as He is given to man. He can have the Spirit only as He is continually given to him. Spirit is the event of the gift of life whose subject is God; and this event must be continually repeated as God's act if man is to live. In this sense Spirit is the *conditio sine qua non*EN52 of the being of man as soul of his body. There is value in reminding ourselves, of course, that the same is also to be said of the beasts. It is only by the Spirit of God the Creator that they also live and are soul of their body. What distinguishes man from beast is the special movement and purpose with which God through the Spirit gives him life; and, connected with this, the special spirituality of his life, which is determined by the fact that God has not only made him in his constitution as soul of his body, but destined him in this constitution for that position of a partner of the grace of His covenant. We know nothing of such a double determination in respect of the beasts; and hence we do not understand the manner of their life or of their souls (though we cannot dispute that they have them) and at very best can only intuit. So far as we know, they lack that second determination by the Spirit which is primary

---

EN52 necessary condition

and peculiar. Men and beasts can be born, but men alone can be baptised. Yet in the relation Spirit-life and therefore Spirit-life-body as such, there is no difference between men and beasts. The unfathomable free act and attitude of God the Creator is here too the *conditio sine qua non*[EN53] of the life and therefore the being and existence of His creatures. The Spirit is also Judge of the life and death of man. He is this not only in the historical sense already considered, but also in regard to the natural constitution of man. In this respect already Spirit means that he may live, and lack of the Spirit that he must die. [360]

The biblical statements about the Spirit as the principle of the existence of man in the covenant of grace are related to those about the Spirit as the principle of his creatureliness in such a way that the former include the latter as presupposition and also as promise: as presupposition, in so far as the latter show and explain how man (together with the beasts) already stands as a creature under the same judgment and what will be his being as partner of the covenant of grace; as promise, in so far as man has a certain hope in and for his creatureliness—the hope which in the New Testament is described as the resurrection of the dead, the resurrection of the whole man. It follows that the New Testament statements about the Spirit of grace and renewal must always be understood extensively and to the effect that they also refer to man's creatureliness and indirectly explain how it happens that man in the simplest and nearest sense of the word may live and need not die. A saying like Jn. 3^8, which says of the Spirit that "it bloweth where it listeth, and thou hearest the sound thereof, but canst not tell whence it cometh, and whither it goeth," not only can be made of the Spirit that awakens creaturely life, but also, since it refers to the Spirit of renewal, does actually refer to the creative Spirit. He comes—whence? and goes—whither? We put these questions if we do not know the ground of our life. For what is real between the two questions, as the mysterious birth by the Spirit that comes and goes, is the life of man, man as soul of his body. So, too, the saying in Jn. 6^{63} (cf. also 2 Cor. 3^6): "It is the spirit that quickeneth; the flesh profiteth nothing," while it is meant soteriologically, has an indirectly anthropological significance. We have also anthropological instruction in Rev. 11^{11}, where of the two dead witnesses it is said that, after three and a half days, "the spirit of life from God" entered into them, "and they stood upon their feet; and great fear fell upon them which saw them." Reference may also be made to Rom. 8^{10-11}: "And if Christ be in you, the body is dead because of sin; but the Spirit is life because of righteousness. But if the Spirit of him that raised up Jesus from the dead dwell in you, he that raised up Christ from the dead shall also quicken your mortal bodies by his Spirit that dwelleth in you." With its mention of the name of Jesus Christ and the opposition between sin and righteousness which dominates the first sentence, the saying obviously has in view the dispensation of the covenant of grace, the threat of death by sin on the one side and the promise of life by righteousness on the other, with Christ between and looking forward, His back to the one and His face to the other. But the second sentence points beyond the present into the future, and therefore just as clearly includes also the creaturely reality of man. For the Spirit of God, who is also creative Spirit, there is, so long as He dwells in us, a mortal body, but one quickened and again and again maintained alive in its mortality; and it is this that He will manifest and vindicate in man as the Spirit of Him who raised Jesus from the dead in defiance of sin and death. Or Gal. 4^6: "And because ye are sons, God hath sent forth the Spirit of his Son into your hearts, crying, Abba, Father"; and also Rom. 8^{26f}: "Likewise the Spirit also helpeth our infirmities: for we know not what we should pray for as we ought: but the Spirit maketh intercession for us with

[EN53] necessary condition

153

groanings which cannot be uttered. And he that searcheth the hearts knoweth what is the mind of the Spirit, because he maketh intercession for the saints." Here it is said of the prayer of Christians, and therefore undoubtedly with reference to the dispensation of grace, that it is not in the power of the Christian to be in prayer his own intercessor before God. In fact, when he prays, the Spirit takes his place and effects in his place the invocation of God the Father which is inexpressible for him, which is then heard and accepted by Him as though it were his own prayer. But this tells us implicitly, yet with unsurpassable precision, how it comes about that a man can exercise with supreme reality what he does not have in himself and therefore cannot produce of himself, i.e., his creaturely life, since the same Spirit of God is not only the Advocate and Representative for his prayer as the Spirit of the covenant but also for his life as the creative Spirit, giving him what he cannot take for himself. We might also think of an Old Testament passage like that which describes the restoration of life to the field of dry bones in Ezek. 37^{1-14}, for what is the awakening of dead Israel or the regathering of dispersed Israel here mentioned if it is not implicitly the very obvious process by which the living breath of God gives life and sustains it?

But the Old Testament especially gives us many direct testimonies to this fact. Who is the God of Israel? Moses and Aaron declare it (Nu. 16^{22}) when, at a moment when the whole community of God is most gravely threatened with annihilating wrath, they cling to this: "O God, the God of the spirits of all flesh, shall one man sin, and wilt thou be wroth with all the congregation?" The God who is invoked in this way cannot will this. He is and acts (Is. 42^5) as He who "giveth breath unto the people upon (the earth), and spirit to them that walk therein." How He did this at the first is plainly described in Gen. 2^7. He breathed the breath of life into the nostrils of the man formed by Him out of the dust of the earth, and the latter thus became a "living soul." The meaning of this is that by the breathing of God man's own breath is set in motion, and thereby his life is aroused, his soul created, his earthly material body made into an organic body. "The Spirit, entering the form of dust, or earthly organism, creates the soul, which thus carries within itself an essentially indestructible because divine power of life … through which it has come into being and consists" (H. Cremer: *PRE³*, Vol. 6, 465). This is poetically illustrated in Prov. 20^{27}: "The spirit of man is the candle of the Lord, searching all the inward parts of the belly." In the Old Testament, therefore, the fact that man lives is directly equated with the fact that he breathes. But he will not breathe without the breath and therefore the Spirit of God who awakened him to his own breathing and therefore to life. As he himself breathes and lives on the basis of the fact that God has breathed into him, he has the Spirit. But that he has the Spirit and therefore breathes and lives demands the continuing work of divine creation. "He giveth to all life, and breath, and all things," as the New Testament has it (Ac. 17^{25}). Hence Job. 33^4 can declare: "The spirit of God hath made me, and the breath of the Almighty hath given me life." Hence also (Ps. 150^6) everything that has breath can be summoned to praise the Lord. To praise God is in fact our natural office.

It should not be overlooked that it is on the basis of God's free operation that man has Spirit and therefore breathes and lives and may be soul of his body; and further that it is under the judgment of God that, as matters stand, he is placed in his creaturely constitution. This is proclaimed in a fact already mentioned, that he has his breath and life, as well as the Spirit, in common with the beasts. For example, Gen. $1^{20,\ 26}$ calls the beasts "living beings" before men; and Gen. 7^{15} calls them expressly "flesh having the breath of life in them." According to the Old Testament, neither soul nor the Spirit can be simply denied to the beasts. To be sure, their creation is not described as an act of special bestowal such as that which takes place in man according to Gen. 2^7. Yet even so the creative Spirit which awakens man to life is also the life-principle of the beasts (and even of the whole host of heaven according to Ps. 33^6). Eccles. $3^{19f.}$ develops this insight in a shattering way: "For that which befalleth the sons of men befalleth the beasts; even one thing befalleth them: as the one dieth, so dieth the other; yea, they have all one breath; so that a man hath no pre-eminence above a beast: for all is vanity. All go unto one place; all are of the dust, and all turn to dust again. Who knoweth the spirit of man that goeth upward, and the spirit of the beast that goeth downward to the earth?" Yes; who knows? Man has no right to find in his own favour in this respect. All that he can really know and expect of himself is that his breath and life, like that of the beasts, will end as it began, and that like the beasts he must die. Thus immediately after the fall he is told (Gen. 3^{19}): "In the sweat of thy face shalt thou eat bread, till thou return unto the ground; for out of it wast thou taken: for dust thou art, and unto dust shalt thou return." This is made even more precise in Gen. 6^3: "And the Lord said. My spirit shall not always strive with man (Germ.: dwell in man), for that he also is flesh: yet his days shall be an hundred and twenty years," a span which Ps. 90^{10} reduces to the familiar seventy or eighty years. God is not bound to let His Spirit dwell in men always, and when He does so no longer, then it is all up with breath and life, with the being of man as soul of his body; he must return to the earth from which he was taken, and die. "Thou turnest man to destruction; and sayest, Return, ye children of men" (Ps. 90^3). This is the divine judgment under which man in his creaturely constitution is placed in virtue of the fact that he can have the Spirit only as He is to be had as the free act of God. Since the Spirit can go as He came, it is a precarious thing to be a man "whose breath is in his nostrils" (Is. 2^{22}). "Verily all that is called man is only a breath" (Ps. 39^6, Zurich version and versification). "If he set his heart upon man, if he gather unto himself his spirit and his breath; all flesh shall perish together, and man shall turn again unto dust" (Job. $34^{14f.}$). Nor is this merely possible, but a fact: "His breath goeth forth, he returneth to his earth; in that very day his thoughts perish" (Ps. 146^4). "Then shall the dust return to the earth as it was: and the spirit shall return unto God who gave it" (Eccles. 12^7). "Thou hidest thy face, they are troubled: thou takest away their breath, they die, and return to their dust. Thou sendest forth thy spirit, they are created: and thou renewest the face of the earth" (Ps. $104^{29f.}$). Observe how in the last passage the relation is reversed, and the withdrawal of the breath of life is succeeded and relativised by a new sending forth. But the seriousness of the withdrawal and therefore of certain death is not thereby diminished. It is certain that there will be this withdrawal; that there will be a new sending forth is something which we can neither decide nor perceive. In both cases God is at work, and in both He is a free Subject. God is He "in whose hand thy breath is," is the warning given to Belshazzar in Dan. 5^{23}. If a man breathes and lives and is the soul of his body, since only the breath and Spirit of God can make this possible, he stands inevitably in God's judgment. Man is, as he has Spirit. But this means that it rests with God alone whether he moves to the salvation or loss of his being. It means that in his creaturely constitution man is absolutely dependent upon God's judicial sentence, and therefore upon the fact that the freedom of this Judge is the freedom of His grace.

This leads us to the final question what it means for man to have Spirit. From what has been said, the definition is primarily very simple. To have Spirit means that he may live, and therefore be soul, and therefore be soul of his body. The "may" demands emphasis. It gives rise to a "can" and the "can" to an actualisation. But the "may" is the basis and beginning of everything else. And when Spirit is ascribed to man it means that this "may" is proper to him. What does man "have"? What he "has" is that he may live and be the soul of his body. This is what is meant when we say that he "has" Spirit. Four delimitations are possible and necessary in the light of this fact.

[362]

[363]   1. That man has Spirit means that God is there for him. Every moment that he may breathe and live he has in this very fact a witness that God turns to him in His free grace as Creator, that He has willed him again and again as a living being, and that He has allowed him to become one. It is not that man, having Spirit, is of divine essence even if only in a part or in the core of his being. On the contrary, the creatureliness of the whole man cannot be more evident than in the fact that he stands in need of this "may," of this freedom to live which is not immanent in him but comes to him from without. It would be more possible to ascribe to him a divine nature in virtue of his spiritual or even his corporeal being than in virtue of the Spirit who makes it possible for him to be soul of his body. But since his life rests on this transcendent enabling, we cannot say this even in regard to his soul and body. We must be content that the whole man lives by the fact that God is there for him.

We read in Ovid (*Ars amandi* III, 549): *Est Deus in nobis et sunt commercia coeli/Sedibus aetheriis spiritus ille venit*[EN54]. This conception of an immanent being of God in us is hermetically excluded by the biblical concept of the Spirit, if only because it is the idea of an activity and not of a being. Since we have the Spirit and may therefore live, God is indeed "in us" according to the Bible. But according to the Bible, the Spirit is always a divine work in man, a divine gift to him. And as God's work and gift, it is always free and superior to him. Because He signifies absolutely everything for man, being the *conditio sine qua non*[EN55] of his fellowship with God and therefore his life, it is impossible that He should be identical with man in any depth of his being and existence, which would involve the transformation of man into a divine being. The relationship between Spirit and man even in its anthropological sense is to be represented on the analogy of expressions used in the soteriological context. He is poured forth upon man, or laid upon him; but He is not to be thought of as changing human nature into divine nature, against which Paul twice (1 Cor. 15^{45}, 2 Cor. 3$^{17\ 18}$) ventures the equation $\kappa \acute{\nu} \rho \iota o s = \pi \nu \epsilon \hat{\nu} \mu a$[EN56]. These passages tell us that this man, because in His humanity He was also Son of God, accomplished and still accomplishes in His own person the mighty quickening action of God in relation to all other men. Jn. 7^{38} can also be adduced in this connexion: "Rivers of living water" will flow from the body of those who believe in Him; but the context ("If any man thirst, let him come unto me, and drink," v. 37) makes it quite clear that this cannot be understood as an identification of human and divine being, but again only as a description of man's being in service of the quickening divine activity.

2. That man has Spirit is the fundamental determination which decisively makes possible his being as soul of his body. The Spirit is in man and belongs to him as the mathematical centre is in and belongs to the circle. The whole man is of the Spirit, since the Spirit is the principle and power of the life of the whole man. Hence he cannot be a third thing beside soul and body. He is rather an augmentation of the stability of man's being. It is the Spirit that brings this into being and stabilises it. He is the "may" on the basis of which the soul is awakened and made soul, and the material body is besouled and thus becomes an organic body and is maintained as such.

[EN54] God is in us, and heaven's wares/Inspiration comes from celestial spheres
[EN55] necessary condition
[EN56] Lord=Spirit

2. *The Spirit as Basis of Soul and Body*

The difficulty of 1 Thess. 5^{23} would be removed if the terms αὐτὸς ὁ θεός, ὁλοτελεῖς, [364] ὁλόκληρον and τηρηθείη EN57 were to be related to one another as in the following paraphrase: "The God of peace sanctify you in the wholeness of your being, and may your spirit (which is the basis and guarantees this wholeness of your being), and with it your soul and body, be preserved without injury until the return of our Lord Jesus Christ." What Paul would then desire for his readers is that the return of Christ and the resurrection of the dead should bring them the renewal and confirmation of that divinely conceded "may," and therefore the freedom to live which He, God alone, has already given them in time, and which He alone can give them again to all eternity. May it bring them the maintenance of their whole being as men by the same Spirit by whom it is already based and constituted. And may this come about through God's sanctifying them in this present being of theirs and thus preparing them for that final salvation and preservation. All other passages which speak of the Spirit of man indicate that the explanation of this saying must be sought along these lines. Whatever else we may be told about the Spirit of man, the reference is always to a centre of his being and existence which is not a third thing beside soul and body but is to be sought in soul and body and at the same time above and beyond them, being understood as the representative of the divine grace of creation over against the whole being and existence of man.

3. Since man has Him, the Spirit is certainly in man—in his soul and through his soul in his body too. It is the nearest, most intimate and most indispensable factor for an understanding of his being and existence. But while He is in man, He is not identical with him. We have seen already that this would imply a transformation of man into God, which is excluded by the fact that Spirit is a conception of activity. The Spirit is not transformed into the soul of man, although He first and supremely creates the soul of man and makes it His own dwelling. Nor does He become corporeal, although as the Spirit of the soul He immediately becomes the Spirit of the body and man is ordained to be not only spiritual soul and besouled body, but also spiritual body. He does not merely become the human subject. He is more than this. He is the principle which makes man into a subject. The human subject is man as soul, and it is this which is created and maintained by the Spirit. But for this very reason the Spirit lives His own superior and alien life over against the soul and the human subject. He is not bound to the life of the human subject. He cannot, therefore, be reached by its death. When the subject dies, He returns to God who gave Him. In distinction from the human subject, He is immortal. Whether or not death is the last word concerning man depends upon whether He is given again and that "may" is renewed.

At this point we must again refer to all the passages in which reference is made to a withdrawal of the Spirit and the death of man which this entails. The sickness of the son of the widow of Sarepta was so grave "that there was no breath left in him" (1 K. 17^{17}). The Spirit must be "discharged" like a strange guest (Mt. 27^{50}), or "given back" like something borrowed into the hands of Him from whom it was received (Lk. 23^{46}). The body without Spirit is dead (Jas. 2^{26}). But the Spirit can be saved when a man is delivered to Satan for the [365] destruction of his flesh (1 Cor. 5^5). Awakening from the dead means that the Spirit returns

---

EN57 the very God, wholly, whole ... be preserved

to the man concerned (Lk. 8⁵⁵), as can sometimes be said in the Old Testament of men who are totally exhausted and apparently dead (Jud. 15¹⁹, 1 Sam. 30¹²). Thus the Spirit, coming and going, lives His own life over against the man. Note must also be taken of 1 Cor. 2¹¹, where an express distinction is made between $\pi\nu\epsilon\hat{\upsilon}\mu\alpha$ $\tau o\hat{\upsilon}$ $\dot{\alpha}\nu\theta\rho\dot{\omega}\pi o\upsilon$ EN58 and man, and it is said of the former that it knows $\tau\grave{\alpha}$ $\tau o\hat{\upsilon}$ $\dot{\alpha}\nu\theta\rho\dot{\omega}\pi o\upsilon$ EN59 as the Spirit of God knows $\tau\grave{\alpha}$ $\tau o\hat{\upsilon}$ $\theta\epsilon o\hat{\upsilon}$ EN60.

4. The Spirit stands in a special and direct relationship to the soul or soulful element of human reality, but in only an indirect relationship to the body. The soul therefore is the life of the body, and therefore the human life as such which man may not only have but be when he receives the Spirit. He may be soul. Thus it is the besouled body that the Spirit chooses and occupies as His dwelling. It is on and in the soul that the act of God, which is the Spirit, takes place in man; and on and in the body through the soul. This is the basis of the order of the relationship of soul and body, and of the superiority of the soul over the body. The soul is *a priori* the element in which the turning of God to man and the fellowship of man with God in some way take place. The same is to be said of the body, but only *a posteriori*. It is as the principle of the soul that the Spirit is the principle of the whole man.

Here we stand before the material justification of the possibility of which Scripture makes such frequent use, not speaking of the soul directly, but of that which grounds and maintains the soul as its principle and that of the whole man, namely, the Spirit. Since the Spirit dwells especially in the soul, and therefore the soul especially is spiritual soul, the Spirit participates in the motions and experiences of the soul, and what is said of the former can be said of the latter. In this sense, Gen. 41⁸ can say of Pharaoh that his spirit was uneasy, and 1 K. 21⁵ of Ahab that he became of an ill-humoured spirit. In the same sense Job (6⁴) can complain that his spirit drank the glowing poison of the arrows of the Almighty; the Psalmist (142⁴, 143⁴) can say that his spirit is cast down in him, or fails him (143⁷), and Is. 57¹⁵ can speak of a contrition and humbling of the spirit. In the same sense, Jesus can be said to sigh in His spirit (Mk. 8¹²), to groan in His spirit (Jn. 11³³), and to be troubled in spirit (Jn. 13²¹). Similarly, 2 Cor. 2¹³ tells us that in certain situations Paul had no rest in his spirit. In the same sense again, it can be said conversely of Jacob that his spirit revived (Gen. 45²⁷); and of the king of Assur (1 Chron. 5²⁶), the Philistines (2 Chron. 21¹⁶) and Cyrus (2 Chron. 36²²; Ezra 1¹) that their spirit was aroused to certain acts and attitudes. We read in Ps. 77⁶ of a spirit which makes diligent search, in Is. 26⁹ of a spirit which desires God, in Is. 38¹⁶ of a spirit which longs for quickening by God, and in Lk. 1⁴⁷ of a rejoicing spirit. In the story of the childhood of John the Baptist (Lk. 1⁸⁰) we read that he grew and waxed strong in spirit. To Daniel (5¹²) there is ascribed an "excellent" spirit, while Ezek. 13³ charges the false prophets with following their "own" spirit. According to 2 Cor. 7¹, there is a filthiness of the spirit as well as of the flesh, whereas 1 Cor. 6²⁰ tells us that God can be glorified in our body and in our spirit, and 1 Cor. 7³⁴ that Christians can be holy in body and spirit. Eccles 7⁸ compares a "patient" and a "proud" spirit. The Jew Apollos (Ac. 18²⁵) was "fervent in spirit"; and Prov. 16² can speak of a weighing of spirits. It may be seen how the Spirit stands for soul in this sense from Gal. 6¹⁸, where Paul's desire for his readers is that the grace of Jesus Christ may be with their spirit, or from Rom. 8¹⁶, which speaks of the Spirit of God bearing witness to our spirit. In all these

[366]

EN58 the spirit of man
EN59 the things of a man
EN60 the things of God

passages we obviously have to do with man as such, and with man in his natural relationship and orientation to God. Even in those passages we cannot of course forget that according to many other clear contexts the Spirit is not man as such, but the divine gift of life which makes him man, and therefore something foreign and superior to the whole man. Yet while this gift does not cease to be a gift, it is really given to man as such and belongs to his very essence. This strange and superior thing is at the same time nearest and most intimate. And this is expressed in the Bible in the fact that man—and therefore man primarily as soul—can be considered and described in terms of that which divinely grounds and maintains him. Note that here again there is no thought of an equation of Spirit and man. Here again the case is different from that of soul. Man "has" the Spirit, but it cannot be said that he is spirit. Yet to have the Spirit is so essential that what he is, and especially his soul, can also be simply described and denoted from the standpoint of this having, and this having, this divine "may," must be understood on all sides as participant in the ebb and flow of the life of his soul and his whole creaturely life. Something of the divine condescension already apparent in the sphere of creation is undoubtedly revealed in the distinctive ambiguity of the biblical terminology at this point. So long as man lives, God has evidently declared Himself in solidarity with him by constantly giving him His Spirit. It is not too trifling a thing for Him to empty Himself and tread with him the different paths of his soul, whether they lead into the heights or the depths. When the Corinthians (1 Cor. 3^{16}, cf. also 2 Cor. 6^{16}) are exhorted by Paul to know that they are the temple of God and that God dwells in them and when the following interpretation is given in 1 Cor. 6^{19}: "What? know ye not that your body is the temple of the Holy Ghost which is in you, which ye have of God, and ye are not your own?"—the primary reference is of course to Christians as members of the body of Christ, but it has also a more extensive anthropological truth and significance. The Holy Spirit is immediate to the soul, but through the soul He is also mediate to the body, and He is thus the basis and maintenance of the whole Christian and therefore of the man who does not belong to himself. But if by Spirit we understand the creative Spirit, the "may" which goes forth from God and by which man has life, then the relationship of this creative Spirit to the soul and body of the natural man is described in this saying of Paul. As He dwells in man and primarily in his soul, the body as the body of this soul is indirectly the property and sanctuary of God, and even as body man is really withdrawn from his own disposal and power and with his soul made the dwelling of the sovereign Spirit.

3. SOUL AND BODY IN THEIR INTERCONNEXION

We now turn to the question what it is that by God and therefore through the Spirit is grounded, constituted and maintained as human creatureliness. This is the question of the inner structure of this creatureliness. It subdivides into the three questions of its inner unity, its inner differentiation, and its inner order. That is to say, it is a matter of soul and body in their interconnexion, in their particularity, and in their material relationship.

We must first address ourselves to the first of these subsidiary questions—that concerning the inner unity of human creatureliness and therefore soul and body in their interconnexion.

In the preceding sub-section we made it clear that human creatureliness is [367] essentially conditioned by the free action of God the Creator. Man is, as he is from God and through God, i.e., as he has Spirit. This is in some sense the sign which stands before the brackets in which we have to see and understand the being of man. We have now to ask what stands in these brackets and therefore under this sign, taking up the question of the being of man as such. But here we are confronted by the remarkable fact that within these brackets we have to do with a whole, but with a whole in which there is antithesis, and therefore with a duality; with something resembling at least the distinction between God and the creature in the case of the creature, or Spirit and man in the case of man. Man is twofold. He is soul of his body, as we must put it on the basis of our understanding of the Spirit and the fact that he is conditioned by the action of God. But he is these two things in differentiation: both soul and body.

We may provisionally paraphrase as follows the results of our first proposition. Man is (1) creaturely life—life which by the will and act of the living God is awakened, created and called into temporal existence as the individual life of a body. He is *living* being. And he is (2) creaturely being—being which by the will and act of the same God has a certain spatial form or besouled body. He is living *being*. To put it in another way, he is (1) there, and has existence, and in this respect is soul; and he is (2) there in a certain manner and has a nature, and in this respect is body. It is obvious that this entails duality, that these determinations and elements of his being are not identical, and that neither of them can be reduced to the other. Soul is not organic body; for life is not corporeal body, time is not space, and existence is not nature. Similarly, body cannot be soul.

The contrast is so great that the question arises whether in this differentiation within human creatureliness we do not really have a form of the distinction between Creator and creature, Spirit and man. But to ask this question is to answer it. The distinction between Creator and creature is unique and unrepeatable. In expounding our first proposition, we had to emphasise the fact that man neither is nor becomes the Spirit, but that he acquires and has Him, and that the creative turning of God to man, the gift of the Spirit, means that God is for man, but not that man is in any respect or in any part or moment of his natural condition identical with God. God remains God and man man when this turning takes place and the being of man is grounded, constituted and maintained by God. From the very outset, then, the possibility is ruled out that in this inner differentiation within man's being we really have to do with a form of the distinction between Creator and creature, Spirit and man. The being of man in its totality is creaturely being, and, however great and important the inner differentiation, it can never extend to nor include the differentiation in which God confronts human and all created being alike as its Creator. The latter antithesis is absolute and final, the former relative and provisional. The antithesis of soul and body, like that of heaven and earth, is an antithesis within creation and immanent in the world. This does not mean that it is invalid or unworthy of notice. But it does mean that the whole which stands within those brackets, the whole man who is of and through God and is born

[368]

of the Spirit, must at any rate be seen together as God and man cannot be seen together except in Jesus Christ. Apart from Jesus Christ, God and man are neither one person nor one thing. A master concept including them both can result only in the denial of the existence and being of both. It can only be the concept of a false God or a non-existent man. But the soul and body of man are the one man, as heaven and earth as a whole are one cosmos. The differentiation of soul and body is not denied by this consideration, but set in its proper place. Only in this place can both be seen in their differentiation.

The comparison of the relationship between soul and body with that between Creator and creature does of course contain a *particula veri*EN61 which is not suppressed by this consideration. Even the antithesis between heaven and earth is not identical with that between Creator and creature nor equal to it; yet it is an attestation and reflection of this higher antithesis. But it is incontestable that between heaven and earth on the one hand, and soul and body on the other, there is a similarity; and while we need not on this account adopt the speculative view that man as soul of his body is the "microcosm," the world in miniature, we must always take this similarity into account. The antithesis between Creator and creature is not in any case an antithesis without relation, for in the person of Jesus Christ it is not only bridged but annulled, and at this point the Creator and His creature are to be seen as one. Hence we need not be surprised if we come across certain traces of this fundamental antithesis even on the side of the creature, finding an analogy and copy, if not the antithesis itself or its equivalent, both in the structure of the cosmos (heaven and earth), and in the being of man (soul and body). The correspondence consists in the fact that in the relation of soul and body too, in irreversible order, there is a higher and a lower, a quickening and a quickened, a factor that controls space and one that is limited by it, an element which is invisible and one which is visible. Does not this inevitably remind us of the relation of Creator and creature as that of heaven and earth with its closer correspondence inevitably reminds us of the basic antithesis?

It belongs to the creatureliness of all creatures, and therefore to that of man, that even though they cannot reproduce they can copy and attest the differentiation and relation of God towards them in the inner differentiations and relations of their own being. To the absolute antithesis between God and man [369] (with one great exception), there can correspond in man himself only a relative antithesis of two moments which in him are finally and originally bound together and united. The creature is first and last and in all his differentiation *one*, whereas God and His creature in all the relations that exist between them are always and necessarily *two*, even in their unity in Jesus Christ. Thus body and soul belong together otherwise than Creator and creature. In the one case, it is grace that Creator and creature belong together; but in the case of soul and body, it is nature. In the former case, the interconnexion is grounded

---

EN61 grain of truth

in the free creative will of God; in the latter in the creature itself, of which it is the *ratio essendi*[EN62] from which it cannot escape without forfeiting its being.

But this negative affirmation has a more important positive side. It is not the case that the creature is deprived of anything by being unable to repeat that original antithesis; for it could not be good for it to do so. On the contrary, the goodness of its creation is seen in the fact that it is given to be only relatively distinct within itself, to belong together by nature in its inner antithesis, and to have its *ratio essendi*[EN63] in this interconnexion. The thought of man in his differentiation as soul and body really having to repeat the differentiation between God and the creature is not only an arrogant but a terrifying thought. It would mean—and here perhaps we can first see why it is forbidden—that in every minute of his existence and being man himself must undertake to bridge the chasm which God Himself bridged by calling the creation out of nothing into a reality distinct from Himself. In other words, man would necessarily be placed continually in the position and role of a *creator ex nihilo*[EN64]. As soul, he would be the absolute lord of his body, absolutely responsible for it, and therefore his own creator; and as body, he would be the absolute object of his soul, absolutely dependent upon it, and therefore his own creature. He would then have to attempt the hopeless task of being man, and he would have to be equal to God to be able to be true man. He would inevitably be torn asunder by this contradiction even if for a moment he successfully undertook to live in it. It is really for his salvation that the theories about soul and body which directly or indirectly amount to the fact that man as soul is his own creator, and as body his own creature, are merely theories which have never really been put into practice, except in certain experiments or approximations. It is bad enough that sinful man actually finds himself on a way corresponding to one of these theories, and that this usually leads in practice to such dreadful consequences both inward and outward. But it is for man's salvation that he cannot continue this way to the end; that he cannot be what he is not, his own creator as soul and his own creature as body. He may be creature alone and no more. It is the grace and kindness of the Creator that he may be this.

[370]   And therefore in his creatureliness, for all its inner differentiation, he may be a solid inner unity, a whole. That he is soul and body does not threaten him with an infinite contradiction which he would have to meet with an achievement of which only God is capable. That he is soul does not burden him with the task of being his own creator, nor that he is body with the fate of being his own creature. However great and important the antithesis between soul and body, it does not have this intolerable width. Man is one in his being as soul and body. He can and may be wholly and simultaneously both in the peace of his self-united being: soul, without that absolute responsibility for the body;

[EN62] ground of being
[EN63] ground of being
[EN64] creator from nothing

and body without that absolute dependence upon the soul. It is not the case that man is his soul alone, his body being a distinct reality produced and to be controlled by it as such. This is just what man is graciously spared by the fact that he is creature and not creator. It is possible to be man. To be man is not an extravagant task necessarily leading to despair. It appears as though it were so only in many theories about man and the many experiments in living corresponding to these theories. Human reality is neither so powerful nor so powerless. Naturally the perverted will for life produced by these theories and experiments will avenge itself. Death is the final and conclusive result of the delusion in which man wants to be both creator and creature. In death as the unnatural division of soul and body this sin is paid for. But death, too, makes it clear that this undertaking is a delusion and nothing else. The ostensibly all-powerful soul becomes completely impotent in death because it becomes bodiless. But this does not mean that the body becomes all-powerful in death. In death, the organic body as such decays, becoming a mere material body and merging into the surrounding world of material bodies. Even the misery of death is not so great that the delusion is a reality in its inverted form. Even in death, the human reality cannot fail to return to the infinite and intolerable tension between Creator and creature. The difference and antithesis between soul and body is as great in death as it can possibly be within the created world. In death man is only the spent soul of a spent body, and he cannot live at all unless the God who let him live and then die gives him new life. But the fearful thing which would befall him if he succeeded in being both creator and creature cannot befall him even in death. Sin receives its wages in death, but it does not reach its objective. The difference and antithesis between soul and body remains relative; and it is a gracious preservation in the grounding, constituting and maintaining of man that the difference between soul and body never becomes that basic antithesis but is always and in all circumstances relative.

But we can and must say something better. The fact that it is given to man to be only relatively different in himself, to belong together by nature in his inner antithesis, is the positive benefit of his creation because by it he is one—an [371] inwardly united and self-enclosed subject. He is not one, of course, in the sense that God is one. The oneness of God is certainly not without its inner differentiation. But there are no different things in God, there are no individual perfections which are not in and for themselves the one totality of His Godhead, the sum of all His perfections. Yet we cannot say of the human soul that it is also the human body, nor of either soul or body that one or other is in itself the whole man. Again, for all the rich differentiation of God, there is no higher and lower in His unity, no prior and posterior in His individual perfections. There is order in God, but no subordination or superordination. The order of man, on the other hand, entails the latter. We speak equivocally when we say that both God and man are one. We may and must say of man that he is one; just as we may and must say that the cosmos is one, although it is composed of heaven and earth. Man cannot succeed in making an absolute separation of soul from body, nor can this come upon him. Their interconnexion and therefore his inner coherence may be powerfully challenged by himself and then by God, but the God whose creature he is has made them indestructible. Even in death there is only a relative differentiation in man. He can and must die; but even in death he cannot and must not suffer the destruction of this interconnexion. For even in death God watches over him. And as on either side of death he may live by the gracious will of God, God not only watches over him but awakens him to this interconnexion and then speaks and deals with him as the one who lives in this interconnexion: the God who is one in Himself with the man who is one in himself even in his purely creaturely completeness; one Subject with the other. It is no more and no less than the being of man before God, his intercourse with Him, which is radically made possible by the fact that for all the differentiation of his being as soul and body it is given to him, not to be two things, but in these two one. This is one of the natural points of contact for the covenant of grace. Indeed, it is the basic one. This is a strange fact, for God is one, a Subject, in a totally different way from man. It really rests upon His creative initiative and action that there may be anything in common between God and man at all. Even the knowledge of this common factor presupposes the covenant of grace and therefore God's revelation to man. Yet for all that it is so strange, it is a real fact. God can be for man and man for God, because in his place and way man is no less one than God. It is not only preservation but the positive blessing of this benefit that man's being and existence as soul and body cannot repeat in itself the absolute opposition of Creator and creature.

We recall that we are required to speak at once not only of the interconnexion but of the unity of soul and body. It is true humanity in the person of Jesus which allows us no other starting-point but bids us commence at once with this knowledge. And in any case we should be hard put to it to find a better or more relevant point of departure. We best keep ourselves from prejudice, abstraction and one-sidedness if we proceed from the concrete reality in which man neither lacks the inner differentiation of soul and body, nor is mere soul or mere body, nor merely a combination and association of the two, but wholly and simultaneously both soul and body, always and in every relation soulful, and always and in every relation bodily. We cannot cease to see both and therefore these two; for the unity of soul and body does not consists in their identity, or in the interchangeability of soulful and bodily. But again we cannot cease to see both, and therefore the two together; for the unity of soul and body does not consist in the union of two parts which can always be seen and described separately. It is this double stipulation which makes difficult our present inquiries and representations, and especially the first in which it is a matter of the unity. On no side may we evade this difficulty. It would naturally be easier and more agreeable if we could skip the differentiation of soul and

[372]

body and speak simply of man as such, as made and willed by God. But then we should not have man as such before us; for the concrete reality of man consists in his being both, and only in both one. Again, it would be easy and simple if we could speak comfortably of the soul first and then of the body, and in this succession and combination of man as such. But we should then miss man as such; for his concrete reality consists in his being absolutely one, and only in this way both. No mitigation is, in fact, possible except at the cost of the thing itself. And a third stipulation is to be added at the start, which makes the thing no easier and which is to be observed just as carefully. This is that in the unity and differentiation of man we do not have a symmetrical relation. That he is wholly and simultaneously both sou and body does not exclude the fact that he is always both in different ways; first soul and then body. It would again be easier and more suitable if instead of this we could reckon with an equal division of weight and worth between the two moments. But this we may not do. We should again abandon the concrete reality of man if we did not reckon from the very outset with the inequality of that which in man is different and yet one.

We begin then, as is proper, with a statement about man's soul. We recall our proposition concerning the Spirit, that as the creative action of God He arouses the soul as the life of man, but that He is not for that reason identical with it. Applying this statement to the soul, we must first say concerning it too that it is not identical with the Spirit. It owes its being and existence to the Spirit. It is spiritual soul. But it is not a kind of prolongation or continuation of that divine action. It is the creature grounded by this action, and the action of this creature.

It is not the effecting of life but life in being (H. Cremer). In the concrete language of the [373] concepts and outlook of the Old Testament, it is not the quickening breath of God but that which lives by it, man's own breath awakened by it. We have already seen how close the connexion is. Since the soul is spiritual soul and entirely from the Spirit, the Old and New Testaments can often speak of the spirit where the wording and context of the passage make it plain that only the soul can be meant. The breath of the creature is never more than the answer to the breathing of the Creator. Occasionally then, though remarkably seldom, the LXX can venture to render *ruah*[EN65] directly by $\psi\upsilon\chi\acute{\eta}$[EN66]. But the converse is never true that the soul is spoken of where the Spirit is unambiguously meant. The breathing of the Creator cannot be understood as an answer to the breath of the creature, or the work of the Creator as an answer to the work of the creature. There is in fact no case where the LXX translates *nephesh*[EN67] by $\pi\nu\epsilon\hat{\upsilon}\mu\alpha$[EN68]. Even these Alexandrian Jews had a sharp perception that the interchange of the ideas is possible from above downwards but not from below upwards. The condescension of the Spirit has no parallel in the elevation of the soul.

But we cannot complete this delimiting statement about the soul without immediately speaking of the body as well. The soul is not a being for itself, and

---

[EN65] spirit
[EN66] soul
[EN67] soul
[EN68] spirit

it cannot exist for itself. Soul can awake and be only as soul of a body. Soul presupposes a body whose soul it is, i.e., a material body which, belonging to soul, becomes an organic body. Soul is inner—how could it be this if it had no outer? Soul is movement in time—how could it be this if it did not have an inalienable spatial complement, if it had no place? Soul fulfils itself in specific perceptions, experiences, excitations, thoughts, feelings and resolutions—how could it do this if it had no means in and through which it could exhibit itself? But all these, outwardness and space and means, it does not have of itself. All these constitute its body. Thus in being soul, it is not without body. It is, only as it is soul of a body. Hence every trivialisation of the body, every removal of the body from the soul, and every abstraction between the two immediately jeopardises the soul. Every denial of the body necessarily implies a denial of the soul. It is in this, when seen from below, that the difference between soul and Spirit consists. The Spirit cannot be said to need a body. It is divine action. It is the free act of grace on the part of the Creator. It needs a body as little as God needs the world. The converse is true that the world needs God, and the body needs the Spirit because it needs the soul. Without the Spirit, it could only be a material body, not the body of a soul, not a quickened and living body, and therefore not an organic body. Man is soul of a body and therefore necessarily both soul and body. This is what distinguishes him from the Spirit, and what distinguishes the act of his existence from the creative act on which his existence is based. Thus the first delimiting definition would be impracticable if it did not also contain the idea of the body.

[374]   Soul is "life as it stirs in the individual and quickens the material organism which serves as a means for its activity." Soul is "the inner being of man which on one hand bears the Spirit, and on the other is distinctively determined by the fact that this Spirit is the principle of a corporeal being" (H. Cremer). In the plastic language of the Old Testament, that which according to Gen. 2^7 is created by the breath of God could not enter into being, or would immediately cease to be, if this product of the breath of God were not related to a product of His hands: "And the Lord God formed man of the dust of the ground." Note that this formation, a material body which has not yet become an organic body, is already called "man." He can be called this, only in view of what follows concerning the breath of life which God breathes into the nostrils of this formation. But it is worth noting that this formation is in fact called "man," that the one man can obviously be seen and understood wholly from this bodily side. Man in his totality offers this aspect too. The materialists are quite right: he is wholly this living bodily organism, this corporeal life as well. And this distinguishes his soul from the volitional act of God, from the Spirit, by whom it is awakened and created.

We move on from this delimitation. Soul is life, self-contained life, the independent life of a corporeal being. Life in general means capacity for action, self-movement, self-activity, self-determination. Independent life is present where this self-movement, self-activity, and self-determination are not only the continuation and partial appearance of a general life-process, but where there is a specific living subject. Not every corporeal being is living. Purely elementary corporeal beings are not this. They lack the capacity for action. To ascribe soul to corporeal beings like a stone or a mass of water or a puff of wind or a flame would be an absolute *contradictio in adiecto*[EN69]. We do not know what we are talking about if we try to do this. Soul is life. What is lifeless is soulless. Again, there are corporeal beings of which there can be no doubt that they are living but real doubt whether their life is independent and not merely the partial appearance of a general life-process. We cannot know whether a specific plant is a subject. We say more than we can answer for if we speak of plant-souls. Independent life, the life of a specific subject, does not emerge except where the capacity for action of a corporeal being is not bound to a specific point in space. The capacity for action of the beast and of man is independent life of this kind. Here again, however, we must make the qualification that, although we recognise the life of the beast as such, we do not know but can only surmise or suspect that it is an independent life, the life of a specific subject. The life of man, and man alone, is for us the object of true and direct knowledge. What we mean when we speak of soul, we can strictly know only when we speak of the human soul. Soul is independent, the life of a particular subject. I know it as such independent life as I know myself. I know life as mine, as the life proper to myself as a subject. With this life of mine I may also be the continuation and partial appearance of a general life-process. But at any rate, as I know myself, I know my life as my own and myself as the subject of my life. Whether the beast is engaged in such self-knowledge or is even capable of it, I cannot know, because the beast cannot tell me any thing about it. I myself say [375] to myself that I am engaged in this self-knowledge and therefore capable of it. All the acts of my life consist also at least in the fact that I say this to myself. And my fellow-man tells me—he too with all the acts of his life—that he is engaged in the same self-knowledge and is capable of it. On the basis of this agreement, it is a reasonable hazard to ascribe to him as to myself, and therefore to man as such, independent life and therefore soul.

But this process whereby we become conscious of ourselves, of our independent life and therefore of our soul, is not merely an act of soul, whether in subject or in object. It is indeed true that both in subject and in object it is wholly an act of soul. As I live and am therefore soul I find myself able to become conscious that I am soul. And as I make use of this ability, my life itself and therefore my soul executes a return movement to itself. I come to myself, discover myself and become assured of myself. It belongs to my capacity for action that I continuously do this, that I am continuously engaged in the act of becoming self-conscious and therefore in this return movement. It all takes place in me and therefore in my soul. Yet it cannot be denied that this act in which my soul is at once subject and object is also wholly a corporeal act. The life which I live, and to whose fulfilment this return movement belongs, is in none of its moments other than the independent life of my physical body. I am not this material body of mine; it is not this material body that lives. But I do not exist without also being this material body. I do not live otherwise than as I

[EN69] contradiction in terms

live in my body. As certainly as it is a capacity of my soul, this capacity of mine for that return movement is bound up with the fact that I am also a material body, and that as I make use of the capacity, and perform that movement, I necessarily perform also a corporeal act. It would be very hazardous even to affirm that for this return movement I do not need my corporeal senses. Without having some command and making some use of them, I cannot be aware of objects different from myself. And without being aware of objects different from myself, I cannot distinguish myself from others as the object identical with myself, and cannot therefore recognise myself as a subject. In the delimitation and determination of myself as an object of my knowledge, which is decisive for the fulfilment of my self-consciousness and which is necessarily presupposed in my self-knowledge as a subject, I thus have great need even of my corporeal senses. It may well be true that this act of knowledge is not seeing, hearing or smelling or any perception communicated by my physical senses, but an inner experience of myself. Yet it is just as true that this experience, while it is internal and a moment in the history of my soul, is also external and a moment in the history of my material body. Were it not the latter, it [376] would not be the former. If as soul I were not also my material body, I should not be at all. If I did not live as my material body, I should not live at all. Did I not know myself in the common act of my soul and my material body, I should not know myself at all. And if I do in fact know myself, and am engaged in the process of my self-consciousness and therefore come to myself, discover myself and find assurance of myself as happens in every act of my life, the end thus reached, the discovery made and the assurance obtained is certainly my soul, my independent life, I myself as the subject of this life, yet at the same time it is never merely my soul, nor is it my soul alongside or even in my material body (like an oyster in its shell), but it is my soul as the independent life of this material body of mine, and therefore absolutely with this body, and therefore I myself as the subject of my life which is also wholly and utterly a corporeal being. I have not come to myself, discovered myself or received any assurance about myself, if I have not perceived myself as the soul of this material body and therefore my soul as its independent life and myself also as this corporeal being. Thus in both subject and object the act in which we become conscious of ourselves, in which we are known with our soul and therefore with the soul generally, is wholly and at the same time both a soulful and a corporeal act, or, more accurately, a soulful act which directly includes a corporeal. If it is not both, the one within the other, then it does not happen at all. We are not then conscious of ourselves, and we do not know what we are talking about when we speak of soul.

These noetic facts are grounded in ontic. Soul is independent life. But independent life in itself would be an empty and impossible concept. What is life without something quickened and living? We say nothing at all in the words "life" and "independent," if we do not speak immediately and simultaneously of something quickened and alive. Even when we try to define independent life as the self-movement, self-activity and self-formation fulfilled by a specific subject, we clearly presuppose not only the time but also a place and a material in and on which this movement, activity and formation is accomplished. And when we speak of a subject's independent life, and therefore of soul, we presuppose that there is a spatio-material system of relations which is no less proper to this subject, which is lived and quickened by it, and which by the self-contained life of this subject is alive for its own part, i.e., one in which the self-movement, self-activity and self-formation of this subject fulfils and realises itself, and which thus acquires a share in this life of which in itself it is not participant. This spatio-material system of relations is the material body. Independent life is not for itself; it is the independent life of a material body. Soul is not for itself; it is the besouling of a material body. In the material body it has the problem to which it replies, the object in relation to which it is subject, the sphere of action in which it is at work. The material body may be generally defined as a spatio-material system of relations. It is spatial, i.e., it is essential to [377] it to be at its own specific point in space. It is material, i.e., it is essential to it to be distinct from other bodies in virtue of its own specific material mode or composition. It is a system of relations, i.e., it is essential to it to have a specific spatial and material structure, not free in its inner relation, but forming a specific composition. Soul is the besouling of such a body and therefore the principle of its becoming and being alive. Soul is, as it is the soul of such a body, as it is alive in it and for it, thus rendering alive that which as mere material body is not alive. As we have seen, it does not belong to the concept of material body to be alive, and even less to be alive in an independent way and therefore to be besouled. On the contrary, it belongs to the concept of material body, and primarily of every material body, not to be for itself but at best only to be able to become. Again, it does not belong to the concept of any material body that it can be alive and even besouled. It is with the plant that the possibility of a living material body begins, with the beast that of an independent organic body, and with man that of the perceptibility and comprehensibility of an independent organic body. Soul and therefore besouling is in no sense a general determination of the world of bodies, but a matter of selection from among bodies. It thus implies a lack of reflection to speak of a world soul or of all cosmic reality as besouled. All material bodies are spatial and material systems of relations, but not all of them can be alive, let alone alive in an independent manner. This is not even possible for them all. The selection of those that can be has been made and is fixed. A plant will never live in an independent manner; to do so it would have to be transformed into a very different material body. A stone will never live at all; to do so it would have to cease to be a stone and adopt the spatiality and corporeality, the system of relations, of a very different material body. On the other hand, the animal body, and distinctly and recognisably the human, will always have at least the possibility of independent life, of being the body of a soul. When a material body is besouled, it does not cease to be material body, but only to be merely material body. As a problem answered, as an object in relation to a subject, as a sphere of action filled and controlled by deed, it becomes organic body. Hence we do not describe real man correctly if we call him soul of his material body, or soul and material body. As man lives, as the material body is his material body and therefore the material body of his soul, the latter is more than material body. It is his organic body, and man must therefore be described as soul of his organic body or as soul and organic body.

It is remarkable and regrettable that the important distinction, material and organic body (*Körper* and *Leib*), cannot be reproduced in Greek, Latin, French or English, and therefore two meanings which in this connexion are fundamentally distinct must be linked with the same word (σῶμα, *corpus*, *corps*, body).

[378] The organic body is distinguished from the purely material body by the fact that as animal or at all events human body—we hardly speak of the organic body of a stone or plant—it is besouled and filled and controlled by independent life. By its selection from among all other material bodies, and without ceasing to be a material body, it can be taken up into unity with a soul and in all respects share its being and willing, though without itself becoming soul. As the organic body of a soul, it is no longer merely an object of its self-movement, self-activity and self-formation; it is always this of course, but it now moves, activates and develops itself with it. As it may live through and with it, it is no longer for itself—if it were it would not be alive—but is for the soul as the soul is for it. It is and works with the soul. But since the soul is independent and therefore the life of a particular subject, this means that it is not now a mere object—though it is always this—but also a subject. When a living corporeal being says I, this I, as that of its soul, is also that of its body, and not merely of some privileged part of its body, but of its whole body in which there are indeed centres and peripheries, but no parts which are simply excluded from the besouling of the whole. It has also to be considered from the standpoint of the soul that if the body is not organic body but purely material body when it is without soul, so the soul is not soul but only the possibility of soul when it is without body. I may be identical with my soul, but my soul is not for itself, but is the besouling of my body. To this extent I am identical as soul with my body, and my movement, activity and development are never merely soulful, but as such are also bodily. I cannot be without or against but only for my body, as it can only be for me, as it cannot live without me and therefore without my soul, and as it is actually for me, constituting my only possibility of expression without which I could not be even inwardly. I cannot answer for myself without at the same time answering for my body. I cannot express or represent myself without the participation of my body and without its co-responsibility for the manner and genuineness of my expression and representation. In every respect I can only work as this spatio-material system of relations, which as my organic body is my material body, is real, i.e., participant in my work and therefore in my subjectivity. All rejection of this interconnexion, and all attempts to

deny it in theory or practice, can only mean a distortion of the nature of man and precipitate it from one disorder into another.

The Old Testament *nephesh*[EN70] is just as strictly and fully the life of the body as the New Testament ψυχή[EN71]. This sense does not exhaust the term, but it is always present in all its other uses. The Greek conception of the soul as a second and higher "part," as an imperishable, if possible pre-existent, and in any case immortal spiritual substance of human reality, contrasted with the body as its lower and mortal part—the conception of the soul as a captive in the prison of its body, is quite unbiblical.

The Old Testament sees the soul as the life of the body and therefore in conjunction with it. *Nephesh*[EN72] like *ruah* means breath, but now concretely—the breath which comes and goes in a human throat, and which distinguishes the living being from the dead. The word *naphash* must not be forgotten. Where breathing is present or restored, there is soul, but there must also be a body in which it takes place. When someone loses patience (e.g., the people in the desert, Num. 21⁴, or Samson with Delilah, Jud. 16¹⁶), then his breath "is shortened." If someone comes to himself after deathlike weakness (e.g., the son of the widow of Zarephath, 1 K. 17²¹), then his breath returns to him. But breath is only the representative and linguistic cipher for the bodily life as such. Since *nephesh* is bodily life, the soul can "long" and "be satisfied" or "hunger" and "be filled" (Ps. 107⁹); it can also be chastened by fasting (Ps. 69¹⁰) and polluted by forbidden food (Ez. 4¹⁴). Hence "to save his soul" means simply to "go for his life" (like Elijah in 1 K. 19³). Similarly, a man risks his soul, i.e., his life (in a heroic deed, as in 2 Sam. 23¹⁷); a word can cost a man his soul, i.e., his life (Adonijah, 1 K. 2²³); the soul, i.e., life (A.V. "ghost"), is "breathed out" (Jer. 15⁹) or "poured out" (Lam. 2¹²), or it can "depart" (Gen. 35¹⁸). This just means that the soul dies (Jud. 16³⁰; Ez. 13¹⁹). That is, it can die or be "devoured" (Ez. 22²⁵), i.e., be killed (Num. 31¹⁹), as certainly as it is created (Is. 57¹⁶; Jer. 38¹⁶) and is the life of the mortal body. The Old Testament is at its most emphatic on this point in Lev. 17¹¹. The soul of the flesh is in the blood, and immediately after (v. 14) there is the rather sententious repetition: "the soul (A.V. "life") of all flesh is the blood thereof" (cf. Deut. 12²³). Hence all shedding of blood, whether permitted or not, is an act of the highest significance, and the eating of blood is forbidden. Just as *nephesh* as bodily life can always mean the life of an individual corporeal being, so it can always mean the living individual himself. Thus *kol ha'nephesh*[EN73] in Josh. 10²⁸ denotes the complete human and animal population of a city. Again, in the numbering of the people (e.g., Num. 31³⁵), souls are numbered instead of men. Again, the slaves whom anyone has won can be called "souls" (e.g., Gen. 12⁵). In the long run, "soul" can simply indicate a being or individual, e.g., one who sins (Lev. 4²), and even paradoxically one who is dead (*nephesh met*, Num. 6⁶). Even in the important verse in Gen. 2⁷, where it is said that man became a "living soul" by the *ruah*[EN74] breathed into him, we have to do with this diluted sense of the concept. And in some emphatic passages *nephesh* can be used for "I myself" or "thou thyself," and therefore as the personal pronoun. The only point to remember is that it is the subjectivity of a corporeal being which is denoted by the term.

We could not claim that the sense and use of ψυχή[EN75] in the New Testament is essentially different. It is striking that the term is particularly frequent in Acts, and here it obviously bears the Old Testament meanings of life, individual life and individual. But even in the rest

[379]

[EN70] soul
[EN71] soul
[EN72] soul
[EN73] all the souls
[EN74] spirit
[EN75] soul

of the New Testament there are few passages where there is even the slightest suggestion of the Greek conception of the soul. When the ψυχή [EN76] is spoken of as loving, finding, preserving, gaining, saving, finding peace and prosperity, forfeiting, losing, perishing, being exterminated and departing, there are no grounds for thinking of anything other than simply the life of man in contrast to his death. Even Mt. 10^{28} does not say that the soul cannot be killed, but only that no man can kill it, while God has the power to cause both soul and body to pass away and be destroyed in the nether world. Hence we do not have here a doctrine of the immortality of the soul. The difference from the Old Testament consists in the fact that the forfeiture of life to death on the one hand, and the promise and hope of a deliverance of life from death on the other, are now much more strongly bound together. But here, too, the ψυχή [EN77] is the whole man, the life of his body, he himself as he exists in this bodily life. And the content of the promise and hope given to man is not its immortality but its future deliverance in the resurrection from the dead.

[380]   The one man is wholly and simultaneously soul and body. In the light of this fact three delimitations are demanded.

1. We necessarily contradict the abstractly dualistic conception which so far we have summarily called Greek, but which unfortunately must also be described as the traditional Christian view. According to this view, soul and body are indeed connected, even essentially and necessarily united, but only as two "parts" of human nature. Of these, each is to be understood as a special substance, self-contained and qualitatively different in relation to the other. The soul is spiritual, non-spatial, indissoluble, and immortal; the body material, spatial, dissoluble and mortal. If this is the case, if soul and body are two "parts" of which man is "composed," if these two "parts" are two self-contained substances, if these substances are quite different and even opposed in nature, and if this involves an opposition of the worth of the one (the soul) to the unworthiness of the other (the body), what are we to make of their alleged connexion and unity, and therefore of the unity of man's being? Is this affirmation of unity more impressive if the unity is called a "mystery" and compared with the unity of the two natures of Christ? Is it not clear that in these circumstances soul and body neither have nor can have anything in common, but can only be in conflict and finally part from one another? From the understanding already attained, we may deny that the doctrine of these two shadowy substances is the Christian understanding of man, although for many years it has been self-evidently accepted as such.

"Human nature consists of body and soul" (B. Bartmann: *Lehrbuch der Dogmatik*, 1928, Vol. I, p. 271). Taught by Plato and Aristotle, the fathers, schoolmen and orthodox theologians of older Protestantism all held and taught this view, believing that the anthropology of the Old and New Testaments was to be expounded along these lines. This is the view of man which Roman Catholic dogmatics still represent as the normative Christian understanding. The connexion between soul and body is affirmed by understanding the soul, like Aristotle,

---

[EN76] soul
[EN77] soul

as the ἐντελέχεια σώματος^{EN78}, the *forma corporis*^{EN79}, a formula which was raised to the status of a dogma in the *Conc. Viennense* (1311–12, Denz. *No.* 841). The connexion was described as a co-existence of two substances, nor was there any hesitation in saying that the connexion is total, and therefore that the soul, even if not in a local sense, is *tota in toto corpore et tota in qualibet parte corporis*^{EN80} (Voetius, *Disp. theol.*, 1648, 767). Mediation was obviously sought between the two spheres by distinguishing within the soul between an *anima vegetativa, sensitiva* and *intellectiva* (*rationalis*) ^{EN81}, the implication being that on the last and highest level the soul of man is distinguished from that of the animals by its *facultas apprehendendi verum et appetendi bonum*^{EN82} (P. v. Mastricht, *Theor. Pract. Theol.*, 1698 III, 9, 6). But in respect of this supreme and distinctively human capacity, it is now described, with Plato, as οὐσία ἀσώματος αὐτοκίνητος^{EN83} as a *substantia talis naturae, quae a corpore etiam separari et subsistere per se posset*^{EN84} (Polanus, *Syn. Theol. chr.*, 1609, col. 2060). The central affirmation in this whole anthropology is that of the immortality of this rational thing, the human soul; and immortality is a property which does not come to it by the special grace of God, but dwells within it by nature, so that it can be proved not only by Holy Scripture but on general rational grounds. Such a proof is given, for example, by P. v. Mastricht (*op. cit.* III, 9, [381] 17), and it takes the following form: 1. the soul is spiritual, and therefore not material, dissoluble, nor mortal; 2. the righteousness of God requires the preservation of the soul through death for the purpose of the eternal reward and punishment of man; 3. the wisdom of God cannot permit that the end of man be the same as that of a beast, and his soul must therefore be immortal; 4. all religion would cease if we were faced with the fact that only the decaying body remained of man and thus his soul too were mortal. *Corpore igitur distracto, discerpto, manet anima substantia, manet cogitans, manet id, quod voce hac "Ego" significatur, nil diminutum, nisi quod integumento suo exuitur*^{EN85}. (H. Heidegger, *Corp. theol.*, 1700 VI, 87, quoted by Heppe, p. 181). So strange to one another are soul and body according to this doctrine, that in death they can part from one another in this manner. So little force has the affirmation of the soul as *forma corporis*^{EN86} that the body on the other hand can become the mere *integumentum*^{EN87} of the soul. In this doctrine of the immortality of the soul, an over-estimation of the first moment of the human reality betrays and establishes itself which necessarily leads to an almost wholly negative estimation of the second, and to a trivialising or minimising or ignoring of the problem of corporeality. Hence the anthropology of the older dogmatic becomes remarkably sparing of words, and the little it says remarkably gloomy, when it begins to say that which *in thesi*^{EN88} it does not deny but emphasises solemnly as a great mystery, namely, that in the end man is not only a psychical but also a physical being. Polanus is an infrequent exception (*op. cit., col.* 1900 f.) when he accords to the human body as such three whole chapters of his exposition, and even develops an

---

^{EN78} form of the body
^{EN79} form of the body
^{EN80} wholly in the whole body and wholly in every part of the body
^{EN81} vegetative, sensitive ... intellective (rational) soul
^{EN82} capacity to apprehend the true and desire the good
^{EN83} a disembodied, self-moving substance
^{EN84} a substance of such a nature as to be able also to be separated from the body and subsist by itself
^{EN85} Thus when the body has been torn apart or mutilated, the substance of the soul remains, the thinking subject remains, that which is designated by the term "I" remains, in no way diminished, except that it has cast off its covering
^{EN86} form of the body
^{EN87} covering
^{EN88} in propositional form

§ 46. *Man as Soul and Body*

Anatomia theologica partium humani corporis[EN89], in which he tries to show, in a series of astonishing allegories, that we are instructed by the composition of the human body *de rebus divinis, nempe de Deo, eius essentia, attributis, operibus, beneficiis, iudiciis, etc., de Christo Mediatore, de Angelis, de Ecclesia, de officio nostro, quod debemus cum Deo tum proximo nostro, de aliis denique rebus praeclaris, quibus ad Deum mentes nostrae attolluntur*[EN90]. A few examples may be taken from the plenitude of his fancies. Thus the form of the human heart, broader above and narrower below, reminds us that while we keep to things below, to that which is earthly, temporal and visible, we should be wide open to higher, heavenly and eternal things. Again, the systole and diastole of the heart remind us of the wisdom of avoiding everything which is superfluous and unhelpful in our worship of God and of zealously making our own that which is necessary for the love of God and our neighbour. Again, the form of the human skull, in contrast to that of the animals, is an imitation of the globe and cosmos. Our forehead reminds us warningly that we may have no connexion with the city of Rome, the whore on whose forehead, according to Rev. 17[5], "Mystery, Babylon the Great" is written. Again, the fact that we have two ears but only one mouth signifies that we should listen more than speak. The ears are more important than the eyes, since it is with the ears and the ears alone that we come to understand doctrine, wisdom, and above all the Word of God. But the mouth is also valuable for proclaiming the Word of God; nor is it forgotten that it is also of value for breathing and the taking of nourishment. Strict Calvinist that he is, Polanus discourses for two columns about the different kisses that appear in the Bible (from the apostolic *osculum caritatis*[EN91] to the Old Testament *osculum valedictionis*[EN92]). It is clear that the existence and activity of the different "spirits of life," with which Polanus deals in accordance with the physiological knowledge of his day, give occasion for significant sidelights on the work of the Holy Spirit. We need not waste time in showing how dubious is this whole line of investigation. I seriously wonder whether my illustrious predecessor did not fall victim occasionally in this chapter to the spirit of the Basel *Fastnacht*[EN93], and quite deliberately indulge in pious witticisms. At all events, his work does not form any very useful contribution to an alleviation of the problem. Yet, though we shake our heads at his "theological anatomy," we must remember that the dogmatics of the Early Church did not even accord to the human body this allegorical attention, but treated it only as the boundary of the problem of the soul, which was its only real interest. It will be conceded to Polanus that this stepchild of anthropology, which otherwise was mostly despised, did at all events occupy him in its way, and that he did at least attempt to help it to the honour which was otherwise denied it. In general, the character and result of this anthropology are marked by a separation of soul and body, an exaltation of the soul over the body, a humiliation of the body under the soul, in which both really become not merely abstractions but in fact two "co-existing" figments— a picture in which probably no real man ever recognised himself, and with which one cannot possibly do justice to the biblical view and concept of man. It was disastrous that this picture of man could assert and maintain itself for so long as the Christian picture. We must earnestly protest that this is not the Christian picture.

[382]

2. On the other hand, we cannot accept the reactions in which the attempt

---

[EN89] Theological Anatomy of the Parts of the Human Body
[EN90] about matters divine, especially about God: His essence, attributes, works, benefits, judgements, etc.; about Christ the Mediator, about Angels, about the Church, about our duty (what we owe to God and our neighbour), and also about other wondrous things, by which our minds are brought near to God
[EN91] kiss of peace
[EN92] kiss of farewell
[EN93] lit. 'Fasting Eve,' a Mardi Gras type celebration in German speaking countries; Fat Tuesday

has been made to set over against the abstract dualism of the Greek and traditional Christian conception a no less abstract monism.

There is first monistic materialism. This is the theory according to which the one substance of man consists in his corporeality, while the soul is treated in practice as at most the boundary of the only real problem, that of the body, and its particular existence is flatly denied. On this view, the real is only what is corporeal, spatial, physical and material. What cannot be brought under this denominator is either mere appearance, imagination, illusion, an irrelevant by-product or "epiphenomenon" of corporeal causes and conditions, or, more mildly conceived and expressed, its subjectively conditioned and necessary phenomenal form. In the true and proper sense, there is in man no soul and nothing spiritual; he is body only; besides the causal sequence of material change and other bodily functions, there are only certain processes in the brain and nerves which we are wrong to interpret as actions *suae originis et sui generis*[EN94], as thoughts, decisions, feelings and the like, as an independent being over against that of the body, and for which it is only in enslavement to mythological notions that we feel it necessary to posit a basis in the soul as a genuine element of reality.

This, then, is the materialistic counter-attack. It is historically quite understandable. It does not rest primarily on scientific considerations, but on a certain kind of honesty and sobriety (recognisably antithetical to the Greek and traditional Christian view) in face of the actual course of individual and social life. This is what gives materialism old and new its surprising and confusing power in spite of its theoretical weakness. The Christian Church is forced by this opponent to investigate more seriously the tenability of the abstract dualism of its own conception, since on its side too the connexion of soul and body is continually asserted but cannot really be exhibited within the framework of its conception. Indeed, the contrary thesis cannot be simply or finally denied, for rather disquietingly the biblical picture of man, and especially the resur- [383] rection hope of the New Testament, forces us to think along the lines to which materialism now points in one-sided but complementary opposition, but not without right and necessity.

Yet it is obvious that we must also contradict materialism with our statement that man is wholly and simultaneously soul and body. The appropriate philosophical criticism does not interest us here. Our argument against it is simply that its conception does not enable us to see real man. Man is also, and indeed wholly and utterly, body. This is what we must be told by materialism if we have not learned it elsewhere. But there is no sense in trying to seek and find man only in his body and its functions. For if he is really seen as body, he is seen also as soul, that is, as the subject which gives life to his material body, to the spatio-material system of relations which physiology describes, thus distinguishing it as an organic body from a purely material body, and giving it stability even as a

---

[EN94] having their own origin and of a distinct type

material body. Man's material body, its matter and energies, are those of his living organic body. To be sure, man is identical with this living because quickened body in all its organs and with all its functions, actions and passions, but only as the continuously living and quickening subject of his body, only as this body of his continuously becomes identical with him, and he with it. We obviously do not see man if we will not see that, as he is wholly his body, he is also wholly his soul, which is the subject, the life of this body of his. Because materialism will not see this, it is unacceptable, and we have to ask whether it is not even more guilty of the very illusionism with which it charges the Greek and traditional early Christian conception, since the latter does not deny or suppress the problem of corporeality even though it cannot do justice to it, whereas that of the soul is completely eliminated under the hard fists of the materialists. With them, the two figments of the Greek tradition and early Christian conception become one. This is not an advance. They would be right if only they did not want to be exclusively right. But they want to be exclusively right, and therefore they are wrong.

"Materialism" is not a product of modern times alone. As is well known, it played a role in the different phases of ancient philosophy, from Thales and the other Ionians by way of Democritus to Epicureus. Thus it confronted Christian theology not only in the 17th and 18th centuries but long before. For example, at the beginning of the 16th century it confronted it in a form in which it ought to have engaged its attention. In 1516, the same year in which Luther delivered his famous lectures on the Epistle to Romans, there appeared a work by the Italian philosopher Pietro Pomponazzo entitled *De immortalitate animae*, in which the Aristotelian statement, *anima forma corporis*[EN95] (and therefore the dogma of 1311), was interpreted to mean that the soul belongs to the body, is inseparable from it, cannot persist without it, and therefore, as a mode of its existence, must fade and die with it. The most that Pomponazzo could allow was that, though human knowledge is certainly not a purely imma-

[384]

terial activity, there takes place in it a certain ascent from sensible representations to universal ideas and therefore to eternity, so that the human soul resembles the immaterial and immortal without belonging to it, and thus stands nearer to it than anything else. The sphere of our existence, and of the tasks, duties and hopes in which each and every individual soul is determined, is the here and now, which stands in face of the eternal and hereafter, but is not coincident with it. Pomponazzo did not deny the hereafter. It seems that he did not even deny the resurrection of the dead (as the resurrection of the whole man). But in fact his doctrine of the soul is materialistic. He understood it as only *forma corporis*[EN96], and not as a substance independent of the body, different in attributes, immaterial and immortal. Many things would have been different, and many embarrassments would have been avoided in the 18th and 19th centuries, if three years before at the 5th Lateran Council (Denz. *No.* 738) the Roman Church had not dogmatically declared the immortality of the intellective soul, or if Reformation theology at least had girded itself for a new understanding at this point. This philosophical thesis might well have shown it how to apply its Scripture principle seriously in this matter, and thus to institute certain necessary and overdue investigations into the biblical as opposed to the Greek picture of man, especially in relation to biblical eschatology. On such a basis, it would not have needed to accept the materialism of Pomponazzo, but it

---

[EN95] the soul is the form of the body
[EN96] form of the body

would have had a better conscience in relation to this and all other materialism both before and after. Failure in this matter was probably a just consequence of the fact that the Reformation had too little time or understanding for biblical eschatology, and therefore saw no occasion to undertake a revision of the traditional anthropology. At all events, even Calvin (*Instit.*, I, 5, 6) identified himself at once with the Roman Catholic rejection of the thesis, his only argument being the platonic rather than biblical consideration that in the reason which encompasses heaven and earth, in its agility in investigating time and space, and in its endowment with free fancy as manifested in dreams and many works of art, we have clear and indestructible signs of the immortality of the human soul. Calvin even wrote expressly: *Certa sunt divinitatis insignia in homine*[EN97]. Following him, Ursin (*Loci theol.*, 1562, p. 559, quoted by Heppe, p. 179) and the theologians of the 17th century could only deny the thesis *a limine*[EN98]. In this respect, the Cartesians among them were even more decided than the Aristotelians, and A. Heidan (*Corp. Theol. chr.*, 1686, I, p. 335) could go so far as to say that apart from the denial of the existence of God no thesis was more morally dangerous than this which would put man on the level of the beasts. Christian theology thus dismissed the problem. But with such answers it could not adequately deal with the practical reality of human life in every century, with the contemporary development of speculation about nature, or least of all with the questions arising from the Bible. And so it had to be prepared for the fact that, in virtue of the *particula veri*[EN99] which cannot be denied, materialism would arise in a new and even more difficult form—as in fact happened.

As an example of the specifically modern form in which it appears as it were in the springtime of its sins, and in which in the middle and the end of last century it evoked as much enthusiastic applause on the one side as anxious shock or angry rejection on the other, we may take the conception in which it was introduced by the Jena zoologist, Ernst Haeckel, in his book *Die Welträthsel*, which first appeared in 1899 and was later very widely publicised. A similar Bible of modern materialism, *Kraft und Stoff*, had already been written in 1855 by a tutor at Tübingen, Ludwig Büchner, who was dismissed because of it. In the same year Karl Vogt (a German exile in Geneva) had published his work *Köhlerglaube und Wissenschaft*, in which there occurs the contemptible sentence that "thoughts are related to the brain in much the same way as gall to the liver and urine to the kidneys." In the middle of the 19th century, Jakob Moleschott, another German tutor, had also emerged as a champion of similar views and was disciplined in consequence. During the forty years between these men and Haeckel, the philosophy of L. Feuerbach was at work on the frontiers of materialism. Man is (*ist*) what he eats (*isst*), was the ingenious formula with which he enriched future discussion. In the work of his old age, *Der alte und der neue Glaube* (1872), D. F. Strauss finally broke with absolute Idealism and crossed over with flags flying into the camp of this very different system. The vote of Haeckel was the last and the most massive and impressive word in the matter. His exposition in chapters 6–11 of his book is as follows. What is called "soul" is a natural phenomenon. Psychology is thus a branch of physiology. The basis of all spiritual events in both man and beast is "psychoplasm," an egg-white carbonic compound. What we call experiences, motions, reflexes, ideas, memories, instincts, conceptions, emotions and decisions, as also what we finally and supremely call self-consciousness, are mere functions of the animal organism alive in virtue of this plasm. Their differences are only steps on a scale rising from the protozoon to man, and they are all subject to the law of the one moved and self-moving material substance. Psyche is only a collective concept for the totality of these functions. The soul comes into being (i.e., the course of these functions begins) in the

[385]

[EN97] The marks of immortality in humanity are certain
[EN98] from the outset
[EN99] grain of truth

moment of copulation, in which the male and female cell-kernels come together to form the nucleus of a new body, which is in this sense inherited. With the other vital activities of the organism, this then follows its individual development from the unself-conscious condition of the newly born to the senile decay which hurries on to the dissolution of self-consciousness. Hence man's soul is only the last and supreme form in the history which leads from the soul of the cell by that of a union of cells to the soul of a complete structure, then to the soul of plants and beasts, and in the latter sphere from the soul of primitive animals to that of the higher mammals and finally to man as the highest. Even consciousness, the "central psychological mystery," the "strong citadel of all mystic and dualistic errors, against whose mighty walls all attacks of the best-armed reason are threatened with ruin," is a natural phenomenon, which like all others is subject to the law of substance. It is explained by the fact that in the brain of mammals, in the zone of gray crust which covers the brain, there are not only "sense convolutions" but also four special "thought convolutions" or association centres, of specially developed structure in the case of man, in which the soul has its locus and from which all its phenomena can be explained. Stimulation, numbing and disease of these portions of the brain result in consequential changes in consciousness. Consciousness begins, grows, fails and finally expires in the individual ontogenes. From the consciousness of the amorba to that of the cultured man of the present day, it develops in the universal phylogenes. Hence it follows that this, too, is a physiological function of the brain, and therefore not the immaterial and immortal being of a soul distinct from natural matter. The doctrine of immortality ("athanism") is an illusory opinion which stands in irresoluble contradiction to the most certain affirmations of modern science, which cannot be justified in face of physiology, histology, pathology, ontogenetics or phylogenetics, and for which finally no serious rational ground can be supplied.

The materialism of the middle and later 19th century was only in a very qualified sense the result of modern natural science, as it was only in a qualified sense that in its earlier form it was connected with a supposedly deeper and more exact knowledge of nature in different fields. There can be no doubt, of course, that the natural science of the 19th century, which was so much more thorough-going than ever before, had a general tendency in this direction, the public being specially aware of it in the bearing of its doctors; and that conclusions, such as those which Büchner, Vogt, Moleschott and finally Haeckel proposed, found an immense number of exponents and prophets among the *clerus minor*[EN100] of the world of culture with its contemporary interest in natural science. But it is also true that the leading and famous investigators and teachers in natural science, however much they might be inclined to think along similar lines, displayed strikingly little inclination in general for the conclusions of those who precipitated strife or for the proclamation of a dogmatic materialism. Nor was this because they were hampered by the powers of the state, society and the Church and could not summon up courage, but clearly because of the obvious insight so appropriate to the laboratory that, though these conclusions might seem to be suggested by their science, they could not be drawn by it. The step from affirming that human consciousness is a function of the brain to affirming that it is *only* a function of the brain, from stating that the soul is materially conditioned to stating that it is materially *constituted*, and therefore to materialistic monism, was and still is a $\mu\varepsilon\tau\acute{\alpha}\beta\alpha\sigma\iota\varsigma$ $\varepsilon\acute{\iota}\varsigma$ $\mathring{\alpha}\lambda\lambda o$ $\gamma\acute{\varepsilon}\nu o\varsigma$[EN101], which, when it is to be carried out, requires another justification than natural science can provide. Haeckel's "psychoplasm" has never actually been seen by mortal eye. Those who noticed that we must here believe, speculate and philosophise if we are to know, did not see a basis for their materialism—if they took this view—in their natural science, but were more likely to find in

[386]

EN100 lower clergy
EN101 change of categories

178

it a pretext for not committing themselves to materialism or making its proclamation a duty. It is also the case—and Haeckel himself deplored it loudly—that at this time some of those who bore names most prominent in natural science, such as Rudolf Virchow, Emil Dubois-Reymond, Wilhelm Wundt, and also George Romanes, the Englishman whom Haeckel specially prized, held publicly aloof from the systematising and dogmatising of materialism, although in their earlier years they had apparently or genuinely favoured it. The big event in the story of this contradiction was Dubois-Reymond's lecture to the *Naturforscherversammlung* in Leipzig on 14th August 1872, *Über die Grenzen des Naturerkennens*, in which he indicated that the connexion between matter and power, and that between our spiritual activity and its material conditions, constitute the limits beyond which the human spirit cannot go even in the most advanced natural knowledge: *ignoramus—ignorabimus!*[EN102] Haeckel declared to Dubois-Reymond and his other colleagues, with firmness and friendliness, that their position was explicable only by a psychological metamorphosis caused by the advancing predominance of age. But when they adopted this position these men had no intention of confessing the spiritualism and dualism of the Early Church, as this had been passed on to them through the decades. Their aim was rather to indicate the reservations which must be made, if science is to be true to itself, against a leap which might perhaps appear to be a close consequence from it, but which can in no case be claimed as what it is usually called a "finding" of science.

But the modern materialism which particularly interests us cannot be dismissed in this way. It had and has the power, not of true science, but of a comprehensive view of the world; and the emergence and composition of this view rest on the very real "psychoplasm" of very powerful emotions which for their part are related to certain undeniable historical, ethical social and facts. This holds good, not for His Excellency from Weimar, Haeckel, personally, but for the vexatious popular applause which both he and his older spiritual companions found for their poetry. It seems to be a fact that human reality represents itself to the naive consideration of most men of all ages in a form which is far closer to the materialistic picture than to that of Christian dualism. And there can be no doubt that, as the result of rapid social progress since the 17th century, from 1830 at the very latest, a form of life began to distinguish itself which must and did speak with primitive weight in favour of a materialistic anthropology. The general rationalisation of human life in the sense of this progress which had begun in the 18th century, very clearly and decisively involved in the practice of the 19th its subjection to economics, its commercialisation, industrialisation and mechanisation, and therefore its obvious materialisation. At the beginning of the century, the Idealists, e.g., Schleiermacher as a moralist, had still visualised the powerful onslaught and victory of spirit over nature and matter. But the real picture which soon presented itself to all strata of [387] the civilised nations except the dreaming philosophers, poets and unfortunately theologians, was very different. The first railways began to rattle across Europe, the first steamships to cross the Atlantic, the first electric telephones to operate, the first forerunners of the modern photograph to immortalise the physical countenance of man as he is. There began a direction of enormous interest on the part of a noteworthy proportion of the Western intelligentsia towards technics with its promise of substantial rewards. There began the corresponding mass movement of town and country into the factories, forges and mines. The figure of the human robot, who neither asks nor is asked about his soul and therefore cannot ask about that of others, who by an anonymous centre of power is made, moved, regulated, used and then discarded and replaced from an anonymous centre—this materialistic human figure was now arising. Here it had the form of the great industrial and bank magnates, there that of the unperceptive co-operating middle-class townsmen, there in the

---

[EN102] we do not know - we shall not know

machinerooms and under the waterline of the great liners—"For some are in darkness and others in the light; and one sees those who are in the light but not those who are in darkness"—the new form of the modern proletariat. The real foundation of modern materialism, and the explanation of the validity and expansion which it has enjoyed in and in spite of its scientific weakness, are not to be found in the researches and results of biology and physiology, but in the rise of this form of humanity, in which everyone who lives with open eyes in and with his time must willingly or unwillingly recognise a little of himself. "And so I solve the problem: only he who lives in prosperity lives agreeably"—so thinks the big man contentedly and the little man discontentedly, except that the big man is perhaps seldom honest enough to admit to himself that this is how he thinks. What need is there for biology and physiology to prove to both of them that man must be thought of materialistically? They do this already. Nor do they do so only in the 19th century but earlier. The 19th century merely brings it to light.

This is where what is called "historical materialism" comes in. For it, what we have hitherto spoken of under the name of materialism is only a necessary weapon and an indispensable apologetic and polemical ally. The doctrine of Karl Marx, which is identical with this historical materialism, is undoubtedly materialism in the sense in which we have used the term, and in practice it stands or falls with the fact that it is so. Yet it is so only *per accidens*[EN103] and not *per essentiam*[EN104]. It is certainly one of the historical limits of Marxism that it has bound itself so closely with the dogma of ostensibly scientific materialism. But we quite misunderstand it if we take it to be grounded on this, or adopt the view of older theological polemics that it is one of its evil moral fruits. The very opposite is the case, namely, that ostensibly scientific materialism, at any rate in the 19th century, acquired weight only as it was discovered, appropriated and employed by historical materialism. Over against it, historical materialism is a construction with its own origin.

In face of the modern development of community, historical materialism is 1. the affirmation in which the child at last acquires a name, namely, that the whole history of mankind at its core is the history of human economy or economic history, and that everything else, the achievement of civilisation, science, art, the state, morality and religion, are only phenomenal accompaniments of this one reality, expressions of the current relations of economic forces, attempts to disguise, beautify, justify, and defend them, occasionally perhaps even expressions of its discontent, instruments of its criticism, means of its alteration, but at all events secondary forms or ideologies from which economics is differentiated as true historical reality. The figure of man which arose in the 19th century seemed unambiguously to prove this. At any rate, this is how it was interpreted and understood by Karl Marx.

[388]   Historical materialism is 2. a critique of the previous course of human history interpreted in this way. As economic history, it is the history of a struggle between the ruling and ruled strata or classes of the community, i.e., between the economically strong and the economically weak, between the invariable possessors of the earth and all the other means of production and the others who invariably do the work which is economically productive in the true sense. In this struggle, the latter, the workers, have always been the losers, and, under the characteristic modern dominance of anonymous capital striving only for its own increase, they are the losers with an accentuated necessity—the expropriated and exploited. Those ideologies have in fact shown themselves to be only accompanying phenomena which can neither render impossible nor stop the class war which is waged with such unequal weapons, but in different ways can only confirm and further it. How very differently does Karl Marx

---

[EN103] accidentally
[EN104] essentially

view what the Idealists only a few decades before had celebrated as the victory of the spirit over nature!

Historical materialism is 3. a prediction concerning the future course of the history of mankind. The dominance of the possessors, which has to-day become the dominance of anonymous capital, will necessarily lead to continually new crises of production and consumption, to warlike developments and revolutionary catastrophes. Thus with an inner necessity, it moves towards a final upheaval. The proletarianisation of the masses becomes sharper and sharper, and encroaches upon greater and greater levels even of the modern middle class. The class of the oppressed, thus increasing, will gradually be automatically compelled to unify itself, and to recognise and seize the power which really lies in its hands, in order finally and conclusively to make political, and if need be forceful, use of it, and to set up its own dictatorship in place of that of the anonymous tyrant. It expropriates those who have so far expropriated. It erects the economic and welfare social state in which there are no more exploiters and therefore no more exploited, in which all other social sicknesses vanish with their common cause, and in which morality, which in the present class-state is possible only in the form of hypocrisy, can become a genuine reality. Again, it will not be ideologies that will lead mankind to this end, but only economic material development as this is rightly understood and therefore directed at the right moment by the right intervention. This was the hope, the eschatology, which Karl Marx gave to his followers as the supreme good and as the appropriate driving motive for socialist action on the way to it.

Historical materialism is 4. a summons. It is not issued to all, and therefore not to the dominant middle class. Historical materialism has nothing to say to the "bourgeois," since *a priori*EN105 it does not expect that it will permit itself to have anything said to it or to learn anything, imprisoned as it is in the presuppositions of its economic position, which are stronger than its deepest insights and its best will. There are fortunate exceptions, and these can be put to good tactical use; but they merely confirm the general rule that there can be no discussion with the middle class as a class. It will have to be reckoned with, and its account finally discharged, but there can be no conversation with it—only dispute. Thus the summons of historical materialism is directed only to the constantly increasing proletariat. It is an appeal to its insight: to openmindedness towards the economic meaning of history in general and the necessity of its critique in the light of the dominating class war: to faith in its necessarily approaching goal; and above all to the restoration, by way of trades unions and co-operatives, of the economic and political solidarity of the working class, with the meaning and intention of a more rapid or more gradual advancing of the dissolution of the present class relationship and a more rapid or more gradual preparation of the construction of the new classless community, and all with careful and flexible regard for the contemporary hour and situation and its special economic, political and ideological circumstances, ideologies, of course, have weight in this practical outworking of historical materialism, yet only as [389] accompanying phenomena which are partly useful and partly useless, partly necessary and partly disruptive, but with no independent significance. It is understandable that to those who stand aloof the doctrine of Karl Marx is usually most impressive and least attractive in this final form as a summons to the warlike solidarity of the working class against them.

It is now clear why the pseudo-scientific materialism of the 19th century, which now concerns us, should acquire so much weight and currency. Marxism as such needed no doctrine of soul and body. For it, speculations along the lines of Feuerbach and Haeckel could only be one middle-class ideology with others. And these middle-class materialists for their part could be notoriously unconcerned with working-class affairs and movements, D. F. Strauss being a fairly bigoted devourer of Socialists. Yet the fact remains that Marxism could use this

---

EN105 unconditionally

doctrine of soul and body, even though it was obviously opposed to its own intentions as with the crude materialism of this particular cult. It did in fact make use of it. It allied itself with it to form what began to be called the "Marxist view of the world." Were not body and soul related to each other in the doctrine of these materialists as economic development to the accompanying ideological phenomena in Marxist doctrine? Did not its doctrine affirm of the human individual and the human race as a whole what was Alpha and Omega to Marxist doctrine in relation to the social structure of its history? It thus came about that the scientifically inadmissible deduction that the soul is material because materially conditioned became the received dogma of historical materialism. There thus arose the equation, practically sacrosanct even to-day to orthodox socialism, that Marxism is science, i.e., natural science, i.e., the natural philosophy of the cult of Haeckel. There thus arose the mass emotion which first gave to the materialism of the cult of Haeckel its distinctive popularity. It lived and continues to live on the attraction of the class war in the Marxist sense, of which it has proved itself to be a useful and even indispensable ideological instrument. But we must go deeper and say that it lives on that which in historical materialism is not merely a compelling construction but genuinely historical. It lives on the factual existence of that soulless figure of man so forcefully revealed in the 19th century. Marxism with its exclusively economic view of human affairs and all the theoretical and practical consequences, is a violation of history which in its way is no less bad than that which Haeckel and his associates imposed on human nature. Obviously it was and is a congeniality in error which caused Marx to ally himself with this doctrine of human nature. Obviously it is a curse lying on this matter, which will one day avenge itself, that the most determined, consistent and orthodox representatives of the Marxism based on this alliance take on more and more of the spirit, or lack of spirit, of that robot man. But we need not be surprised that this happened when the real life not merely of the Marxist opposition, but of the whole modern community, showed (and still shows) such strong characteristics pointing unmistakeably in this direction. The Christian Church need not be surprised at this, nor that it has come under the fire of Marxist polemic, nor that it must now hear its faith denounced as a "relic of capitalism" in the service of restraint and therefore of reaction. In all the centuries, what has it done positively to prevent the rise of that figure of the soulless man? Has it not always stood on the side of the "ruling classes"? At any rate, has it not always been the surest guarantee of the existence and continuance of an order of classes which technically cannot be understood otherwise than as the order of superiority of the economically strong? And has it not with its doctrine of soul and body at least shown a culpable indifference towards the problem of matter, of bodily life, and therefore of contemporary economics? Has it not made a point of teaching the immortality of the soul instead of attesting to society, with its proclamation of the resurrection of the dead, that the judgment and promise of God compass the whole man, and therefore cannot be affirmed and believed apart from material and economic reality, or be denied or pushed aside as ideology in contrast to material and economic reality? When the masses fell victim first to economic and then to the related pseudo-scientific materialism, as though they had become accustomed to hear from the Church of the day only irrelevant middle-class ideology; and when the dismayed Christian world could do little more than complain and scold in face of this double defection, was not this the penalty for the fact that quite unthinkingly, and certainly not in obedience but in disobedience to Scripture, it had prescribed that abstract dualism of soul and body, and that even in the time of the Reformation it had not dug very much deeper into this matter? Against the rise of that materialistic figure of man, it was thus completely impotent. And against the convincing power which both the Marxist doctrine of society and the pseudo-scientific doctrine of soulless man necessarily acquired in the realistic light of this human figure, it had nothing whatever to say from the traditional standpoint. Nor will it have anything to say in the future, but will always have a bad conscience in face of both materialisms and therefore of the so-called "Marxist view of the world," so long as it does not undertake an energetic revision of its anthropology at this point in the light of its eschatology, thus arriving at a very different practical position towards the whole complex. In this sense, it has to be said that even to-day we are by no means done with the materialism of the cult of Haeckel, for all its obvious theoretical weakness. It reminds the Church and theology of debts which they have by no means paid.

3. Reaction against the Greek traditional Christian dualism can, however, come from quite another quarter than materialism. Indeed, monistic materialism past and present obviously calls for the counter-attack of a monistic spiritualism, which takes the opposite view that the soul is the one and only substance of human reality. The advantage which materialism possesses, its greater nearness to the biblical picture of man than abstract dualism, its refusal to allow body and soul to fall apart, its realisation that man is at all events a unity—this advantage belongs also to spiritualism, with of course the difference that whereas for the one the soul is pure appearance and the body the real thing, for the other the body is pure appearance and the soul the real thing. The historical necessity of this reaction is understandable; and so long as materialism is present and the abstract dualism of the Greek traditional Christian conception is not purified, it will always have a relative justification. The concrete reality of man now demands expression on the other side. Man is not swallowed up as a subject, as obviously happens in materialism. His unity with himself does not go by default, as is the case in the Greek and traditional Christian conception. Here we have to do with a kind of triumph of the distinctive subject, man as posited and known by himself. In contrast to this, the being of the same name which according to materialist doctrine emerges and disappears in the ongoing stream of common organic animal life, is so miserable a being that, given the choice between the two systems, one tends to opt for spiritualism out of regard for man as such. And there may well be the added reason to-day that a quite unexpected ally can be found for this view in physics, which [391] has undergone so revolutionary a renew al in the last decade. Indeed it may even be supported by a more exact appreciation of the facts as these may be demonstrated without the help of physics.

In this respect, the exposition of Paul Haeberlin (*Der Leib und die Seele*, 1923) demands our attention.

We learn from him that nothing is real but the effective and functioning subject or soul, which I perceive in myself as I identify myself with myself, and which I recognise as the first reality without the co-operation of my corporeality. If I recognise another person, or indeed anything, as real and therefore as a functioning subject, this means that I overcome the boundary set for me by the corporeality concealing his soul. Everything is corporeal only in so far as it remains external to the contemplating subject, not yet perceptible as a real and therefore a functioning subject, and thus surrounded for the contemplating subject by this boundary. Corporeality is only the garment, appearance, expression and symbol of the real, the form which its externality takes. Everything is real, as I am, only in so far as it is spiritual. Thus only the spiritual, the non-spatial, the non-sensible, the immaterial is real, while the spatial, the sensible, the material and therefore the corporeal is not real, and in scientific knowledge must be seen, understood, interpreted or sensed at least as merely the external form of the real. All science, including natural science, is therefore psychology. Only as such can it bring all objects under one denominator, as is proper for science. Only as such is it the synthesis of all real perceptions. If it remains the science of things or bodies and claims to be a synthesis as such, this is only at the cost of strict understanding and therefore of its scientific character. Only as psychology can and will it be true to the task of the understanding in its totality, and therefore real science. Since corporeality does not belong to the character of the real, it is scientifically irrelevant. Body is the essence of the total corporeality of a maximally understood being—of the kind of being which we understand as spiritual and in this way, to the exclusion of its corporeality, as real. Body is thus the purely transparent appearance of a being, whether we actually recognise or merely sense it as such. Thus soul and body are distinguished as the fully understandable and the half understandable parts of man. In reality, man (like all real things) is soul and only soul. As soul, he is fully understandable to himself; as body, as expression of the soul, he is only half understandable, as experience shows. To be sure, his body must be taken into account both by himself and others. Yet merely as body he is relatively, i.e., spiritually alien to himself and others. Even as body, in fact, he is only his own sensible image which simply requires a right interpretation to be recognised as soul. The body is no objective magnitude. It is only the subjectively determined figure of the human personality as this is still relatively alien to ourselves and others. The body is only the psychological shadow of the spiritual reality of man, as from a different standpoint it is only its expression and representation.

No mention need be made of the many difficulties from which this thesis would free us at a single stroke. Yet we cannot accept it. It is too good to be true. We have to ask how, when man perceives himself and identifies himself with himself, he comes to recognise his soul as the first reality, and to see in it the essence of all that is real, and in his understanding the measure of all that is real. Who or what justifies this basic ontic and noetic assumption? The real man is naturally soul, subject, he himself. But he is not this alone. He is not this without conditions or limits. As he is body, yet not body alone but also soul, so he is soul, yet not soul alone but also body. To be sure, he is soul first and then body. He is the soul of his body. But soul of his body, he is no less really his body too. In this respect spiritualism would do well to allow itself to be corrected by materialism. Man himself is also his body. And his body is also himself. As his body, man is certainly more than his material body. Yet it is true that he is also a material body, spatial and sensible. He does not become pure soul in virtue of the fact that he is besouled. He is also that which is quickened and lives, and this as such remains different from the soul as that which quickens. Too much is made of the strict relation of the subject to what is quickened by it, and too little is said of the body, if the latter is regarded only as the expression and representation of the soul, only as its appearance, its external form, its symbol, its psychological shadow. At a pinch we can accept these descriptions. But they cannot signify that the body is fundamentally unreal. They can only signify that the body is these things too in relation to the soul. But they must imply that even as these things the body is real: as real as the soul, which it partly reveals and partly hides; as real as the man himself who is the soul of his body. He is not the one without the other. And he is the one not only as the reflection of

[392]

the other. If the body is not without the soul, neither is the soul without the body. The one whole man, to which spiritualism rightly has regard, would not be real, if the body of man, as the revelation and veiling of his soul, as the expression of his inward being, as quickened and living through his life, were not in its own way equally real with his soul.

In sum, if materialism with its denial of the soul makes man subjectless, spiritualism with its denial of the body makes him objectless. Thus both result in a new and fatal division of man, although both are monistic in intention and the declared purpose of both is to demonstrate the unity of the human reality. But this demonstration may not be pursued at the cost of the reality of either of the two elements, reality being found either in body or soul and appearance either in soul or body. A one-sided view of this kind is an act of violence. The Greek and traditional Christian doctrine inevitably leads us to one or other form of this one-sidedness. It is itself fundamentally one-sided, in the direction of spiritualism. It never quite denied the reality of the body, but, with its interest in the immortal and if possible divine soul, it was always on the point of doing so. And when it was attacked by materialism, its lack of understanding for the concern of the latter, and the nervousness with which it reacted against it, showed that it was incapable of providing a really penetrating insight into the whole problem. So long as soul and body are spoken of as two independent and distinct substances, no real insight is possible. Against this abstraction, the [393] concrete reality of the one man must continually and disquietingly call for expression from the one side or the other, and real justice can be done to it only by carrying through the abstraction to its logical but absurd conclusion, i.e., by minimising and if possible juggling away the soul in favour of the body or *vice versa*. What then survives is not alas! the concrete reality of the one man which was sought, but a substance of soul or body which is rendered spectral by this minimising and juggling. Who could recognise his neighbour, or himself, or any of the great or small figures among the actors of real human history, in man as thus described by materialism or spiritualism? Over against these opposed abstractions, the Greek and traditional Christian doctrine can always claim a relative justification, since *in thesi*[EN106] at least it maintains the counter-proposition of the unity of human nature. But we cannot help but see that it gives rise to the two errors. We are, in fact, caught in an endless spiral, so long as the idea of the two substances is not wholly abandoned, and the concrete reality of the one man set up definitively at the start, in the middle and at the end of all consideration, soul and body being understood, not as two parts, but as two moments of the indivisibly one human nature, the soul as that which quickens and the body as that which is quickened and lives. It is to this concrete monism that we found ourselves guided by the biblical view and the biblical concept of the "soul." The abstract dualism of the Greek and traditional

---

[EN106] in principle

Christian doctrine, and the equally abstract materialist and spiritualist monism, are from this standpoint a thoroughgoing and interconnected deviation.

The question how such a deviation was and is possible may be answered as follows. Our statement that man is wholly and at the same time both soul and body presupposes the first statement that man is as he has Spirit. We saw in our second sub-section that it is the Spirit, i.e., the immediate action of God Himself, which grounds, constitutes and maintains man as soul of his body. It is thus the Spirit that unifies him and holds him together as soul and body. If we abstract from the Spirit and therefore from the act of the living Creator, we necessarily abstract between soul and body. If we consider man for himself, i.e., without considering that he is only as God is for him, he is seen as a puzzling duality, his mortal body on the one side and his immortal soul on the other, a totality composed of two parts inadequately glued together, of two obviously different and conflicting substances. And however much we then try to persuade ourselves that this duality is the one man, we stand in the midst of Greek and every other form of heathenism, which sees neither the real God nor real man, and cannot do so, because knowledge of the Spirit is needed for this purpose and this is incompatible with heathenism. Our only relief will then be found in the see-saw movement between ideas and appearance, thinking and [394] speculation and so on, which pervades the history of philosophy in every age. If there is no knowledge of the Spirit, even the practical recollection of the one man can only lead to the materialistic or spiritualist reaction, and therefore to the realm of spectres. What is needed to avoid this whole deviation is simply a refusal to let go of the premise that man is as he has Spirit. Out of this premise arises, in contrast to all abstraction, the conrete and Christian dualism of soul and body. Here human speech is, as often, wiser than human thought. It is a remarkable thing that, in our use of the decisively important personal pronouns, we do not even remotely imagine that our expressions refer to the existence and nature of two substances or merely to one or other of them. On the contrary, we say with equal emphasis and equal right: "I think" and "I see," "I know" and "I have toothache," "I hate" and "I am operated on," "I have sinned" and "I am old." Fundamentally, we know very well—and we cannot dissuade ourselves of it by any synecdochic interpretation, however cunning— that all these things, though some are spiritual and others bodily, concern me myself. They are affairs of the one subject I, which is the soul of its body and for this very reason is wholly and at the same time soul and body. For who, when he speaks, ever thinks of dividing himself or another into soul and body, or of claiming to consider himself or another only as soul or only as body? At a pinch, therefore, we could give the following prescription for avoiding this deviation—that to be secure against it we must simply hold to the greater wisdom of our speech. Yet the fact remains that we must first know of the Spirit if we are to make illuminating use of this argument.

4. SOUL AND BODY IN THEIR PARTICULARITY

We come to the second subordinate question. It concerns the inner differentiation of human creatureliness, and asks concerning soul and body in their particularity.

The inner unity of human creatureliness and therefore the interconnexion of soul and body consists in the fact that in man the soul is the quickening factor aroused by the Spirit and the body is that which is quickened by it and lives. But this differentiation within the concept of life obviously cannot exhaust our description of the differentiation within human creatureliness and the particularity of the soul and body of man. We could very well halt here if we were merely dealing with an animal. What we perceive in an animal is indeed the connexion of an independent life with that which is quickened and lives by it. The supposition that the animal, too, is soul of a body is tempting at this point. But as we have seen we do not know what we are really saying if we accept this supposition. We do not know the particular element in the independent life of an animal. We do not know how it happens that an animal is self-animating. Nor do we know the particularity in which it is both self-animated and living. Whether and how the animal may be soul and body is hidden from us, since we can neither take the place of the animal and see and appreciate its content from inside, nor can we set up such communication with an animal as would enable it to give us information on the point. But in our own case, and in that of other men, we perceive not only the difference between what animates and what is animated, but also how that which animates and that which is animated are different from one another, what is the peculiarity of each, and what is therefore the particularity of soul and body. In the case of man, we can clarify what we mean when we speak of soul and body in their differentiation. In the case of man, we must transcend (without forgetting) the unity of soul and body which he has in common with the animal, and give appropriate expression to the differentiation which in the case of the animal is hidden from us but in the case of man is not so hidden. Even the animal has spirit. But we do not know how it has Spirit, i.e., what it means for the animal that through the Spirit it is the soul of a body. We can know, however, what it means for man, and we must make this clear. To do so is the further task which now faces us.

Man has Spirit, and through the Spirit is the soul of his body. This means at least that, by reason of his creaturely being, he is capable of meeting God, of being a person for and in relation to Him, and of being one as God is one. He is capable of being aware of himself as different both from God and from the rest of the created world, yet also bound up with God and with the rest of the created world. He is capable of recognising himself and of being responsible for himself. He exists in the execution of this self-recognition and self-responsibility before his Creator. As far as the animal is concerned, we do not even know whether its being fulfils itself in a corresponding or similar or very

[395]

different action. Yet we know it of man as certainly as we know His Creator who is not silent to him at least, as certainly as we know the Word of this Creator. Man exists in this Word; i.e., he is, as over against this Word he is conscious of himself and responsible. We know of this human constitution of ours. But in this knowledge is included the knowledge that we are capable of this activity in which we consist, i.e., that we are qualified, prepared and equipped for it. That we are capable of this is the essence of our human creatureliness. That man has Spirit means, whatever it may mean for the animal, that he is capable of executing this activity. He can recognise himself; he can be responsible for himself. Whether or how the animal can do this is not apparent to us. It may be that, in a way not apparent to us, it can do so. But we know neither whether nor

[396] how it can. In the case of man, on the other hand, there is no question whether he can or cannot. We must replace man by a quite different being if we are to question whether he has this ability. His creatureliness, what he is through the Spirit, is in itself and as such this ability. As he is caught up in this action and continuously involved in self-recognition and self-responsibility, he is man, and he continuously affirms his ability for it, and therefore the particularity of his human creatureliness. If man is the soul of his body—and this we can say of the animal only with the reservation of ignorance—then in his case at least the meaning is that he is qualified, prepared and equipped for this activity. Soul and body, as the essence of human nature, are in any case the presupposition and precondition, the potentiality, which underlies the actuality of his being in the Word of God.

We turn to Gen. 2⁷. When God breathes His breath into the nostrils of man and thus makes him a living being, He seems to be doing materially the same thing as might be said of animals. It is merely a matter of form that it is said specially of man. The material difference emerges only in the fact that the continuation of the story is the history of the covenant and salvation, not between God and animals, but between God and man. The course of events described in Gen. 3ff. occurs between God and man, not between God and animals. This shows what is involved in the fact that God gave man the Spirit. He gave the Spirit to animals also, but obviously not in the same way. Man is the being between whom and God such events can take place. Only in regard to man is it understandable that in the Old and New Testaments the same word *ruah* and πνεῦμα can denote both the prophetic and the creative Spirit, or that the creaturely soul can be summarily and compendiously described as spirit. The Spirit given to man, and grounding, constituting and maintaining him as soul of his body, has *per se*ᴱᴺ¹⁰⁷ an affinity to the prophetic Spirit, by whose operation the actuality of his being in covenant with God arises out of the potentiality of his creatureliness. Thus man's soul *per se*ᴱᴺ¹⁰⁸ has an affinity to the Spirit by whom it is made. And thus it is created *a priori*ᴱᴺ¹⁰⁹ in this affinity, i.e., for the realisation of a connexion between man and his Creator. This is the factual explanation of these very striking linguistic usages of the Bible. In regard to animals, they would both be inexplicable, because a retrospective consideration of animals, looking from salvation history back to their nature, is impossible for us. In regard to

---

ᴱᴺ¹⁰⁷ in itself
ᴱᴺ¹⁰⁸ in itself
ᴱᴺ¹⁰⁹ unconditionally

man, both are readily explicable, since we not only can but must understand human nature from the standpoint of salvation history.

We shall now try to see what is to be seen from this standpoint concerning the particularity of man as soul of his body.

Man meets God and stands before Him. God calls him by name and claims his obedience. God takes account of his own decisions, and everything that He does will either be directly revealed in his decisions or will have connexion with them. There will be a correspondence. It will mean that they are confirmed or condemned, rewarded or punished by God. This includes the fact that the independent life of the human creature is the life of a subject to whom God can entrust and from whom He can expect this partnership in intercourse with Him. Man is a subject of his own decision. He forms his own centre and his own periphery. Further, he is aware that he does this. He posits himself   [397] as such a centre. He posits himself in connexion with his environment. He posits himself in relation to God. In this way he is the soul of his body. That he is soul means that he is such a centre: the subject of specific engagements, opinions, views and resolves; a subject which is ordained for action and from which actions are therefore expected. That he is body means that as such a centre he has a periphery, that he can take action appropriate to this determination, that from this centre he can display a specific attitude in the creation around him, that from this point he can take a specific path and thus outwardly represent himself to be a person. It is not that he merely is this, or that it merely happens and occurs to him. Rather, in it all he knows himself and recognises himself to be both centre and periphery. In it all he posits himself wholly and simultaneously both inwardly and outwardly, from within outwards as the person he is and as the representation of this person. To him as a being capable of this existence, it is entrusted and accorded that he should meet God and stand before Him and be His partner. As this being, he may and should be man in the action of self-consciousness and responsibility. In this sense, he, man, is wholly and simultaneously soul, self-animating, and body— self-animated and alive. Human life is independent life. We can and must know that man's life is independent life. We cannot know this of animals. We can and must know it of man, because we know of his confrontation by God, and because in this confrontation with God there is entrusted and accorded to him that he may not only live but live independently. As God gives him soul, making him a soulful being, a besouled body and therefore a true body, man becomes a subject of this kind.

We notice at once that in this peculiar way man is one, a totality. He is independent as he can represent himself independently. His engagements, opinions, views and resolves are displayed in the attitudes and actions in which they are expressed. He lives his life, as he is soul of his body. Conversely, what he represents he is. His attitudes and actions are distinguished from any kind of movements in the realm of nature by the fact that they are the expression of his engagements, opinions, views and resolves. He lives his own specific and independent life as he is soul of his body. Not as soul or as body, but in the unity and totality of the two, it is entrusted and accorded to him to meet God and stand before God. And in their unity and wholeness we have to recognise his creaturely nature.

But we notice—and this is our present concern—that the two moments in this human creaturely nature are differentiated. The centre is not as such the periphery. The person is not as such the representation. The inner is not as such the outer. The soul is not as such the body. That it could not be without it is of course true. But it is not for this reason directly identical with it. It is in the body and the body in it. The soul is with it. It has and uses it. The body serves it, as it is its body. And as this happens, man is the soul of his body. Similarly, the periphery is not as such the centre, but presupposes it. There is no periphery where there is no centre. But in this relation of condition and dependence, the periphery is different from the centre. Similarly, although the person itself cannot be thought away from any of his representations, it is not exhausted in its expression, but remains itself even as it represents and expresses itself, and even though without this it could not be itself. Similarly, the outer is not simply the inner, though the inner needs the outer in order to be the inner. Similarly, the body is not directly the soul. Yet as the body is in the soul and the soul in the body, as the body is used and possessed by the soul and serves it, it takes place that man is the soul of his body and therefore identical with his body too. Man is wholly and simultaneously both soul and body. But the soul and the body are not for this reason identical, in spite of the well-known mathematical rule. On the contrary, they are distinguished from each other as subject and object, as operation and work.

Not without his body, yet not as body but as soul, man is the subject of his own decision. To be this is entrusted to him and expected of him in his relation to God. Not without his body, yet not as body but as soul, he is conscious of what he does and posits himself as such a centre and periphery in relation to his environment and even to God. Not without his body, but as soul and not as body, he fulfils the various engagements, holds the various opinions and forms the various views and resolves in which he lives his personal life. For again it is not without his body, but as soul and not as body, that he is person, and is thus determined and fitted to live his life as an independent life. The body can and must assist him in this. But the body cannot on its own account be the primary factor. It cannot represent the soul or displace it or render it superfluous. It must follow it, and can only follow it.

The same distinction, however, applies also from the other side. Not without his body, but as body and not as soul, man must execute the decisions entrusted to him and expected from him in his relationship to God. He forms not only a centre of his own but also a periphery of his own. This periphery implies not that he is soul but that he is body. Not without his soul, but as body and not as soul, he is able to display a specific attitude corresponding to his self-consciousness, to strike out along a specific path, representing himself outwardly. Not without his soul, but as body and not as soul, he executes the actions in which what he is inwardly attains expression and form. Not without his soul, but as body and not as soul, he lives the independent life for which as soul he is determined and fitted. In all these things the soul, or rather he himself as soul, can only give guidance and direction to his life. But in matters of execution the soul, or rather he himself as soul, cannot displace the body, [399] nor do for it what only the body can do. It can as little dispense with the body as the body with it. It must precede the body, but can only precede it.

This is, in general terms, the differentiation within the unity of soul and body as invisible in animals but visible in man, and very clearly visible in the light of what is entrusted to him and expected from him in his relationship to God. We distinguish within the one man, not two substances, but two moments of his creaturely reality. For within man the animating factor and the animated, the soul and the body, diverge and are distinct from one another in this way. But a more precise exposition is required at this point. As man meets God and stands before Him, two definite presuppositions emerge in regard to his creaturely nature.

1. The first is that man is capable of perceiving the God who meets him and reveals Himself to him; that he is capable of distinguishing Him from himself and *vice versa*; that he can recognise His divine being as such, and His Word and His will; and that he can understand the order which subsists between himself and God. In dealing with man, God appeals to this ability. He presupposes that in man as the subject of a decision of his own, in his existence as his own centre of his own periphery, this ability at least may be appealed to. Without this ability, every appeal would obviously be without object; and the meeting between God and man, as it took place in the history of the covenant, would obviously be impossible. If God created him to have his being in His Word and as His partner, it is already decided that He created him as a percipient being. As he is ordained and it is given to him to perceive God, he is ordained and it is given to him to perceive generally, to be percipient. To perceive means to receive another as such into one's self-consciousness. To be percipient thus means to be capable of receiving another as such into one's self-consciousness. A being capable only of a purely self-contained self-consciousness would not be a percipient being. Man is not such a self-contained being. He is capable of self-consciousness, but he is also capable of receiving another as such into this self-consciousness of his. Man can not only posit himself. In so doing, he can also posit another, and therefore himself in relation to this other and this other in relation to himself.

He can be aware of another and he can think it. The idea of perception divides into these two functions when applied to man. That man is percipient implies both. We believe that we can see and know that there is awareness in animals. But we do not know whether they think. Not knowing this, we do not really know whether their awareness is not very different from man's. Hence

191

we do not really know whether and in what sense an animal is a percipient being. But we do know that man perceives. That is, we know that this per-
[400] ception always takes place in a compound act of awareness and thought. It is not a pure act of thought, for in a pure act of thought we should not surmount the limits of self-consciousness and so we should be unable to receive and accept another as such into our self-consciousness. Neither is it a pure act of awareness, for when I am merely aware of something and do not think it, it remains external to me and is not received into my self-consciousness. Only the concept of perception can be divided in this way. And it is only for an understanding of the concept that we can allow the division. But the perception proper to man is itself an undivided act, in which awareness makes thinking possible and thinking awareness. The thinking becomes possible and the awareness real as the act of receiving another into the human self-consciousness. As a being capable of such perception, man is claimed in his relation to God, and it is the ability for such perception that has to be ascribed to him through the fact that he is claimed in this way. When we speak of man, to have the Spirit means in the first place to be able to perceive in this sense, to perceive God first and foremost, but because God, therefore and therewith another in general. Existing as man and so as person, man always executes this act of perception. It is thus proper to him to be capable of this act.

Superficially we can recognise the two moments of human nature, body and soul, in the division of the idea of perception into awareness and thought. It is natural and in a certain sense justifiable to say that awareness belongs to the body, i.e., its sense organs, and thought to the soul, so that the act of perception, which is single, has to be understood as an act of the whole man in the sense that one had to understand body and soul in him to be in a kind of distributed co-operation. But the situation is more complicated than this. I am not only my soul; I am my soul only as I am also my body. I am not only my body; I am my body only as I am also my soul. Hence it is certainly not only my body but also my soul which has awareness, and it is certainly not only my soul but also my body which thinks. There can thus be no question of a simple distribution of the two functions in the act of perception to soul and body, or of the simple notion of co-operation between the two. The situation is rather that man as soul of his *body* is empowered for awareness, and as *soul* of his body for thought. Understood thus, the two are different and cannot be interchanged.

Awareness is not only with the body. How could the body or the sense organs have awareness of themselves? What makes man naturally capable of awareness is simply that this body is his body, the body of his soul. Yet he does not execute this act as soul, but as body, by means of his organs; and in these the soul as such has no part, but they must be supplied by the body. That he is body makes it possible for another as such to enter his consciousness, for him to
[401] posit another as possible. How could his soul have awareness in and (for itself when as such it is inward and not outward?

4. *Soul and Body in Their Particularity*

Again, thinking is not only with the soul. How could his soul think, if it were not the soul of his brain, his nerves and his whole organism? Even when he thinks, man lives the life of his body. Even his thought is necessarily disturbed by the disturbance of the life of his body; and it necessarily ceases if he is deprived of his body. Even his thinking is executed as it is accompanied and assisted in one way or another by the action of his whole body. In thought he brings it about that what comes into his consciousness is received there as his self-consciousness, is posited by this as real, is recognised as another, and is understood in its relation to him. Yet he does this, not as body, but as soul, in the form of an act which certainly has accompanying bodily phenomena and conditions, but which is not for this reason an external and bodily act, but an internal act of the soul. As he thinks, he must necessarily live the life of his soul. How could his body as such, or any of his organs, even the highest, think of itself when as such it is outward and not inward?

Hence the two functions of perception cannot be distributed as though one were of the soul and the other of the body. But it can be affirmed that a special relation to the body is proper to the one, and a special relation to the soul to the other. Both are functions of both soul and body. We must even say of both that they are primarily of the soul and secondarily of the body, since in both man is the soul of his body and not the body of his soul, the body functioning only as the indispensable participant and the soul as the real bearer of the action of perception.

But a special relation to the body can be ascribed to the act of awareness to the extent that it is in fact the outer and not the inner side of perception. In this act, the other which I perceive comes to me in order that it may then and on this basis come into me. The soul has awareness, but this is possible only in so far as it has in the body its outer form and is thus open to the other of which it is aware. Body is the openness of soul. Body is the capacity in man in virtue of which another can come to him and be for him. Man has awareness, therefore, in so far as he is the soul of his *body.*

So, too, a special relation to the soul can be ascribed to thinking inasmuch as it is in fact the inner and not the outer side of perception. When I think, the other which I perceive comes into me, after it has come to me. The soul does not think without the body, because even thinking can take place only when it is accompanied by the functions of the whole body. It can think only in so far as it is the inner form of the outer, the place in which the other can be received for which it is now open, thanks to the body. The soul is man's self-consciousness taking place in the body. The soul is the capacity in virtue of which he can make another his own, in virtue of which the other can be not [402] only for him but in him. Man thinks, therefore, in so far as he is the *soul* of his body.

It is the biblical anthropological view of perception which we have before us in these statements, and which compels us to formulate the matter in this and not in another way.

§ 46. *Man as Soul and Body*

In the Old and New Testaments we look in vain for any abstract interest in the rational nature of man, in his sensible and (in the narrower sense) rational apperceptive capacity. We look in vain for any abstract doctrine of this object. And if our present concern with the matter is theological, we must take our stand on the fact that abstract attention to the sensible-rational capacity of man as such necessarily means inattention when measured by our task. The concrete attention demanded of us befits the man who meets his God and stands before his God, the man who finds God and to whom God is present. What interests the Bible, and therefore ourselves, in dealing with the matter, is that even man's ability to perceive is one of the properties presupposed in his meeting with God, his standing before Him and his finding Him present, which we must thus regard as essential for his creaturely nature. He is one who perceives in the fact that God, who will deal and treat with him, can be for him and in him, and can approach and enter him. He should and can perceive God. For this reason his nature, and he himself as soul of his body, is rational nature. It is this, and not any autonomous rationality, which marks him off from the animals and the rest of creation. His rationality is constituted by what he needs, has and employs as the partner of God in His action as the Lord of the covenant between Himself and man. Hence there is hardly a passage in the Bible which, when it speaks of man's own capacity of awareness and thought, of observation, reflection, recognition and knowledge, does not directly or indirectly mean his capacity to be open to the will and action of God and to give God a place within himself.

Man may sense and think many things, but fundamentally the perceiving man is the God-perceiving man. It is true, of course, that the other which he perceives is not identical with God, and that he continuously perceives other things as well as God. But when the Bible speaks of perceiving man, there is nothing else which it is important or necessary for man to perceive. Man perceives and receives into self-consciousness particular things—the action and inaction of his fellow-men, the relations and events of nature and history, the outward and the inward sides of the created world around him. But these are important and necessary for man only because God does not usually meet him immediately but mediately in His works, deeds and ordinances, and because the history of God's traffic with him takes place in the sphere of the created world and of the world of objects distinct from God. Basically, however, it is only in connexion with this history that this world of objects and therefore perception of the reality distinct from God becomes important and necessary for man. First and last and all the time his perception has properly only one object, of which everything else gives positive or negative witness. Man perceives this witness when he perceives particular things. He may and must be open to this witness and give it place. Thus in, behind and over the other things which he perceives by sense and thought there always stands in one way or another the Other who through other things approaches and enters him, who wills to be sensed and thought by him, to be for and in him, not casting him off, not leaving him to himself, willing rather that man should be with Him and that He should be received and enclosed in his self-consciousness. In order that this may take place, man is percipient. Thus he does not have an abstract capacity of awareness and thought, but the concrete capacity to sense and think God. This is the object and content in virtue of which and in relation to which his nature is a rational nature. This carries with it the fact that he rationalises generally, and that by awareness and thought he can make his own other things beside God. But the general capacity does not come first, so that, among other things, he can make God and the witness to God his own. On the contrary, the general is contained in the particular. The general capacity is given for the sake of the particular, and always first and last in connexion with the particular.

It is thus that the representative men of the Bible perceive. There can be no question of a general rational capacity prescribing the framework and standard and rule for a religious rational capacity. But as they obviously have the special capacity to perceive God and His

[403]

194

witnesses, they have also the general capacity, and we see them using it. If there is also in the biblical sphere a purely general perception, i.e., a perception loosed from that particular object and content, if even here men sense and think the creaturely in itself and as such, these are deficiency phenomena, and such perception must be described as improper, as abnormal rather than normal. We have here an awareness and thinking which is basically darkened, false and corrupt. Of course, this exists. Percipient man in the Bible is concretely sinful man, the man who would like to escape perception of God, who contradicts his human nature, and who does not behave wisely and rationally, but for all his ostensible wisdom and pretence of reason behaves as a fool and simpleton. He denies his rational nature. This does not mean, however, that he can alter it. It itself judges and condemns him. It is always directed to God even when he will not have it so and acts as though it were not so. The perception which he then chooses is improper and abnormal, depriving itself of its first and last object and being abstractly directed to other objects. Such a perception can only be deranged and per verted. Neither in the Old Testament nor the New does the Bible recognise such human perception which is estranged from its first and last object and therefore improper and abnormal, but proper and normal in respect of other objects. It knows no reality which is not the creation of God; and equally it knows no rational activity, knowledge, philosophy or the like which is loosed from the perception of God and yet intrinsically good, useful, valuable and praiseworthy. It certainly gives evidence of knowing that there is in fact a human perception that is loosed from the perception of God. But I know no text or context where it may be taken to recognise and approve this abstraction. On the contrary, it constantly undermines the autarchy of a general human reason loosed from God as its origin and object, and protests against the banishment of the perception of God into a religious corner. Only thought and awareness of God are comprehensive, proper, normal and therefore sound thinking and awareness. This is the first and most important lesson to be learned from biblical anthropology.

But when we have learned it, we can understand to what extent even on the biblical view the act of perception is in fact twofold but not divided, an act of awareness and thought. God wills both to approach and to enter man. He wills to be both known and recognised by man as God. From this angle, this is the meaning of the event of the covenant between God and man for which man is made. What kind of a being is it to which this event can happen? Clearly the presupposition made on the side of man is that he is capable of letting God approach and enter him. This capability is his capacity of awareness and thought. He is a percipient person in this twofold sense. It is essential that he should be it in this twofold sense.

God is not in him as a matter of course. He would not be creature, but himself the Creator, if God were in him from the very outset, if it belonged to his nature to be master of God, if he did not stand continually in need of God's giving Himself to be his, of God's approaching him from outside and giving Himself to be known by him just because He is not his as a matter of course. That God does this is described in the Bible in the story which tells how God bears witness to Himself before men in the midst of the created world. This witness man does not already have, nor can he give it to himself. It must come to him from outside, as [404] another, in order to enter into him. If he perceives God, then, his perception must he fundamentally an act of outer awareness. He meets God and stands and walks before Him. He sees and hears Him in one of His witnesses. God makes Himself known as One who not only is, but is for him.

But clearly this is inadequate, nor is it the whole of the process concerned even according to the biblical description. Self-evidently man would still be withdrawn into himself if God only approached him and did not enter into him, if He did not make Himself his in such a way that man might recognise Him and know himself claimed and blessed by Him and set in relation to Him. It is in this way that God bestows Himself upon man. Man still remains in need of renewed meeting with Him; but whatever may be his attitude, he is met and reached by Him. Even if only as Accuser and Judge, God takes up His dwelling in him. In some way, God's witness is powerful in man. If he perceives God, this act must be decisively an inner act, i.e., an act of his thinking. He finds God, and in God's presence finds himself. God is not only for him. He is in him, as he perceives Him.

To be capable of this twofold act of awareness and thought makes him a percipient person. Neither aspect may be lacking. In neither by itself would he be a rational nature. Neither permits replacement by the other. Neither can be interchanged with the other, though each takes place with the other in a single differentiated but not dissociated act. Since this is true of man's perception of God, it is true of his perception in general, and his perception of other things is always twofold, both awareness and thought. It is in the perception of God, in which this order is essential, that man's perception of everything, his reason as such, has its source and rule. Because it is first and last perception of God and as such unfolds in these two moments, it is bound to this development, so far as it is proper and normal perception. And again we have to say of the representative men of the Bible that their perception too stands under this order. They are neither pure empiricists, nor pure thinkers. They live wholly with their eyes and ears, and at the same time in the faith of their hearts. They are always wholly and at the same time engaged in awareness and thought. It is for this reason that they are so seldom of use and of so little value from the standpoint of pure empiricism or pure philosophy. And again it is to be observed that the possibility of living only with eyes and ears, i.e., by awareness, or only in the faith of the heart and therefore by thinking, that every attempt at a diminished perception, can only be a deficiency phenomenon in the sphere of the Bible. Both are possibilities only for sinful man; both are therefore in the highest degree imminent and common. For man in himself, indeed, they are the only imminent possibilities. Human perception, when displayed as his own act, is indeed a divided capacity. But this division has nothing to do with human nature. It is the consequence of the fact that human perception is accustomed to evade its first and last object and content, i.e., God, and thus becomes improper and abnormal in relation to all its objects and contents. But this does not affect its nature in the very slightest. Man cannot change into a being to whom it is natural to perceive in this divided way. Nor can he prevent intending and missing unity, and reaching out for it, in all his dividedness. Biblical man, the prophet and the apostle, reveal to us something of what natural perception is, for their awareness and thinking obviously take place in a single act.

In the same context we have also to understand the proper relation between awareness and thinking on the one hand, and body and soul on the other. The biblical man ordained for encounter with God is everywhere the whole man. Violence was done to the biblical text when in the last two centuries the salvation history to which it witnesses was construed as a kind of history of piety, when the things recorded as happening to man were reduced to [405] purely religious experiences, when the external was internalised, when it was increasingly forgotten that the Old and New Testaments deal with pure events, which certainly engaged the soul of the man concerned, but for that very reason claimed also his flesh and blood. The biblical men did not so much experience in their relation to God; it is much truer to say that they simply lived, and no less fully on this side than the God of whom the texts speak on His. But this means that biblical awareness and thinking are always understood as both of soul and body, as both an outer and an inner act. Both the biblical languages are, of course, acquainted with the terms by which the two functions are distinguished as outer and inner, sensuous and mental, physical and psychical. But the meanings of these terms are much closer than appears from Greek thought. And there is no way of denoting the two extremes of pure external observation on the one hand or pure internal reflection on the other. In

4. *Soul and Body in Their Particularity*

the strict sense. Hebrew possesses no equivalent for the pure idea of thinking. The only possible term is *binah, sakar* being the concrete consideration and *hashab*[EN110] the equally concrete contriving or inventing of a matter. In the New Testament, it is only infrequently that the term νοῦς carries a suggestion of its use in this sense in classical Greek. As a rule it does not have a theoretical but a practical meaning, and it is a function of the heart. The term *jada'*[EN111] is, of course extremely important, but it indicates a knowledge in which our concepts of awareness and thinking are coupled together. Again, the Old and New Testament ideas of "hearing" and "seeing" do not merely denote external, sensuous or bodily perception. We have only to consider what is meant by the context when the biblical "See" is uttered, or what the Old Testament understands by a "seer," or how comprehensive is the biblical "Hear," which certainly speaks of an act of awareness effected by the bodily ear, but in most cases carries the further thought of inner acceptance, of understanding, appropriation and recognition, indicating that something is taken to heart. Where, then, is that which is purely of the soul or purely of the body? In the Bible percipient man has decisively to do with God, who made him as soul of his body. It cannot well be otherwise than that the one always goes along with the other.

At both points, then, we have to do with the act of man in its totality. But this means that, according to the biblical understanding of this action, we must speak of a primacy of the soul in relation to the two functions of awareness and thinking. The soul—the soul of the body, but still the soul and not the body—is the man himself, the human subject. He not only thinks, but it is he who also senses. He might obviously have eyes and yet not see or ears yet not hear, as is said of the foolish, unperceptive people of Judah (Jer. 5²¹). "He that hath ears to hear, let him hear." This is the call which must particularly go out in the New Testament. Not for nothing man must be continually exhorted to see what is before his eyes. It is evidently not a matter of course that the fulfilment of the outer function immediately implies a fulfilment of the decisively inner function, or that what is sensed by man is also thought by him. Failure to see and hear in spite of the possession of eyes and ears can be an inevitable consequence of divine hardening (Is. 6⁹ᶠ·). The man himself, and therefore his soul, must have awareness if he is to be a real percipient. As he is soul, he stands before God, and it is to his soul, and therefore to himself, that God wills to be present as his blessing, his will, his law and his promise. He himself summons his soul (Ps. 103¹), and therefore himself, to praise of the Lord. This is the normal result of real human perception, although and as this is everywhere a bodily act, just as this praise of the Lord, while it is an act of the soul, must also be a bodily act. From this there follows necessarily what we must describe, not indeed as a distribution of awareness and thought to body and soul, but as a special relation of the former to the body and the latter to the soul. When biblical man perceives, when he properly and normally perceives God in all that he perceives, he is open as whole man; and again as whole man he is the open place in which God is present in His witnesses and takes up His habitation. His awareness then attains its goal and is itself a thinking. His body stands wholly at   [406] the service of his soul. His thinking arises from his awareness, and is itself simply a completed seeing and hearing. His soul is wholly that for which it is determined by the action of his body. Yet it is still the case that in this event he executes two different functions: the one as *what* he is, the function of awareness in which it becomes possible and actual on his side that God should approach him, and give Himself to him for recognition, this being the special function of the body; the other as *who* he is, the function of thinking (in biblical language, his heart), in which it becomes possible and actual on his side that God should approach him, and become object of his recognition, or perhaps of his non-recognition, but

---

EN110 mind
EN111 to know

197

in either case the object with which now he has to come to terms, this being the special function of his soul. He has awareness as he is the soul of his *body*; he thinks as he is the *soul* of his body. In this differentiation the one act of perception is the act of the whole man, as in the Bible we see him confronted with God.

2. We turn now to the second great presupposition made concerning human nature, and therefore concerning the soul and body of man, by the fact that it is entrusted and accorded to man to be God's partner, to meet God, to stand and walk before Him, to be right in self-reflective responsibility before Him. That he can perceive God is only a first point that calls for consideration in this respect. The second is that, in relation and correspondence to what he perceives of God, he can be active. In His dealings with man, God summons him to this ability. He presupposes from the very outset that even on man's side the fellowship between man and Himself must not be limited to a fellowship of knowledge, but that it can become a fellowship of action. If man is summoned to personal knowledge and responsibility over against his Creator, besides the bare perception of God, which is of course an indispensable and most important presupposition, he is summoned to decisions. And if this does not take place in vain, if it is really possible and not impossible for him to make decisions, to do this or that, and thus to be obedient to the summons which he meets and hears, this means that God has made him an active being. Again it is the case that as he is determined and it is given to him to be active in answer to the summons of God and in encounter with Him, he is determined and it is given to him to be active in general, to be a doer and not a non-doer. To act generally is to set oneself freely in motion in relation to another. A doer is always one who is capable of such free movement in relation to another. A being immovable in relation to another, or capable only of movement that is not free and not self-initiated, is not an active being. Even if capable of being moved, it cannot act. Man can be moved. But he can also take up an attitude towards others which involves action as well as perception. In his co-existence with the other he can desire and will. Thus in the concept of activity as in that of perception, both understood as possibilities given to man, we have to do with two different functions. Desiring and willing characterise man as the distinct subject that he is. In this respect, too, it is instructive to compare him with animals. We think that we see and know that animals desire. But we do not know for certain whether they will. Since we do not know this, fundamentally we do not know whether animal desire—however often human desire may remind us of it—is not something quite different. Thus we really do not know whether and in what sense animals are active beings. The interpretation which ascribes this to them can be as right or as wrong as that which denies it to them. But we know that man is active, and in what way. That is, we know that this takes place in a single act of desiring and willing of whose occurrence and interconnexion we are well aware.

It does not take place in a pure act of will. Pure volition would take place to some extent in a vacuum, since as such it would have no object, and no other

[407]

in relation to which to exercise itself. What was purely willed would necessarily be purely internal to us. Pure volition is in fact a movement incapable of execution and can have nothing to do with activity.

Nor is it fulfilled in a pure act of desire. Pure desire would certainly have an object. But it would not as such be our movement in relation to this other. What was purely desired would remain as external to us as something purely sensed. Pure desire, too, is a movement incapable of execution and can have nothing to do with activity.

So again we can quite well divide the concept—but only the concept—of activity into the ideas of desiring and willing. But the activity proper to man is itself the undivided act in which desire makes the willing possible and the willing makes the desiring actual, the possibility and the actuality being the free movement of a man in relation to another. Man in his relation to God is claimed as one capable of such activity. It is the ability for such activity that this engagement ascribes to him and presupposes in him. Therefore when we say of man that he has Spirit, we mean in the second place that he can be active in this sense first and last in relation to God, and for this reason generally in relation to all else. Existing as man and therefore as person, he constantly executes this act, his own action. It is indeed proper to him to be capable not only of perceiving but also of doing, of perceiving as the presupposition of doing, and doing as the end and goal of his capacity for perceiving.

We interject that it is as essential for man to be capable of perceiving as it is of doing, and of doing as perceiving. Between the two presuppositions, there exists the same relation as between sensing and thinking and desiring and willing. The real life-act of real man can and will never consist in pure perception or pure activity. Perception is itself wholly and utterly human activity. Without desiring and willing I cannot sense and think. But again all my activity depends absolutely on the fact that I perceive. Without sensing and thinking I should not desire and will. A perception which had nothing to do with my activity, or stood in contradiction with it, would not be real, or at any rate would be incomplete. If my activity took place without my perception or stood, wholly or partly in contradiction to it, then it would reveal that it was either not at all or only incompletely my real activity. All distinction between perception and action, all abstraction to the advantage and disadvantage of one or [408] the other, all action and reaction between *vita contemplativa*[EN112] and *vita activa*[EN113], between "intellectualism" and "voluntaryism"—all these, so far as they succeed, can only lead to all kinds and forms of inhumanity. But the enterprise is impossible on both sides. The really human person is the one who both perceives and acts in each of his life-acts. This reality will always be the refutation of all the distinctions and oppositions which are futilely proposed and championed in this connexion.

In the case of desiring and willing, too, we face the question whether we have to apportion these two characteristic functions of human activity to the soul and the body. The answer can and must be fundamentally the same as in the case of sensing and thinking. There is indeed a special relation of desiring

---

[EN112] contemplative life
[EN113] active life

to the bodily nature of man, and of willing to the soul. But there is no partition. On the contrary, we have to understand both desiring and willing as both soulful and bodily, both being primarily of the soul and secondarily of the body.

The case of desiring is as follows. It is intrinsically a bodily process that I desire, wish or long for (or negatively fear, shun or avoid) another, or a certain relation between me and another, or that it arouses my liking (or dislike). In this process, besides the nerves of my brain, those of the most diverse other organs can participate in greater or less measure. A particular sensible experience can let loose in me a particular urge of liking or dislike. This bodily urge as such is in some sense the necessary material of my desiring. To this extent we can and must affirm a special relation between desiring and the body. But the urge as such, the bodily liking or dislike, does not constitute the desire or aversion. If I am to desire or shun, it is necessary that I not only be aware of the urge concerned but that I affirm it, making it my own and committing myself in some sense to it. I can do this. But I can also ignore and disavow it. I am able not to desire (or to shun), though I am urged to it. I can thus accept that material or leave it. That I experience liking or dislike for another is not simply an affair of my nerves. It is this, but it is also my own affair. This constitutes what is obviously the most decisive participation of my soul in my desiring—however true it may be that without my body I am quite unable to desire at all.

The case of willing is as follows. It is a matter of the soul that I allow another to be not merely the object of my desiring (or shunning), but go beyond this to make it an object of my will; that I have a certain intention and come to a resolution with respect to it or to my relation to it; that I set it before me and put myself into the corresponding movement in relation to it. My desiring—which itself has a soulful element, as we have seen—is naturally presupposed. Where I have no desire, I cannot will. But I do not by any means will everything which I desire or for which I admittedly have a liking; nor again do I not will [409] everything for which I have no liking. When I will, I make up my mind. I myself, as soul, make up my own mind as the physico-psychical being provisionally united in like or dislike. I subject the provisional pact between my physical urge and my psychical agreement or rejection to a second proof. I choose, i.e., I determine myself and my activity for the execution or non-execution of my desiring. I prescribe for myself a specific attitude to the desired object. My desiring alone cannot do this. Desiring alone does not lead to any attitude. This is a process of soul. It is also true, of course, that it can be realised only because I am the soul of my body, and that my body too has not only a passive but an active part in my willing. But the activity of the body is at this point purely accessory and dependent. The body itself does not decide or determine, though it offers to me the material for my desiring in the form of an urge. It is I who decide and determine in relation to my desiring, not without parallel physical phenomena and conditions, but in such a way that I elevate myself above myself, above my physico-psychical desiring and therefore above my body, so that I am my own master and the master of my body. If this were not so, I should obviously not yet be willing but only desiring, confronting myself and my desiring in neutrality. I should not then be aware of myself in distinction from my desiring or of my power over it. I am aware of myself only when I realise the distinction between me and my desiring and make use of my power over it. This I do when I will; for then I abandon my neutrality towards myself and my desiring and take position over against them both. But this abandonment of neutrality and occupation of position is as such my act, the act of my soul, in just the same way as must be said of thinking in relation to awareness.

If we are not to lose touch with biblical anthropology, we must maintain this unity and differentiation of soul and body in respect of the active man as well.

And above all we must again take note of its basis. We observe that in this respect, too, the Bible has no abstract interest in the rational nature of man (and here especially his capacity for action); or in a formal antithesis between the sensibility and externality of desire on the one hand and the spirituality and freedom of the will on the other. Here, too, it views man in his concrete wholeness. It does this because it sees him first and foremost in his relation to God, as one who in this relation acts and desires and wills. That he is one who desires and wills is important in the biblical texts because God deals with him, and his own capacity for action is thus presupposed. Man should and can decide for God. God the Other is that Other in relation to which man's desiring and willing is a relevant matter. What distinguishes man from animals and the rest of creation is that he can desire and will in relation to God. The action expected of him is that he acknowledge God. He is man as in and with all he does he stands under the demand that he hear, believe and love God. For this he is claimed by God Himself through His covenant with him. The significance of his nature as active nature is that he can do this. Directly or indirectly, it is always this ability that is concerned when such a nature is ascribed to him. Thus his work has no immanent importance, justification and worth; it acquires these as in some way it is done in relation to the work of God. Thus the character of his work as good or bad, salutary or destructive, is dependent on no other [410] criterion than what it represents and means in this relation. Of course man also desires and wills in other connexions. Of course the other in relation to which he wills and affirms is always directly this or that component of his natural and historical environment, and therefore of the world of objects distinct from God, over against which he never stands merely in awareness and thought but always in some sense in activity and therefore in desire and volition. But on the biblical view this world of objects distinct from God is itself simply the sphere in which the history of the covenant between God and man unfolds. What meets man in this sphere as the possible object of his desiring and willing does not belong to him (for it is not his creation), any more than it belongs to itself (for it did not create itself). What can meet him in this sphere belongs to God and is His creation. When man is active in relation to it, he is active in relation to God. He acts in one way or another as the partner of God; and therefore his action is in one way or another measured by what it represents and means in its relation to God. Again, therefore, man has first and fundamentally the ability to be active in relation to God, and only then and for this reason to every other "other." Here, too, the general is contained within the particular, and not *vice versa*.

The idea of a special religious activity is just as strange to the Bible as that of a special religious perception. The people of Israel is not first of all and in general a people which as such unifies, asserts and propagates itself, which seeks a country and a habitation and nourishment in this country, which constructs its order of life, and then in addition to all this has a particular faith, follows a particular worship, and is thus active in a particular sphere in relation to God. On the contrary, the significance of the existence of Israel is that precisely in its general activity, in its unifying and asserting and propagating of itself, its finding of a country and in that country its habitation, nourishment and order of life, it is active in relation to its God, a relation which is expressed in its particular cultic acts, but is materially a total life-relation. This is even more true of the followers of Jesus Christ, the members of His community. They are not first of all and in general men with all kinds of urges and tendencies, and only then representatives and preachers of the Messiah Jesus and faith in Him, and in this particular respect active in relation to God. A Paul acts and lives "in the flesh" and therefore in general; but this he does in the faith of the Son of God (Gal. 2^{20}); and whether Christians eat or drink or whatever they do, they do it in all cases under the law of thankfulness and under the determination that everything takes place to the glory of God (1 Cor. 10^{31}). There is no place for a general human activity beside what is here done in relation to God. For the sphere of the general is determined and limited by this particular. If Christians also come together in particular, eating and drinking particularly in remembrance of the Resurrected, speaking particularly with one another and with God, it is not this that makes them Christians. In this way they merely confess that they are Christians. They are Christians as in the whole range of their humanity they are active in relation to God in ways determined by Christ. Hence the Bible knows of no general idea of right human conduct loosed from relation to God. Of course it knows that such conduct is continually possible and real, or may become so even in Israel and the Christian community. Of course it knows the constantly recurring attempt of man to withdraw his activity from this fundamental relation and to set up between himself and the world of objects a kind of closed circle in which man's desiring and what he desires, man's willing and what he wills, man's work and its several objects, form among themselves a kind of neutral sphere over against God. Of course it knows that man constantly strives after an intrinsic well-being, a self-grounded fortune and greatness, in the belief that he is commanded, compelled or justified therein, quite apart from the question of his relation to God. And finally of course it knows of the artifice with which man allows [411] himself such an autonomous, self grounded and self-enclosed desiring and willing and then brings all into a kind of relation to God by also engaging privately or publicly in religious activity. But it is characteristic of the Bible that it inexorably criticises as a deficiency phenomenon any desiring and willing which thus tries to loose itself from relation to God, whatever the necessity from which arises, whatever right it invokes, however morally enlightening the character it bears, and quite irrespective of any religious appendix which it may or may not have. It condemns it as a false and perverted desiring and willing and doing, just as it sees that all sensing and thinking which tries to loose itself from God as its proper object is in all circumstances folly rather than wisdom. It does this because it regards man as actually unable to renounce that fundamental relation of his activity. It sees and affirms that he is of course constantly engaged in the attempt. But even in this attempt, it sees him constantly refuted and judged by his own nature, which he can certainly alienate and violate but cannot alter, and which gives him the lie if he is false to it. It measures him by the fact that in his activity he belongs wholly and utterly to God. For this reason it cannot abandon him to any sphere of neutral righteousness. It cannot concede to him that any action in which he denies that he belongs to God can be a right action. At once and necessarily it sees that such action is evil and pernicious. This explains why it is that neither in the Old Testament nor the New is there any praise of man *in abstracto*[EN114], but even where judgment is withheld the refer-

---

[EN114] in the abstract

ences to man's undertakings and performances as such are so cool. Just because it is moved to participate so deeply in the activity of man, it maintains an attitude of great concern for the fundamental relation in which alone it can be right action. It demands desiring and willing that is liberated in this decisive respect. Since it does not meet with, and since it cannot content itself with anything less, it cannot praise man. Here, too, it disturbs his autarchy, the false self-contentment of a general human activity alienated from its proper object., Here, too, it protests against the hypocrisy which on the one side would like to endorse and co-operate in this alienation, but on the other is not prepared to surrender the relation of the active man to God, but justifies human desiring and willing as such, supplementing it by a well-meant but useless religious activity. The biblical texts forbid us to call sound what is sick. The desiring and willing is sick in which man in any respect makes the futile attempt to conduct himself as though in this or that matter he had not to do with God. It is sick because the attempt can never succeed, but can only lead to crippled and convulsive acts unworthy of the name. The proper, normal and sound desiring and willing is that in which the real state of the case, that God first and last constitutes its only object, is conceded, recognised, respected and honoured. The Bible looks to this sound human activity when in so striking a way it looks away from what men do in general.

But this also explains why it is that without division human activity occurs in the twofold function of desiring on the one side and willing on the other. This is true because God, as man is first and last active in relation to Him, wills not only to be willed but first to be desired by man, and not only to be desired but then also willed. To express it in the concrete content of biblical speech, God wills not only to be feared but first to be loved, and not only to be loved but then also to be feared. Man is the being capable of this twofold act in his relation to God and therefore generally. He is in this twofold sense an active person.

In respect of the One who in the Bible is called and is God, man must desire Him wholly, properly, purely, supremely and genuinely, and therefore love Him. This is because, as Calvin strongly emphasises at the very beginning of the *Institutes*, He is the *fons omnium bonorum*[EN115], and means not only this and that for man's life but absolutely everything, because man cannot be without Him, because without Him he would be cut off from the source of all that is good for him. That he exists as man and that he stands in need of God, are not two things but one and the same thing. The well-known opening to Augustine's [412] *Confessions* is relevant in this connexion, and it is a correct interpretation of the biblical concept of man: *Quia fecisti nos ad te, et inquietum est cor nostrum, donec requiescat in te*[EN116]. (*Conf.* I, 1). This need of man for God is not just one—perhaps the deepest—need among others; nor is it to be explained by any individual need, though it can express itself in every individual need of human life. The "disquiet" of the soul referred to in Pss. 42 and 43 is not a specific disquiet, though it can represent itself in every highest or smallest human disquiet, beginning with bodily hunger and rising to the anxiety of the man who knows that he is hopelessly guilty and lost. Because God is man's Creator, and as such the source of all that is good for him, we have to do here with *the* human need and *the* human disquiet as such—the need which man cannot not have, and the disquiet in which he cannot not find himself. Just because there is nothing human that is more constitutive than man's need for God, his activity must be fundamentally and decisively a desiring of God. That man desires means that he cannot be self-satisfied but needs another for the satisfying of his need. If he could be self-satisfied, he could not and would not desire. Whenever he desires, he begins to notice that he is unable to satisfy himself, and he undertakes the attempt to transcend himself with a view to satisfying himself from elsewhere. But here it becomes evident that genuine and

---

EN115 source of every good thing
EN116 Since You have made us for Yourself, our hearts are restless until they rest in You

proper desiring can only be desiring of God. It is God the Other and He alone who is the true and complete Other that as such can be the object of genuine desiring. No created thing can be this for man. Fundamentally he does not stand to any created thing in such a relation that his desiring of it cannot again turn out to be the demand for some kind of self-satisfaction, or the fulfilment of his desire for it cannot again complete itself in the form of a kind of self-satisfaction. No created thing, not even the sweet sun itself, stands as an other in such a relation to man that it is wholly and fundamentally withdrawn from his power and his service, or that he does not know how to make it of use in one form or another. In the created world, man with all his neediness is always also the lord and master who knows how to make use of created things. Towards them he is not capable of genuine desiring—or only when he has apprehended that even in his desiring of created things he can first and last desire only their Creator. But in relation to the Creator, there is no self-satisfaction, no utilising, but only genuine desiring, since all human lordship and mastership is here *a priori*^{EN117} and absolutely excluded. Here man is not only accidentally but necessarily needy, i.e., of God. Hence he does not desire accidentally but necessarily. Yet only God can be the object of this genuine, proper and pure desiring. From this there follows the constant presupposition of the Bible, that wherever and however he desires, fundamentally he must necessarily and not just accidentally desire God, that he is caught in the most profound self-misunderstanding in all desiring loosed from the desire for God, and that all other desiring of this kind is only a perverted desiring. Hence when the Decalogue forbids desire for the possession of the wife of another, it does so because such desiring has loosed itself from the desire for God and thus manifested itself as a perverted desiring. If in many passages in the New Testament the word ἐπιθυμία^{EN128}, with or without further specification, signifies evil and sinful desiring; if lust is described in 1 Jn. 2^{15–17} as the form of the passing cosmos in contrast to which only he who does the will of God remains to eternity; if in Rom. 7⁷ and 13⁹ the Old Testament command is given a shorter and yet more comprehensive form as οὐκ ἐπιθυμήσεις^{EN119}, the reference is not to desiring as such, but to the human desiring that is loosed from its proper object and has degenerated into a carnal, worldly, irrational, bad and corruptible, in short one's "own" (2 Tim. 4³; 2 Pet. 3³) desiring. On the other hand, the Prodigal (Lk. 15¹⁶) desires to eat of the husks of the swine-trough and Lazarus (Lk. 16²¹) of the crumbs that fell from the rich man's table. Again, Jesus can say: ἐπιθυμίᾳ ἐπεθύμησα^{EN120} to eat this passover with you (Lk. 22¹⁵), and Paul (1 Thess. 2¹⁷) that he endeavoured ἐν πολλῇ ἐπιθυμίᾳ^{EN121} to see the community again, or (Ac. 20³³) that he desired the gold or apparel of no one. According to 1 Tim. 3¹, a man can wish for the office of a bishop and in so doing desire a καλὸν ἔργον^{EN122}. All these passages remind us of the natural and by no means pejorative sense of the word. Again, in Mt. 13¹⁷ we read of many prophets and righteous men who desired to see and hear what the disciples see and hear; and in 1 Pet. 1¹² of the angels who desire to look into the things revealed to the Church by the preaching of the Gospel; and again in Lk. 17²² of the disciples, that the days would come when they would desire to see one of the days of the Son of Man. Further, Paul in Phil. 1²³ desires to depart and be with Christ. The writer of Hebrews (6¹¹) desires that everyone in the Church might show the same diligence to the full assurance of hope unto the end. Gal. 5¹⁷ speaks not only of the desire of the flesh against the spirit, but also of the desire of the spirit against the flesh. In these texts we are obviously confronted by the proper, original and

[413]

---

^{EN117} unconditionally
^{EN118} desire
^{EN119} you shall not desire
^{EN120} with desire I have desired
^{EN121} with great desire
^{EN122} good work

4. Soul and Body in Their Particularity

comprehensive sense of the term, in which it indicates the desire of man for encounter with God in relation to which evil desiring is not natural but supremely unnatural. Man in the Bible is the being for whom, whether he knows it or not, it is necessary and essential to desire God; and he is the being who by his creation is capable of this. Man can love. The activity of desiring in its genuine, proper and pure form is that he can love, i.e., desire in its otherness another over which he is not lord and master, which he cannot make a means to his own self-satisfaction, but by which he can attain satisfaction and through which he can actually be satisfied. Man can love God. God and God alone—or the witness to God in the created world—is the other which he can desire in its otherness, through which, just because it is always another, he can be satisfied, and which therefore he can really love. It may thus be seen that just because he can desire and love God he can desire and love in general. "In general" does not mean another beside and outside God, but another in God and for the sake of God, God Himself in this other, because this other, God's creation like himself, is God's witness. In practice, he can and will always desire and love God Himself only in such another, in His witnesses, as the God who is active, visible, audible and tangible in His works, as the God who approaches him from outside, entering the sphere of his outer perception. He who in the Bible is called and is God is not a God to be directly experienced, inwardly present to man and possessed by him; He is always the God, strange and mighty, who approaches him from outside. If we think or speak of the matter differently, we must take good care that we have not interchanged God with our own psychical basis and therefore with our self-consciousness and therefore with ourselves, with a suppositious God whom one cannot really desire or really love, to deal with whom is always to be caught again in self-satisfaction and therefore to be worlds away from all real satisfaction. The God of the Bible wills to be perceived, desired and loved in His visible, audible, tangible witnesses. That is why the Bible speaks so anthropomorphically of God's speech and conduct, His coming and going, His action and inaction, His heart and eyes, His arms and hands and feet, as though the reference were to a creature like man. That is why He is described as the Other who can be perceived, desired and known by man (himself only a creature and not the Creator) in the midst of the created world. His creaturely witnesses and demonstrations.

But it is obviously not enough that man can desire Him, just as it is not enough that he can perceive Him. It is only half the matter that man can desire the One who stands over and approaches him as the strange and mighty Creator, even if we understand the term desire in its deepest sense of love. If this were all, we should not have the full idea of an active person. To desire and love God is in itself only his inner activity, and therefore not the complete activity in which God is always present to him purely outwardly—not an activity which can be quite visible in its relationship to God. He who in the Bible is called and is God is the One whom man must also will and therefore fear just as absolutely and supremely as he desires and loves Him. He is responsible to Him. His willing must consist in surrendering himself to One to whom he belongs. We can again refer at this point to the passage in Calvin already cited, for it is simply an interpretation of the biblical concept of man. Man is *iure creationis addictus et mancipatus*EN123 to God. He is under obligation to Him for his life. What he undertakes and does must be positively related to Him if it is to be rightly undertaken and done. He acts in obedience to Him, or else his conduct is perverted. The will of God is his *lex vivendi*EN124. From the standpoint of the biblical concept of man, these are no florid exaggerations, but sober affirmations of the facts of the case. That he wills and that it is in the fear of God that he wills, are not two things, any more than his existence and his need and therefore his desire for God are two things. They are one and the same. He cannot will as

[414]

EN123 by right of creation bound and subject
EN124 law of life

such and in general and then also will God, i.e., will what God wills. This is no less true than that he cannot desire as such and in general, and then also desire God among other things. Since he can purely desire God alone, he can purely will God alone. Since he is in truth engaged in this desiring, his decision and his own confession with reference to his desiring can consist only in this willing and can be only the affirmation of this desiring. Wherever the human will recognises and affirms human desiring, man's desiring stands before the question whether it is of such a kind that this may happen, that it may, must and can be endorsed, because it is this pure desiring. And wherever the human will declines and rejects human desiring, it is itself confronted by the question whether it is a pure will, whether it is really an impure and not perhaps a pure desiring which it is in process of rejecting. The question is always posed from both sides. As man wills, he becomes in one way or another responsible for his desiring, for the decision is his. His decision may not merely fall in with his desiring. It depends on whether or not he wills what he desires. But in this decision and resolve he is responsible to God, he lives in or outside the fear of God, and he begins to act, the occurrence of history between God and him being enacted on his side too as his own action. There thus comes into being what he is or is not in his relation to God. Both become possible in his desiring in itself and as such. That he be satisfied is related to his desiring; that he on his side in return satisfies the God who first satisfies him, is related to his willing. His proper and genuine willing can thus only be the willing bound to God. Man can owe to no creature what he owes to God—himself in his totality. Nothing can claim from him that he serve its satisfaction. When a created thing imposes this demand on man, and when man recognises the demand, we have nothing but the invalid claim of false gods. No created thing can substantiate the Creator's right over man. Thus no created thing can become for him the object of pure willing. He must really will only what he must will in his relation to God. This and this alone can he himself will in freedom. This and this alone is the willing that corresponds and conforms to his nature. On the other hand, everything in his relation to God which is superfluous to it and excluded by it, and everything not demanded by God or contradicting the demand of God, whether in false agreement or in false conflict with his desiring, can be based as such only on the same self-misunderstanding to which his desiring is exposed. Then man in truth does not yet or any longer will genuinely and properly. His will is a corrupted and perverted will, and it is clear that, since he cannot satisfy God with such a will, he is cut off on his side from satisfaction by God; and what occurs to him in the history between God and himself can only be the painful experience of divine judgment which he cannot escape, so long and so far as he wills something other than God. But man's pure and right will is a will obedient to God. As he is capable of this will, he is capable of will in general. As God made him free for Himself, He made him free in general. The energy of every human decision and every human resolve, the energy of the person deciding and resolving, has its origin and basis in the fact that man first and foremost can fear God, and therefore can purely and rightly will He does not will this and that, and then perhaps once in a while will the one pure and right thing, namely, God and himself for God. On the contrary, he can will this or that because he can will this one thing first and foremost. He thus makes use of his freedom of will only when in all things, even when he wills this or that, he wills this one thing. He neglects his ability, and denies and forfeits it, when, instead of the one thing, he wills only this and that. But the merely apparent freedom of his thus perverted will, and his energy in evil, bears witness in its very "involuntariness" to the way in which he comes to be able to will, though only apparently, impurely and wrongly. He can will, i.e., he can decide and resolve concerning his desiring, and he is an active person, as he is directly determined to and for God. That is, he can decide and resolve for his desire for God and against his godless desire. As he can do this, he can be man in the biblical sense. God appeals to this ability as He claims him for Himself, calling him and giving him His command and promise.

[415]

4. *Soul and Body in Their Particularity*

God elects man in order that he may elect Him in return, and therefore on the presupposition that man is capable of this election, not only of desiring (*ḥamad, awah, baqash, araq,* and
ἐπιθυμεῖν), but also of willing (*abah, ja'al, ḥapaz,* βούλεσθαι and θέλειν), in which he takes
up a positive or negative position to his desiring, "pulling himself together." In this pulling of
himself together, he is an active person and therefore a man. He makes decision about
himself, as his will and so his election is or is not identical with the fear of God.

This enables us to understand finally the relation of desiring and willing on the one side
and body and soul on the other. The biblical man determined for God is the whole man in
his activity too. The Old and New Testament terms for man's activity to which we have
referred are all closely akin and merge into one another, like those for his perception. Just
because they directly or indirectly characterise all the active relation of man to God, his
action within the history of the covenant of grace, there is no genuinely neutral zone within
their compass.

The man whom God will have for Himself is of course the man who wills and therefore
desires; he is man active in the unity of desiring and willing. Hence the Decalogue speaks not
only of stealing and adultery, but also with equal emphasis of the corresponding desire; and
we recall that it is precisely this aspect which is drawn out and emphasised in Jesus' Sermon
on the Mount (Mt. 5²⁷ᶠ·). Man in the whole of the Old Testament is so emphatically made
accountable not only for his decisions and resolves, but also for the inclinations and tendencies that precede them, and in the whole Bible it is so emphatically maintained that God will
have man for Himself in this sphere too, that it may well be asked whether the relation
between soul and body is not reversed, the desiring being understood as the essential and
psychical function of active man and willing as the merely incidental outward and physical
function. There can be no doubt at least that biblical anthropology completely forbids any
abstract understanding of desire as a mere outward and physical function. There can be no
doubt that in this sphere, too, we have to do not only with the soul, but with a primacy of the
soul. It is not for nothing that there is in the Old Testament a whole series of passages in
which *nephesh*[EN125] is designated as the subject of feeling and affection, joy and sorrow, longing and love, hatred and contempt, aversion and disgust, and yet not only of the animal
impulses as one might suppose, but also of the true desire of man for God. In the language
of the Bible I can never interpret the fact and object and manner of my desiring as a business
of my in some sense independently self-stimulating and self-motivating bodily organs, but
only as my very own business, in which I do not merely have a physical part but am myself the
one who desires. Here I myself am engaged; here my soul is revealed before God in its
orientation, its nature or degeneration; here I say Yes or No to God; here I am in one way or
another answerable and responsible for the fact that I am this desiring being. That this is the
case is exemplified by the fact that in the Bible bodily hunger and thirst as such are not
trivialised but always taken seriously, and can thus be applied at once (and not merely as a   [416]
picture) to the vital need of man for God. The bodily and the soulful together form a coherent sphere in which there is nothing of the body that is not also of the soul. On the biblical
view, the body, even in respect of its desiring, has no life of its own apart from the soul It
continually has the soul to thank for the fact that it is an organic and not a mere material
body, for the functioning of its organs and for the fact that it can desire. That it desires can
only mean that it puts into effect the desire of its soul, just as its awareness can only mean
that it puts into effect the awareness of its soul. For this, of course, the soul needs a body. But
it is the desiring of the soul which is put into effect by the body.

The primacy of the soul does not consist merely in the fact that man decides and resolves
concerning his desires in a volitional act which is purely of the soul. For his soul, i.e., he

---

[EN125] soul

himself, is the subject even of his desiring as this faces the decision of the will. The higher significance of volition as compared with desire is simply that in it the soul comes to a decision concerning itself, undertaking and executing a work corresponding to its tested desire. In this alone consists the differentiation between the element of soul and that of body in the active man. The active man is the man who exercises not only his desire but also his will. He needs soul and body to be able to desire and to will. And he needs both again to exercise his desire and his will. But he needs the body, because it is only as body, i.e., as something, that he can desire and therefore will or not will something else. He needs the body, because he can be induced to desire only in his bodily impulses, only as he lives in them, only through them, i.e., by their agency; and because he cannot will without being accompanied by these bodily impulses and without using, controlling and guiding them. Again, he needs the soul because he is not merely something but himself, and because his desiring is not alien to him but his own, something that ho practises in the fact that in the act of volition he decides and resolves with respect to it, affirming in the willing of a specific act an independence of his desires which is not based upon his body or its impulses, but has, its own order for all its interconnexion with these impulses. We can sum up the whole matter in the concluding formula that man desires as the soul of his *body*, and wills as the *soul* of his body.

To summarise, we have asked concerning the inner differentiation of human creatureliness, and we have now seen both the fact and the nature of the distinction between soul and body, between the animating and the animated in man. They are distinguished in the particular way in which he is a percipient and an active being—a way which in the case of the animal is at least not manifest but hidden. The fact that man has Spirit, and that through the Spirit he is the soul of his body, means that he can perceive and be active in this special way. He is the percipient and active soul of the body which puts into effect his perception and action. We have not deduced this from an abstract consideration and assessment of man. We have not given it a basis in scientific or cultural studies, but in theology. The starting-point was that man stands before God, who is his Creator. We brought out the presuppositions which result in respect of his creatureliness. We asked concerning that which is thereby credited to man and expected from him. We tried to understand man's special nature in the light of the fact that at all events it had to be so [417] constituted as to comprise within itself the ability corre sponding to his special relationship to God. We then affirmed in general that human life, being wholly and at the same time both of soul and of body, is a subjective life with subjective representations, subjective in so far as it is of soul, and with subjective representations in so far as it is of body. Man is capable of standing before God because he can live this kind of life. The rest was merely a development of this basic understanding. As the soul precedes the body, but can only precede and cannot exist as such without the body, so the body follows the soul, but can only follow and cannot exist as such without the soul. The two indissolubly connected moments of human creaturely reality consist in this preceding and following of these two moments. The one never is without the other. Since they are not interchangeable with one another, the one always preceding and the other following, we must accept a differentiation between soul and body, while never speaking of two distinct substances. We have found this to be substantiated in our analysis of the two concrete presuppositions of intercourse between God and man. That is to say, in relation both to human perception and human activity we have encountered a duality exactly corresponding to the dualism of body and soul. In man as he stands before God, we have had to distinguish sensing from thinking, and desiring from willing, in order to construct a complete view and conception of the fact that man is capable of standing before God. However it may be with animals, awareness and thought are different in man, and only when both combine in a single act does human perception take place. And however it may be with animals, desire and volition are different in man, and only when both combine in a single act does human activity take place. We must emphasise in both cases that it is only as they combine in a single act, for we cannot distinguish awareness and desire as an act of the body and thought and volition as an act of the soul. The biblical conception of man is there to warn us that we must also ascribe awareness and desire in their own way to the soul, and thought and volition in their own way to the body. The concrete differentiation is that they must be ascribed in their own distinctive ways which are not the same. The relationship cannot occasionally be reversed. On both sides of the duality we have come upon the primacy of the soul. At no level have we ever found it alone without the body. Nor could we restrict ourselves to the statement that the soul thinks and wills. We had to enlarge it and say that the soul also senses and desires. Only the soul can be meant when we speak of man as an independent subject. The human body cannot be meant, though man is always his body too. But even in the outward fulfilment of his perception and his activity, even in awareness and desire, he is the soul of his body. He expresses himself as such as he goes beyond the outward and thinks and wills, taking up a position in relation to his own awareness and desire, and treating them as his own business and activity. He is not cap-   [418] able of this as body, though for it he stands in need of his bodily life. He does not think without sensing, nor will without desiring. But when he thinks and wills, he stands at a distance from his sensing and desiring. He passes himself under review. He becomes an object to himself. In this freedom to stand at a distance, pass under review and become object, he conducts himself as soul of his body. The body lacks this freedom. It can only participate in it. In and by itself, it does not possess it. But the soul does. The soul is itself the freedom of man, not only to sense and desire, but in thinking and willing to be able to stand at a distance from himself and to live his life as his own. The body on its side is man in so far as it enjoys this primacy of his soul as a corporeal being, being not merely something but the something which is himself. For he could not be himself without this something; he could not be a real person without this outward form and activity. His body is the organ through which his ability to perceive and do is exercised. It is the bearer and the representation of his thinking and willing. On both sides it is the openness of the soul without which it could not be free. This is its dignity, which in its own way is not less than that of the soul. That man is the soul of his *body* is the secondary fact which is no less indispensable to real man than the first, namely, that he is the *soul* of his body.

5. SOUL AND BODY IN THEIR ORDER

We could not complete the exposition of our third statement without reaching and indeed anticipating the final point which must now claim our specific attention. From the particularity in which man as soul of his body is a perceiving and active being there arises a particular relation between soul and body. From their inner differentiation there arises the inner order of human creatureliness. We cannot analyse the two great presuppositions constitutive of the relation of man to God on the side of man, i.e., that he is a percipient and an active being, without coming upon what we have called the primacy of the soul. In the last analysis we have found the distinction in unity between the two in the fact that the soul *precedes* in its perception, both as awareness and thought, and its activity, both as desire and volition, and that the body follows. But since this matter is decisive for the picture of man as soul and body, we must give it special consideration. We remember the decisive importance of this point, of the phenomenon of order, in the anthropology of Jesus with which we started in our first sub-section. But the formula of the primacy of the soul which is our starting-point can only suggest what we have now to affirm, namely, that the nature of man as soul and body is not an accidental conjunc-

[419] tion, a mere juxtaposition, or a hostile *contretemps*[EN126], but an intelligibly ordered association of these two moments; that it is not a chaos but a cosmos, in which there rules a Logos; that there is control on the one side, i.e., that of the soul, and service on the other, i.e., that of the body. As this takes place man is fully man in the unity and differentiation of his soul and his body. As he is grounded, constituted and maintained by God as soul of his body, and thus receives and has the Spirit, there occurs the rule of the soul and the service of the body. And in this occurrence man is a rational being.

We use this term in a very comprehensive sense. The German word *Vernunft*[EN127] has something inexact and misleading about it. By linguistic relationship and widespread usage it refers only to the ability to understand (*vernehmen*), which is only one among the many capacities of man. In addition, the term is often one-sidedly used to denote merely the human ability to think. As we use it here, we are giving it the comprehensive sense of the Latin *ratio* and the Greek λόγος. We understand by it a "meaningful order," so that when we say that man is a rational being, what we mean is that it is proper to his

---

EN126 confrontation
EN127 reason

nature to be in rational order of the two moments of soul and body, and in this way to be a percipient and active being.

For all its ambiguity, we prefer the term "rational being" (*Vernunftwesen*) to a foreign or a coined word. But we always understand by it a rational or logical being in the true and comprehensive and not a restricted sense of *ratio* and λόγος.

We thus understand man as a rational being with regard not only to his soul but also to his body. For in virtue of his soul, his body also has a full participation in his rationality. It is ruled by the soul and serves the soul. Therefore it, too, is not non-rational but rational, in so far as it finds itself together with the soul in and under that meaningful order. For in its relation to the soul, *ratio* or λόγος is no less proper to it than to the soul, and dwells no less in it. That man is a rational being we also understand as an event, in accordance with the fact that the presupposition of the whole, namely, that he receives and has Spirit, is also an event, a divine action. We speak of a ruling and of a serving, and therefore of an act in which the whole is engaged. We speak of the real man whose existence is his own act and whose being can therefore be revealed and understood only in this act of his. Man lives as man in a meaningful order. He recognises it and subjects himself to it. He himself establishes and observes it. He is man as it is valid; and he makes use of its validity in human perception and activity. As this happens, i.e., as he himself brings it about, he is a rational being.

At this point we must again remember and maintain that we have no information whether animals are or are not also rational beings in the sense described. We have information about man only as we look at this event and are engaged in it, in the act of human existence, in the fulfilment of that rule and service, in living under and in that meaningful order. If we could and had to observe man too only from outside, it could and would have to be a mere hypothesis for us that man is a rational being. The very thing that we cannot know about animals is whether there is something like that rule and service in their existence. We can know this only as we do it, as we are ourselves engaged in the event, and can thus recognise it in other beings, as is possible and necessary between man and man but not between man and animals. The evidence for this cannot be used for both man *and* animals, nor of course for man *against* animals. It can be used only without reference to animals for man, and for man only as he conducts himself as a rational being. If he does not do so or tries not to do so—and we think sorrowfully of the great number engaged in this attempt—and if he then tries theoretically to contract out of the fact that he always acts as a rational being, attempting to regard himself and his fellow-men from outside as we can only regard animals, then he need not be surprised to discover that the evidence for his rational nature does not apply in his case either. All possible doubts about man's rational nature, and all false or partly false theories about the relation of soul and body, have their basis here. To a terrifying extent man can attempt in practice to act otherwise than as a

[420]

rational being, and he can then attempt in theory to observe himself and his fellow-men from outside and not first and foremost from inside, in the fact that he and unmistakeably his fellows, as men, act as rational beings. This theoretical attempt is foolish, and far from commendable for all its apparent objectivity and freedom from presuppositions. For in this ostensible objectivity we lose sight of the object which we are supposed to know and discuss, namely, the real man, who even in this observation of himself from outside acts as a rational being. And the ostensible freedom from presupposition involves the very worst presupposition that is possible in this matter, namely, to think it possible the more concretely to see and understand man the more we abstract from the fact that we are ourselves what we wish to see and understand. As man acts as a rational being—and he does so in some measure as he senses and thinks, desires and wills, in contradiction of all practical attempts not to do so and all theoretical attempts to persuade himself that he does not do so—he gives proof of the fact that, however it may be with animals, he is a rational being. He gives it not only by approximating to the ideal of a rational being, to a perfection of that ruling and serving, but also by moving away from or falling far short of it. He gives it even in his omissions and mistakes. He gives it even by caricaturing himself. He gives it even when he appears to exist as a complete denial of his rational nature. Strictly speaking, he never gives it except in a

[421] nega tive form, in the form of all kinds of deficiency phenomena, some worse, some not so bad, some almost tolerable. Yet he gives it none the less factually and evidently, whereas we cannot say whether animals, unknown to us, give it or not. That is to say, man always exists as the soul of his body, whereas we do not know whether an animal is also the soul of its body or merely the vegetative body of its soul. Whether he considers or respects it or experiences it or not, man is always first of all himself: this subject, who thus or thus rules, determines, stamps and guides himself and with himself his body; who as this person thinks and wills in his willing, pulling himself together, deciding and resolving who he is and then and on this basis what he is bodily in the service of himself and his soul, as that which, used and fashioned by himself and therefore by his soul, represents himself and his soul. As we ourselves exist, and exist with other men, we do in fact continually exemplify this distinction and reckon with this order, superordination and subordination. In fact, the soul rules and the body serves with whatever incompleteness or confusion. We see ourselves and other men actually engaged in a relation concerning which we have in the case of animals no information—not of course the negative information that this relation does not hold good for them too, but no information at all. But in the case of men, ourselves, we have this information. We supply it ourselves as we exist as men.

It is to be observed, however, that this information is certain and convincing, and the proof that man is a rational being is final and conclusive, only when it is given theologically. We may seriously ask: Who or what compels man to make this recognition of his own rational nature, and therefore of the order in which soul and body stand, however infinitely near it may seem to be? Who or what compels him to take himself and his fellow-men really seriously in the action of their existence, however integrated they may in fact be in this act? Who or what compels him really to abstain from that observation of man from without, in which his own rational nature must appear as dubious to him as that of an animal? Who or what compels him instead resolutely and finally to acknowledge what can and apparently must be recognised by him as that order, rationality or logicality of his existence? Who or what forbids him occasional vacillation between these two modes of observation as though one were as possible as the other, or even perhaps the acceptance and assertion of ambivalence between an inner and an outer picture of human existence? Who or what commands him to regard the inner picture as the truth and the outer resolutely and finally as error? We can hardly overlook the fact that it is of some importance for the cause of humanity whether this last question must be left open, the only final answer being a "Perhaps, perhaps not," or whether there is a compulsion, a prohibition and a command binding us to a recognition plausible in itself. No man, and humanity even less, lives as if it were self-evident to make this recognition, or as if the proof of our rational nature   [422] which we continually give by the mere fact that we are men were sufficient of itself. On the contrary, real human existence, both individually and as a whole, develops in such a way that the proof is obviously given, yet also in such a way that the proof seems not to be taken with final seriousness but is constantly given in vain. The cause of humanity is in fact constantly threatened, and most severely threatened, by the fact that a true compulsion to decide for the inner picture and therefore for the truth, and against the outer picture as a pernicious error, that a strict prohibition and command, does not seem by a long way to be recognised by us. Is there such a decisive prohibition and command? This is the question to which even the most well-meaning non-theological anthropology can give no answer. In the last resort it is simply referred to man himself, and its demonstration of the demonstration will finally consist only in the call and summons that man, to be man, should value and respect the obvious fact of his rational nature and therefore of that order, that in his being and conduct he should take account of this nature of his and therefore of the law of his better self. This imperative, the recognition and observance of which would actually serve the cause of humanity, can obviously be formulated very categorically. But it cannot really become or be categorical, since to the category of the imperative there belong not only a command but supremely one who commands and who has the competence and authority, the will and the voice, to do so. Where the last word in face of that open question can only be the pious wish that man should command himself, taking himself seriously as the rational being as which he acts, we cannot truly speak of a categorical imperative. How is man to be able to ascribe to himself, i.e., to the inner picture of his false existence, the absolute significance which he must have for himself in order to be able to command himself categorically? He must be categorically commanded categorically to command himself if he is to have this ability. To answer that final question, theological anthropology is needed, for this alone knows of a decisive prohibition and command, and of One who commands with competence and authority, at the point where the only other alternative to that interchange and ambivalence of the two ways of consideration is the pious wish that man himself should attempt that command and prohibition, himself making the decision for truth and against error. If we are interested in the statement that in the sense expounded man is a rational being, it is as a theological statement, i.e., in the form in which it is guaranteed in face of that final question, and in which alone it is ultimately well founded.

Man is a rational being because he is addressed as such by God, and because—we must again draw the same conclusion as we have worked with hitherto—it is thus presupposed that he was created as such by God.

[423] The imperative which commands us always to understand and conduct ourselves as rational beings is thus categorical. But it is categorical not in so far as it is the imperative which man imposes on himself, but so far as it is the imperative which God imposes on him. Imposed by man on himself, it would not be really categorical. But it is this as it is imposed on man by God. Thus imposed by the Creator on His creature, it is not a kind of question to which different answers could be given and which could be finally evaded. It is rather the affirmation concerning his being or non-being. For as the imperative of the Creator to His creature, it does not only command, but in so doing contains and reveals a knowledge of the being of the one whom it commands, the one being beside which he has no other. In this one being of his, the Creator claims the creature. If the creature perceives this claim, it has no choice between life and death with respect to the way in which it must understand and conduct itself. What it is in reality lies before it clearly and plainly, unmistakeably and incontestably. And what it is not, what it is only in its own illusion, flees before it like mist before the sun. There thus remains only one truth about man. There is no second truth beside it. Beside it there is only falsehood. Man has thus to choose between truth and falsehood in his knowledge, and between being and non-being in his conduct. The neutrality in which he thinks he can now take himself seriously and now not as a rational creature, being right in both cases and living under both signs, is quite impossible for him when he is claimed by God. The only choice which now remains for him is to take and conduct himself seriously as a rational being, or to fall into complete error in relation both to God and to himself, electing to defy the revelation and will of God and therefore choosing his own nothingness. It can only be the choice between life and death. Since theological anthropology understands man simply from the standpoint that he is called and claimed by God, the possibility of understanding him as a rational being attains the character of an absolutely decisive necessity.

Theological anthropology cannot go behind this necessity because without this recognition it cannot even begin to consider man at all. The proof of his rational nature which man gives by the fact that he exists as a rational being is convincing for it, and all doubt concerning it on the basis of a purely outer consideration of man is dismissed, not because it thinks that man himself can make this decision in virtue and in the light of his own existence, nor because it ascribes an absolute significance to the inner picture in which he distinguishes himself as man from the animal, but because, behind and above the factual existence of man, and behind and above this inner picture, it sees the competence and authority of the commanding person of God the Creator, by whose claim on man the whole question is answered as it is raised. On this basis the command that man take himself seriously in his factual existence becomes a categorical command. On this basis there is a strict prohibition and command. On this basis an irrevocable decision is taken at the absolutely decisive point. For on this basis the internal proof for man's rational nature is *a priori*[EN128] strong, and the external questioning of this knowledge *a priori*[EN129] weak. On this basis the pious wishes, which are the last word of even the best non-theological anthropology, that man would be so good as to adhere to that external proof, are superfluous. On this basis the cause of humanity, which depends on the fact that there is here no open question, is *a priori*[EN130] secured. On this basis there is a barrier to the otherwise unavoidable vacillation between the inner picture and the outer, between humanity and inhumanity.

[424]

As God addresses man, he treats him as a being who can rule himself and serve himself. He thus treats him as a rational being. And it is thus evident that he was created a rational being. We shall develop what is to be said about man as rational being under three heads.

1. If man understands himself in his relation to God as ordained not by himself but by God, he cannot in any sense understand himself as purely soul or as purely thinking and willing subject. As he is created by and for God, the fact that he receives and has Spirit, and is thus a being which lives spiritually, a spiritual soul, is a specific activity in a specific sphere. He is not simply soul. Soul is life. Its thinking and willing (together with its sensing and desiring) is simply the human act of living. The sphere, or at least the proximate and specifically allotted sphere of this act of living, in which it always takes place and to which it always refers, is the body of this soul. It is indeed active in general. Its thinking and willing has an object, and can thus become actual as well as purely potential. For it there can be another, God first and then the world. But all this is dependent on the fact that it is not bodiless but the soul of its body. It is this, however, as it is first active in this sphere in a specific manner—a ruling manner. It is in this way, as one who rules himself, that we find man addressed

---

EN128 unconditionally
EN129 unconditionally
EN130 unconditionally

by God and claimed by Him. Before God, he is not an improper but a proper, i.e., a free subject. He is identical with his body, in so far as he is its soul. He thinks and wills and therefore fulfils the human act of living; and in so doing he treats his sphere, i.e., his body, as his own domain, and controls and uses it, striding ahead of it in precedence. And because in this he is still identical with his body, it may be said that in his relation to his body he goes ahead of himself, preceding himself, giving himself guidance and direction as his own lord and ruler. His soul is his freedom over his body and therefore over himself. As he acts in this freedom, as in thinking and willing he is his own lord and director, he is spiritual soul. For in order to be active in this way, he is given Spirit by God and through the Spirit he is awakened to be a living being. In this activity, in a specific thinking and willing and so in the specific act of his living, he is undoubtedly summoned and claimed by the Spirit of God, as God has dealings with him. He lives as man so long and so far as he is not only capable of such activity but actually engages in it. Death, in which the soul is alienated from the body and the body from the soul, is the end of such activity. Death puts an end to his freedom, to the lordship of his soul over the body and therefore to its direction, so that further life-acts are made impossible. Unless, therefore, there is deliverance from death, it is simply the end of man. Man is the ruling soul of his body, or he is not man. We know no being which we must address and can designate as man, to whom must be denied this ruling soul, for we know no man to whom, since God calls and claims man, it is not to be ascribed. This is the first thing which we have to say theologically concerning man as a rational being.

[425]

2. If man understands himself in his relation to God as established and ordained by God, he can in no case understand himself merely as body, merely as a sensing and desiring subject. That he receives and has Spirit distinguishes him *a priori*[EN131] from a purely material body. It is what makes him an organic body, which means of course a soulful body. Even the fact that he is an organic body signifies a specific activity in a specific sphere. He is not simply body, but that which is animated and lives by soul. His sensing and desiring (along with his thinking and willing) is again nothing but the human life-act. Its sphere— here we must say its sole sphere, the sphere in which alone the human life-act can take place on its bodily side—is the soul whose body it is. It is not without the sensing and desiring of the body, yet not as body but as soul, that man has a sphere wider than himself, and that there is for him another, God and the world. Since the body is body in and through the soul, receiving its determination from the soul, we may say that man is identical with it. Man is also through and through body. This is revealed in the fact that he is wholly addressed and claimed by God as one who has to serve himself. How could he be a genuine free subject if he could not at the same time be a genuine obedient object? This ability—one may and must describe it as a freedom—is the

---

[EN131] unconditionally

bodily moment of his being. As he senses and desires, it is also true that he serves himself in ruling himself. The same sphere which from the standpoint of the soul is the domain in which man must rule, is from the standpoint of the body the domain in which he may be subject to himself and serve. As body he does not dispose of himself, but stands at his own disposal; he does not use himself, but is used by himself. As body he does not go beyond himself, for it is not as body but as soul that he is immediate to the Spirit and therefore to God. As body, then, he cannot precede himself, but only follow. He is spiritual soul. That he is also spiritual body is not apparent to him, and we cannot speak of it   [426] if we speak of his natural condition, since it will be the gift of grace of future revelation. What is now apparent to us is that he is soulful body and therefore limited and determined by the soul, the body of his soul. The body, the whole man, has his value even according to the bodily moment of his being in the fact that he is active as soul of his body. Certainly as God has dealings with him he is called by God's Spirit to this serving activity which is indirect in relation to the Spirit. Certainly he is called to the sensing and desiring of the soul. Man lives, so long and so far as he is bodily capable of such activity and engaged in it. Death, which makes an end of the soul as the life of the body, is also the end of what is animated and alive through it, and therefore of the body. Where there is no more ruling, there is no more serving; and on this side too—unless there is deliverance from death—we are confronted with the end of man. He is the serving body of his soul, or he is not man. For we know no man who is not called and claimed by God in his totality, and therefore in this moment too. This is the second thing which we have to say theologically concerning man as a rational being.

3. If man understands himself in his relation to God as established and ordained by God, in relation to soul and body as the two moments of his being he can in no case understand himself as a dual but only as a single subject, as soul identical with his body and as body identical with his soul. Soul and body are not two factors which merely co-exist, accompany, supplement, sympathise and co-operate with one another, but whose intentions, achievements and sufferings have different origins, ends and meanings. The one man is the soul of his body and therefore both soul and body. In the relation thus determined, in the order, rationality and logicality which obtains at this point, the one man is just as much soul from head to foot as he is body from the most primitive acts of sensing and desiring to the sublimest and most complicated acts of thinking and willing. He and he alone is subject in both the moments of his being. He rules himself, and again he serves himself. He is free to dispose of himself, and he is also free in standing at his disposal. It is he who thinks and wills, but he too who senses and desires. He always does the one as he does the other. As soul of his body, he is neither in a foreign land, nor in a prison, nor even in a vessel, but wholly in his own house and wholly himself. Again, as body of his soul, he is not merely external; he does not cling to it accidentally; he is not merely its accompanist. Again, he has in it that which is his own, and is in it

himself. Man does not exist except in his life-act, and this consists in the fact that he animates himself and is therefore soul, and is animated by himself and is therefore body. His life-act consists in this circular movement, and at every point in it he himself is not only soul or body, but soul and body. He is indeed the one for and by the other, but always soul first and then body, always the ruling soul and the serving body. It is thus that he is claimed by God. Obviously there is not a double divine call, one side applying only to his body and the other only to his soul, with something special intended for each, possibly a higher and a lower, or an essential and an incidental, a final and a transient, pure inwardness and pure outwardness. On the contrary, the one divine calling encounters the one man, who is able as soul to rule himself, and as body to serve himself, and in executing this life-act to correspond to the divine calling, to be there, i.e., to be active as a creaturely person for the person of the Creator. Engaged in this one activity, he is fitted as the creature of God to be also the partner of God. God can meet the one who is engaged in this one activity, giving him His promise and His command; and God can make Himself like him, treating with him on an equal footing, binding Himself to him and having a common history with him.

[427]

We may now return to the analogies suggested earlier. The man engaged in this activity, as the unity of a ruling soul and a serving body, is in himself a likeness of the fellowship of God and man. This nature of his is itself in image form an anticipation of his historical determination, that God wills to be with him and he may be with God, that God wills to rule him but he may serve God. It is also in image form an anticipation of the final and decisive fulfilment of this historical determination of his, namely, of the relation between Christ and His community, in which ruling and serving are distributed in the same way between Christ and the community, and both together form a single coherent activity, the one irreversible but indivisible life-act of reconciliation. Again, man as preceding soul of his succeeding body is a picture of what Scripture describes in the relation of man and woman as the divine likeness of man's being fulfilled only in this duality, to the extent that even in this fulfilment ruling and serving are distinguished and yet wholly integrated as the work of the one man. We have not deduced our understanding of man as soul and body from these similitudes. They say both too much and too little to permit us to draw direct conclusions about man from them. But as we draw our understanding of man from his historical encounter with God, we cannot help observing how the relation between the ruling soul and the serving body is more or less clearly illuminated by these similitudes. In them there is shed at least a supplementary light on the fact that it was not by accident that God the Creator and Reconciler, with whom we have to do even in this wider sphere, ordained as His partner and covenant associate the man who exists as ruling soul of his serving body.

To exist as man is to exist in the order, rationality and logicality which consists in the ruling and serving which so mysteriously pervade the whole work of the Creator with His creation. Only death, i.e., only the end of man's existence, could destroy and dissolve the order. And if there is deliverance from [428] death, a death of death, then this order has the last word, even against death itself. Man is, as he is in this order. Otherwise we must again conclude that he is not man. In addressing ourselves or others as men, we reckon with the validity of this order. We do not do this arbitrarily but necessarily, for God reckons with it, and the being with whom God willed and still wills to keep company is undoubtedly the one which exists in this order, not a dual being but the one being who as soul must rule himself and as body may serve himself.

Our only remaining task is to state that on the basis of these conclusions we must reject and abandon not only the materialistic and spiritualistic doctrines, but also all those expositions of the relation of soul and body which would apportion their activity to two different series of activity, whether independent of each other or connected by reciprocal causal links. We have chiefly to deal with the theories of psycho-physical parallelism and psycho-physical alternation. They were constructed and expounded in the 19th century with the intention of mediating between the materialistic and the spiritualistic views, or rather of surmounting and surpassing both. Both contain elements of truth. If we must here dissociate ourselves from them, it is because both start from the $\pi\rho\hat{\omega}\tau o\nu\ \psi\epsilon\hat{v}\delta o\varsigma$ EN132 that man can and must be understood in abstraction from his historical relation to God, and therefore logically also from the $\delta\epsilon\acute{v}\tau\epsilon\rho o\nu\ \psi\epsilon\hat{v}\delta o\varsigma$ EN133 that he is to be understood not as a simple but as a dual being, not as soul of his body but as soul and body alongside one another.

The theory of parallelism was propounded under the stimulus and direction of Spinoza by Gustav Theodore Fechner, Wilhelm Wundt, Friedrich Paulsen and others. It understands the psychical and physical events in man's existence as two "parallel" series which never meet, but whose courses, while mutually independent, must mutually correspond. Thus to every increment and alteration on the one side there must correspond an increment and alteration on the other, although there is never any direct connexion or influence at any point. Only the one X of human existence holds them together, and this has two sides, as a curve has a convex and a concave side. As we see it, the strongly maintained identity of this X is clearly the element of truth in this theory. For the rest, however, we can only say that the positive assertion of two corresponding but not intercommunicating series or sides serves only to mark off the problem. It speaks of two natural human determinations which are most closely related and mutually and irresistibly accompany one another. But it does not speak of the one man. With its mere positing of an X it fails to answer the question concerning the one who exists in these two series or sides. The soul of real man is not simply the constant companion of its body, nor the body of its soul. This is true enough. But it cannot be supposed that it is the whole truth about real man. We have to recognise the essence of real man in his activity, and his activity does not merely consist in his being his own *alter ego* as soul and body.

The other theory, propounded among others by H. Driesch and H. Rickert, is that of intercommunication. It, too, proceeds from the idea of two series or sides in the event of human existence. But it does not understand their relationship merely as a factual co-existence. Hence it is not content merely to refer to an X holding them together, and to the fact of their parallel development. It perceives and emphasises their connexion, and understands it as a causal determination and influence on both sides. Physical causes

---

EN132 first falsehood
EN133 second falsehood

impinge upon the life of the soul, both to stimulate and prosper on the one side and to disturb and restrict on the other. Conversely, the life of the body is exposed to the influence of specific advantageous or injurious activities and passivities of the soul. For example, physical pain is not merely a conceivable but a verifiable consequence of psychical defects, and psychical treatment can be used to cure it. In place of mere parallelism we have to set the notion of a widespread correspondence which may very well be represented in the form of a kind of transformation of energy on the frontiers of the two spheres. From our standpoint, we welcome the attempt obviously made here to speak of an activity of soul and body proceeding not in a puzzling duality alongside one another, but in a certain unity of thrust and counterthrust. But unfortunately, to obtain this, the theory is forced to withdraw or let go of the insight concerning the identity of the human subject which the theory of parallelism maintained at least in the form of its assertion of an X. For now the differentiation and even disparateness of the two series or sides is more sharply emphasised than before, as when it is sometimes said that the plan for the two series in their unity embraces two polar opposites. The purely philosophical objection concerns the nature of this unity and the way in which anything like intercommunication can really be possible and actual in these circumstances. But that is not our business. We have to ask: Who or what operates from one side or the other? Where is real man in this play of thrust and counterthrust? Is he on the one side or the other? Is there a decision on this? Or is he on both sides? And if so, how is he the subject of such a criss-cross and competitive activity? And if no answer is to be given to these questions, what is really meant by intercommunication? Or does man stand somewhere in the middle between the two interacting series? And if so, how is he related to their operation? The theory of intercommunication obviously does not lead us beyond the fatal co-existence of two human activities, an idea behind which there stands concealed the old doctrine of two independent and exclusive substances of soul and body.

Nor is it easy to see what advance is made if we follow the latest attempt (welcomed on the theological side, for example, by A. Titius) to mediate between the theories of parallelism and interaction by combining the idea of two no less homogeneous than heterogeneous activities beginning simultaneously and following a common course, with the idea of a mutual contact and influence between both. Can they really be combined? Not unjustly, it has been maintained in face of this attempt that we must choose between parallelism and interaction, since the idea of parallelism excludes that of interaction and if the latter is emphasised there is no place for the former. But this must be settled between the advocates of the attempt and their critics. Our question simply concerns the simple human subject; and this question cannot in any case be answered by this attempt.

We cannot participate in the solving of the riddle which seems to burden and engage the participants in this discussion. In face of the whole discussion we can only declare our fundamental objection that the soul and the body of the man of whom they speak are the soul and body of a ghost and not of real man. To dispute concerning these and to throw light on their co-existence and relationship is necessarily a waste of time and effort. We can only oppose to all these theories that the soul and body of real man are not two real series or sides existing and observable in isolation. They are the two moments of the one human activity, which as such do not merely accompany each other and cannot influence and condition one another as though there were on both sides an active and passive something. We do not have the body here and the soul there, but man himself as soul of his body is subject and object, active and passive—man in the life-act of ruling and serving, as the rational being as which he stands before God and is real as he receives and has the Spirit and is thus grounded, constituted and maintained by God.

To say this is to bring out again the theological presuppositions of the anthropology here presented. Non-theological anthropology lacks this presupposition. In the last resort, there is something tragic in every non-theological anthropology. This finds expression in the fact that such ghostly pictures of the relationship between soul and body are proposed in these [430] theories. It is to be noted that the advocates of the theories just mentioned are distinguished from others by the fact that they profess to be aware of the one-sidedness of both materialistic and spiritualistic views and that they make a real effort to consider and to take seriously both sides of man, doing equal justice to both the physical and psychical series and to their interconnexion. Yet they can only offer parallelism or interaction. They can only present the two accompanying or corresponding forms of real soul and real body, of which we can never know for certain which is merely the shadow of the other. They can only have reference to an X in which the two may be one and the same and therefore real man. They can give no decisive and final information whether man is or is not a rational being. And on that basis, we can think of no better counsel. Inevitably this is how things work out even in the best non-theological anthropology. Where the question of the confrontation of the human creature by his Creator is handled as a *cura posterior*EN134, from whose consideration we must look away in favour of a prefabricated conception of science, there is no need to understand man from the standpoint of Spirit, and therefore as ruling soul of his serving body, and therefore as rational being. The categorical imperative laid upon the investigator to see man *a priori*EN135 in this unity drops away, and it cannot be replaced by corresponding pious wishes.

In these circumstances, if we avoid the one-sidedness of materialism and spiritualism, we are left with two things, with soul and body as two series which are real in themselves and finally as two parts which we exert ourselves in vain to reassemble when we think we have taken them apart and considered them separately. From the world of the purely psychical—if there is such a thing, or if such a thing is fancied—there is no bridge to the world of the really physical. If we think that we can see one, we shall finally end up in spiritualism, for which the body is only an appearance and no reality. Conversely, from the world of the purely physical—if there is such a thing, or if we are convinced that it is real and can be considered as such—there is no bridge to the shore of a world of the really psychical. Once we are rashly compromised on this point, we shall logically end up in some form of materialism, for which the mind is only an appearance and no reality. But the advocates of the doctrines of parallelism and interaction do not improve matters by accepting the false assumptions of both those conceptions. They are more far-seeing than the spiritualists and the materialists in their desire to do justice to the twofold aspect of human reality as this is actually given, but they are less far-seeing in their refusal to see that we cannot divide the one human reality into two and then hope to put it together again. They have the same blind spot as spiritualists and materialists, for they do not think that they can begin with an unshakeable conception of the rational nature of the whole man as soul and body, but think it necessary to take as their axiom and starting-point the fact that the rational nature of man is an open question and that its reality has still to be established. But in this question the end must inexorably correspond to the beginning and the result of the investigation to its starting-point. From the supposed reality of the soul we inevitably finish up with the soul as the only reality, and from that of the body with the body as the only reality. And if we begin more critically but less logically somewhere in the middle with the problem of both realities, we can only finish up in face of the same problem. Thus it seems as though we could and really should begin at quite another point—with the obvious reality of the rational being of man himself, with the capacity with which we actually find ourselves possessed as ruling soul and serving body when we raise the question concerning man and therefore concerning

---

EN134 afterthought
EN135 unconditionally

ourselves, with the life-act as such in which we are finally engaged even as we undertake and carry through this investigation. Are we soul only in this act? or body only? or only two parallel series accompanying or corresponding to each other? Can we speak of two worlds, one of which calls the reality of the other in question? Must not our first enquiry be for a bridge from the one to the other? Are we not equally present to ourselves as soul and body? Are we anything but the psycho-physical rational being of man which as a unit, though in irreversible superordination and subordination, senses and thinks, desires and wills, is subject and object, active and passive? It is here that we should begin. It is to this object that we should apply anthropological analysis. Obviously an analysis of this object will necessarily lead us back to the corresponding synthesis, the end again corresponding to the beginning. Why should we not accept this object? Are we prevented by the scientific requirement that we put this object out of mind in order first to consider the external aspect in which soul and body each appear to form a world of their own? So it is said. But can it be good science in which we arbitrarily force ourselves to begin with an aspect which even as we select it we must necessarily regard and describe as a mere appearance in relation to the rational nature which we still exercise in our selection? Who are we to make this outer aspect with its obviously phenomenal character the measure of all things? Should we not rather relate the obviously incontestable data of this outer aspect—everything which an external consideration of our psychical or physical existence has to teach us—to the reality of our rational existence as such? Should we not rather explain the data from the latter instead of giving ourselves the fruitless trouble of trying to deduce the latter from the data and thus to erect the one real world out of two obviously phenomenal worlds? What is there really to prevent us, as real men, from trying to investigate real man as such?

But we will not labour the point. For it is obvious that non-theological anthropology is not wholly arbitrary in its constant decision not to begin with real man but with one or other outer aspect, nor in its consequent ending up with spectres instead of returning to real man. If we disregard man's relation to God, there is no obligation to accept what is to us the obvious object of anthropological investigation, nor is there the boldness always to begin where the investigator finds himself, namely, in the middle of his life-act as rational being and man, in the middle of the reality of the ruling soul and the serving body. If man will not understand himself as through and through the being confronted by God, it is only natural that he should suspect and question himself as rational being. And the inevitable result is that the outer aspect of the two series in which he appears to exist gains power and might over him. That is, it then presents itself to him as the aspect which, even if only in phenomenal form, contains the mystery of human reality. To get behind the appearance, to get behind this aspect, then seems to be the only possible scientific task, and the only question is then whether we shall decide for a materialistic or spiritualistic solution, or for one of the proposed compromises. If we are not permitted or obliged to take with absolute seriousness the inner aspect in which man actually finds himself as psycho-physical rational being, we have no freedom to begin at this point and to use the data of the outer aspect as contributions to an anthropology proposed from this standpoint instead of making them something for which they are not fitted, namely, an anthropological basis. We then necessarily lose ourselves to that outer aspect. Yet we cannot stand under this obligation or have this freedom if we will not come to terms with the theological presupposition that in his confrontation with God man is claimed as rational being and imperiously commanded to take himself with absolute seriousness as such. In these circumstances we cannot begin at this other place. We may thus agree that apart from this presupposition the only advice we can give is to decide for one of the remaining ways or evasions. But since we ourselves make this theological presupposition, we regard ourselves as absolved from the task of judging which of these ways or evasions is relatively least unsatisfactory.

5. *Soul and Body in Their Order*

The phenomena to which those theories refer in detail cannot of course be overlooked or denied. There are undoubtedly correspondences and connexions, agreements and relationships between psychical and physical conditions of sufficiency or lack, health or sickness, [432] strength or weakness, soundness or degeneration, between psychical and physical actions and passions, conditions and experiences, achievements and omissions. They form a whole field of undeniably genuine human living reality. It is the business of non-theological science, of psychology, physiology and biology, to establish and evaluate these facts. From the standpoint of theological anthropology, we have least reason of all to wish that the facts were otherwise, or to want to shut our eyes to them. On the contrary, we are tempted to suppose that this field is even greater than is now accepted, and that it will be seen to be much more extensive than is the case to-day. Our own expectation is that in much greater measure and with much greater strictness it will be perceived that the whole of human life both in particular and in general is governed by these correspondences and connexions, and that in no ostensibly psychical phenomenon do we have to do only with the soul, and in no ostensibly physical phenomenon only with the body, but always and at every point with both soul and body. Whether regarded from this side or from that, only the whole man is the real man. Lévy-Brühl has reduced the picture of man in what is called "primitive" religion and the "primitive" outlook to the formula that in it nothing is represented as wholly material and nothing as purely spiritual. If this is correct, we can say that the "primitives" have maintained or anticipated the view which is lost to "higher" religions and outlooks with their different abstractions, but which may be one day taken for granted again when these phenomena are better and more fully understood and have passed into the general consciousness. We do not really question the data of the outer aspect of human reality, but we regret that they are not seen together in a very different way and applied as contributions to an anthropology based on the inner aspect of this reality. Thus we do not dissociate ourselves from the facts brought to light by modern science, but only from the one-sided and the mediating interpretations which it has hitherto given them. Our opinion is that these very facts are susceptible and worthy of a better interpretation. Our formula that man is the ruling soul of his serving body has admittedly and consciously a theological basis, and can have no other. But in our view it does better justice to the facts. It turns attention from the first upon the whole man, and upon this man in his activity, in the life-act in which he is always soul and body, but each in its proper way. And each in its proper way does not mean each for itself, but always the one in the appropriate relation to the other. Nor does this relation consist in a mere reciprocal association of two partners unrelated in themselves. The human existence of the one man is that he stands in this relation, and that he is the soul of his body and then also the body of his soul. Nor does this relation and therefore human existence consist merely in a mutual acting and suffering of these two partners. It is the one man who in this relation is both the doer and the sufferer.

Our interpretation of those phenomena, formulated as briefly as possible in four propositions, would be as follows.

1. The soul does not act on the body, but the one man acts. And he does it in that as soul he animates himself and is acting subject, but always as soul is soul of his body, animated by himself, determined and enabled to act, and engaged in action.

2. Again, the soul does not suffer from the body, but the one man suffers. And this takes place in that as soul (namely, as acting subject) he is fundamentally exposed and susceptible to such hindrances and injuries, but as soul of his body must actually experience them.

3. Again, the body does not act on the soul, but the one man acts. He acts in that as body he is animated by himself, determined and enabled to act, and engaged in action, but as body of his soul, animating himself and acting subject.

4. And again, the body does not suffer from the soul, but the one man suffers. When this takes place, it means that as body he really experiences such hindrances and injuries, but that as body of his soul he must really make them his own.

[433]

The one whole man is thus one who both acts through himself and suffers in himself, but always in such a way that he is first soul (ruling, in the subject) and then body (serving, in the object)—always in this inner order, rationality and logicality of his whole nature. This is the interpretation of those phenomena which from the standpoint of our presupposition we must oppose to the doctrines of both spiritualism and materialism, of both the parallelism and the interaction between psychical and physical reality, and which we in any case regard as in closer correspondence to the facts to which these theories relate. It would naturally be the business of an extensive psychological, physiological and biological science, on the recognition of the basic viewpoints indicated, to procure for itself a freedom which it has to-day only to the extent that in spite of its enslavement to those theories it engages in the investigation and presentation of the facts as such.

It is again the biblical view of man which has been our guide and which we must now consider in detail. We remember that we shall search the Old and New Testaments in vain for a true anthropology and therefore for a theory of the relation between soul and body. The biblical texts regard and describe man in the full exercise of his intercourse with God. Their authors have neither the time nor the interest to occupy themselves with man as such, nor to give to themselves or their readers a theoretical account of what is to be understood by the being of man. We have thus to be content with purely incidental and self-evident presuppositions if we seek information from them on this question, and we must not be surprised if this information seem to us to be unsystematic, defective, partial and even contradictory. The fact is that the biblical authors knew very well what they were talking about when they spoke about man, that there was substantial unanimity among them and that everywhere in their statements we have a much more fundamental and truly systematic treatment than appears at first sight.

We may begin with a general historical characterisation. With respect to the relationship between soul and body, their representation of man is on the whole that of primitive man. This representation knows the double-sidedness of the being of man. It knows what we have called the two moments of the human life-act. It reckons with both. But it knows of no division between them. It knows of no bodiless soul and soulless body. It knows only of the one whole man seen from both sides. It thus parts from the Greek picture of man, and therefore from that which was normative for so long in the Christian Church and theology, and which, basically uncontested, has formed the presupposition of modern discussion concerning soul and body. In classing the biblical picture of man with that of primitive man, we cannot see any reflection on its value. From our whole consideration of the matter, it appears that the supposed "primitives" are in this matter more sophisticated than the sophisticated whose approach has so successfully superseded their own in the civilised west and cultures influenced by it. It is no discredit to the Bible but a point in favour of the so-called primitives that the biblical presuppositions concerning soul and body are in considerable material agreement with theirs. The practical result of such a comparison can only be that, if we look away from the Bible, we have more to learn from the so-called primitives in this matter than in the school of Plato and all his followers.

Of course, the biblical picture of man is marked off from that of the primitives by a distinctive quality which is not easily defined but must always be noted. It is of a piece with the basis proper to the general outlook of the Bible. It sees and knows man decisively, and in the last resort exclusively, in his relation to God, to the God of Israel who is absolutely gracious towards man but also makes an absolute claim upon him, not in any kind of neutral activity, constitution or capacity, it sees and knows him in the responsibility which this imposes on [434] him. It understands what he is from the fact that he has the Spirit. In conformity with this, its view of the inner order of his constitution, of the rule of the soul and the service of the body, has a precision in its representation which it cannot have where this presupposition is not accepted. It has a fundamental precision at this point, even where it is not specially emphasised. But this means that the view of the active unity of soul and body is here fundamentally secured. The same cannot be said of the picture of man of the so-called primitives. From the latter it was and is basically possible to slide over into a picture of man like that of the Greeks with its divisions, because the order of soul and body, though perceived by them, is not fundamentally secured. In passing over from the biblical to the Greek picture of man, there occurs not merely a deviating transition, but a fundamental misunderstanding and a lapse from truth into error. This means in practice that in order to win back the true picture of man we must let ourselves be taught not by the primitive but solely by the biblical picture, and ultimately regard the former only as a confirmation and illumination of the latter.

In accordance with what was earlier said about *ruaḥ πνεῦμα*^{EN136} and *nephesh ψυχή*^{EN137}, the basic outline of biblical anthropology to which we must refer again in this final connexion is as follows.

It is obvious that the Bible treats the body and the bodily organs of man not only as the locus but as the object of his capability and activity as soul. As body, he has no proper persistence or significance. That he lives and moves, experiences good and ill, is healthy and sick, and in the end dies, is not at all an affair of his as mere body. Rather in all these things there acts and suffers the human subject, and therefore the soul of man, with his experience, his thinking and willing, his rejoicing and setbacks, his wants, desires and possessions, and in his temporal limitation. When it is seen on this side one might be inclined to call biblical anthropology far too spiritualistic. Is not its only interest in the body the fact that in its totality it is a besouled body?

But the matter must also be seen and described from the opposite side. It is just as obvious that the Bible regards the body as the locus, even the subject, of man's capability and activity as soul. Where is there here a persistence and significance of the soul? That it wants, desires and possesses, grieves and rejoices, is on the right or wrong way, lives and dies, even that it is before and with God, is not its own affair. It is rather the affair of the body and its organs in and through which all this takes place. When it is seen on this side, could not biblical anthropology be claimed with equal right to be far too materialistic? Is not its only interest in the soul the fact that in its totality it is the life of the body?

Both these extremes have to be held in view if we are to see clearly at this point. We have to realise that it can only be a matter of these two extremes. At a pinch biblical anthropology can be called both spiritualistic and materialistic. On the other hand, we look in vain here for any trace of the theories of parallelism and interaction. In reality, of course, the Bible does not think either spiritualistically or materialistically. In contrast to both, and in contrast to all theories deduced from Greek presuppositions, its conception has been called "realistic." This may be allowed, if we give it a systematic name, and if real man must be regarded as a *res*^{EN138}. On the other hand, we must be clear that in making this connexion we still move fundamentally within the schema of Greek thought to the extent that in some measure of actuality and significance, even though repudiated by the realists, a *res*^{EN139} of man always

---

^{EN136} spirit
^{EN137} soul
^{EN138} thing
^{EN139} thing

seems to be confronted by an *idea* or *nomen*[EN140]. The Bible does not think in terms of this opposition. The real man who would have to be a *res*[EN141] on this view is not a *res*[EN142] but the human person self-animating and self-animated in the act of existing under the determination of the Spirit. The Bible has to do with this person. Hence its statements concerning man are to be understood as both spiritualistic and materialistic, but as either they can only be misunderstood, since they are con cerned with neither the soul nor the body in themselves, but always with man, and with him as the soul of his body. If we want to give a very suitable name to this biblical conception, our best plan is simply to call it "anthropology," and not to attempt any systematic addition.

[435]

We shall now present this basic outline in the form of a brief glance at the way in which the Bible actually describes the activity of the body and its organs wholly as that of its soul, or conversely, and in the same terms, the activity of its soul wholly as that of its body.

We may begin with the most striking passages. According to Ps. 84[2], it is the flesh that cries out for the living God, and according to Ps. 63[1] it is again the flesh that longs for Him in a dry and thirsty land without water. In passages like Eccles. 4[5] "flesh" can also designate the human person. According to Ps. 6[2], man's bones can be vexed, and according to Isa. 58[11] they can be strengthened by God. According to Ps. 32[3], they wax old when a man keeps silent about his guilt before God, and according to Ps. 51[8] they rejoice when God satisfies him with joy and gladness. When the prophet sees the destruction of his people drawing near, his bowels are pained, according to Jer. 4[19]. Job (30[27]) complains that his bowels boil without rest within him, and we read in Lam. 1[20]; 2[11] that they are troubled. The word "bowels" appears in passages like Gen. 43[14] as equivalent to compassion, a usage which is continued in the New Testament employment of $\sigma\pi\lambda\acute{a}\gamma\chi\nu a$[EN143] and $\sigma\pi\lambda\alpha\gamma\chi\nu\acute{\iota}\zeta\epsilon\sigma\theta\alpha\iota$[EN144]. When the reference is to the innermost element of man, which others cannot fathom but which is open to God, the Bible speaks of reins, e.g., in Jer. 11[20], Ps. 7[9] and Prov. 23[16]. As the seat of life which can be mortally wounded, Prov. 7[23] can also speak of the liver. In all these equations of soul and body, it is futile to ask whether the emphasis is such as to describe the bodily quality of the soul or the soulful quality of the body. Nor is it much help to seek important material nuances behind the different terms. They all have much the same significance. It is always in some way the whole man who is revealed by the fact that reference is made to his body, but as a besouled body, or to his soul, as a bodily soul. To be sure, the language is poetic; but it is not purely figurative. To see mere figures, the bodily as a mere expression of the soul and therefore what is said about the bodily as mere description of what are properly processes of the soul, is to interpret the statements on the basis of a very different understanding of man from that presented in the texts, and therefore to misunderstand them. They must be taken seriously in what is always the double sense of the verbal expression, or they cannot be understood at all.

More frequent, comprehensive and emphatic than all these other terms is the heart. The Bible speaks of the heart when it wants to speak particularly impressively of the active and suffering man. The passages are too numerous for us to discuss them in detail. *Leb* or $\kappa\alpha\rho\delta\acute{\iota}a$[EN145], is really much more than is usually indicated in the lexicons and text-books. It is more than merely the "locus" or "centre" of the mental and spiritual powers and possibilities of man, of his excitations, thoughts, inclinations, resolves and plans. It is more, too, than the "place" of his decisions, the crossroads, so to speak, from which his ways in relation

---

[EN140] concept or name
[EN141] thing
[EN142] thing
[EN143] compassion
[EN144] to show compassion
[EN145] heart

to God and man usually part for good or evil. All this is also true. But when we say it we must be careful not to re-introduce a division between the reality of soul and that of body which it is the intention of this idea to exclude. On the one side the biblical "heart" is undoubtedly identical with what is always called this anatomically; and everything that is said about the activity of the heart, its experiences and undertakings, its purity and evil, its fidelity and infidelity, its joy and sorrow, must undoubtedly be related to what we describe physiologically as the activity of the heart. On the other side, in all that is said of the heart, the reference is to the human subject, the subject existing in the activity and suffering of his bodily heart. Thus man does not only have a heart as his locus, place or centre. He really is what man is in his heart. In his heart, because man as body—as ancient and primitive anatomy and physiology [436] already knew quite well—lives by the heart, animating himself in its diastole and being animated in its systole. The heart is, as it were, the body in the body; and understood in this way, the expression "centre" is justified. But for this reason, if we are true to the biblical texts we must say of the heart that it is *in nuce*EN146 the whole man himself, and therefore not only the locus of his activity but its essence. Always, in every beat of his heart, he is ruling soul and serving body, subject and object. "With all thine heart" necessarily means "with all thy soul" and therefore "with all thy might" (Deut. 6⁵). What a man is, or confesses, or does "from the heart" counts before God as done responsibly before him. What a man takes "to heart" he takes to himself. The mouth speaks out of the fulness of the heart (Mt. 12³⁴). When a man hardens his heart, he is rejected by God; and on the other hand, those who are pure, i.e., open, in heart, will see God (Mt. 5⁸). That there should be a circumcision of the heart (Ez. 36²⁶, Rom. 2²⁹) is the positive content of the proclamation of the coming day of God. Thus the heart is not merely *a* but *the* reality of man, both wholly of soul and wholly of body. Who would want to say from his heart that it is the one more or less than the other or without the other? Of this term which in the first instance is wholly physical, but is then given in the Bible a content which is wholly of soul, we are forced to say that it speaks with particular plainness of the order in which man is soul and body, of man as a rational being.

EN146 a nutshell

INDEX OF SCRIPTURE REFERENCES

INDEX OF SUBJECTS

INDEX OF NAMES